The
GIANT
Encyclopedia
of
Art & Craft Activities

The GIANT

Encyclopedia of

Art & Craft

Activities

for Children 3 to 6

More Than 500 Art & Craft Activities
Written by Teachers for Teachers

Edited by Kathy Charner

Illustrations by Jane Yamada

gryphon house
Beltsville, Maryland

dedication

Many thanks to the hands, hearts, and creative minds who made this book possible.

Published by Gryphon House, Inc.
10726 Tucker Street, Beltsville MD 20705

Cover Illustration: Beverly Hightshoe
Text Illustration: Jane Yamada

Library of Congress Cataloging-in-Publication Data

The giant encyclopedia of art & craft activities: for children 3 to 6 more than 500 art & craft activities written by teachers for teachers / edited by Kathy Charner; illustrations by Jane Yamada.
    p. cm.
  Includes index.
  ISBN 0-87659-209-4
  1. Early childhood education--Activity programs--Handbooks, manuals, etc. 2. Creative activities and seat work--Handbooks, manuals, etc. 3. Art--Technique--Handbooks, manuals, etc. 4. Art--Study and teaching (Early childhood)—Handbooks, manuals, etc. 5. Artists' materials—Handbooks, manuals, etc. 6. Artists' tools—Handbooks, manuals, etc. I. Title: Giant encyclopedia of art and craft activities. II. Charner, Kathy.

LB1139.35.A37 G52 2000
372.5'2044--dc21   00-024529

Gryphon House books are available at special discount when purchased in bulk for special premiums and sales promotions as well as for fund-raising use. Special editions or book excerpts also can be created to specification. For details, contact the Director of Marketing at 10726 Tucker Street, Beltsville, MD 20705

table of Contents

table of Contents

table of Contents

table of **Contents**

table of Contents

table of Contents

table of Contents

introduction

Every day wonderful, dedicated people use their talents and energies to teach young children. To help these teachers share their work with others, we conducted a national contest asking teachers to send in their best art and craft activities. We selected the very best entries to create this book of over 500 art and craft activities to use with children 3 to 6 years old. This book is packed with days, weeks, and months of activities and ideas that teachers around the country have used successfully with the children they teach. We trust that you will benefit from the years of experience reflected in this book.

This book contains both art and craft activities. The art activities, which are child-centered, are those that do not have a pre-set outcome. They encourage the child to decide what the end result will be. The craft activities, which are teacher-directed, are those that have a specified outcome.

Keep in mind the following suggestions when involving children in art and craft activities:

- Encourage all children to participate, both during the activities and when preparing for them.

- Let children touch, smell, and look at the art materials without "producing" anything.

- Let children experiment with the activities and with the materials; they have great ideas.

- Allow children to use their imagination and creativity for all the activities, even the crafts.

- Organize art and craft materials so children can get the materials they need on their own.

- Use open-ended questions to ask children to tell you about their work. Sometimes "Tell me about your picture (or boat, or windsock, or puppet, etc.)" is all that is needed to get them started. Or try, "How did you make such a big picture?" or "What part do you like best?"

how to use this book

The *Giant Encyclopedia of Art and Craft Activities for Children 3 to 6* was created by experienced teachers who contributed their original ideas. Each activity uses some or all of the following sections.

Age
The age listed is a suggestion. Each teacher is the best judge of the appropriateness of an activity, based on his or her prior knowledge of the children and the children's responses to the activity.

Materials needed
Each activity includes a list of readily available materials. Investigate all possible sources of free materials in your community, including donations from paper stores, framing shops, woodworking shops, lumber yards, and, of course, parents.

What to do
The directions are presented in a step-by-step format. Patterns and illustrations are included where necessary.

More to do
Additional ideas for extending the activity are included in this section. Many activities include suggestions for integrating the art or craft activity into other areas of the curriculum such as math, dramatic play, circle time, blocks, language, snack, and cooking.

Related books
Under this heading are titles and authors of popular children's books that can be used to support the art or craft activity.

Related songs and poems
Familiar songs related to the original art or craft activity and original songs and poems written by teachers are in this section.

Indexes
This book has two indexes. One is an alphabetical index of the activities by the name of the activity, and the other one is an index of the materials used in the activities.

A Bag Full of Air!

Materials
Trash bags, preferably transparent
Collage materials such as bright colored streamers, tissue paper, stickers
Glue
Tape
String

What to do
1. Give each child (or pair of children) a plastic bag, preferably outdoors. Encourage them to fill the bags with air. They will quickly and joyfully begin to empty and fill, empty and fill, while running around.
2. Invite the children to decorate the bags with collage materials. If the bags are transparent, they can decorate the inside, fill them with air, and have an adult tie a knot to seal them. If the bags are opaque, they can decorate the outside after the bags are blown up and sealed with a knot.
3. Display bags by hanging them from the ceiling.

More to do
Language: Emphasize *more* or *less*, *empty* or *full*, and *big* or *small* when filling the bags with air.
Outdoor play: Use the bags of air to play a game of catch.

Related books
Gilberto and the Wind by Marie H. Ets.
The Wind Blew by Pat Hutchins

 *Barbara Reynolds, Smithville, NJ*

Soda Straw Painting

Materials
Manila paper
Masking tape
Tempera paint
Plastic soda straws, one per child

What to do
1. Use masking tape to fasten the paper to the table.
2. Place a spoonful of tempera paint near the bottom of the paper.
3. Invite the children to blow through the straws, moving the paint without touching it.
4. Show them how to create a design by moving the straws and changing the direction of the air.
5. They should continue to blow until the paint is evenly distributed.
6. Encourage the children to name their creation. Does it look like a spider, an octopus, a tree?

More to do
More art: Use black tempera paint to make trees. When the paint is dry, tissue paper scraps may be pasted onto the branches. Use light green and pastel blossoms for spring or autumn colors.
Science: Use the activity to illustrate the power of moving air. For older children, compare results of blowing with or without the straw. Which is easier? Which has better results? Why? (Channeling the air increases the pressure and gives better control.)

Related book
Mouse Paint by Ellen Walsh

Mary Jo Shannon, Roanoke, VA

Paper Bag Kites

Materials
Paper bags, any color, one per child
Crayons or markers
Stickers
Hole punch and reinforcements
String or yarn, 24" (60 cm) pieces, one per child

What to do
1. Invite the children to decorate a paper bag with crayons or markers and stickers.
2. Punch a hole in the center of one side, about one inch (three centimeters) from the edge, and reinforce it.
3. Show the children how to attach the string by pushing it through the hole and tying it securely.
4. The children will enjoy "flying" the kites by holding the string and running so the bags fill with air.

More to do

More art: Use bits of paper and yarn to make faces and hair on the bags.

Outdoor play: Have a kite race.

Science: Talk to the children about how air occupies space inside the bag. Perhaps conduct other experiments involving air.

Mary Jo Shannon, Roanoke, VA

Windsocks

Materials

Construction paper
Pastel tempera paints
Marbles
Shallow box top
Crepe paper streamers, different colors, 18"-24" (45-60 cm) long
Stapler
Tape
Hole punch
String, one per windsock, 12" (30 cm) long

What to do

1. Place a piece of construction paper in the box top.
2. Invite the children to dip the marbles in the paint and place them in the box top, on top of the construction paper.
3. The children can take turns rolling the marbles back and forth until they make imprints on the paper.
4. Let the paint dry, then roll the painted construction paper lengthwise into a tube (painted side out) and staple or tape together.
5. Have the children attach different color streamers to one end of the tube using tape.

6. Punch two holes at the other end of the tube and tie the ends of a string to each hole.
7. Hang the windsocks outside of a classroom window on a dry but breezy day so the children can watch the wind make the streamers move.

More to do
More art: Use various mediums to decorate the windsock (tissue paper, sponge paint, markers, string paint). Cut various types of paper to use as streamers.
Science: Hang the windsock near a fan and talk about the movement of air and how it affects the windsock.

Related books
Gilberto and the Wind by Marie H. Ets
Millicent and the Wind by Robert Munsch
Sasha and the Wind by Rhea Tregebov
The Wind Blew by Pat Hutchins

Kaethe Lewandowski, Centreville, VA

Bubbles, Bubbles, Bubbles

Materials
Old shower curtain
White construction paper
Scissors
Cups, one per child
Water
Liquid detergent
Food coloring or liquid watercolor
Bubble wands

What to do
1. Cover a table or the floor with an old shower curtain.
2. Cut white construction paper into large circles, one per child.
3. Fill each cup with water (about one-quarter full).
4. Add a small amount of liquid detergent and different food colorings or liquid watercolors.
5. Give each child a bubble wand and a piece of round construction paper.
6. Invite the children to dip the bubble wands in the colored water and then blow bubbles onto the construction paper.

7. The bubbles will land on the paper and make bubble prints.
8. The children may dip their wands into other cups for different colored bubbles.

More to do:

More art: Put out one large piece of paper and let children take turns blowing colored bubbles on to it to create a group picture.

Outdoor play: Make or purchase regular bubble solution and take children outside to blow bubbles in the air.

Related book

Bubble Factory by Tomie DePaola

 Sandra Fisher, Kutztown, PA

Catch the Wind

4+

Materials

Contact paper, one square 12" x 12" (30 cm x 30 cm) per child
Poster board

What to do

1. Take the children outside to a park or field on a windy day. This is a lot of fun on a warm, fall day when lots of leaves are blowing in the wind.
2. Give each child a sheet of contact paper with the protective backing removed.
3. Show the children how to hold the sheet open, with the sticky side facing away from them.
4. Invite them to run and play in the wind, twirling and dancing, while holding the contact paper. They can hold the paper over their heads, in front of them, or swing it from side to side.
5. Tell them they can try to catch some of the things that the wind picks up and tosses around, such falling leaves, or they can just wait and see what surprises the wind blew on to their sticky paper.
6. Back in the classroom, tape the sheets of contact paper on to poster board and display.

Related books

Dancing With the Wind by Sheldon Orser

Snowsong Whistling by Karen E. Lotz
When the Wind Stops by Charlotte Zolotow

Gryphon House Staff

Parachute People

5+

Materials
8"-10" (20-25 cm) squares of lightweight cloth or tissue paper, white or colored. Cheesecloth will also work as long as the weave isn't too loose and open.
12" (30 cm) lengths of thread, 4 per parachute
Beeswax or clay

What to do
1. Tie the thread to the four corners of the cloth by scrunching up each corner, wrapping one end of the thread around it a few times, and tying a knot. Leave the other end of the string free.
2. Attach the other three strings. Gather the loose ends together and tie them into a knot.
3. Embed the knot in a ball of beeswax or clay (a pencil point helps with this), and if you like, form a little person. Just make a very general shape; don't make it too detailed.
4. The older children will be able to make these on their own. The younger ones will need some help or may just want to play with them after you've made them.

Note: You can help the children cut their own string by taping a piece that is the correct length on the table. They can use it as a measuring gauge.

More to do
More art: Decorate the cloth before assembling the parachute.
Science: Drop different objects at the same time and observe the results.

Related book
The Wing Shop by Elvira Woodruff

Carol Petrash, Kensington, MD

(Reprinted from *Earthways* by Carol Petrash)

Alphabet Rubbings

3+

Materials
Large pieces of cardboard
2 clothespins, spring-type
Newsprint or other paper
Tag board letters
Crayon pieces with paper removed

What to do
1. Clip the newsprint to the cardboard using the clothespins.
2. Have the children lift the paper, insert several letters, and return the cover sheet.
3. The children can use the crayon on its side to rub from top to bottom, left to right.
4. They will notice the letters appearing on the top sheet of paper.

More to do
Language: Put magnetic letters on the side of a file cabinet or on a refrigerator. Encourage children to spell their names.
More art: Use a number of different colored crayons for an artistic effect.
Science: Collect leaves and do leaf rubbings using the same process as the alphabet rubbings.

Related books
Animal Action ABC by Karen Pandell
Anno's Alphabet by Anno Mitsumasa

 Mary Jo Shannon, Roanoke, VA

Green Glitter Ghosts

3+

Materials
White paper
Green finger paint
Green glitter
Scissors
Markers, optional

What to do

1. Talk to the children about the sound of the letter *G*. Tell them that the words *green, glitter,* and *ghost* all begin with the letter *G* and that today they are going to make green glitter ghosts.
2. Invite the children to finger paint a piece of paper with green paint.
3. While the paint is still wet, have the children sprinkle their papers with green glitter.
4. After the paper dries, the children can cut out one large or several small ghost shapes. Some of the children may wish to draw on facial features using the markers.

More to do

Language: Ask the children to name other things that start with the *G* sound.
Snack: Give children cookies cut in a ghost shape, green frosting, and green sprinkles. The children can spread the frosting on the cookies, add green sprinkles, and enjoy!

Related books

ABC I Like Me! by Nancy Carlson
Z Was Zapped by Chris Van Allsburg

Suzanne Maxymuk, Cherry Hill, NJ

Alphabet Quilt

Materials

26 felt squares, 6" x 6" (15 cm x 15 cm)
Felt alphabet letters
Fabric glue
Letter for parents
Large-eyed needles
Yarn or thread

What to do

1. Ahead of time, glue one felt alphabet letter to each felt square using fabric glue.
2. Send an alphabet square home with each child along with a letter asking the parents to help the child find and draw items that have that letter sound, glue one picture onto the square, and then have the child return the square to the classroom. Depending on the number of children, some may take home more than one felt square.
3. When all 26 letter squares are returned, invite the children to help you sew the squares together to make a class alphabet quilt.

More to do
Language: Display the alphabet quilt and use it as a visual aid when teaching letter recognition.

Related books
Eating the Alphabet: Fruits and Vegetables from A to Z by Lois Ehlert
The Keeping Quilt by Patricia Polacco

Kaethe Lewandowski, Centreville, VA

Fun With Initials

4+

Materials
Letter stencils, large
Scissors
Tagboard
Paint and paintbrushes
Decorative materials such as glitter, pompoms, felt
Glue

alphabet

What to do
1. Have the children trace and cut out the initials of their names from the tag board. Younger children may prefer to just do the initial letter of their first name.
2. Invite the children to paint their letters.
3. When the paint is dry, the children can glue on decorative materials.

More to do
Circle time: Ask each child to hold up an initial and name the letter. Then have the rest of the class repeat the letter in unison.
Game: Put all the letters in a pile. Select a child to come up and pick the initials of someone in the class. The first person to correctly name the child whose initials are presented gets the next turn.
Music: Have the class sing the "ABC" song, with each child holding up a letter when it appears in the song.

Related books
Dr. Seuss's ABC by Dr. Seuss
Eye Spy: A Mysterious Alphabet by Linda Bourke
Pigs From A to Z by Arthur Geisert

Deborah Hannes Litfin, Forest Hills, NY

Detective Letters

Materials
White construction paper
Ink pad

What to do
1. Ask the children to look at the underside of their fingertips and tell you what they see.
2. Give each child a piece of white construction paper.
3. Encourage the children to press one finger on the inkpad and then on the paper.
4. Invite them to form the first letter in their names by pressing their fingerprints on the paper.
5. Some children may wish to write their names using their fingerprints.

More to do
More art: Encourage the children to make simple designs using their fingerprints. Make an entire hand print.

Science: Use a magnifying glass to look at the lines on a fingertip. Discuss what types of lines are found on a fingerprint and why fingerprints are important to detectives.

Related books
The ABC Mystery by Doug Cushman
Detective Donut and the Wild Goose Chase by Bruce Whatley and Rosie Smith.

Sandra Fisher, Kutztown, PA

ABC Tree

Materials
Chicka Chicka Boom Boom by Bill Martin, Jr., and John Archambault
Light blue construction paper
Brown paper strips, 1" x 4" (3 cm x 10 cm)
Small green leaves (4 or 5 per child)
Glue or glue stick
Small alphabet stickers (1 sheet per child)

What to do
1. Read *Chicka Chicka Boom Boom* by Bill Martin, Jr., and John Archambault.
2. Invite the children to glue the brown strips and green leaves onto the blue construction paper to form a "coconut tree."
3. The children can decorate the tree using the alphabet stickers.

More to do
Games: Play alphabet bingo.
Language: Retell the story using a flannel board. Encourage the children to add new adventures to the story.

Related books
Eating the Alphabet: Fruits and Vegetables From A to Z by Lois Ehlert
Tomorrow's Alphabet by George Shannon

Linda N. Ford, Sacramento, CA

Letter B Butterflies

Materials
Uppercase letter *B* pattern on tag board
Construction paper, 9" x 12" (23 cm x 30 cm)
Scissors
Pipe cleaners, cut in 2" (5 cm) pieces
Glue
Butterfly stickers
Pencils

What to do
1. In advance enlarge the letter *B* on tag board and cut it out.
2. Fold a piece of construction paper in half like a card.
3. Trace the letter *B* pattern against the folded edge of the paper. Make one card for each child.
4. Encourage each child to cut around and in the holes of their letter, but not along the folded edge.
5. Then have them open the letter up to form a butterfly.
6. Give each child two pieces of pipe cleaner. Show the children how to glue the pieces on one end to look like antennas. Let dry.
7. Finally, add an assortment of butterfly stickers for decoration.
8. Hang from ceiling and voila! You have beautiful butterflies breezing through your classroom.

Related books
Butterfly Alphabet by Jerry Pallotta
The Very Hungry Caterpillar by Eric Carle

Quazonia J. Quarles, Newark, DE

The Colors of Nature

3+

Materials
Photographs of vividly colored saltwater fish
Construction paper
Scissors
Play sand
Washable tempera paints
Containers for mixing paint with sand
Large brushes
Blue paper for bulletin board
Light brown paper for bulletin board

beach

What to do

1. Ahead of time, cut out ocean-and beach-related shapes from the construction paper such as fish, starfish, and lobsters, and have at least one for each child to decorate.
2. Mix several spoonfuls of sand in with each different color of tempera paint.
3. Look at the photographs of tropical (and other) fish and invite the children to paint onto the shapes as desired, imitating the vivid colors of nature!
4. Dry thoroughly.
5. Display these works of art on a bulletin board of blue paper with a light brown border to simulate the seashore!

More to do

Environment: Add different toy sea creatures or objects to the sand to create a "sand dig" experiment. For an environmental effect, add bits of trash and explain why keeping the beaches and oceans clean is so important to us and especially to the animals that live there.

Sensory: Add sand to your sensory table. Add water and small plastic cups to it one day and make mini-sand castles. The sand will dry out as the children play with it and should be completely dry in a day or two.

Related Books

At the Beach by Huy Voun Lee
At the Beach With Dad by Mercer Mayer
Beach Day by Catarina Kruusval
Homer the Beachcomber by Janet Craig

Tina R. Woehler, Oak Point, TX

Everything's Just Beachy!

Materials

Large sandbox or a portion of sand-covered playground
Spray bottles
Food coloring, blue
Water
Garden hose and outside faucet
Seashells
Seaweed or sea kelp (real, if possible, if not, you can make these out of crepe paper)
Sand shovels

Sand pails
Sand molds
Playdough or clay that will harden in air

What to do

1. First, read a book about the beach (see suggestions under Related books below). Ask the children if they have ever been to a beach. Allow them time to tell their own beach stories.
2. Explain that because there is no beach nearby, they are going to make their own beach.
3. Use your large sandbox for the next steps. If your entire playground is sand, then use rope or heavy yarn to mark off a large area. You will need lots of room!
4. Ask the children to describe what a beach looks like. As they talk, begin to mark off the areas of your sandbox that will represent each aspect of a real beach.
5. Mark a line in the sand that shows where the sand and ocean water on the beach meet. Explain that this is called the shoreline. Give several children spray bottles filled with water, which has been colored a bright blue with food coloring. Have them spray the "ocean" part of your sandbox bright blue.
6. As those children are working, have other children spread seashells and sea kelp or seaweed over the "beach" area. Let them freely choose where they want to place things. They can also use a shovel and pail to move the sand around to form sand dunes, and the sand molds to make sand castles.
7. While these two groups are working, a third group of children can be molding fish, octupi, sea lions, oysters, snails, and other sea-dwelling creatures from clay or playdough. These creations can be placed on the beach or in the "water" as the children desire. They will air dry quickly.
8. Stand back and enjoy your huge work of art!

More to do

Dramatic play: Plan a beach party day. Invite parents to come and have a picnic lunch. Encourage them to bring their lawn chairs or beach blankets and invite them to lounge around INSIDE your artwork.

Related books

At the Beach by Anne Rockwell
A Beach for the Birds by Bruce McMillan
Castle Builder by Dennis Nolan

Virginia Jean Herrod, Columbia, SC

Sand Art

3+

Materials
Sand
Bowls
Spray bottle with water
Food coloring
Stirring utensil
Funnel
Salt shakers
Glue
Paper

What to do
1. Put sand in several bowls (use as many bowls as you have colors).
2. Invite the children to help you spray the sand until it is slightly damp, and mix the food coloring thoroughly with the sand. Allow the sand to dry. (Sun or an oven will speed up the drying process.)
3. When the sand is dry, use the funnel to put it in salt shakers. You can use different shakers for different colors, or mix up the colored sand in one shaker.
4. Have children dribble a design on paper using the glue, then shake the colored sand on top for a lovely effect.

More to do
More art: Use holiday shapes, let dry, and then decorate.

Related books
The Art Lesson by Tomie de Paola
Little Blue and Little Yellow by Leo Lionni

Sandra Hutchins Lucas, Cox's Creek, KY

Fish Stencil Resist Painting

Materials

Clean Styrofoam meat trays
Exacto knife (teacher only)
Pencils
White paper
Light-colored crayons
Very thin blue paint (Test paint
   to make sure the crayon will
   resist it.)
Sponges or brushes

What to do

1. Ahead of time, cut fish-shaped stencils out of Styrofoam trays using an Exacto knife (adult only).
2. Invite the children to place fish stencils on top of paper and trace to create fish outline.
3. Demonstrate how to color, pressing FIRMLY inside fish shapes with light-colored crayon.
4. Ask the children to use sponges or brushes to paint a thin wash of the blue paint over the whole scene, creating a sea.

More to do

More art: Make stencils of other sea creatures or vegetation. Use a large paper to make a "deep sea" mural.

Related books

My Visit to the Aquarium by Aliki
The Rainbow Fish by Marcus Pfister

Deborah Bauer, Tempe, AZ

Beachcomber's Wreath

4+

Materials
Seashells
Tempera paints
Paintbrushes
Styrofoam wreaths
Glue
Raffia

What to do
1. If possible, take children to the beach to collect seashells. Otherwise, provide the children with a variety of small seashells.
2. Give the children Styrofoam wreaths to paint with tempera paints in any color they choose.
3. When the wreaths are dry, invite the children to glue shells all over them.
4. Help children tie a raffia ribbon into a bow to glue at the top or bottom of the wreath.

More to do
Blocks: Build pretend sand castles with blocks.
Dramatic play: Create a beach in the classroom by laying a blue sheet on the floor as the ocean, and setting up a lifeguard chair. Give the children beach towels, sunglasses, and empty bottles of sunscreen.
Science: Examine different kinds of seashells.

Related books
At the Beach by Huy Voun Lee
Sand Cake by Frank Asch

Lisa M. Chichester, Parkersburg, WV

Fossil Fun

Materials
Fossils or pictures of fossils
Clay or other modeling compound
Seashells, preferably scallop shells with a ribbed design

What to do
1. If possible, show the children samples (or pictures) of fossils, and discuss what fossils are.
2. Give each child a lump of clay and a seashell.
3. Invite the children to press the shell into the clay and carefully remove it, leaving an impression.
4. If using Sculpey, follow the directions for baking.
5. Otherwise, let the clay air dry.

More to do
Sand table: Hide the fossils in the sand table and have the children pretend to be paleontologists searching for fossils.

Related books
Fossils of the World by Chris Pellant
Until I Saw the Sea: A Collection of Seashore Poems, edited by Alison Shaw

 Mary Jo Shannon, Roanoke, VA

Sea Collage 4+

Materials
Cardboard pieces, approximately 8" x 10" (20 cm x 25 cm)
Sponges, small
Water
Dry tempera paint, blue and green
Glue
Small shells, sand, bits of driftwood, pebbles from the beach

What to do

1. Invite the children to dip a damp sponge in the dry tempera paints and gently paint the cardboard.
2. Let cardboard dry.
3. Encourage the children to select from the available shells, sand, driftwood, and pebbles that they would like to use in their collage.
4. Demonstrate how to dribble glue on the cardboard, then press the natural materials into place.
5. Allow the collages to dry, and then shake off any excess sand.

More to do

Sand: Hide seashells and rocks in the sand table or sandbox.
Science: Have children bring in their special seashells or rocks to show to the class.

Related books

How to Hide an Octopus: And Other Sea Creatures, by Ruth Heller
Life in the Sea by Eileen Curran
Seashore by David Burnie

Mary Jo Shannon, Roanoke, VA

Colored Sand Jars

5+

Materials

Baby food jars with lids
Paintbrushes
Tempera paints, wet and dry
White sand
Bowls for mixing sand
Spoons
Stickers

What to do

1. Invite the children to paint the lids of the baby food jars and put aside to dry.
2. Give them several bowls with white sand and ask them to stir in a little dry tempera paint (the color of the sand should be strong).
3. Encourage the children to fill their baby food jars with the colored sand, alternating colors or creating a pattern. Remind the children not to shake their jars!

4. When the jars are full to the top and the lids are dry, the children can cover their jars and then place a decorative sticker on top.

More to do
More art: Provide children with other types of clear containers, such as plastic soda bottles, to fill with sand. Children can add layers of tiny shells or pebbles.

Related books
Sylvester and the Magic Pebble by William Steig
Until I Saw the Sea by Alison Shaw

Melissa J. Browning, Milwaukee, WI

Beach Pebble Mosaic

Materials
Shallow, pliable plastic bowl
Plastic wrap
Pebbles from a beach
Plaster of Paris
Bowl or basin
Scissors

What to do
1. Ahead of time, line the bowl with plastic wrap if it is not sufficiently pliable.
2. Talk to the children about the pebbles and how the water has made them smooth. Help the children sort the pebbles by color and size.
3. Invite the children to draw the outline of a picture, like a drawing in a coloring book. Lay the picture in the bottom of the bowl.
4. Have the children fill the picture in with pebbles, giving consideration to the size and color of the pebbles. For example, dark-colored pebbles could represent the spots on a dog or the color of someone's eyes.
5. Mix the plaster in a bowl or basin. Carefully pour it on top of the pebbles, covering the picture.
6. Let the plaster dry for several hours, then gently tap the bottom of the bowl and turn it over to release the mosaic. Carefully manipulate the bowl if you cannot remove the mosaic at first.
7. Trim any excess paper from the edge of the mosaic.

beach

8. If they are able, invite the children to create their own mosaic.

More to do
More art: Share examples of mosaics with the class. Design mosaics with an assortment of materials. Use paint and other materials to decorate rocks.
Science: Examine a collection of rocks and pebbles with a magnifying glass.

Related books
Anansi and the Moss-Covered Rock by Eric A. Kimmel
Sylvester and the Magic Pebble by William Steig

Jean Potter, Charleston, WV

Teddy Bear Patchwork

3+

Materials

Teddy bear silhouette, about 4" (10 cm) high
Cardboard
Marker
Scissors
Masking tape
Crayons in a variety of colors, with paper removed
Construction paper, 12" x 18" (30 cm x 45 cm), or typing paper

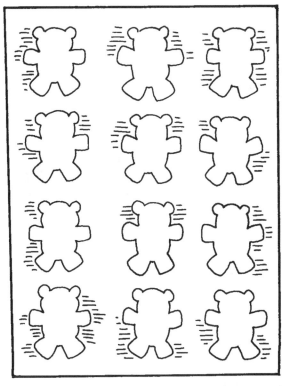

What to do

1. Ahead of time, cut out a teddy bear silhouette about 4" (10 cm) high from cardboard, and glue it to a larger rectangle of cardboard. Cardboard from shirts or cereal boxes works fine. If there is no time to glue, rolls of masking tape will hold the bear to the backing.

2. Talk to the children about patchwork quilts and how, on some quilts, one design is a repeated over and over in different colors. Their rubbings will look like a teddy bear patchwork.

3. To keep cardboard from shifting, tape it to the table. Place paper over the cardboard. To check paper position, ask children to "feel the bear under the covers."

4. Invite the children to rub the side of a crayon back and forth several times over the bear until the image appears on the paper. Children can help each other—one holds the paper while the other rubs. After a good image has been produced, have them choose a new color crayon and shift the paper over slightly to begin the next "patchwork" block. (Older children may want to start at one corner of the paper, so they can add bears in a row.) Repeat rows (or random groupings) of bears in a variety of colors.

5. After filling the paper, use a dark crayon to add features such as eyes, nose, and mouth (a simple "V" can be used as a mouth, or use two "*Js*" back to back to form a teddy bear smile).

6. To give the impression of a really big quilt, hang the pictures with their edges touching.

More to do

More art: Using the technique on the previous page, make teddy bear placemats (for extended use, laminate or cover with clear contact paper). Make the cardboard teddy bear relief in three sizes (big, medium, and small) so children can make rubbings for "Goldilocks and the Three Bears," adding details from the story.

Related books

Bear Shadow by Frank Asch
The Keeping Quilt by Patricia Polacco
The Quilt Story by Tony Johnston

Tina Slater, Silver Spring, MD

Teddy Bears' Picnic

Materials
Paper plates
Scissors
Stuffed bears
Crayons or markers
Tape
Stapler
Hole punch
Old towels, blankets, or tablecloths
Playdough in assorted colors
Rolling pin
Plastic knives
Small plastic plates, margarine tub lids, or Styrofoam trays
Music
Lunch or snack, optional

What to do
1. Beforehand, cut a slit from the edge of each paper plate to the center. Also, ask the children to bring a stuffed bear from home, if possible.
2. To make the bears' party hats, have the children decorate a paper plate with crayons or markers.
3. When they are finished, twist the plate into a cone shape and secure it with tape or staples.

4. Next, ask the children to choose whether they would like to make a dress-up collar or a bowtie for their bear.

5. To make a collar, fold the paper plates in half and, beginning at the slit, cut a hole in the middle of the plate.

6. Have the children decorate the collar with crayons. Let them punch some holes so the collar appears to be made of lace.

7. To make a bow tie, follow the same steps as above, then cut out the shape of a bowtie where the ends of the collar meet.

8. Have the children decorate the bow tie with crayons.

9. When they finish the party hats and a collar or bow tie, have the children dress their bears and set them on picnic blankets around the room.

10. Invite the children to prepare a picnic with playdough. Show them how to roll the playdough flat with a rolling pin and cut shapes for bread, lunchmeat, and pie crust. Have them roll balls of dough for fruit and doughnuts or a tubular shape for pickles and cucumbers. Provide them with play cookie cutters. Encourage them to decorate the cookies and cakes with little bits of playdough.

11. Ask the children to serve the food to the bears on trays or plastic dishes. Play some music and perhaps serve lunch or a treat to the children as well.

More to do

Circle time: Invite the children to introduce their bear friend to their classmates.
Language: Prepare invitations to the picnic.

Related books and song

Happy Birthday, Moon by Frank Asch
The Teddy Bears Picnic by Jerry Garcia and David Grisman
Song, "The Teddy Bear's Picnic"

Tina Slater, Silver Spring, MD

Teddy Bear Paper Dolls

Materials
Teddy bear pattern
Oak tag or poster board
Crayons
Markers

bears

Safety scissors
Watercolor paints
Paintbrushes
Glue
Moveable eyes
Pompoms
Construction paper, various colors
Glitter

What to do

1. Have the children trace the pattern of a teddy bear doll on oak tag or poster board and cut it out.
2. Give the children watercolors and invite them to color their paper teddy bears.
   The children can glue on moveable eyes and pompom nose, and draw on a mouth with markers.
3. Give the children construction paper and safety scissors; invite them to cut out clothing that they think will fit their paper teddy bears. They can decorate the clothing any way they like using crayon, marker, glitter, or paint.

More to do

Dramatic play: Children can use their dolls to act out stories, such as "The Three Bears."
More art: Children can make families of paper teddy bears.

Related books

Golden Bear by Ruth Young
Ira Sleeps Over by Bernard Waber
When the Teddy Bears Came by Martin Waddell

Lisa M. Chichester, Parkersburg, WV

Stuffed Teddy Bear

Materials

Brown paper grocery bags
Crayons
Stapler
Newspaper, shredded

bears

What to do

1. Cut out teddy bear shapes from paper bags (two for each child, one for the front and one for the back).
2. Color the teddy bear shapes, one for the front of the bear and one for the back.
3. Crinkle teddy bears, then smooth out (this makes the paper bag softer and easier to stuff).
4. Place the two sides together and staple along the edges, leaving an opening for stuffing.
5. Stuff the bear with shredded newspaper.
6. Finish stapling bear closed.

More to do

Snack: Follow this activity with a teddy bear picnic day. Children bring in their favorite teddy bears and enjoy a picnic-style snack, with milk and bear-shaped cookies.

Related books

Corduroy by Don Freeman
My Friend Bear by Jez Alborough
Teddy Bear, Teddy Bear by Michael Hague
Teddy Bear's Picnic by Bruce Whatley
Who Wants an Old Teddy Bear? by Ginnie Hofmann

Deborah R. Gallagher, Bridgeport, CT

Feathered Friends

Materials

Construction paper
Scissors
Glue
Craft feathers
Medium-sized googly eyes

What to do
1. Cut out a bird shape for each child from the construction paper.
2. Invite the children to spread the glue onto the paper where desired.
3. Let the child place the feathers on top of the glue.
4. Put glue onto the back of a googly eye and place it on the bird's head.
5. Let the bird dry completely.
6. The birds may be hung from the ceiling with yarn. If you decide to hang the birds, invite the children to decorate both sides.

More to do
Science: Make a bird feeder using a grapefruit. Cut the fruit in half and scoop out the insides. This may be eaten or discarded. Afterward allow the rind to dry out about 24 hours. Then punch several holes around the edges for hanging purposes. Afterward, thread the yarn through the holes and secure together. Place any type of birdseed or sunflower seeds inside and hang in a visible tree area so the children can monitor its use. If no tree is available, then just take a walk outside and spread some seed on the ground and the birds will probably find it.
Sensory: Add birdseed to your sensory table.
Snack: Make a wormy snack by mixing prepared chocolate pudding with crushed chocolate sandwich cookies. Place the mix in a small cup and then garnish with gummy worm candies. Push the worms down into the pudding mixture to invite the children to pull them out just like the birds.

Related books
Are You My Mother? by Philip D. Eastman
The Best Nest by Philip D. Eastman
A Nest Full of Eggs by Priscilla Belz Jenkins

Tina R. Woehler, Oak Point, TX

Bird-watching Binoculars

Materials
Cardboard toilet paper rolls (two for each child)
Tape
Hole punch
Glue
Scissors

Markers
Paint
String

What to do

1. Take two toilet paper rolls and tape them together, side by side.
2. Punch a hole on the outside edge of each roll (at the same end).
3. Ask the children to decorate their binoculars. They can be painted, colored with markers or crayons, or decorated with stickers.
4. Tie a string through the punched holes to make a handle.
5. Go outside and look for birds!

More to do

Dramatic play: Have real or toy binoculars available during play.
Science: Long paper tubes can be made into telescopes. These can be used with camping units or space units.

Related books

A Bird's Body by Joanna Cole
Birdsong by Audrey Wood
Grandmother's Pigeon by Louise Erdrich

Sandra Nagel, White Lake, MI

Nesting Bags

Materials

Plastic netted bag (such as onions, oranges, or potatoes are packaged in)
Small pieces of yarn

Shredded paper
Colored wrapping paper scraps
Dryer lint
Scissors
String or cord

What to do

1. A week or so before the project, post a sign asking parents to save the plastic netted bags and send them in for making nesting bags.
2. Tell the children they are going to make nesting bags, which are like gift bags for the birds. Talk with the children about how birds make their nests by picking up miscellaneous materials they find and taking them, one by one, to their nesting sites.
3. Invite the children to select, from the nesting materials you have made available, a nice assortment that they can use to stuff in their netted bags.
4. Be sure to cut a slit or two on the sides of the bags to allow the birds to get the items out.
5. Tie the bags on tree branches and watch for signs of birds "stealing" the items to make their nests.
6. The birds will love it!

More to do

Science: Make a bird feeder by using an empty plastic gallon jug with a handle. Cut a section out of two sides of the jug. Cut the bottom of the handle away from the jug in order to place it onto a tree branch. Fill the jug bottom with birdseed (NEVER use rice as this kills the birds). Watch for signs of birds using it. Fill as necessary. Be sure to put it in a very popular place used by birds.
Snack: An edible variation can be made if desired. Melt a bag of butterscotch chips in the microwave and add canned chow mein noodles. Mix with a spoon and place by spoonfuls onto wax paper until hardened. Then color two cups (500 mL) of coconut green by placing it into a zip-closure bag with a few drops of green food coloring. Shake. Add the coconut to the chow mien nests before hardening is complete. Then add a few jellybeans to each nest. Enjoy!

Related books

Feathers for Lunch by Lois Ehlert
The Robins in Your Backyard by Nancy Carol Willis

Original fingerplay

I Wish I Were a Little Blue Bird (to the tune of the "Oscar Mayer Wiener Song")

Oh, I wish I were a little happy blue bird.
Oh, that is what I'd really like to be.
For if I were a little happy blue bird,
I would build my nest up high in the tree.

Oh, I wish I were a little baby blue bird.
Oh, that is what I'd really like to be.
For if I were a little baby blue bird,
I'd hatch from my egg in that tree.

Oh, I wish I were a Mommy blue bird.
Oh, that is what I'd really like to be.
For if I were a Mommy blue bird,
A worm would feed my babies in the tree.

Tina R. Woehler, Oak Point, TX

Cookies for the Birds

3+

Materials
Large cookie cutters in simple shapes
Stale bread
Peanut butter
Plastic knives
Birdseed
Plastic drinking straws
String

What to do
1. Invite the children to choose a cookie cutter to cut a design from a slice of bread.
2. Let the children spread peanut butter on the bread "cookie" they have just made.
3. Give them birdseed to sprinkle over the peanut butter.
4. Gently lift the shape and let the excess seeds fall off.
5. Have the children poke a hole close to the edge of their shapes with a drinking straw.
6. Allow the shapes to dry over night until hard.
7. Tie a loop of string through the hole for hanging.

8. Hang these bird cookies from the branches of a tree or bush that can be seen from the classroom window.

Related books
Outside the Window by Anna Egan Smucker
The Robins in Your Backyard by Nancy Carol Willis

Rebecca McMahon, Mobile, AL

Pinecone Feeders

Materials
Pinecones (white pines work well)
String
Peanut butter
Small spreading knives
Birdseed
Aluminum pie plates or trays

What to do
1. Fill aluminum pie plates or trays with birdseed.
2. Tie a string at the top of each pinecone.
3. Invite the children to spread peanut butter over the cone, gently pushing it into the crevices.
4. Next, have the children roll their cones in birdseed.
5. Take the children outside and let them pick low branches on which to hang their pinecone feeders.

Related book
Birdsong by Audrey Wood

More to do
Science: Watch the birds. Keep a bird picture journal of who comes to eat at the feeders.

Linda Atamian, Charlestown RI

It's for the Birds

Materials

Found items:
> Pine or regular straw
> Bits of fabric
> Bits of thread
> Twigs, broken into very small pieces
> Dryer lint
> Bits of grass
> Craft feathers or real bird feathers

Petroleum jelly

Homemade glue (recipe on the following page)

Large mixing bowl

What to do

1. Read *The Magpies Nest* by Joanna Foster. Talk about the nest that the birds built. Ask children if they would like to try to build a nest just like the birds did.
2. Send a letter home to the parents asking them to send in items listed above, noting that you will need lots of stuff as the children are going to make a larger-than-life-size nest.
3. After you have gathered enough items to build a nice nest, make your glue. Use the recipe on the following page.
4. Coat the inside of the mixing bowl with petroleum jelly and then apply a thin layer of the glue mixture. It will be hard to do, but keep at it.
5. Dump your found items out on a table. Sort out the lint and feathers and set them aside to be used last.
6. Invite the children to begin to add the found items to the mixing bowl. Have them press the material firmly against the glue mixture. Continue to layer the glue and nest materials, always pressing them firmly against the sides of the pan. Keep the shape as round as possible. Remember to fill in the bottom.
7. Keep going until you have used up all the materials and glue. Last, add the feathers and lint to line the nest just as a real bird would.
8. Let your nest dry for several hours in a warm place.
9. Remove the nest from the mixing bowl. It will probably still be a little moist and messy. Place it on a sturdy surface where you can leave it, such as on a work tray. Push down on the bottom to flatten it slightly and lift up on the edges to make them a nice, round shape. It will continue to dry over the next couple of days.

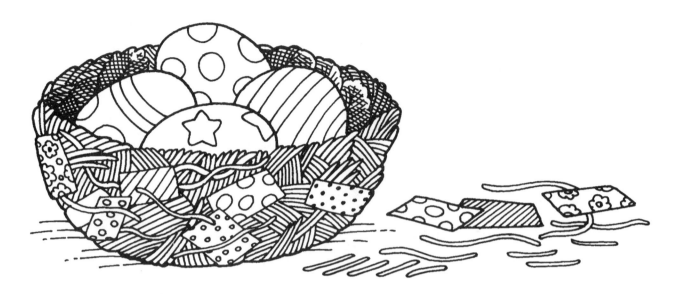

Recipe for Glue

Ingredients:
¼ cup (60 mL) sugar
¼ cup (60 mL) flour
½ teaspoon (2.5 mL) alum
1 & ¾ cups (450 mL) water

Mix the sugar, flour, and alum in a pan. Gradually add 1 cup (250 mL) of water and stir briskly. Heat to boiling and boil until the mixture is clear and smooth. Add ¾ cup (200 mL) water and stir. (Double or triple this recipe as needed according to the size of your nest. This recipe is for a small nest.)

More to do

Dramatic play: Pretend to be birds and fly to music.
Field trip: Go bird watching.
More art: Children can decorate eggs to be placed in the nest. Use old plastic Easter eggs. Let the children decorate them any way they please and put them in the nest. Make birds out of clay or playdough to sit on your nest.

Related books

The Magpies' Nest by Joanna Foster
No Roses for Harry by Gene Zion

Virginia Jean Herrod, Columbia, SC

Sock Birds

5+

Materials
Socks, brightly colored
Yellow felt
Scissors
Googly eyes
Feathers
Glue

What to do
1. Show the children what the sock bird will look like by placing one you have already made over your hand, then laying it flat so that the children can see how the "features" are placed.
2. Help the children cut a large folded beak from the yellow felt to place inside of the sock bird's mouth at the end.
3. Have the children glue googly eyes on top of sock.
4. Give each child two or three brightly colored feathers to glue on the sock bird's head. Feathers can also be added on the bottom of the sock for a feather-covered body.

More to do
Dramatic play: Set up a puppet theatre and invite the children to put on a show with their new sock bird puppets.
More art: Give children socks and a variety of decorative materials and colorful markers. Invite them to make "crazy" birds by

decorating them in funny and original ways.

Related books

About Birds by Cathryn Sill
Owl Babies by Martin Waddell

Lisa M. Chichester, Parkersburg, WV

Creative Clown Hat

3+

Materials
Markers, many colors
White sturdy paper bowls, 7" (18 cm) diameter
Pompoms, I" (3 cm) size (metallic type is best)
White glue
Yarn, any color, cut in 15" (40 cm) lengths
Hole punch

What to do
1. Give each child a paper bowl that has two holes punched near the edge for yarn.
2. Invite the children to turn their bowls upside down and then decorate them using different color markers. They might draw stripes, polka dots, or shapes.
3. When their marker designs are dry, have them glue on a pom-pom in the center.
4. Give each child two pieces of yarn, and show them how to tie one in each hole on the side of the clown hat. Glue short ends inside the hat.
5. Invite the children to put on their colorful clown hats, tying them under their chins.

More to do
Dramatic play: Have a circus. Invite the children to do funny clown routines while wearing their hats.
Game: Cut big feet or shoes out of cardboard or felt. Write a numeral on each foot or shoe. Place them randomly on the floor. Start the music. Children walk around stepping only on the feet. When the music stops, each child says the number that he is standing on.

Related book
A Three Hat Day by Laura Geringer

Circus

Original song

I Am a Clown (sing to the tune of "You Are My Sunshine")

I am a clown, a funny clown.
I make you laugh all the day.
See my hat and my red nose.
And my suit is bright and gay.

I have big feet and fuzzy hair,
And I like to jump around.
I ride in a tiny car,
And do tricks with squeaky sounds.

Come to the circus or an ice show,
And lots of clowns you will see.
I hope you like my big smile,
And are happy just like me.

Mary Brehm, Aurora, OH

Elephant Footprints

Materials
Shallow tray of mud
Long strip of paper
Eager group of children

What to do
1. This is an activity best done outdoors on a warm day.
2. Let the children help you stir dirt and water together in a shallow tray to make mud.
3. Have the children take their shoes and socks off and hold their hands while they step into the tray of mud. (It gets pretty slippery.)
4. Let them walk across a long strip of paper to create elephant tracks!

More to do
More art: Let the children dip their hands in the mud and make handprints on a sheet of paper.
Science: Create a "feely" bag. Put several different textured items such as a pinecone, wool, or a

feather in the bag and let the children use their sense of touch to guess what's inside.

Related books
Little Elephant by Tana Hoban and Miela Ford
Mud Pies and Other Recipes by Marjorie Winslow
Pigs in the Mud in the Middle of the Road by Lynn Plourde
Rain by Peter Spier

Cindy Winther, Oxford, MI

Clown Ties

3+

Materials
Felt or real cloth ties (donated by parents)
Scissors
Squeeze paint
Glitter
Pompoms
Sequins
Yarn

What to do
1. Cut pieces of felt into a tie shape or collect used ties.
2. Encourage the children to decorate the ties using squeeze paints, jewels, glitter, pompoms, and sequins.
3. If using felt, fold over top and put a piece of yarn through to tie on.

More to do
Dramatic play: Set up a circus. Hang a parachute from the ceiling. Make cages out of boxes. Let the children bring in "wild" animals to place in the cages.
More art: The ties make a nice gift for Dad on Father's Day.

Cindy Winther, Oxford, MI

Circus

Class Clown

4+

Materials
Markers or crayons
Butcher paper

What to do
1. Have one child volunteer to lie down and be traced on butcher paper to make the outline of the clown's body.
2. Cut out the outline into six pieces: head, body, two arms, and two legs.
3. Divide the children into five groups.
4. Have each group color their part of the clown as colorfully as they can. Encourage pattern-like stripes, dots or other shapes.
5. Decorate the head with a typical clown face.
6. Have the children help re-assemble the clown and tape him on a wall in the classroom, complete with his creatively colorful clown outfit.

More to do
Dramatic play: Place colorful clothing and clown wig in dramatic play area for kids to dress up. Remember, the more colors the better!
More art: Do clown face painting.

Related books
Circus! by Peter Spier
If I Ran the Circus by Dr. Seuss

Suzanne Pearson, Winchester, VA

Balloon Clowns

4+

Materials
White balloons, one per child

Red yarn, cut into 12" (30 cm) lengths
Pompoms, red
Markers, black and red

What to do

1. Blow up and tie one balloon for each child.
2. Encourage the children to glue red yarn on top of the balloons for hair.
3. The children can glue a red pompom nose on their clown's face.
4. Invite the children to draw eyes on their balloons using black marker.
5. The children can draw on a big clown smile with the red marker.

Related books

Harvey Potter's Balloon Farm by Jerdine Nolan
The Well-Mannered Balloon by Nancy Willard

 *Lisa M. Chichester, Parkersburg, WV*

Lion With a Curly Mane 5+

Materials

Pictures of lions in wild and in circus
Construction paper, 9" x 12" (23 cm x 30 cm) in light brown, yellow, and orange; one sheet per lion
Paper strips, 12" x 6" (30 cm x 15 cm) in light brown, yellow, and orange; about 15 per lion
Scissors
Crayons

Circus

Jumbo crayons (for rolling paper strips)
Glue
Damp paper towels

What to do

1. Talk to the children about lions
   and their habitats, prides,
   appearance, and other
   characteristics. Show
   some pictures of lions in
   the wild and in the circus.
2. Give each child a large
   sheet of construction
   paper. Have the chil-
   dren draw a large cir-
   cle or oval shape on
   the paper for the lion's
   face. They can add facial features (no manes) with crayons
   and then cut out the face.

3. Show the children how to add a mane to the face of their lion by tightly rolling a strip around a jumbo crayon. Hold it for a moment and then slip the crayon out, keeping the curl intact. Put a small amount of glue on the inside edge of the curl. Slip the glued end under the lion's face so that the curl winds up and over the edge of the lion's face.
4. The children can repeat with other strips, curling and gluing them all around the lion's face. Provide damp paper towels for finger wiping. Allow glue to dry before displaying.

More to do

Circle time: Ask the children to bring toy lions from home to show and tell about.
Dramatic play: Pretend to be lions and lion tamers. Add circus animals and encourage circus activities.

Related books

Circus! by Peter Spier
If I Ran the Circus by Dr. Seuss
Johnny Lion's Bad Day by Edith Hurd
A Lion Named Shirley Williamson by Bernard Waber
Nanta's Lion: A Search-and Find Adventure by Suse MacDonald

Susan O. Hill, Lakeland, FL

My Favorite Clothes

3+

Materials
White construction paper
Crayons or markers
Scissors
Clothespins
Clothesline

What to do
1. Ahead of time, draw the outlines of children's clothing on white construction paper. You might draw pants, shorts, shirts, dresses, hats, coats, and swimsuits.
2. Invite the children to tell about their favorite kinds of clothing.
3. Give each child an outline shape of her favorite kind of clothing.
4. Encourage the children to decorate the plain clothing outlines to look like their favorite piece of clothing.
5. Have the children cut the decorated clothing items out with scissors.
6. Give them clothespins and tell them to hang the items on a length of clothesline strung along a classroom wall.

Related books
Jesse Bear, What Will You Wear? by Nancy W. Carlstrom
Max's New Suit by Rosemary Wells
Mrs. McNosh Hangs Up Her Wash by Sara Weeks

 Nancy Dentler, Mobile, AL

Meat Tray Prints

3+

Materials
Paper
Pencil
Scissors
Styrofoam meat trays, one per child
Fabric paints

clothes

T-shirts, one per child

What to do

Note: For this activity, you might wish to work with one child at a time, helping that child print her own drawing on a T-shirt.

1. Ask a child to make a pencil drawing on paper.
2. Cut away edges of the meat tray to make a flat surface.
3. Using a pencil, trace the child's original drawing onto the meat tray.
4. Paint the meat tray drawing with fabric paints. It helps to decide on colors prior to painting. Put a small amount of the chosen colors on a clean meat tray and have multiple paintbrushes to allow for a quick application of the paint to the child's drawing.
5. Invite the child to carefully flip the painted drawing and print it onto the T-shirt. The drawing can be outlined with black fabric paint for accent.

More to do

More art: Set out an old bedsheet and let the children work together to print designs on it. This activity could also be done with tempera paints on paper, if desired.

Related books

Froggy Gets Dressed by Jonathan London
Pelle's New Suit by Elsa Beskow

Ann Wenger, Harrisonburg, VA

Sew Buttons

Materials

Plastic needles
Yarn
Squares of plastic canvas
Plastic 1" (3 cm) buttons

What to do

1. Thread plastic needles with yarn.
2. Give each child a piece of plastic canvas, a threaded needle, and some buttons.
3. Show the children how to sew buttons onto the canvas and encourage them to sew on some buttons by themselves.

More to do
Game: Play "Button, Button, Who's Got the Button?"
Math: Sort buttons by color or the number of holes it has.

Related books
Bit by Bit by Steven Sanfield
The Button Box by Margarette Reid
Corduroy by Don Freeman

Sandy Lanes, Silver Spring, MD

Mitten Friends

Materials
Winter mittens or oven mitts
Yarn, buttons, felt scraps, pompoms, rickrack, and other notions and trimming
Scissors
Glue
Fabric paint
Glue gun

What to do
1. Invite the children to decorate a mitt or mitten with the various sewing notions and fabric paint.
2. Help the children glue the decorations on; afterward, secure the decorations to the mitten with a glue gun, reminding the children that only an adult may touch the glue gun.
3. If they choose, invite the children to create a second character on the other side of the mitten, to be worn on their opposite hand.

More to do
More art: Create finger puppets with old film canisters.
Language: Using mittens, create characters from nursery rhymes or favorite stories, and recite the words with your mitten friends.

Lisa M. Chichester, Parkersburg, WV

clothes

Bonnet Bouquet

Materials
Construction paper or poster board
Scissors
Wallpaper sample book
Scraps of gift wrapping paper
Glue
Hole punch
Ribbon

What to do
1. Before class, cut a wide-brim hat from construction paper or poster board for each child.
2. Invite the children to cut up scraps of wallpaper or gift wrap and arrange, then glue them on their hat.
3. When they are finished, help the children punch a hole at the bottom of the brim on both sides of the hat.
4. Cut ribbon into short pieces and show the children how to tie the ribbon to each hole.

More to do
More art: Create a still-life picture of a flower vase or a garden scene using the same technique. Decorate straw hats with artificial flowers. Make silly paper plate hats with collage materials.

Related book
Jennie's Hat by Ezra Jack Keats

Inge Mix, Massapequa, NY

Cereal Box Tote Bag

Materials
Old magazines
Scissors
Empty cereal boxes
Glue thinned with water
Pencil
Ribbon or cord
Paintbrushes
Decorative items such as lace, buttons, stickers

What to do.
1. Have the children cut out pictures from magazines.
2. Give each child an empty cereal box.
3. Show them how to tuck in the flaps and secure with glue if necessary.
4. Using the point of the pencil, help the children poke a hole through each side of the box.
5. Have the children cut equal lengths of ribbon or cord for the handles.

6. The children thread the ribbon or cord through the holes, making a knot on either end to secure it (some children may need help with this).
7. Using a paintbrush, the children spread glue on both sides of the cereal box.
8. The children arrange and apply the magazine pictures to the glued surface.
9. When they are finished, have them spread another coat of thinned glue over the entire box and allow to dry.
10. The children may add other objects to decorate and personalize their boxes.

More to do
Holidays: Give these tote bags as gifts for Mother's or Father's Day.

Related books
The Big Green Pocketbook by Candice Ransom
I Need a Lunchbox by Jeannette F. Caines
Lady With the Alligator Purse by Ernest Finney
Lilly's Purple Plastic Purse by Kevin Henkes

Nicole Sparks, Miami, FL

Giant Paper Dolls

Materials
Roll of brown butcher paper or a similar kind of paper
Chalk
Drop cloths such as old blankets and sheets
Tempera paint in Styrofoam trays
Liquid soap
Small sponges
Scissors
Round sticky labels
Oil pastels
Miscellaneous materials such as fabric, felt, yarn, ribbon, wrapping and construction paper, pompoms, and cotton balls
Glue
Stapler

What to do
1. Invite the children to take turns lying on the butcher paper while one of their classmates traces the outline of their body with chalk. When the outline is complete, encourage the children to sketch in details on their own paper doll such as pants or a dress and shoes. Tell the children that their doll can represent them, someone they know, or an imaginary person.
2. While they are working, cover the floor with drop cloths. Pour a small amount of paint into each tray, adding a bit of liquid soap to extend the paint. Provide a sponge for each tray.
3. When the children are ready, set the trays on the floor and have the children lay their dolls on the floor around the trays.

4. Encourage the children to work with one color until they are finished with it, then start a second color. When they are finished painting, set the dolls aside to dry.
5. Afterward, help the children cut out their doll outside the outline.
6. Invite the children to use round labels, oil pastels, or other materials to add features and clothing accessories. Suggest that the children make props from paper such as a football, a book, a pet, or a favorite belonging.
7. Display the paper dolls along a wall, holding hands.

More to do
More art: Have the children sit beneath the display of paper dolls and take a photo; invite the children to create a frame for their group photo. Create portraits with oil pastels.
Language: Have the children introduce their paper dolls and write or dictate a few sentences about them.

Related book
Cherry Pies and Lullabies by Lynn Reiser

 Tina Slater, Silver Spring, MD

Baker's Hat 5+

Materials
White, unruled sentence strips
Scissors
Markers
Stickers
Sheets of white tissue paper
Glue
Scissors

What to do
1. Cut sentence strips in half lengthwise to make hatbands, and give one to each child. Invite the children to personalize their hatbands using markers and stickers.
2. Show the children how to fold one full sheet of tissue paper in half, then in half again to form a complete square.
3. Cut the ends off so when opened it will be a large circle.
4. Invite the children to glue the edges of the circle to the hatband, scrunching the tissue so the entire edge of the circle is glued on the band; then have them glue the ends of the hatband

clothes

together. You may need to help the children with this step.

5. Show the children how to puff the center of the hat by gently pushing the tissue from the inside of the hat or placing crumpled tissue paper inside the hat to help hold the structure.

More to do
Dramatic play: Children can pretend to be bakers in the Housekeeping Center.
Snack: Children can put on their hats and mix real bread dough, kneading it on a clean surface until it is ready to bake. Serve warm!

Related books
Aunt Flossie's Hats by Elizabeth Fitzgerald Howard
Caps for Sale by Esphyr Slobodkina
Felix's Hat by Catherine Bancroft
Walter the Baker by Eric Carle

Nicole Sparks, Miami, FL

Kente Cloth Weaving

5+

Materials
Kente Colors by Debbi Chocolate
Cardboard looms (purchased or made by teacher)
Yarn, assortment of bright colors
Scissors

What to do
1. Read the book *Kente Colors* by Debbi Chocolate to the children.
2. Talk about cloth and how it is woven.
3. Show the children how to wrap their cardboard looms.

4. Show them how to weave under and over and tie new colors as needed.

5. When completed, help the children cut and tie the fringed ends.

More to do

Field trip: Visit a textile museum or professional weaver.

Related books

Abuela's Weave by Omar S. Castaenda

The Quilt Story by Tony Johnston

Linda Atamian, Charlestown, RI

Bath Sponge Painting

3+

Materials
Washable paints
Paint trays
Bath sponges in a variety of
   shapes
Paper

What to do
1. Fill paint trays with paint.
2. Place a bath sponge in each
   paint tray.
3. Hand a piece of paper to each
   child, or attach a large sheet
   of paper to the wall for a
   cooperative project.
4. Encourage the children to create a painting with the bath
   sponges.

More to do
Language: Encourage older
children to paint letters or their
name. Provide them with
sponges cut into alphabet shapes.
Math: Encourage younger children to create big designs or little designs, or provide them with
different size sponges to reinforce a lesson on size.
Music: Play music while the children paint, altering the tempo.

Related books
No More Water in the Tub by Tedd Arnold
Of Colors and Things by Tana Hoban
The Tub People by Pam Conrad
Who Said Red? by Mary Serfozo

Barbara J. Lindsay, Mason City, IA

Rolling Ball Painting

3+

Materials
Paper
Shallow boxes
Tempera paint
Spoons
Marbles or golf balls

What to do
1. Place a piece of paper in a box.
2. Invite the children to spoon two or three colors of paint onto the paper.
3. Have the children drop three or four marbles or golf balls in the box, then tilt the box back and forth and sideways. The balls will create a design as they roll through the paint.

More to do
More art: Do the same activity using large boxes so that two or three children can make a design together, or cover the bottom of a small plastic swimming pool with paper, squirt paint on the paper, and add tennis balls; encourage the class to work together.
Movement: Have the children roll balls back and forth indoors or outside.

Related books
Frederick by Leo Leonni
Growing Colors by Bruce McMillan
Of Colors and Things by Tana Hoban

Audrey F. Kanoff, Allentown, PA

Plastic Wrap Painting

3+

Materials
Tempera paint
Plastic spoons
Paper
Plastic wrap

Colors

What to do

1. Have the children spoon two or three colors of paint onto their paper.
2. Cut a piece of plastic wrap slightly larger than the paper.
3. Lay the piece of plastic wrap over the paper.
4. Encourage the children to gently rub and twist the wrap with their fingertips, squishing the colors together.
5. Let the painting dry with the plastic wrap on it. The plastic wrap will stick, creating an interesting effect.

More to do

Language and Math: Older children can write alphabet letters and numbers with their fingers.
More art: Provide the children with fingerpaint and trays for a similar project.

Related books

Little Blue and Little Yellow by Leo Lionni
Mouse Paint by Ellen Stoll Walsh
Who Said Red? by Mary Serfozo

Audrey F. Kanoff, Allentown, PA

Tissue Paper Collage

Materials

Liquid laundry starch
Containers
Tissue paper in various colors
Scissors
White construction paper
Small brushes

What to do

1. Before class, pour about 2" (5 cm) of liquid starch into each container.
2. Cut the tissue paper into 2" (5 cm) squares, or tear the tissue into small pieces.
3. Show the children how to apply the starch to the paper with the brush.
4. Have them lay squares of tissue paper where they have applied the starch, overlapping the squares to create new colors.
5. When the first area is covered with squares, have the children brush another area with starch and begin again.

6. When the construction paper is covered with tissue paper, lay it on a flat surface to dry.

More to do
Games: Play color lotto or color dominos.
More art: Make playdough in three colors; encourage the children to mix the dough and make new colors.
Water table: Fill pitchers with water and food coloring, and supply the children with ice cube trays and eyedroppers. Invite them to make colorful ice cubes.

Related books
Color Dance by Ann Jonas
Little Blue and Little Yellow by Leo Lionni
The Mixed-Up Chameleon by Eric Carle

Cory McIntyre, Crystal Lake, IL

Coffee Filter Art

Materials
Watercolor paints
Water
Bowls
Paintbrushes
Coffee filters

What to do
1. Place paint, brushes, and small bowls of water on the table.
2. Give each child a coffee filter.
3. Have the children moisten their brushes and dip them into the paint. Encourage them to paint designs on their filter and watch the colors spread.

More to do
More art: Add water and food coloring to ice cube trays and let the children experiment with color using eyedroppers.

Colors

Related books
Brown Bear, Brown Bear, What Do You See? by Bill Martin, Jr.
Color Dance by Ann Jonas
Mouse Paint by Ellen Stoll Walsh

Cory McIntyre, Crystal Lake, IL

Roll-on Painting

Materials
Construction paper
Scissors
Empty roll-on deodorant bottles
Paint in various colors, mixed to medium consistency

What to do
1. Ahead of time, cut any shape from construction paper, one shape per child. Examples include animal, flower, insect, or seasonal shapes.
2. Clean the bottles by removing the ball. Dry completely.
3. Pour a different color of paint into each bottle, then replace the ball.
4. Have the children use their new paint bottles to paint the shape.
5. Hang to dry.

More to do
More art: Punch a hole in the top of the shape and attach a piece of yarn or string to create a holiday or window ornament. Use the paint bottles to create a mural on large craft or butcher paper.

Related books
All I See by Cynthia Rylant
Mouse Paint by Ellen Stoll Walsh
Who Said Red? by Mary Serfozo

Tina R. Woehler, Oak Point, TX

Color Wheel Game

Materials
Poster board circles, one per child
Paint and paintbrushes
Spring-type clothespins
Sample color wheel

What to do
1. Beforehand, draw six equal segments on the poster board circles. Pour red, blue, yellow, orange, purple, and green paint into containers. Paint six clothespins for each child in the colors listed.
2. Show the children a color wheel and have them paint their wheel in the same manner. Allow the color wheels to dry.
3. Distribute the clothespins.
4. Invite the children to match the clothespins to the correct color segment on the wheel by clipping them along the rim.

More to do
Games: Create a giant color wheel for the floor; players hop from one segment to another as they answer questions about color.
More art: Make additional color wheels with other colors. Let the children design their own wheels. Have the children cut pictures from old magazines and place them on a color wheel in the classroom.

Related books
Appelemando's Dream by Patricia Polacco
Mouse Paint by Ellen Stoll Walsh

Elaine Commins, Athens, GA

Colors

Colorful Bags 3+

Materials
Zip-closure bags, sandwich-size
Shaving cream
Red, yellow, and blue food coloring
Masking tape, optional

What to do
1. Help the children squirt about ½ cup (125 mL) of shaving cream into their zip-closure bags.
2. When they are ready, ask the children to choose two of the colors. Have them add five or six drops of each color to the shaving cream.
3. Show the children how to squeeze the excess air from their bags and zip them closed.
4. Seal the edge with masking tape, if desired.
5. Invite the children to gently squish the bag in their hands to mix the shaving cream and food coloring. Have them identify the new color they made.

More to do
Science: Make predictions about the combinations and record them on a colorful chart. After the experiment is finished, record the results.

Related books
Color Dance by Ann Jonas
Little Blue and Little Yellow by Leo Lionni
Mouse Paint by Ellen Stoll Walsh

Nancy Tatum, Williamsburg, VA

Change That Pumpkin 3+

Materials
Bright pink copy paper
Yellow watercolor cakes, one per child
Paintbrushes
Water

72

What to do

1. Ahead of time, cut pumpkin shapes from the copy paper.
2. Give each child a pink pumpkin cutout and ask him or her to guess how to change the pumpkin's color to orange.
3. Hand each child a cake of yellow watercolor paint, a paintbrush, and water. Have them paint their pumpkins and observe how the pumpkins change color.

More to do

Cooking: Bake pumpkin bread and have it for snack.
Gardening: Plant pumpkin seeds and watch them grow.

Related books

Apples and Pumpkins by Anne Rockwell
The Biggest Pumpkin Ever by Stephen Kroll
It's Pumpkin Time! by Zoe Hall
Of Colors and Things by Tana Hoban

Linda S. Andrews, Sonora, CA

Rainbow of Hands

Materials

Fabric paints in basic colors
Pie plates or paint trays
Newspaper
White T-shirt for each child

What to do

1. Ahead of time, pour fabric paint onto plates or trays, and cover a work area with newspaper. This project should be conducted near a sink.
2. Place a T-shirt on a flat surface in front of each child. Insert a piece of newspaper between the front and back of the shirt to prevent color from transferring.
3. Encourage the children to dip one hand in paint and then make a handprint on their shirt. Have them make a new print with each color, rinsing their hands each time.
4. Allow 48 hours to dry.

More to do

More art: Make a handprint on paper at the same time, then use for a greeting card or book

Colors

cover. Frame the print for a special occasion. Have the children create a border for the bulletin board with their handprints. Create fingerprint drawings.

Related books
Chidi Only Likes Blue: An African Book of Colors by Ifeoma Onyefulu
Hands by Lois Ehlert
Here Are My Hands by Bill Martin, Jr., and John Archambault
Planting a Rainbow by Lois Ehlert

Lisa M. Chichester, Parkersburg, WV

Color Blending

Materials
Little Blue and Little Yellow by Leo Lionni
Fingerpaint in blue, yellow, and red
Fingerpaint paper

What to do
1. Read *Little Blue and Little Yellow* to the class.
2. Give each child a piece of paper. Place a glob of blue fingerpaint on the left side of each paper and a glob of yellow paint on the right side.
3. Encourage the children to mix the colors together with their fingers.
4. Repeat steps two and three using yellow and red or blue and red paint.
5. When the paintings are dry, display them around the room.

More to do
Water table: Add drops of blue and yellow food coloring to the water table.

Related books
Brown Bear, Brown Bear, What Do You See? by Bill Martin, Jr.
Little Blue and Little Yellow by Leo Lionni
Who Said Red? by Mary Serfozo

Ann Wenger, Harrisonburg, VA

Tissue Paper Prints

3+

Materials
Brightly colored tissue paper
Scissors
White construction paper
Spray bottles
Water

What to do
1. Ahead of time, cut the sheets of tissue into small pieces.
2. Provide each child with a piece of white construction paper and a tightly sealed spray bottle containing a small amount of water.
3. Invite the children to create a design on their paper by arranging the bits of tissue paper.
4. Once their arrangement is complete, have the children spray the tissue paper with water.
5. Place the pictures on newspaper and allow them to dry overnight.
6. When the children return to class, tell them to remove the pieces of tissue paper and see the colorful imprint left behind.

More to do
More art: Cut the tissue paper in different shapes depending on the occasion or season, such as egg shapes at Easter time or leaves in the fall.

Related books
My Crayons Talk by Patricia Hubbard
Of Colors and Things by Tana Hoban

 Rebecca McMahon, Mobile, AL

Roller Printing

3+

Materials
Yarn, cut in 1' (30 cm) lengths
Scissors
Glue

Colors

Toilet paper tubes, one per child
Tempera paint
Paint trays
Paper

What to do

1. Have the children cover the yarn with glue and wrap it around the toilet paper tube in any design. Let the glue dry for at least one hour.
2. While the tubes are drying, pour tempera paint into trays and give each child a sheet of paper.
3. When the tubes, or paint rollers, are dry, have the children place their index and middle fingers inside the tubes and roll them through the paint. Some children will prefer to roll the tube with the palms of their hands.
4. Show the children how to lift the roller from the paint tray and roll it back and forth on their paper, creating a design.

More to do

More art: Working in small groups, create large rollers from wrapping paper tubes. Brush paint on the tubes and roll the paint onto large sheets of craft paper. Use for murals, a bulletin board, or wrapping paper.
Movement: Encourage the children to find a partner and roll a ball back and forth.
Outdoors: Invite the children to lie on their sides and roll down a hill at the schoolyard or at home.
Science: Build ramps using blocks or small slides and roll balls, trucks, or cars down the slope.

Related books

Abuela's Weave by Omar S. Castaneda
Who Said Red? by Mary Serfozo

Constance Heagerty, Westboro, MA

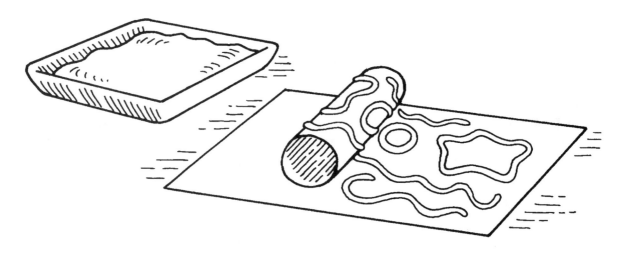

Squirt Bottle Art

3+

Materials
Red, blue, and yellow tempera paint
Small trigger squirt bottles
Easels
Large newsprint or construction paper in light colors

What to do
1. Pour tempera paint, mixed to a thin consistency, into the squirt bottles.
2. Set up easels in the classroom or outdoors.
3. Ask the children to choose one color and squirt it on their paper.
4. When they are finished with the first color, ask them to choose a second color, spray it over the first, and then repeat the process with the third color. Allow their pictures to dry.

More to do
Language and Math: Provide older children with alphabet or number stencils and create flash cards.
More art: Tape stencils or paper shapes to the paper. Squirt paint on the paper, then remove the shape, leaving an impression there.

Related books
Brown Bear, Brown Bear, What Do You See? by Bill Martin, Jr.
Little Blue and Little Yellow by Leo Lionni

Cory McIntyre, Crystal Lake, IL

Wet Paper Towel Prints

3+

Materials
Newspaper
Water
Dishpan
3 pie tins
Powdered tempera paint in 3 colors
Paper towels
Construction paper

Colors

What to do
1. Ahead of time, cover the work area with newspaper and fill a dishpan with water.
2. Add powdered tempera to pie tins, one color per tin.
3. Supply each child with a paper towel and construction paper.
4. Invite the children to dip a paper towel into the water, then wring the excess water from it.
5. Ask them to dip a corner of the paper towel into one color of paint, then dab paint onto their construction paper.
6. Repeat the process with the other two colors.
7. Allow the paintings to dry.

More to do
Games: Invite the children to play a lotto game with only blue, red, and yellow items.
More art: Use only black, white, and one other color of paint to introduce the concept of shading. Set out playdough in the colors you have chosen to work with.

Related books
Little Blue and Little Yellow by Leo Lionni
The Mystery of the Stolen Blue Paint by Steven Kellogg
The Sky was Blue by Charlotte Zolotow

Cory McIntyre, Crystal Lake, IL

Warm or Cool Pictures

Materials
Newspaper
Smocks
A color wheel
Heavyweight art or watercolor paper
Small paper cups or shallow plastic trays
Water
Watercolor paints
Paintbrushes
Large sponges cut into 2" (5 cm) cubes
Cloth towels

What to do

1. Cover the work area with newspaper and have the children put on their smocks.
2. Show the color wheel to the children and ask them to say which colors make them feel warm and which ones make them feel cool. Help them identify red, yellow, and orange as warm colors and blue, green, and purple as cool colors; explain that a painting with only warm or cool colors is called a wash.
3. Fill the small cups or trays with water.
4. Demonstrate how to dip the paintbrush into the water and wet each color in the watercolor tray.
5. Have the children dip the small sponge into the water and wet their paper completely. The children can dry their hands on the towels before continuing.
6. Before the water dries, have them dip their brush into a warm or cool color, coating the brush, then brush color in broad strokes across the paper.
7. Continue painting in this manner, using only warm or cool colors, until the paper is covered in color. Allow sufficient time for drying.

More to do

More art: Make another wash, using the opposite of the colors they used the first time. After the painting has dried, draw a design on it in black crayon.

Related book

The Art Lesson by Tomie DePaola
Colors Everywhere by Tana Hoban
Night Sounds, Morning Colors by Rosemary Wells

Barbara Saul, Eureka, CA

Fingerpaint Collages 3+

Materials

Smocks
Two dishpans
Fingerpaint paper
Sponge
Small bowl of water
Fingerpaints, such as liquid tempera mixed with liquid starch
Tablespoon
Bath or paper towels
Art paper

Crayons, markers, or pencils
Scissors
Glue

What to do

1. Fill one dishpan with soapy warm water and the other with clear warm water. Place the towels next to the dishpans. Have the children put on their smocks.
2. Supply each child with a sheet of fingerpaint paper, shiny side facing up. Have the children dip the sponge in the bowl of water and wipe their paper with the sponge to wet it.
3. When the children have finished, place two tablespoons of paint in the center of each paper. Invite the children to paint a design or pattern with their fingers, covering the entire sheet of paper. The paint will begin to dry in about five minutes.
4. Have the children wash their hands in the dishpans.
5. When the children are finished and back at their seats, distribute the art paper. Show the children examples of collages, such as the illustrations in Eric Carle's *The Very Quiet Cricket* and *The Grouchy Ladybug.*
6. Have the children draw a large shape on their paper.
7. Help the children cut their fingerpaintings into small pieces and glue them onto their drawing. Encourage them to fill in the shape completely.

More to do

More art: Draw a background for the collage paintings using felt-tip pens. Cut the shape out and punch a hole, then attach yarn or string for hanging.

Related books

Brown Bear, Brown Bear, What Do You See? by Bill Martin, Jr.
The Grouchy Ladybug by Eric Carle
The Very Quiet Cricket by Eric Carle

 *Barbara Saul, Eureka, CA*

Dye-dip Flowers   3+

Materials

Red, yellow, and blue food coloring
Water
Small paper cups

Spoon or stirring straw
Paper coffee filters
Green construction paper
Scissors
Stapler

What to do

1. Ahead of time, mix food coloring and water in paper cups, keeping the colors separate.
2. Distribute the coffee filters and show the children how to fold their filter in half three times. The filter should be folded into eighths when they are finished.
3. Invite the children to dip the point of the filter into one of the colors, then watch the liquid color spread up the paper. Encourage the children to dip the filter's other corners and edges into different colors. The colors will blend and form new colors.
4. When they are finished, have the children gently unfold their filter and let it dry.
5. While the filters are drying, hand out the scissors and construction paper.
6. Help the children cut leaves and stems from the paper. Attach them to the dye-dip flowers with a stapler.

More to do

Circle time: Talk about which secondary colors were created when the red, blue, and yellow dyes blended together. Use color transparencies or colored cellophane to demonstrate.
Gardening: Bring in packets of flower seed and sort by color, then plant in separate containers.
Language: Have the children dictate a story or sentence about their flower as you write it down, then mat their papers on dye-dipped paper towels.
More art: Attach string to the dye-dip flowers and hang as ornaments. Use paper towels or napkins instead of filters and make gift wrap. Bring fresh flowers to class and make a colorful, three-dimensional chart on poster paper, classifying the flowers by color.
Outdoors: Go for a walk and find flowers of different colors.

Related books

Growing Colors by Bruce McMillan
Planting a Rainbow by Lois Ehlert

Barbara Saul, Eureka, CA

Colors

Yarn Mosaic

3+

Materials
Yarns
Scissors
Glue, small squeeze bottles
Paper plates

What to do
1. Ahead of time, cut up the yarn (use a variety of textures, colors, and widths) in small pieces.
2. Help the children write their names on the backs of the paper plates.
3. Tell the children to turn the plates over and encourage them to create a design on their plates with glue. You might want to suggest that they use glue dots and lines rather than glue lakes and puddles.
4. Have the children place the yarn scraps onto the wet glue.
5. Allow the decorated plates to dry.

More to do
More art: Add yarn hanging cords and decorate a tree outside with hanging plates.

Related books
Aabuela's Weave by Omar S. Castameda
Bit by Bit by Steve Sanfield
The Mitten by Jan Brett

Dani Rosensteel, Payson, AZ

Colors

Ice Painting

3+

Materials
Paint aprons
Ice cubes, ice chips
Dry tempera paint
Small shallow cups
Plain paper
Spoons or popsicle sticks

What to do
1. Help the children write their names on their papers and put on aprons.
2. Put tempera powder in shallow cups with spoons.
3. Have the children sprinkle the dry powder onto their paper in small quantities. Popsicle sticks work best with younger and special needs children due to the fact that they can only retrieve small quantities at a time.
4. After the sprinkling process, have the children select an ice cube and rub it around on the paper until all of the powder has become wet and soaked into the paper.

More to do
More art: Have the children sprinkle dry powder on their papers, add a few ice chips on top, and set by a sunny window. After a few minutes, they can check to see how the melting ice chips have made a painting!

Related books
Colors Around Us: A Lift-the-Flap Surprise Book by Shelley Rotner and Anne Woodbull
Growing Colors by Bruce McMillan

Dani Rosensteel, Payson, AZ

Spray Paint Lift-off

4+

Materials
Brownie or cake pan, 9" x 12" (23 cm x 30 cm)
Water

Colors

Glycerin (optional)
Spray paint in assorted colors
Paint stirrers
Plain paper or construction paper, 8½" x 11" (21 cm x 25 cm)
Tongs and chopsticks
Art drying rack with clothespins

What to do
1. Help the children write their names on their papers and turn them over.
2. Fill the pan with 1" (3 cm) of water. A small amount of glycerin can be added to water for a long-lasting product.
3. Encourage the children to choose a color. An adult should then spray the surface of the water with the chosen color.
4. Encourage the child to stir the paint with a stick (the paint will float) and then, using tongs, gently slide the paper into the pan on top of the water so that the paper lays on top of the paint.
5. Have the child gently pull out the paper and watch as paint is lifted from the water onto the paper.
6. Place the artwork on a drying rack to dry.

More to do
More art: Use the colored paper for other purposes such as drawing, painting, card making, and book covers.

Related books
It Looked Like Spilt Milk by Charles Shaw
Of Colors and Things by Tana Hoban

Dani Rosensteel, Payson, AZ

Blow Me a Picture

Materials
Straws
Scissors
Red, yellow, and blue paint
Paint cups
Eyedroppers
Paper

What to do

1. Before class, cut a tiny snip in the straws about half-way up in case the children try to suck up the paint.
2. Pour the paint into cups.
3. Have the children squeeze droplets of color onto their paper using the eyedroppers, then ask them to blow the paint around the paper with their straws, blending the colors.

More to do

More art: Add different colors to the choices. Cut paper into the shape of an object or animal and have the children paint it with straws. Cut a chain of paper doll shapes and drop a different color of paint onto each doll, then ask the children to blow the paint with their straws, creating colorful outfits for their paper classmates.

Related book

Little Blue and Little Yellow by Leo Lionni

Melissa J. Browning, Milwaukee, WI

Tie-dyed Butterfly

4+

Materials

Red, green, yellow, and blue food coloring
Water
Bowls
4 suction-cup soap dishes
4 eyedroppers
White paper towels
Spring-type clothespins

What to do

1. Mix food coloring and water in small bowls. Place four suction-cup soap dishes on a table with the suction cups facing upward.
2. Have the children dip an eyedropper into the colored water and squeeze a drop of the liquid into a suction cup. Have them do the same until each suction cup has a drop of color in it.
3. Close the spring-type clothespin on the paper towel, forming two butterfly wings.
4. Invite the children to dip one wing into a cup or cups of colored water, then do the same with

Colors

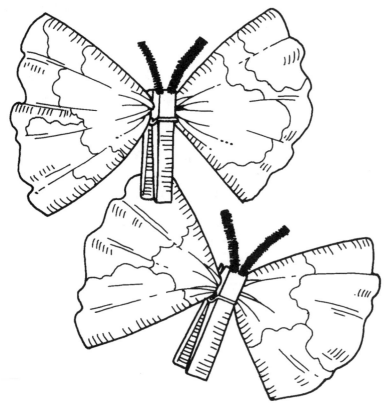

the second wing. Have the class watch the towels absorb the water and color, then hang the towels to dry.

More to do
More art: Attach a magnet to the clothespin for hanging on the board or a refrigerator. Design a butterfly garden on a mural or bulletin board, then add the children's tie-dyed butterflies.
Outdoors: Plant a butterfly garden with the other classes at your school.

Related books
Colors Everywhere by Tana Hoban
I Wish I Were a Butterfly by James Howe

Diane M. Leschak, Chisholm, MN

Shades of Color

Materials
Paint
Paintbrushes
Containers
White or off-white construction paper
Water

What to do
1. Beforehand, choose one color to use throughout the project. Set out containers of black and white paint as well as containers of paint in the color you have chosen. The color blue is well suited to this project.
2. Show the children how to mix either black or white paint with the color blue to create lighter or darker shades of blue. Demonstrate how to rinse the brush with water each time you change colors.

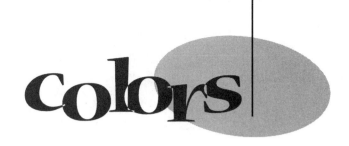

3. Provide the children with brushes and paper and encourage them to create several shades of the color, reminding them to rinse their brushes in the water.

More to do
More art: Provide paper "pallets" for experimenting. Divide construction paper into squares with a pencil or marker and have the children fill in the spaces with different shades of one color for a surprisingly colorful design. Challenge the children to number their shades from lighter to darker.
Games: Have the children paint matching pairs of cardboard squares and play a matching or memory game.

Related books
All I See by Cynthia Rylant
Colors Around Us: A Lift-the-Flap Surprise Book by Shelley Rotner and Anne Woodhull
The Color Wizard: Level One by Barbara A. Brenner
Little Blue and Little Yellow by Leo Lionni
The Mixed-Up Chameleon by Eric Carle

Shirley R. Salach, Northwood, NH

Still-life Paintings

Materials
Still-life subjects
Still-life art prints or posters
Watercolor paints and brushes
Paper

What to do
1. Ahead of time, set up a display of still-life subjects. Some familiar objects might include a teapot and cups, a baseball mitt and glove, some children's blocks and a beach ball, and a grouping of teddy bears.
2. Show the children examples of still-life drawings or paintings.
3. Invite the children to choose the subject they would like to paint.
4. Provide the children with paint, brushes, and paper and encourage them to paint their still-life subject.

Colors

More to do

Dramatic play: Hang the children's work and art posters, then pretend you are visiting a gallery. Take turns as docent, artist, and visitor, then enjoy a snack in the café.

More art: Repeat the activity using different media such as crayons, tempera paints, chalk, colored pencils, and markers. Frame the children's artwork and create an art gallery or exhibit. On another day, create portraits, landscapes, or abstract art.

Music: Play quiet music while the children paint.

Related books

Bonjour, Mr. Satie by Edward Lear and Tomie DePaola

Come Look with Me: Enjoying Art with Children by Gladys S. Blizzard

Picture This by Felicity Woolf

Shirley R. Salach, Northwood, NH

Adventure in Purple

Materials

Harold and the Purple Crayon by Crockett Johnson
Purple crayons
Large paper banner

What to do

1. Read and discuss *Harold and the Purple Crayon* by Crockett Johnson.
2. Invite the children to create a character like Harold and give him or her a name. Lay the banner paper on the floor or a long table.
3. Decide what your character will do first, and draw a simple picture using straight or wavy lines in purple crayon. Invite one of the children to continue telling the story and add some lines to the drawing. When the first child is finished, invite the rest of the class in turn to finish the story and drawing.

More to do
Language: Have the children dictate their own story and design a book of their own with white paper and a crayon.

Related books
Cherries and Cherry Pits by Vera B. Williams
My Crayons Talk by Patricia Hubbard

Nancy Dentler, Mobile, AL

Cool Colors

Materials
Red, yellow, and blue food coloring
Water
Ice cube tray
Small clear plastic cups
Plastic spoons
Paintbrushes
White construction paper

What to do
1. Ahead of time, make red, yellow, and blue ice cubes with food coloring and water.
2. Have the children transfer the ice cubes with spoons to the plastic cups, encouraging them to pair different primary colors in the cups.
3. As the ice melts, ask the children to identify the secondary color they have made by combining the pair of primary colors.
4. Invite the children to dip the paintbrushes in the cups and make watercolor paintings.

More to do
Language: Assemble the watercolor paintings in a book and have the children tell how the colors were created.
More art: Put out a large piece of paper and invite a group of children to make a watercolor painting together.

Related books
Mouse Paint by Ellen Stoll Walsh
Red Is Best by Kathy Stinson
Who Said Red? by Mary Serfozo

Lyndall Warren, Milledgeville, GA

Crayon Etchings

Materials
Courier and Ives art poster
White art paper
Crayons
Paper clips

What to do
1. Show the children an example of an etching such as the Courier and Ives print.
2. Supply the children with art paper and crayons.
3. Have the children color their paper in any design with different colors. Encourage them to press hard and cover the entire surface.
4. When they have finished, show the children how to cover their design completely with black crayon, again pressing very hard.
5. Straighten the paper clips to form a point on one end. Hand one clip to each child.
6. Invite the children to etch a design or picture in the black crayon using the paper clip.

More to do
Circle time: Show the children a dollar bill and explain how the design is etched in metal, then printed onto paper. Brainstorm about everyday examples of etchings.
Field trips: Visit an off-set printing shop for a demonstration. Tour the art department at a nearby high school to see how etchings are made.

Related books
Beady Bear by Don Freeman
Lunch by Denise Fleming
A Rainbow of My Own by Don Freeman

Barbara Saul, Eureka, CA

Build a Bridge

Materials
Construction paper
Markers
Glue
Popsicle sticks
Toothpicks

What to do
1. Have the children think about bridges that they would like to build. What does the bridge connect? What does it cross over? Is it a walking bridge or a driving bridge? Who might go on it?
2. Give the children construction paper to use as a background for their bridge scene.
3. Have them use magic markers to draw the scenery, such as grass, the sky, the ocean, sidewalks, parks, etc.
4. Invite the children to build their bridges by gluing popsicle sticks and toothpicks on their scene.
5. After the glue is dry, suggest that the children draw people, cars, or animals crossing their bridges.

More to do
Blocks: Encourage the children to make bridges with hollow blocks and unit blocks. Suggest that they try crossing them with their cars and trucks.
Field trip: Visit a real bridge.
Language: Set up a balance beam as a bridge and encourage the children to dramatize the story of *The Three Billy Goats Gruff*.
Social studies: Show the children pictures of different kinds of bridges.

Related books
Richard Scarry's Cars and Trucks and Things That Go by Richard Scarry
The Three Billy Goats Gruff by Paul Galdone

Related song
"London Bridge Is Falling Down"

Linda N. Ford, Sacramento, CA

Cotton Swabs and Tongue Depressors

3+

Materials
Tempera paint
Bedpans or shallow trays
Tongue depressors or craft sticks
Cotton swabs
Paper

What to do
1. Show the children the cotton swabs and tongue depressors. Talk about what happens in a doctor's office.
2. Pour tempera paints in bedpans or shallow trays.
3. Put tongue depressors, cotton swabs, and paints on the table.
4. Let the children explore painting with these tools on paper.
5. Encourage them to use different colors and different techniques to create unique designs.

More to do
Dramatic play: Set up a pretend doctor's office or hospital in the classroom.

Related books
Going to the Hospital by Fred Rogers
Madeline by Ludwig Bemelmans

Vicki L. Schneider, Oshkosh, WI

Junk Mail Collage

3+

Materials
Junk mail from home
Construction paper
Glue
Scissors

What to do
1. Ask the children ahead of time to bring in junk mail from home.
2. Lay the junk mail, unopened, out on the table.
3. Give each child a piece of construction paper, some glue, and a pair of scissors.
4. Let the children open the envelopes and choose which papers they would like to save for their collage.
5. Have the children cut the paper that they have saved into interesting shapes and glue them to the construction paper to make their collages. Encourage them to use lots of colorful pieces and to overlap them on the paper.

More to do
Language: Set up a letter-writing table. Put out stationery, pens, pencils, a typewriter, envelopes, holiday seals that resemble stamps, old greeting cards, stickers, and a mailbox. Encourage the children to think about whom they would like to write to. Encourage them to use their own (developmentally appropriate) writing.

Related books
The Post Office Book by Gail Gibbons
Tortoise Brings the Mail by Dee Lillegard

Barbara Reynolds, Smithville, NJ

Creative Community

3+

Materials
Shoeboxes, one per child
Construction paper

Scissors
Markers
Glue

What to do

1. Give each child a shoebox.
2. Have the children plan what buildings and sites they would like to include in the community that they will create in the shoebox.
3. Provide the children with construction paper, scissors, markers, and glue so that they may cut out buildings, trees, landmarks, etc., decorate them, and glue them in their boxes.
4. Show the children how to fold the bottoms of their cutouts to form a "lip" with which to glue them to the inside of the boxes.

More to do

Field trip: Go on a walking tour of your community. Visit places such as the local bakery, police station, fire station, and doctor's office.

Social studies: Have the class work together to make a map of the community or neighborhood. Let the children draw streets, buildings, and parks. Encourage them to add their homes to the map.

Related books

Aesop's Fable: City Mouse and Country Mouse
I Know a Lady by Charlotte Zolotow
A Year on My Street by Mary Quattlebaum

Amy Melisi, Oxford, MA

Brick Making

4+

Materials
Dirt
Water
Plastic bucket
Muffin tins or ice cube trays

What to do
1. Put dirt in a plastic bucket and mix in just enough water to form a mud ball.
2. Press the mud into muffin tin cups or ice cube tray sections.
3. Place the tins or trays in a warm place for about ten days, or bake at 250° F (130° C) for 15 minutes.
4. When cool, drop the "bricks" on newsprint on the floor and see which ones break and which ones hold together. Use the solid bricks for building.
5. Make as many bricks as possible for the most fun in building.

More to do
More art: Add a little plaster of Paris to the mud mixture so it will hold together better. Attach bricks and other items together in a free-form building using plaster of Paris mixed to a runny consistency. Build with wood scraps and glue.

Related books
Richard Scarry's Busy Town by Richard Scarry
The Three Little Pigs by Joseph Jacobs in Tomie dePaola's *Favorite Nursery Tales*

MaryAnn Kohl, reprinted from Preschool Art

In the Neighborhood

4+

Materials
White construction paper, 8" x 10" (20 cm x 25 cm)
Markers
Scissors
1 large piece of poster board or cardboard

Glue
Sponges, cut into small rectangles

What to do

1. Give the children markers and construction paper, and have them draw pictures of their homes.
2. Have the children cut their houses out of the drawings. If they have included other things in the drawings, such as people and pets, cut those out too.
3. Follow the next set of directions in order to assemble the neighborhood on a large piece of poster board or cardboard.
4. First, have the children choose several houses to be in the back row. They should glue these down in a straight line near the top of the cardboard, leaving some room to make the sky.
5. Then have them choose some houses for your next row. Glue a small sponge to the back of each, and let them dry. After they are dry, glue them in front of the first row.
6. Repeat steps 4 and 5 with the rest of the houses, until you have used them all.
7. Have the children draw some clouds, rainbows, the sun, birds, etc. Cut these out and glue a small sponge to the back of each. Have the children glue them to the sky portion of the scene.
8. Glue a piece of sponge on the back of any people the children have drawn and cut out. Glue these people to the very bottom of the neighborhood scene.

More to do

Field trip: Take the class on a walking field trip through the neighborhood.

Related books

I Got Community by Melrose Cooper
Night on Neighborhood Street by Eliose Greenfield
One Afternoon by Yumi Heo
Rum-A-Tum-Tum by Angela Medearis
Sweet Dream Pie by Audrey Wood
Tales of Trotter Street by Shirley Hughes

Virginia Jean Herrod, Columbia, SC

Blueprints

Materials

Architect's drawing (optional)
Large white paper
Blue pens

Blue pencils
Blue crayons
Blue markers
Rulers
Yardsticks
Empty paper towel tubes

What to do

1. If possible, bring in an architect's drawing of a house and show it to the children.
2. Give each child a large piece of white paper.
3. Put blue pens, blue pencils, blue crayons, blue markers, rulers, and yardsticks on the table.
4. Ask the children to use these items to draw a picture of a building that they would like to build, just like an architect would.
5. Roll them up and keep them in empty paper towel tubes.

More to do

Blocks: Encourage the children to take their blueprints to the block area and build their buildings.
Field trip: Visit an architect's office or construction site.
Language: Have the children write advertisements for their buildings.

Related books

Building a House by Byron Barton
The Little House by Virginia Lee Burton
Mike Mulligan and his Steam Shovel by Virginia Burton

Sandy Lanes, Silver Spring, MD

Give-a-Hand Bookmarks

Materials
Pencils
Scissors
Poster board
Pens
White paper
Tempera paint
Lids from margarine tubs
Glue

community *helpers*

What to do

1. Have each child trace one handprint on a piece of poster board and cut it out. If there are more than 12 children doing this activity, you will need each child to cut out two handprints.

2. Next, invite the children to go around and get their hands autographed, front and back, by the other children. Explain to the children that they are to sign their name on one of the hand's fingers. Nine other children can sign the fingers and two can sign the palm.

3. Make bookmarks by cutting paper into rectangles that are 8" x 3" (20 cm x 8 cm). Write the word *"Thanks"* in dots on each bookmark.

4. When all the hands have been signed by the other children, give out the bookmarks.

5. Pour some paint in margarine lids.

6. Have the children dip their thumbs in the paint and press over the dots of each letter in *Thanks*.

7. When the bookmarks are dry, have the children glue them to the bottom of the hands.

8. Give these bookmarks as gifts to people who have volunteered in your classroom or to community helpers in your town.

Related books

Louise's Gift by Irene Smalls
My Dog Never Says Please by Suzanne Williams

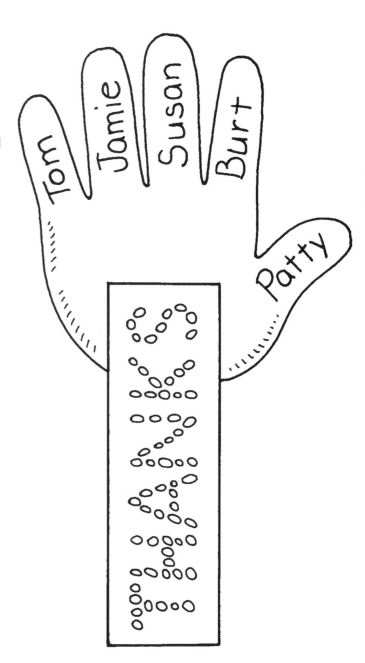

Kathy Brand, Greenwood Lake, NY

Lumber Town

5+

Materials
Night on Neighborhood Street by Eloise Greenfield
Safety goggles
Thick work gloves
Scraps of lumber
Wood saw, nails, and hammers for the older group
Wood glue for the younger group
Sandpaper
Paint and paintbrushes
Markers
Magazines
Scissors

What to do
1. Read *Night on Neighborhood Street* by Eloise Greenfield and then talk with the children about neighborhoods. What are they? Who lives in a neighborhood?
2. Ask the children if they would like to build a miniature neighborhood of their own to play with in the classroom.
3. Allow each child to select a piece of lumber from the scraps. As they do, talk about the shape of the wood and what kind of neighborhood building it reminds them of. Remember that neighborhoods are made up of more than just private homes. There are grocery stores, department stores, toy stores, libraries, museums, hospitals, police and fire departments, and so much more. Let children decide what neighborhood building their piece of lumber will represent.
4. The older children can use the wood saw to cut their pieces of lumber into the shapes they desire. They can also use the hammer and nails to add small scraps of wood to their lumber to represent chimneys, etc. The younger children can use wood glue to do the same. Both groups can use sandpaper to smooth the lumber. Make sure children wear protective gloves and goggles whenever they are handling tools of any kind, including sandpaper.
5. Make sure the bottom of each "building" is sanded smooth and flat so it will stand up when added to the neighborhood.
6. When the pieces are ready, the children can use the paint and markers to decorate them to represent the building they have chosen. Decorative windows and doors can be cut out of colorful magazine pages and glued on after the paint dries. Don't forget to label your community buildings.
7. Add the new buildings to the block area.

More to do

Field trip: If possible, plan a field trip to walk (or even drive) around your neighborhood. Look for the types of buildings your children chose to represent with their pieces of lumber. How many stores do you see? What kind are they? Did you find a library, a museum, police or fire department?

Math: Record what you found on the field trip and make a chart or graph when you get back.

More art: Make a neighborhood mat to put your houses on. On a large flat piece of cardboard, draw in city streets and rural roads. Add fields, grassy areas, parks, parking lots, and crosswalks at the intersections.

Related books

I Got Community by Melrose Cooper
My Perfect Neighborhood by Leah Kamaiko
Night on Neighborhood Street by Eloise Greenfield
Tales of Trotter Street by Shirley Hughes

Original poem

The Buildings in Your Neighborhood

These are the buildings in your neighborhood
In your neighborhood, in your neighborhood.
These are the buildings in your neighborhood
The buildings that you see every day.

The Post office is a building in your neighborhood
In your neighborhood, in your neighborhood.
The Post Office is a building in your neighborhood
You take your letters there to mail.

The Library is a building in your neighborhood
In your neighborhood, in your neighborhood.
The Library is a building in your neighborhood
You can read some great books there.

The Grocery Store is a building in your neighborhood
In your neighborhood, in your neighborhood.
The Grocery Store is a building in your neighborhood
You can buy some yummy food there.

Virginia Jean Herrod, Columbia, SC

Caterpillar Cookies

Materials
Flour
Sugar cookie dough
Cookie sheets
Oven
Vanilla icing
Green food coloring
Spoon
Plastic knives
Gum drops
Black gel icing in a tube
Shoestring licorice

What to do
1. Have the children flour their hands and the surface to be worked. Give the children pieces of sugar cookie dough to roll into a snake shape. They should place the snake shapes on a cookie sheet and flatten them until they are about 1" (3 cm) thick.
2. Bake the snakes according to your recipe.
3. After the cookies cool, have the children help you mix vanilla icing with green food coloring so that it becomes a bright green color.
4. Have the children ice the cookies, and stick gumdrops all over them to represent spots.
5. Next, let the children add black gel eyes and insert cut-up shoestring licorice for the legs and antennae.

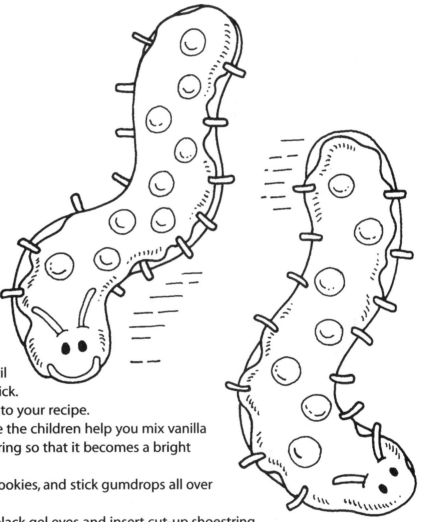

More to do
Outdoors: Give the children magnifying glasses and suggest that they look for caterpillars to examine.

Cooking

Related books
Bugs by Nancy Winslow Parker and Joan Richards
I Wish I Were a Butterfly by James Howe
The Very Hungry Caterpillar by Eric Carle

Lisa M. Chichester, Parkersburg, WV

Spider Bites

Materials
Plastic knives
Cream cheese, softened
Round crackers
Pretzel sticks
Raisins

What to do
1. Have each child spread cream cheese on one round cracker.
2. Tell the children to place another round cracker on top.
3. Give them eight pretzel sticks to stick along the sides of the crackers, into the cream cheese.
4. Have them place two dots of cream cheese on their top cracker, and top those with raisins to resemble eyes.
5. Eat and enjoy!

Related books
Be Nice To Spiders by Margaret Graham
Miss Spider's Tea Party by David Kirk
Miss Spider's Wedding by David Kirk
There Was an Old Lady Who Swallowed a Fly by Simms Taback
The Very Busy Spider by Eric Carle

Kaethe Lewandowski, Centreville, VA

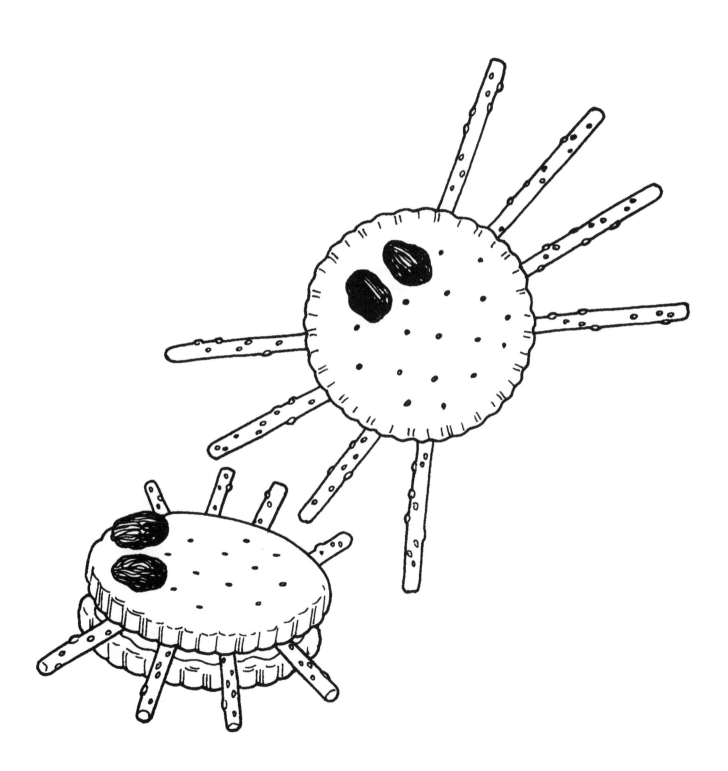

Cooking

Bread People

Materials
Loaf of bread
Toaster
Cookie cutters, shaped like people
Cream cheese
Spreaders
Carrots, celery, and red peppers, cut into small pieces
Olives
Raisins
String cheese

What to do
1. Lightly toast the bread and give a slice to each child.
2. Have the children cut a person out of their bread slice with a cookie cutter.
3. Encourage the children to spread cream cheese on their bread with a spreader, and then decorate the person with the vegetables, olives, raisins, and cheese.
4. Enjoy snack time!

Related books
Gingerbread Boy by Paul Galdone
The Little Red Hen by Byron Barton
Walter the Baker by Eric Carle

Dotti Enderle, Richmond, TX

Pretzel Sculptures

Materials
1 package of dry yeast
1 tablespoon (15 mL) sugar
1 teaspoon (5 mL) salt
1½ cups (375 mL) warm water
Large plastic bowl

Spoon
4 cups (1 L) flour
Paper plates
Vegetables, such as zucchini, carrot, onion, broccoli, green and red peppers,
    cut into small pieces
Cookie sheets
Oven

What to do
1. Let the children help you stir the yeast, sugar, salt, and warm water together in a large bowl.
2. Gradually add the flour.
3. Have the children take turns helping to knead the dough.
4. Give each child a paper plate to work on and a piece of the dough to shape into a sculpture.
5. Encourage them to decorate the sculptures with the vegetables.
6. Bake the pretzels at 425° F (220° C) for 12 to 15 minutes.

More to do
Movement: Have the children sit on the floor cross-legged, so that their legs resemble a pretzel. Now have them lean forward on their hands and try to walk on their knees, while keeping their legs in a pretzel.

Related books
Bread and Jam for Frances by Russell Hoban
Bread, Bread, Bread by Ann Morris
Bread Is for Eating by David Gershator

Jill E. Putnam, Wellfleet, MA

Craft Dough 3+

Materials
2 cups (500 mL) of salt
1 cup (250 mL) of flour
1²⁄₃ cups (415 mL) of water
Saucepan
Spoon
Stove or burner

Cooking

Wax paper
Small objects, such as beads, pebbles, buttons, etc.
Oven
Paint
Paintbrushes

What to do
1. Have the children pour the salt, flour, and water in a saucepan and mix the ingredients well.
2. Cook the dough over a medium low heat, continually stirring, until the dough thickens.
3. Take the dough out of the pan and lay it on a sheet of wax paper.
4. Let the children mold the warm dough into a free-form shape.
5. Provide beads, rocks, peas, macaroni, buttons, etc., for the children to press into the dough.
6. Bake the sculptures at 200° F (90° C) for one hour, or place them in the sun to dry.
7. Suggest that the children paint the finished product.

More to do
Language: Write this recipe on a chart and refer to it while making the dough with the children.

Sandra Hutchins Lucas, Cox's Creek, KY

Thumbprint Cookies

3+

Materials
Measuring cup
Bowl
2 cups (500 mL) of flour
1 teaspoon (5 mL) of salt
⅔ cup (165 mL) of oil
4-5 tablespoons (60-75 mL) of water
Fork
Cooking spray
Cookie sheet
Oven
Jam or peanut butter
Spoons

cooking

What to do
1. Have the children help measure and pour the flour, salt, oil, and water into a bowl. Let them have a turn mixing the ingredients with their hands or a fork.
2. Encourage the children to roll the dough into small balls and lay them on a greased cookie sheet. Have the children push their thumbprints into the balls.
3. Bake the cookies at 325° F (160° C) for 10 minutes.
4. Let the cookies cool, and have the children fill the thumbprint centers with jam or peanut butter.

More to do
More art: Give children ink pads and paper and let them make thumbprint art.

Related books
The Chocolate-Covered-Cookie Tantrum by Deborah Blumenthal
Mouse Mess by Linnea Riley
Tom Thumb by Richard Jesse Watson

Related chant
Who Stole the Cookie From the Cookie Jar?

Sandra Hutchins Lucas, Cox's Creek, KY

Gingerbread People

Materials
The Gingerbread Man, any version
¼ cup (60 mL) butter
½ cup (125 mL) sugar
½ cup (125 mL) molasses
2 large bowls
Spoon
Sifter
3½ cup (875 mL) flour
½ teaspoon (2.5 mL) salt
1 teaspoon (5 mL) baking soda

¼ teaspoon (1 mL) cloves
½ teaspoon (2.5 mL) cinnamon
1 teaspoon (5 mL) ginger
5 teaspoons (25 mL) water
Cookie cutters, shaped like gingerbread men and women
Dried currants, raisins, and store-bought cookie decorations
Cookie sheets
Oven

Cooking

What to do

1. Read *The Gingerbread Man* to the children and tell them that they are going to make their own gingerbread people.
2. Invite the children to help you prepare the cookie dough. Blend the butter, sugar, and molasses in a large bowl. Sift the flour, salt, soda, and spices together in another bowl.
3. Add the flour mixture alternately with the water to the butter/sugar mixture. Knead until smooth.
4. Give the children lumps of dough, and let them press them with the heel of their hands until they are about ¼" (6 mm) thick.
5. Give them the cookie cutters and let them cut out the cookies.
6. Let the children decorate the cookies with currants, raisins, and store-bought cookie decorations.
7. Lay them on a cookie sheet and bake them at 350° F (180° C) for 10 minutes, until lightly browned.

More to do

Games: Go on a hunt for the Gingerbread Man. Read clues to the children that were supposedly left by the Gingerbread Man, leading from one place in the school to another. They might say, for example, "Run, run as fast as you can. You can't catch me. I'm the Gingerbread Man. Look near the slide

Language: Read *The Gingerbread Man* to the children and have them act out the story.

Related books

The Gingerbread Boy by Richard Egielski
The Gingerbread Doll by Susan Tews
The Pancake That Ran Away by Loek Koopmans

Mary Jo Shannon, Roanoke, VA

day and night

Twinkling Stars
3+

Materials
Twinkle, Twinkle Little Star by Iza Trapani
Black construction paper
Star stickers in assorted colors

What to do
1. Read *Twinkle, Twinkle Little Star* by Iza Trapani to the children.
2. Give the children black construction paper and some star stickers.
3. Invite the children to create their own designs by sticking stars on paper.
4. Hang the finished work around the classroom.

More to do
More art: Show the children pictures of constellations. Invite them to create the shape of a constellation such as the Big Dipper using the stickers.
Music: Sing "Twinkle, Twinkle Little Star" with the children.

Margery A. Kranyik, Hyde Park, MA

Star Light, Star Bright
3+

Materials
Black construction paper
Smudge-proof chalk

What to do
1. Encourage the children to envision a nighttime scene. Talk about the kinds of things they see at night (fireflies, stars, the moon, lighted windows).
2. Give the children the paper and chalk and invite them to create a nighttime scene. The white chalk on the black paper resembles the night sky.
3. Display the creations on a bulletin board entitled "Star Light, Star Bright."

More to do
Dramatic play: Act out nighttime routines such as brushing your teeth, reading a bedtime story, and putting on pajamas.

day and night

Language: Create a dream book. Children can draw their favorite dream and dictate a sentence about it.

Related books
Fireflies for Nathan by Shulamith Levey Oppenheim
Good Night Moon by Margaret Wise Brown
The Midnight Farm by Reeve Lindberg
What the Sun Sees/What the Moon Sees by Nancy Tafuri

Amy Melisi, Oxford, MA

Scribble Art Dreams

Materials
Matthew's Dream by Leo Lionni
Permanent black marker
Paper
Colored markers

What to do
1. Read *Matthew's Dream* by Leo Lionni to the children.
2. Invite the children to make pictures like the drawings in the book.
3. Ask each child to make a simple "scribble drawing" on a piece of paper using a permanent black marker.
4. Using colored markers, ask the child to color each section of the drawing in a different color.
5. Notice how the drawings resemble the artwork in *Matthew's Dream* by Leo Lionni.

More to do
Language: Have the children share stories of their favorite or scariest dreams.

Related books
Dreams by Ezra J. Keats
Matthew's Dream by Leo Lionni
There's a Nightmare in My Closet by Mercer Mayer

Ann Wenger, Harrisonburg, VA

day and night

Starry, Starry Night

3+

Materials
White art paper
Crayons
Watercolors
Sponges, cut in 2" x 2" (5 cm x 5 cm)
Containers
Water
Silver or gold glitter and glue

What to do
1. The day before you plan to do this activity, ask the children to look at the night sky and to try to remember all that they see.
2. The next day, invite the children to draw a picture of what they saw in the night sky.
3. Suggest that they color the stars and moon with crayons, pressing hard, but ask them not to color the sky.
4. Give the children watercolors, sponges, and containers of water. Using the sponges, the children should wet their papers entirely and put a black or dark blue "wash" over their pictures of the sky.
5. When the pictures are dry, invite the students to use glitter to make their "Starry, Starry Night" pictures sparkle.

More to do
Dramatic play: Use a refrigerator box to make a "rocket ship" for the play center. Put a journal or plain paper inside for the "astronauts" to record what they see in "outer space."

Related books
My House Has Stars by Megan McDonald
My Place in Space by Robin and Sally Hirst
Twilight Comes Twice by Ralph Fletcher

Barbara Saul, Eureka, CA

day and night

Daytime/Nighttime

Materials
Poster board
Marker
Crayons
Paper
Scissors

What to do
1. Talk about day and night. Name things that we usually do in the daytime, things we do at night, and things we could do during the day or night. You can also name things we could see during the day or night.
2. Draw a Venn diagram of two large overlapping circles on the poster board. Label the large part of the circle on the left "Day" and label the large part of the circle on the right "Night." Label the overlapping part "Day and Night."
3. During the day, children usually eat breakfast, go to school, and play. At night children see the stars, put on pajamas, and go to sleep. During day and night children brush their teeth, eat, and enjoy time with their families. You'll think of many more!
4. Have each child color things they do or see during the day, at night, or both. Cut them out and place on the class day-and-night Venn diagram.

More to do
Science: Talk to the children about animals that are nocturnal and what they do at night.

Related books
Night Is Coming by W. Nikola-Lisa
Rise and Shine Mariko-chan! by Chiyoko Tomioka
What the Sun Sees/What the Moon Sees by Nancy Tafuri

Nancy Dentler, Mobile, AL

day and night

Turning Night to Day

5+

Materials
9" (23 cm) paper plates, two per child
Paint or crayons
Paper fasteners
Scissors

What to do
1. Show the children how to fold both plates in half and use the fold as a guideline.
2. On one plate, have the children draw or paint a picture of a house or any outside scene on the top half, while the bottom of the plate is the ground decorated with grass etc. This is the scene plate.
3. On the top half of the scene plate, trim off all the excess parts of the plate closest to the picture.
4. On the other plate, invite the children to color or paint a day scene on the top half and a night scene on the lower portion.
5. Use the paper fastener to attach the picture plate to the top of the day and night plate.
6. Then turn night into day!

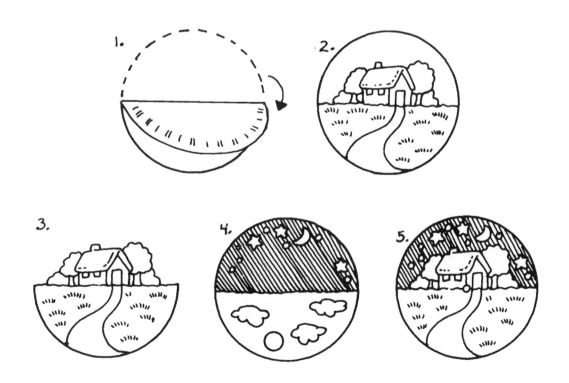

More to do

More art: The scene plate can be changed to animal habitats, various seasons of the year, or even the weather.

Related books

Night Sounds, Morning Colors by Rosemary Wells
The Story of the Milky Way: A Cherokee Tale by Joseph Bruchac
Wind Says Goodnight by Katy Rydell

Nicole Sparks, Miami, FL

Dinosaur Sock Puppets

3+

Materials
Cardboard ovals, 1 ³/₈" x 2" (3.5 cm x 5 cm)
Glue
Old or new socks in solid colors
Fabric
Junk box items, such as packing peanuts,
   buttons, ribbon, popsicle sticks, googly eyes

What to do
1. Help the children glue cardboard ovals underneath the toes of each sock and fold them in half to create the mouths for the puppets.
2. Invite the children to glue fabric and items from the junk box on to the sock to create a dinosaur. Encourage the children to think about what features their dinosaurs need, and what items they could use to create them. For example, packing peanuts may be glued into the mouths for teeth or along the back of the sock for spikes.

More to do
Language: Ask the children to make up a story to go along with their new creations. They can decide on a name for their dinosaur, where the dinosaur lives, what he eats, and what the dinosaur likes to do for fun. Set up a puppet theater and let the children put on impromptu shows with their puppets.

Related books
Dinosaur Bones by Aliki
The Dinosaur Who Lived in My Backyard by B. G. Hennessy
The Magic School Bus in the Time of the Dinosaurs by Joanna Cole

Christine Maiorano, Duxbury, MA

Dino Hats

Materials
Solid-color kerchief or fabric in similar shape
Scissors
Felt or construction paper
Glue
Googly eyes
Pompoms
Fabric paint

What to do
1. Have the children cut small triangles from construction paper or felt. Show them how to glue the triangles, or sharp dinosaur teeth, inside the kerchief along the front; when the child wears the kerchief, he will wear it across his forehead and tie it in back of his head. The teeth will be positioned across the child's forehead when he wears the kerchief.
2. Invite the children to glue googly eyes and pompoms on the kerchief and add a few spots here and there with fabric paint.
3. Set the kerchiefs aside to dry.

More to do
Language: Compose a dinosaur adventure together.
More art: Decorate baseball hats or visors. Design a matching T-shirt. Use a pattern to cut dinosaur shapes in duplicate from fabric or paper; sew or glue the pieces together and fill the dinosaurs with stuffing.

Related books
Time Flies by Eric Rohmann
We're Back!: A Dinosaur's Story by Hudson Talbott

Lisa M. Chichester, Parkersburg, WV

dinosaurs

Dinosaur Sidewalk Shapes

Materials
Enlarged dinosaur shape cut from oak tag or cardboard
Colored sidewalk chalk

What to do
1. Take the children outside to a patio or sidewalk and invite them to trace around enlarged patterns of dinosaurs using colored chalk.
2. If children know the names of the dinosaurs, help them write these next to the outlines.
3. Encourage the children to draw in details or simply color the inside of the outline of the chalk.

More to do
More art: Tell the children to draw their own dinosaurs on the sidewalk without the use of a pattern. Encourage creativity!
Science: Display books about dinosaurs along with puzzles and models for the children to explore.

Related books
Patrick's Dinosaurs by Carol Carrick
The World of Dinosaurs by Melvin Berger

Jackie Wright, Enid, OK

Unique Fossils

Materials
Small objects, such as acorns, rocks, paper clips, buttons, twigs
Plaster of Paris
Water
Styrofoam cup
Small cups from drink mixes, such as Crystal Light

What to do
1. Have each child find a small object to make a fossil out of. They can look for objects in the class-

room or outside.
2. Prepare the plaster of Paris in a Styrofoam cup, according to the directions on the box.
3. Pour the plaster of Paris into each Crystal Light cup, and give one to each child.
4. Have the children place their objects into their cups. The children should press the objects about a ¼" (6 mm) deep.
5. After the plaster of Paris starts to firm up, carefully remove the objects and set the cups aside to dry completely.
6. Have the children remove their "fossils" from the Crystal Light cups.

More to do
Guest: Invite an archaeologist to speak to the class.
Science: Lay out all the fossils and small objects from which they were made, and encourage the children to match the fossil with the object that made it. Bring in real fossils, or pictures of real fossils, for the children to look at.

Related books
Archaeologists Dig For Clues by Kate Duke
Bones, Bones, Dinosaur Bones by Bryon Barton
Digging Up Dinosaurs by Aliki
Dinosaurs Everywhere! by Carol Harrison

Christy Krueger, Evansville, IN

Wear a Dinosaur!

Materials
Plain white T-shirts
White paper
Fabric crayons
Cardboard
Iron and ironing board
Fabric paints

What to do
1. Wash and dry all the T-shirts.
2. Invite the children to draw and color a dinosaur of their choice on the white paper using fabric crayons. Remind the children that they must press hard with the crayons. (You may have to darken some areas before ironing.)

3. Place a piece of cardboard inside each shirt before ironing.
4. Lay each picture face down over the front of a T-shirt.
5. Follow the directions on the fabric crayon box for ironing.
6. After the shirts are cool, let the children create scenery around their dinosaurs with fabric paints.

More to do
Movement: Encourage the children to wear their T-shirts and have a dinosaur parade to music.

Related books
Digging Up Dinosaurs by Aliki
Dinosaur Bob by William Joyce
Dinosaur Days by Joyce Milton
Dinosaurs by Pete Zallinger
A Picture Book of Dinosaurs by Claire Nemes

 Sandra W. Gratias, Perkasie, PA

Dinosaur on the Wall 4+

Materials
Bulletin board paper
Tape
Overhead projector
Dinosaur books
Pencils
Permanent marker
Paintbrushes
Tempera paints
Scissors

What to do
1. Tape a large piece of bulletin board paper to the wall.
2. Have the children choose a picture of a dinosaur from a book. With the help of an overhead projector, have the children draw the outline of the dinosaur on the paper with pencils. Make it as large as possible.
3. Outline the drawing with a permanent marker.

dinosaurs

4. Encourage the children to work together to decide on what features this dinosaur should have.
5. Let the children work in small groups to paint features on the dinosaur. When it is dry, cut it out, and mount it on the wall.

More to do
Blocks: Set up a dinosaur museum in the block area. Decorate the area using the dinosaur mural. Encourage the children to pretend that the blocks are dinosaur bones, and to use them to put together dinosaur skeletons.
Field trip: Visit a natural history museum where there is a dinosaur exhibit.

Related books
Can I Have a Stegosaurus Mom? Can I Please? by Lois G. Grambling
If the Dinosaurs Came Back by Bernard Most
Patrick's Dinosaurs by Carol Carrick

Related song
"Dinorock"—various CDs and cassettes available

Sandra W. Gratias, Perkasie, PA

Dynamic Dinosaurs

Materials
Construction paper
Crayons, colored pencils, or markers
Scissors
Paper fasteners

What to do
1. Divide the children into groups of four or five.
2. Ask each group to create a dinosaur and assign each child in the group a part of the dinosaur body; for example, each child would be responsible for either the head, neck, body, legs, or tail of the dinosaur.
3. Have the children spread out around the room and work apart from their group.
4. Supply the children with construction paper, drawing tools, and scissors. Ask each child to design the body part that they are responsible for without looking at their partners' designs.
5. When the children are ready, invite them to meet again as a group and connect the individual parts with paper fasteners, creating a disjointed dinosaur with a very unusual appearance. Have each group name their dinosaur.
6. Display the dinosaurs on a large wall or mural.

More to do

More art: Create 3-D dinosaurs with butcher paper; cut out two sides of a dinosaur and staple them together leaving an opening, then stuff with newspaper and paint or decorate.

Game: Before you fasten the dinosaur parts together, group the children according to the part of the dinosaur they created and assign each child in the group a number; call out their numbers in sequence and have them assemble a dinosaur—continue until all possible combinations have been made.

Related books

Happy Birthday, Danny and the Dinosaur by Syd Hoff
Tyrone and the Swamp Gang by Hans Wilhelm
We're Back!: A Dinosaur's Story by Hudson Talbott

Tina Nichols, Manchester, MO

Dinosaurs on the Ceiling

Materials
Dinosaur pictures
Large white paper, 18" x 24" (45 cm x 60 cm)
Markers
Paper clips
Scissors
Stapler
Newspaper
String

What to do
1. Display dinosaur pictures in the art area.
2. Give the children large sheets of paper and ask them to choose their favorite dinosaur and draw it with markers.
3. Fasten another sheet of paper to the drawings with paper clips, and cut around the dinosaurs so that you end up with two of each child's dinosaur.
4. Staple each pair together around the outside edge leaving an opening where the children can stuff crumpled newspapers inside to make three-dimensional dinosaurs.
5. Staple the opening closed and add a string at the top to hang the dinosaur.

6. Have the children decorate both sides of the dinosaur shape with bright markers.
7. Hang the dinosaurs from the classroom ceiling.

More to do
Game: Play "I'm Thinking of a Dinosaur" by letting the children take turns giving clues about the dinosaurs hanging from the ceiling, while the rest of the class guesses the name of the dinosaur.

Related books
Dinosaur Roar by Paul and Henrietta Stickland
Time Flies by Eric Rohmann
We're Back!: A Dinosaur's Story by Hudson Talbott

Christine Maiorano, Duxbury, MA

dinosaurs

Dinosaur Eggs

 5+

Materials
Small plastic dinosaurs
Balloons
Papier-mâché
Paint
Paintbrushes

What to do
1. Give each child a small plastic dinosaur and a balloon. Have them put the dinosaurs inside the balloons.
2. Blow the balloons up and tie them (adult only).
3. Let the children put a few layers of papier-mâché over the balloons to form the eggshells.
4. When the eggs are dry, have the children paint them.
5. If the children want, they can make an opening in their egg so the little dinosaur can "hatch."

More to do
Cooking: Invite the children to help make scrambled eggs by cracking and scrambling them.

Related Books
Bones, Bones, Dinosaur Bones by Byron Barton
Count-a-saurus by Nancy Blumenthal
Little Grunt and the Big Egg: A Prehistoric Fairytale by Tomie DePaola
The Magic School Bus in the Time of the Dinosaurs by Joanna Cole
Patrick's Dinosaur by Carol Carrick
Time Train by Paul Fleischman
Tyrannosaurus Was a Beast: Dinosaur Poems by Jack Prelutsky

Elizabeth Thomas, Hobart, IN

emotions

The Mad Monster

3+

Materials
Large monster, cut out of poster board
Glue
Fake fur
Rubber clown nose
Old mittens
Large googly eyes
Markers
Contact paper
Masking tape
Wipe-off crayons
Yarn

What to do
1. Talk with the children about emotions, especially anger. Explain that everyone feels angry sometimes, but we have to find good ways of expressing our anger.
2. Tell the children they will now make a special monster that will help them express their anger in a good way.
3. Show them the monster that you cut out of poster board.
4. Call on the children to help you add the monster's features. They may choose to glue fur on the monster's head, glue on a clown nose, attach the mittens for hands, glue on moveable eyes, or draw on the clothing with markers.
5. Have the children name the monster.
6. Cover it with contact paper, and hang it on the wall. Attach a few wipe-off crayons to pieces of yarn, and attach these to the wall next to the mad monster.
7. Tell the children that whenever they feel angry, they can come over to the monster and use the crayons to scribble out their anger on the monster.

Related books
Glad Monster Sad Monster by Ed Emberley and Anne Miranda
Go Away Big Green Monster by Ed Emberley
Mean Soup by Betsy Everitt

Related song
"If You're Happy and You Know It"

Lisa M. Chichester, Parkersburg, WV

emotions

Squishy Squeezie

3+

Materials
Balloons or rubber gloves
Funnel
Various nontoxic fillings, such as flour, sand, or baking soda

What to do
1. Stretch out balloon or glove, so no parts are sticking together.
2. Using a funnel, help the children pour one of the fillings into their balloons.
3. Stop filling before the balloons are too full, and tie the end in a knot.
4. Encourage the children to squeeze this toy when they have strong feelings or just for fun!

More to do
Games: Set up a beanbag game where children take turns tossing beanbags into receptacles.
More art: Give children stickers of eyes, ears, noses, etc., and let them decorate their Squishy Squeezies.

Related books
Alexander and the Terrible, Horrible, No Good, Very Bad Day by Judith Voirst
Mean Soup by Betsy Everitt
The Temper Tantrum Book by Edna Preston Mitchell
Where the Wild Things Are by Maurice Sendak

Tracie O'Hara, Charlotte, NC

Paper Plate Masks

3+

Materials
Paper plates, with holes cut for eyes
Popsicle sticks
Masking tape
Markers

emotions

What to do

1. Give each child a paper plate, a Popsicle stick, and a piece of masking tape. Help the children tape the stick to the plate as a handle.
2. Invite the children to use the markers to draw a happy face on one side of their plate and a sad face on the other. Encourage creativity! Faces can have tears, teeth, noses, and eyebrows.
3. Encourage the children to act out happy or sad situations using their masks.

More to do

Games: Ask the children a variety of questions beginning with "How would you feel if…" and adding an experience, such as "you got an ice cream cone" or "your cat was sick." Ask the children to turn the mask to the happy or sad side to answer the question.

More art: Suggest that the children make masks portraying other emotions, such as anger, fear, and surprise.

Related books

The Chocolate-Covered-Cookie Tantrum by Deborah Blumenthal
Feelings by Joanne B. Murphy
Frog Is Frightened by Max Velthuijs

Mary Jo Shannon, Roanoke, VA

emotions

Face Puzzles

3+

Materials
Pictures of faces, cut from magazines
Scissors
Glue sticks
Construction paper

What to do
1. Set out magazines and scissors, and invite the children to cut out pictures of faces that express different emotions.
2. Then help them cut each picture into five or six puzzle-shaped pieces (you may need to do this step without their help).
3. Give each child one of the cut-up puzzles and a piece of construction paper.
4. The children can glue the pieces onto a sheet of construction paper to reform the picture.
5. Encourage the children to talk about the different emotions that the pictures are showing.

More to do
Language: Encourage the children to make up stories to go with their pictures.

Related books
I Was So Mad by Norma Simon
Sam by Ann Herbert Scott
Sometimes I Like to Cry by Elizabeth and Harry Stanton

Mary Jo Shannon, Roanoke, VA

Emotion Cubes

4+

Materials
Ruler
Cardboard milk containers, two per child
Pen
Scissors
Paper
Markers

emotions

What to do

1. Ahead of time, make cubes from milk containers. First, measure across the bottom of a milk container. Then measure that same length on all four sides (from bottom to top) and mark. Draw a line around the container at these marks and cut along this line. Cut the other container in the same manner. Place one container into the other, forming a solid cube. Make one cube for each child.
2. Give each child six paper squares cut to fit the side of the cube.
3. Encourage the children to draw six different faces showing emotions on the squares.
4. Invite them to glue one face to each side of their cubes.
5. These cubes can be used as dice or for an emotion game of your choice.

More to do

Circle time: Make an emotion cube to use with the group. The children can use these cubes to try to identify how they are feeling or to play a game where they show their happy, mad, and sad faces.

Language: Make a class book about feelings. Glue drawings of faces on pages and have children dictate stories about when they felt happy, sad, etc.

Related books

Feelings by Joanne B. Murphy
Frog Is Frightened by Max Velthuijs
Glad Monster Sad Monster by Ed Emberley and Anne Miranda
There's a Nightmare in My Closet by Mercer Mayer

Phyllis Esch, Export, PA

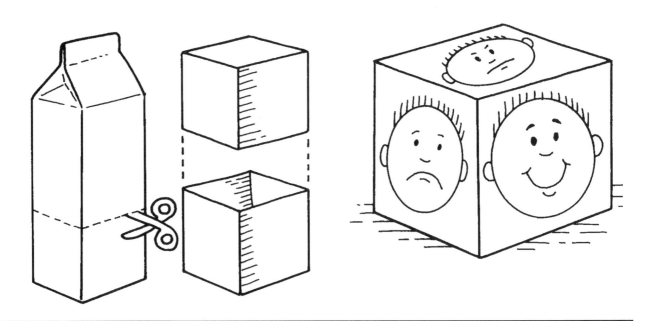

emotions

Feeling Pillows

Materials
Washcloths or other fabric squares
Sewing machine
Fabric paint
Googly eyes
Rickrack, buttons, yarn, felt scraps, and other sewing notions
Pompoms
Filling
Needle and thread

What to do
1. Ahead of time, sew two pieces of cloth together with their wrong sides facing each other; leave one side open to stuff the pillow later, then turn the pillow right side out. Slip some tissue paper or cardboard in between the two pieces of cloth so paint and glue will not transfer from one side to the other.
2. Invite the children to make a happy, mad, frightened, or sad pillow face; if possible, let them make more than one pillow.
3. For the happy pillow face, encourage the children to paint smiling eyes or glue googly eyes or buttons onto the face, then glue a piece of rickrack on, turned up in a smile. Let them add eyebrows, cheeks, a nose, and hair using the assortment of sewing supplies.
4. For the mad face, the frightened face, and the sad face, invite them to add features as above, showing as much expression as possible.
5. When they finish, have the children stuff their pillows with filler. Help them sew the opening closed with needle and thread.

More to do
Language: Have the children maintain a journal using pictures and words to record their feelings.
More art: Let the children sew one expression on each side of their pillow. Paint faces at the easel, adding expression.

Related books
Feelings by Aliki
Grandpa's Face by Eloise Greenfield

Lisa M. Chichester, Parkersburg, WV

emotions

Mixed-up Magazine

Materials
Pre-cut magazine pictures
Paper, cardboard, box lid or paper plate for the base
Paste or glue
Pens or crayons

What to do
1. Choose a magazine picture.
2. Cut an important part from the picture such as the head of a dog, a baby's foot, or a glass of milk. Glue it to the base of the paper or cardboard.
3. Choose another unrelated magazine picture and add a part of that picture to the first part. The idea is to make a silly picture combining unrelated parts such as the head of a dog, the body of a boy, two feet made of bananas, and so on.
4. When a substantially silly picture is complete, dry for an hour or so.

More to do
More art: Glue a part from a magazine picture on a piece of paper. Give the artist the challenge of adding other parts to the pre-glued piece.

Related book
Scared Silly by Marc Brown

Mary Ann Kohl, Reprinted from Preschool Art

Nature's Designs

3+

Materials
Items from nature, such as acorns, leaves, pinecones, shells, seed pods, rocks, or pebbles
Tempera paint
Flat containers, such as Styrofoam trays
Construction paper or tissue

What to do
1. Go on a nature walk and collect lots of small items from nature.
2. On a table, set out the paints in flat containers and an array of small items from nature. Have the children select an object and dip it into the paint.
3. Encourage them to place the object gently on a piece of paper, then lift it straight up without smudging.
4. Encourage them to make as many prints as they wish.

More to do
Games: Set out simple prints of the nature objects, and the objects that made the prints. Mix up the objects and ask the children to match the object and its print.
Math: Invite the children to order groups of acorns according to size, from smallest to largest, shortest to longest, etc.
Science: Look for patterns and shapes in nature's designs. Go for a walk and observe shapes, colors, and patterns in nature.

Related books
I Can Tell by Touching by Carolyn Otto
The Listening Walk by Paul Showers

 Jill E. Putnam, Wellfleet, MA

Sticky Nature Collage

3+

Materials
Clear contact paper
Scissors

environment

Frame, 9" x 12" (23 cm x 30 cm) or larger (make your own out of cardboard or visit your local framing shop to see if they will donate damaged mats and frames)

What to do

1. Cut the contact paper so that it fits in the window of the frame, overlapping the frame a bit so you can stick it down. Peel the contact paper and stick it to the frame so that the sticky side of the paper shows on the front of the frame. Secure the back with masking tape.

2. Take the children to a nice spot on the play yard that has a good combination of grass, dirt, small pebbles, and weeds. Gently brush away any bugs from the area so they will not be harmed.

3. Have the children turn the framed contact paper sticky side down, and gently but firmly press it into the grass and dirt. They should rub their hands over it so that it picks up a variety of natural materials from the ground.

4. Turn it over and see if enough "good stuff" has stuck to it. If not, try again in a different part of the yard to add different plants and pebbles.

5. Continue until you are satisfied with the way the nature collage looks.

6. Use magnifying glasses to inspect the things that are now stuck to the collage.

More to do

Math: Make a graph to represent the variety of items you have on your collage. Label the columns as plants, rocks, twigs, etc. Make a mark or place a sticker in each column for each item of that type you find.

More art: Add a 3-D effect to your frame by gluing on bits of twigs, small pebbles, and leaves. After using magnifying glasses to have a good look at the objects stuck to your collage, have children draw what they see. Post the drawings in the room.

Science: Have a naturalist visit your room to talk to the children about insects that are indigenous to your area.

environment

Related books

Bug Boy by Carol Sonenklar
Dream Meadow by Helen Griffith
Over in the Meadow by John Langstaff

Original poem

I found a little rock in the clover, clover, clover.
I pick up that rock and turned it over, over, over.
I found a little bug and I wanted to play,
But when I reached for it, it hurried away.

Related song

What Can We Find? (sing to the tune of "Mary Had a Little Lamb")

Chorus:
Searching, sifting through the grass,
Through the grass, through the grass,
Searching, sifting through the grass,
To see what we can find.

Timmy found a little rock,
Little rock, little rock.
Timmy found a little rock.
That's what Timmy found.

Chorus

Susie found a tiny bug,
Tiny bug, tiny bug.
Susie found a tiny bug.
That's what Susie found.

(Substitute a child's name and the object he or she found in the verses. Continue until you have sung each child's name.)

Virginia Jean Herrod, Columbia, SC

Ecology Art Creations

3+

Materials
Clean recycled items
Glue
Masking tape
Scissors
Crayons
Construction paper

What to do
1. At home, collect clean items that are usually put in the trash. Items could include empty cracker boxes, a coffee can, an empty milk jug, a soda can, an egg carton, etc. Because these are from you home, you can make sure that they are clean "trash."
2. Talk with the children about how careless people do not dispose of trash properly. Invite them to make art creations out of these clean items.
3. They can make a toothpaste box train, a milk jug animal, a cracker box building, and more! Their creations are based on your recycled materials and their limitless imaginations.

More to do
More art: Have a group of children work together to create a miniature town from clean "trash."

Related books
The Earth and I by Frank Asch
Mr. Willowby's Christmas Tree by Robert Barry

Nancy Dentler, Mobile, AL

environment

Nature Brushes 3+

Materials
Feathers
Pine needles
Sticks
Watercolor cakes
Water
White paper

What to do
1. Place feathers, pine needles, leaves, and sticks within the children's reach.
2. Give each child a paper and watercolors.
3. Invite the children to use the items on the table to paint the picture.

More to do
Field trip: Take the children on a nature walk so they can collect the items that they will use to paint with back in the classroom.
More art: Have the children use other items to paint with, such as kitchen utensils or old tools.

Related books
The Big Book for Our Planet by Ann Durell
Earthdance by Joanne Ryder

Linda S. Andrews, Sonora, CA

Litterbug Bags 3+

Materials
Lunch bags
Black and red construction paper
Scissors
Glue
Markers
Googly eyes

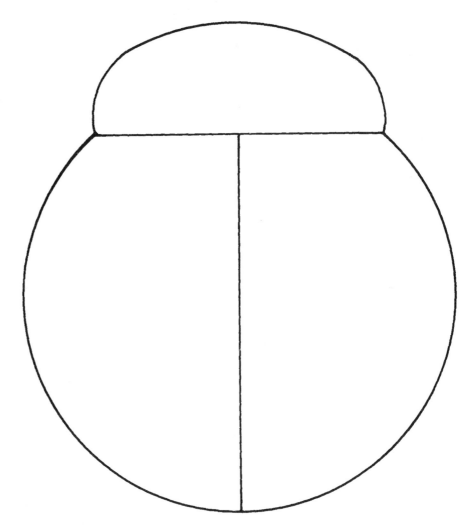

What to do

1. Show the children how to cut out a large ladybug from the construction paper.
2. Invite the children to glue this to the front of their bags.
3. The children can make ladybug dots with markers on the red part of the bug.
4. Show the children how to cut eyelashes from black paper.
5. Have the children glue on the googly eyes and attach the eyelashes just above them.
6. Take the children on a hike with the litterbug bags and encourage them to help clean up their nearby environment.

Related books

Hey! Get Off Our Train by John Burmingham
Home Sweet Home by Jean Marzollo
The Grouchy Ladybug by Eric Carle

Lisa M. Chichester, Parkersburg, WV

Recycle Sam Puppet

3+

Materials
Empty cardboard boxes, such as Girl Scout cookie boxes or cereal boxes
Throwaway junk such as milk tops, plastic lids, paper towel tubes, string
1" (3 cm) strips of colorful scrap paper
Glue

What to do
1. Have the children glue on strips of colorful scrap paper to cover the boxes. (Butcher paper also works well.)
2. Supply children with junk and encourage them to glue it on. Tell them to make arms, legs, faces, etc. with the materials.
3. Show off the creations with a puppet show, and sing "The Recycle Song" below.

More to do
Field trip: Visit your local recycling center.
More art: Invite the children to work together to create a giant puppet or creature from recyclable materials. Ask them to suggest names for the creature and then take a vote to pick one.

Related song
The Recycle Song (sing to the tune of "I've Been Working on the Railroad")

I've been working on recycling
Every single day.
I've been very busy saving
All the things we throw away.
Can't you save those newspapers
Even glass or cans.
Always think of recycling
Give the world a chance.
Give the world a chance.
Give the world a chance.
Don't forget to save your trash.
Don't forget. Don't forget.
You can turn it into cash.
Someone's cleaning up the rivers.
Someone's cleaning up the woods.
Someone's cleaning up the world.
I hope that someone is you!

Synthia Scheck, Mesa, AZ

environment

Nature Bracelets

3+

Materials
Masking tape
Plot of land with bushes, trees, acorns, pinecones, flowers, etc.

What to do
1. Place a piece of tape around each child's wrist, sticky side out.
2. Take a walk with the children in a park or field, and invite them to look for pretty items from nature that they can stick on to their tape bracelets. Encourage them to select lightweight items and to respect the natural environment by not disturbing insects or other living creatures during their search.
3. After the children have filled their bracelets, go back to the classroom, and invite the children to talk about their bracelets and the things they found to go on them.

More to do
Science: Have a variety of books set out for the children to refer to as they attempt to identify items found on their bracelets (e.g., maple leaf, hemlock pinecone, dandelion petal). Ask the children to try to figure out what each item is used for in the wild (e.g., acorns are food for squirrels and chipmunks).

Related books
A Color of His Own by Leo Lionni
Flowers by Ivan Anatta
Fresh Fall Leaves by Betsy Franco
Red Leaf, Yellow Leaf by Lois Ehlert
Squirrels by Brian Wildsmith
The Tiny Seed by Eric Carle
A Tree Is Nice by Janice May Udry

Vicki Whitehead, Ft. Worth, TX

environment

Sticks and Stones Mosaic   4+

Materials
Small stones and sticks
Paper plates
Glue (in small squeeze bottles)

What to do
1. Help the children write their names on the back of the plates.
2. Encourage the children to first use "glue dots" to create a pattern on the plate and then decorate the plate with sticks and stones by pressing them into the glue dots.
3. Allow the creations plenty of time to dry.

More to do
More art: Put out a large piece of poster board. Invite a group of children to work together to create a mosaic of sticks and stones on the poster board.
Field trip: Take a nature walk to collect sticks and stones.

Related books
Have You Seen Trees? by Joanne Oppenheim
Here Is the Tropical Rain Forest by Madeleine Dunphy
Sylvester and the Magic Pebble by William Steig

Dani Rosensteel, Payson, AZ

Shoebox Habitats  4+

Materials
Shoeboxes
Materials to create habitats such as sand, shells, pinecones, grass, rocks, lichen, fabric
Scissors
Crayons
String
Glue

What to do

1. Explain to children the meaning of the word "habitat"—the place where plants and animals live naturally.
2. Invite them to choose a habitat to make, either as a small group project or individually, depending on how many shoeboxes you have.
3. Encourage children to first decorate box with crayons, then use glue to add shells, rocks, and other items. Ask them what creatures live in this habitat and why they choose to live there—what's their food source? What grows there? What's the climate?
4. Poke several holes on the top of the box so children can hang string to dangle various objects down into their habitats.
5. Give the children soft clay or beeswax and suggest that they make the creatures that live in the habitats.

More to do

Field trip: Go for a walk and look at the habitats of insects, birds, and other animals.
Science: Make an enclosed terrarium with real plants and soil. Set out simple picture books about animals and their habitats for children to look at.

Related books

The Earth and I by Franks Asch
Frogs, Toads, Lizards and Salamanders by Joan Richards Wright
Jack's Garden by Henry Cole
The Lorax by Dr. Seuss
The Magic School Bus Hops Home: A Book About Animal Habitats by Patricia Relf
Where Once There Was a Wood by Denise Fleming

Shirley R. Salach, Northwood, NH

Nature Keepsakes

Materials

Items from nature, 2" (5 cm) or smaller
Plaster of Paris
Water
Spoon
Mixing cup
Spices and herbs that smell good

environment

Styrofoam cups, one per child
Sharp serrated knife (teacher only)
Masking tape
Wax paper, cut in 12" x 12" (30 cm x 30 cm) sheets
Cardboard or meat trays, 12" x 12" (30 cm x 30 cm)

What to do

1. Ahead of time, collect materials from nature or take the children on a nature walk and let them collect the items.
2. Using a sharp, serrated knife, cut the bottom out of each Styrofoam cup, leaving the top part about 2" (5 cm) deep (adult only).
3. Help the children write their names on wax-paper sheets and lay them on top of cardboard or meat trays so that they lay flat without bulging.
4. Set the cup rings on top of the wax paper and secure them with masking tape.
5. Invite the children to sprinkle spices in the bottom of their cup ring.
6. Follow the instructions for mixing a small quantity of plaster of Paris (approximately ½ cup at a time) to a semi-soupy consistency.
7. Help the children pour plaster into the cup ring and, working quickly, have them place the nature materials on top of the wet plaster with a sprinkle of spice. Pat them into place.
8. Set the creations aside to dry overnight.
9. Remove from wax paper and remove cup ring from the sides. The children will enjoy taking home their nature keepsakes.

Related books

Everybody Needs a Rock by Byrd Baylor
In the Tall, Tall Grass by Denise Fleming

Dani Rosensteel, Payson, AZ

A Valentine for the Earth

Materials
Newspaper
Blender
Water
Serving spoons
Red food coloring

Framed screen that fits over a bin, tub, or bucket
Heart stencils
Markers

What to do

1. Have the children rip the newspaper into small pieces, as close to 1" by 12" (3 cm by 30 cm) as they can get.
2. Ask a child to place a handful or two of the torn paper into the blender. Add a cup of water, a few drops of red food coloring, and blend (adult operates the blender).
3. Place the screen over the bin. Pour the mixture onto the screen, allowing the extra water to drain into the bin.
4. Spread the mixture over the screen to form a thin layer. Make sure there are no gaps in the mixture. You are making recycled paper.
5. Allow the mixture to drip dry. Then, place some newspaper, several pieces thick, over the mixture and flip the screen over so that your recycled paper comes off the screen and is now on the paper. Leave it there to dry completely.
6. The child can trace a heart stencil on the recycled paper and then cut it out, making a valentine for the Earth (or for a friend).

More to do

Science: The children can also help the environment by collecting cans, selling them to a local scarp yard, and using the money to buy a tree to plant —or just take them to the local recycle collection site. The children could also take a litterbug walk. Pair up the children, give each pair a bag and a pair of metal tongs, take a walk in the neighborhood and look for evidence of litterbugs. Use the tongs to collect trash that is on the ground.

Related books

50 Simple Things Kids Can Do To Save the Earth by The Earth Works Group
For the Love of Our Earth by P. K. Hallinan
Just a Dream by Chris van Allsburg

Ann Gudowski, Johnstown, PA

Leaf Shapes

3+

Materials
Fresh fall leaves
Clear contact paper cut into squares
Scissors
Magnet strip
Glue

What to do
1. Take the children outdoors and have them gather some colorful leaves.
2. When you get back to the classroom, ask the children to tear the leaves into small pieces and place them on a piece of contact paper.
3. Show the children how to fold the piece of contact paper in half and smooth the wrinkles.
4. Cut the contact paper in the shape of a leaf.
5. Help the children attach a magnet on the back of the shape.

More to do
More art: Instead of a magnet, design a mobile with several shapes.
Sand and water table: Place leaves in the water play tub for an interesting sensory experience.

Related books
Apple Pie Tree by Zoe Hall
Red Leaf, Yellow Leaf by Lois Ehlert

Original song
Use movement while you sing:
The leaves are falling down,
The leaves are falling down,
Whirling, twirling all around,
The leaves are falling down.

Cindi Winther, Oxford, MI

Crayon Kaleidoscope Placemats

3+

Materials
Small bags
Colorful leaves
2 pieces of wax paper 12" x 19" (30 cm x 50 cm) for each child
Crayon shavings in small plastic bowls

What to do
1. Bring the children on a nature walk and ask them to collect colorful leaves in a bag.
2. Back in the classroom, supply the children with one piece of wax paper. Let them share the bowls of crayon shavings.
3. Invite the children to arrange their leaves on the wax paper, then sprinkle crayon shavings over them.
4. Have the children slide their paper to you when they are finished.
5. Place the second piece of wax paper over their arrangement and press it with a hot iron. Remind the children that only a teacher or another adult can touch the iron.
6. Let the finished product cool.

More to do
More art: Cut out individual leaves and make a hanging ornament.
Science: Preserve leaves in a book using this technique and identify the leaves.

Related books
Autumn Leaves by Ken Robbins
The Giving Tree by Shel Silverstein
Have You Seen Trees? by Joanne Oppenheim
Red Leaf, Yellow Leaf by Lois Ehlert
Why Do Leaves Change Colors? by Betsy Maestro

Vicki Whitehead, Ft. Worth, TX

Leaf Quilt

3+

Materials
Leaves of various sizes, shapes, and colors
Construction paper cut into squares
Contact paper
Hole punch
Yarn

What to do
1. Have the children place leaves on a square of paper.
2. Help the children remove the backing from the contact paper. Show them how to place the contact paper over the leaves, folding the edges around the construction paper to hold the leaves in place.
3. Punch holes along the sides of each square.
4. Demonstrate how to lace the squares together with yarn.
5. When the squares are laced together, hang the leaf quilt for display. The quilt can be disassembled and individual squares sent home with the children at a later date.

More to do
Math: Count, sort, and match leaves.
More art: For a family-centered project, send instructions and supplies home with the children and let the children make a square with their families, then assemble the quilt in school. Display cloth quilts in the classroom.

Related books
Autumn Harvest by Alvin Tresselt
Marmalade's Yellow Leaf by Cindy Wheeler
The Quilt by Ann Jones
Raking Leaves With Max by Hanne Turk

Sandra Nagel, White Lake, MI

Autumn Wreath

Materials
Natural objects such as leaves, nuts, berries, seed pods, grasses, and twigs
Paper grocery bag
Hot glue gun or a strong adhesive (adult only)
Ribbon

What to do
1. Go for a walk with your class and have the children collect objects from the natural surroundings.
2. When inside, help the children remove the bottom of a grocery bag.
3. Show them how to roll the bag from the top downward, creating a wreath-like form.
4. Invite the children to spread out their treasures and choose where they would like to place them on their wreath.
5. Have the children glue the objects to the wreath or attach them yourself with a glue gun. Remind the children that only an adult may use the glue gun.
6. Help the children tie a bow to the wreath as a finishing touch.

More to do
Math: Collect extra treasures and sort them, then create a picture graph with your results.
More art: Make wreaths in holiday, seasonal, birthday, sports, and other themes. Create candle centerpieces with grocery or smaller bags.

Related book
A Year on My Street by Mary Quattlebaum

Ann Glenn, Memphis, TN

Printing With Leaves 3+

Materials
Leaves of different shapes and sizes
Newspaper
Meat trays
Tempera paint in fall colors
Newsprint

What to do
1. Collect leaves with the children a day or two before you begin the project.
2. Separate the leaves on newspaper to dry.
3. After the leaves are dry, ask each child to select a leaf.
4. Have the children feel both sides of the leaf.
5. Ask the children to lay their leaves on a meat tray.
6. Let the children choose a color of paint and gently fingerpaint the veined side of their leaf.
7. When they are finished, have the children turn their leaf over and press the painted side onto a piece of newsprint, leaving an image of the leaf on the paper.
8. Encourage the children to make as many prints as they can while there is paint on their leaf. Let them experiment with other colors and leaves.
9. Have the children cut out some of their prints, if they choose.

fall

More to do

Language: Record the progress of fall in a journal.

More art: Draw a tree trunk and branches on the bulletin board or a mural and attach the children's leaf prints. Make greeting cards with the leaf prints. Design a leaf scrapbook.

Snack: Have a leafy snack with lettuce and dressing.

Related books

Autumn Leaves by Ken Robbins

Have You Seen Trees? by Joanne Oppenheim

Constance Heagerty, Westborough, MA

Marble Painted Pumpkins

Materials

Pumpkin patterns
Painting paper
Box
Orange and yellow paint
Marbles
Hole punch
Green pipe cleaners

What to do

1. Have the children trace a pumpkin pattern onto paper and cut it out.
2. Ask the first child to place their pumpkin shape into the box and drop a marble into the orange or yellow paint.
3. Invite the child to rock the box back and forth, rolling the marble across their paper, then repeat the process with the second color. When she is finished, ask the next child to take a turn.
4. Dry the paintings thoroughly, then punch two holes in the top of the pumpkin near the stem. Show the children how to slip a pipe cleaner through the holes and twist the ends so they resemble a curly pumpkin vine.
5. Hang the pumpkins on mural paper or a bulletin board.

More to do

Language: Ask the children to describe a pumpkin and write their responses on paper shaped like a pumpkin.

Math: Measure pumpkins using a length of yarn. Estimate the number of seeds inside a pumpkin,

then count them.

More art: Paint a mural of a pumpkin patch or other fall scenes.

Science: Visit a pumpkin patch to see the stages of growth of a pumpkin. Pick a pumpkin from the vine to bring to the classroom.

Related books

Apples and Pumpkins by Anne Rockwell

Pumpkins, Pumpkins by Jeanne Titherington

Kimberle S. Byrd, Kalamazoo, MI

Apple Sachets

Materials

Red felt

Scissors

Safety pins

Needles and thread

Wool

Nutmeg

Cinnamon

Cloves

What to do

1. Ahead of time, cut two red apples from felt for each child and pin them together.
2. Help the children sew the pieces of felt together; have them keep their stitches close to the edge and sew about two-thirds of the way around the apple.
3. Invite the children to stuff the apples with wool, cinnamon, nutmeg, and cloves.
4. When they are finished, they can stitch the opening closed.

More to do

Cooking: Make applesauce or cinnamon apple crisp.

Math: Taste different varieties of apples and make a graph showing the children's preferences.

Related book
Apple Pie Tree by Zoe Hall

Original poem
Way up high in the apple tree,
Two red apples smiled at me.
I shook that tree as hard as I could.
Down came the apples,
Mmmm, they were good.

Linda Atamian, Charlestown, RI

Pumpkin Patch

4+

Materials
Orange paint powder
Pie pan
Cotton balls
Brown construction paper
Glue
Green yarn

What to do

1. Pour the powder into a pie pan.
2. Have the children roll the cotton balls in the powder, coating them.
3. When they are finished, have the children apply dots of glue on the construction paper and set the cotton balls, or pumpkins, in the glue.
4. Finally, have the children glue the yarn, or vines, between the cotton balls.

More to do

Cooking: Make Pumpkin Gelatin Candy with a six-ounce (180 gram) package of gelatin and 1 cup (250mL) of hot water; mix and pour into a pan coated with cooking oil, then chill and cut into pumpkin shapes with a cookie cutter.

Math: Use circles, triangles, squares, and other shapes cut from construction paper to decorate pumpkins.

Related books

The Biggest Pumpkin by Steven Kroll
Pumpkin Fair by Eve Bunting
Pumpkin Pumpkin by Jeanne Titherington

Elizabeth Thomas, Hobart, IN

families

Family Mobile

3+

Materials
Poster board
Scissors
Hole punch
Drawing and writing tools
Laminating machine
Yarn
Clothes hanger

What to do
1. Ahead of time, cut circles from poster board. Punch a hole at the top of each circle.
2. Have the children draw pictures of the people in their family. The children may include extended family, if they choose, and pets. Write the name of the people on the reverse side of the drawing. Encourage them to draw a picture of their house or apartment, or of any place that is particularly important to their family.
3. If possible, laminate the pictures when they are completed.
4. Tie a piece of yarn through the opening in each circle. Attach the opposite end of the yarn to the hanger, creating a mobile.
5. Hang the mobiles around the classroom.

More to do
Circle time: Ask the children to explain who is on their mobile and perhaps invite a family member to introduce to the class.
Language: Have the children write or dictate a sentence or two about someone who is very special to them.
More art: Have the children create characters representing the people in their family from craft sticks or clay and assorted materials such as yarn and googly eyes.

Related books
The Big Green Pocket Book by Candice Ransom
Daddy Makes the Best Spaghetti by Anna Grossnickle Hines
Happy Adoption Day by John McCutcheon

Colleen Hunt, Oxford Mills, Ontario, Canada

families

Thumbprint Families   3+

Materials
Stamp pads
White paper
Pencils
Pens
Markers, thin

What to do
1. Have children press their thumbs on a stamp pad, and then make their thumbprints on a piece of paper.
2. Give the children pens, pencils, and thin markers and encourage them to add facial features, bodies, and clothing to the thumbprints in order to turn them into pictures of their family members.

More to do
More art: Use this idea to create Mother's Day cards. Thumbprints can also be used to create flowers or animals.

Related books
Grandfather and I by Helen E. Buckley
Grandmother and I by Helen E. Buckley
So Much by Trish Cooke
This Is My Family by Mercer Mayer

Mary Jo Shannon, Roanoke, VA

Family Scrapbook   4+

Materials
Poster board
Construction paper
Scissors
Assorted decorating materials such as sequins, pompoms, buttons, beads

families

Glue
Crayons, markers, or colored pencils
Yarn or ribbon

What to do

1. Ahead of time, prepare a blank scrapbook for each child. Cut two covers from poster board and inside pages (the same size) from construction paper. These can be as small or as large as you want. Punch three holes along the left-hand sides of the front and back covers and the pages of the book.
2. Write the words "My Family" on each cover. Invite the children to decorate their covers using the decorating materials and glue. Set these aside to dry.
3. Give the children the inside pages. Tell them they can draw anything they want about their homes and families. The first page could be a picture of their family, the second of their pets, the third of where they live, the fourth of a family trip, etc.
4. For older children, you may want to label the pages with simple words to give them more direction.
5. Assemble the front and back covers and the pages into a book by threading yarn or ribbon through the holes on the left side.
6. Send the scrapbooks home with the children to share with their families.

More to do

Circle time: Invite the children to share their books with the other children and talk about the pictures they have drawn.

Related books

Going Home by Eve Bunting
Lots of Dads and *Lots of Moms* by Shelly Rotner
Noisy Nora by Rosemary Wells
Once There Were Giants by Martin Waddell

Gryphon House Staff

famous artists

Jackson Pollack Tablecloth 4+

Materials
A book about Jackson Pollack
Plastic sheet or drop cloth
White cotton tablecloth
Paint in various colors
Paintbrushes

What to do
1. Use a book such as *Jackson Pollock* by Mike Venezia or poster prints to introduce the class to the artist Jackson Pollack and his method of painting.
2. Hang a plastic drop cloth on an outside wall of the school building using duct tape, then tape a tablecloth to the plastic.
3. Encourage the children to flick paint at the tablecloth with their brushes. This might work best if children do this one at a time.
4. When the painting is finished, allow the tablecloth to dry.
5. Hang the tablecloth on a wall in the classroom to display.

More to do
More art: Substitute large sheets of paper for the tablecloth. Use as a mural or cut into smaller pieces for gift wrap.
Music: Play lively music while the children paint.

Related books
A Blue Butterfly: A Story about Claude Monet by Bijou Le Tord
Jackson Pollock by Mike Venezia
Lives of Artists by Kathleen Krull
Oh, Were They Ever Happy by Peter Spier

Kimberle S. Byrd, Kalamazoo, MI

famous artists

Picasso Portraits

4+

Materials
Art books or posters with portraits, including Picasso's self-portraits
White art paper
Pencils
Crayons
Tempera paints and a brush for each color. In addition to the basic colors, skin tones are
   needed—beige, brown, tan, and black
One large mirror or several small mirrors

What to do
1. Explain to the children that before cameras were invented, people had to have their portraits
   painted if they wanted to have a picture of themselves. Show them pictures from art books. Tell
   them that many artists paint self-portraits by looking in mirrors at themselves.
2. Have the children pair up with partners. Hand out art paper and pencils, and invite the children
   to draw a portrait of their partner. When the first child is finished, the other child gets a turn.
3. Remind the children that a portrait is a picture of the head and shoulders of someone.
   Emphasis should be made on facial features: color of eyes, color of hair and skin, ears, nose, and
   mouths.
4. When the partners are finished, invite the children to look in mirrors at themselves and make
   self-portraits.
5. Mount the partner-portraits and the self-portraits next to each other on a bulletin board and
   compare how they are alike and different.

More to do
More art: Use rulers to make "frames" around the edge of the portrait papers. Decorate the frames
in a pattern or a pleasing design.

Related books
All I See by Cynthia Ryland
Come Look With Me: Enjoying Art With Children by Gladys Blizzard
Getting to Know the World's Great Artists Series by Mike Venezia
Visiting the Art Museum by Laurie Krasny and Marc Brown

Barbara Saul, Eureka, CA

Van Gogh's Sunflowers

Materials
Print of Van Gogh's "Sunflowers"
Vase with real or artificial sunflowers
Construction paper in pastel colors
Pencils
Tempera paint and brushes, crayons, or oil pastels
Felt-tip pens

What to do
1. Invite the children to observe a print of Van Gogh's still-life painting and the vase of sunflowers. Explain what a still-life drawing or painting is.
2. Provide each child with a piece of construction paper. Ask the children to sketch the sunflowers, filling up as much of the paper as possible.
3. When the children have finished their sketches, have them paint or color the flowers, stems, leaves, and the vase. If oil pastels are provided, encourage the children to press hard for vibrant color.
4. Allow the paintings to dry.
5. When the paint has dried, help the children outline their flowers with felt-tip pens.

More to do

Gardening: Plant sunflowers in the spring and harvest them in the fall.

Math: Measure and/or photograph the children standing next to a full-grown sunflower. Ask them to compare their height with the flower's height.

Science: Examine the seed pods in the center of the sunflower seeds.

Snack: Eat sunflower seeds for a snack (older children only).

Related books

Camille and the Sunflowers by Laurence Anholt
Painting the Wind by Michelle Dionetti
Sunflower by Miela Ford
Vincent Van Gogh by Eileen Lucas
Wild Wild Sunflower Child Anna by Nancy White Carlstrom

Barbara Saul, Eureka, CA

Matisse Cut-outs

Materials

Construction paper: full sheets, half sheets, scraps
Scissors
Glue
Hole puncher (optional)
Prints or book showing examples of Matisse's cut-outs

What to do

1. Explain to children that one very famous artist, who lived long ago in France, invented a beautiful art form called "cut-outs."

2. Show examples of some of Henri Matisse's cut-outs, such as in *Henri Matisse Cut-outs* by John Elderfield. Explain that after painting most of his life, he did lots of experimenting with paper while resting in his bed.

3. Demonstrate how holes or even patterns can be cut from paper, then various colors of scrap paper can be placed behind the holes to create a beautiful design. Children have an easier time cutting the spaces if you teach them how to fold and cut a space, rather than punch scissors through the center of paper in order to maintain framed edge.

4. Provide each child with scissors and a full sheet of paper. Allow them to cut their own designs from the whole sheets of paper. Depending on the age of children, you may need to help pre-

vent excessive cutting.

5. Clear table of small scraps, then offer usable scraps or half sheets and glue. Allow children to choose the colors they want to put behind each open space. Suggest that they lay out their work before gluing to be sure they have created the design they want.

6. Edges may need to be trimmed, and you may want to frame cut-outs on larger pieces of paper.

More to do
More art: Hold an art exhibit to display your artwork to other classes, teachers, or parents.

Related books
Getting to Know the World's Great Artists Series by Mike Venezia
Henri Matisse Cut-outs by John Elderfield

Shirley R. Salach, Northwood, NH

farms

Shredded Paper Horses

Materials
White poster board
Scissors
Newspaper or newsprint
Black or brown tempera paint
Large paintbrushes
Glue

What to do
1. Cut one horse shape per child from the poster board (the poster board should yield about four horses per sheet).
2. Give the children newspaper or newsprint and have them tear it into strips approximately 1" by 6" (3 cm by 15 cm).
3. Have the children paint their horses with black or brown tempera paint.
4. Encourage the children to glue the shredded paper to the mane and tail areas for a realistic effect.
5. Display the finished horses on sand-colored paper or on a bulletin board for a Wild West look.

More to do
Dramatic play: Add cowboy hats, bandannas, vests, stick horses, and boots to the dramatic play area of your room. Add horses, barns, and fences to the block area for a ranch.
Movement: Have galloping relays outdoors.

Related books
The Biggest Horse I Ever Did See by Susan Arkin Couture
The Birth of a Foal by Hans-Heinrich Isenbart
The Ornery Morning by Patricia B. Demuth

Tina R. Woehler, Oak Point, TX

Wooly Stand-up Lamb

Materials
Samples of real wool
Pictures of ewes and lambs
Simple templates of a large sheep and a small sheep
Construction paper
Markers
Scissors
Glue

What to do
1. Show the children samples of real wool, together with the pictures of ewes and lambs, and talk about how sheep are sheared.
2. Ask the children to take turns using the templates to trace one big sheep and one small sheep on the construction paper.
3. Invite the children to cut out their sheep, helping them as necessary.
4. The children can draw faces on their sheep and then glue on bits of the real wool for a realistic effect, "matching" the mother and baby if they wish.
5. Enjoy the flock of sheep and encourage the children to appreciate how animals help people!

More to do
Dramatic play: Invite the children to act out "Mary Had a Little Lamb" or "Little Bo Peep."
Snack: Make lamb-shaped sugar cookies for snack.

Related books
The Little Lamb by Judy Dunn
Sheep in a Jeep by Nancy Shaw
The Year at Maple Farm by Alice and Martin Provensen
What a Wonderful Day to Be a Cow by Carolyn Lesser

Mary Brehm, Aurora, OH

Hatching Chick

3+

Materials
Yellow construction paper
Pencil
Scissors
White paper plates, one per child
Construction paper scraps in assorted colors
Glue
Craft feathers, cut into small pieces
2 spring-type clothespins for each child
Playdough
Brown paper bags

What to do
1. Ahead of time, on yellow construction paper, trace the outline of two small shoes, then cut them out and set aside two of the shapes for each child.
2. Show the children how to cut the paper plates in half using a zigzag motion so that they resemble broken eggshells. Set the eggshells aside for later.
3. Hand two of the yellow paper shapes to each child. Explain that the first shape will be the head

and body of the chick.

4. From the construction paper, have the children cut or tear small shapes to represent the beak and eyes of their chick. Let them glue the shapes onto both sides of the head of their chick.

5. Show the children how to cut the second shape in half across its width for the wings. Invite the children to glue pieces of feather onto the wings, then attach a wing to each side of the chick's body.

6. Have the children attach two clothespins for the chick's legs, then mold playdough into feet or a base to help the chick stand on its own.

7. When they finish their chick, have the children tear paper bags into strips for a nest, place the eggshell in the nest, then prop the chick between the two pieces of eggshell.

More to do

Math: Draw a counting line and place it on the table or floor; invite the children to place a chick in each square along the line, counting off as they do so.

More art: Paint a barnyard scene on mural paper. Make a chick from two pieces of felt, then fill with stuffing.

Related books

Animals on the Farm by Feodor Rojankovsky
Barn Dance! by Bill Martin, Jr., and John Archambault
Big Fat Hen illustrated by Keith Baker
Don't Count Your Chicks by Ingri and Edgar Parin D'aulaire

Tina Slater, Silver Spring, MD

Lumpy Horse

Materials

Knee-high stocking (or panty hose cut to similar length)
Rubber bands
Stuffing (cotton, rags, paper towels, toilet paper, or torn/crushed newspaper)
4 spring-type clothespins
Yarn
Felt scraps or construction paper
Glue
Scissors
Optional: playdough

farms

What to do

1. Show the children how to stuff the stocking about three-fourths of the way. Tie off the stuffed portion with a rubber band. The remaining stocking can be the horse's tail.
2. The stuffed stocking will look like a fat sausage. About one-third of the way from the toe end, tie another rubber band to make the horse's head, which may droop down.

3. Invite the children to attach four clothespins on the underside of the horse for legs.
4. The children can cut and glue yarn for a mane and small pieces of felt or paper for the ears and eyes.
5. If they want, the children can make playdough hooves for the bottom of the clothespins.

More to do

Blocks: In the block area, invite the children to build barns for their horses.

Related books

The Big Red Barn by Margaret Wise Brown
The Cow That Went Oink by Bernard Most
Farmer Duck by Martin Waddell
This Is the Farmer by Nancy Tafuri

Tina Slater, Silver Spring, MD

Preening Peacock

Materials

Scissors
Paper plates
Blue, green, and gold construction paper
Tape
Plastic spoon

Blue, green, turquoise, and black markers
Small sticky dots
Glue
Spring-type clothespins
Playdough

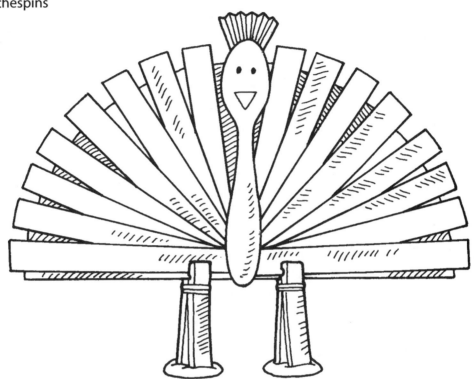

What to do

1. Ahead of time, cut a paper plate in half for the peacock's body. Also, cut paper in one of the three colors into 1" by 3" (2.5 cm by 7.5 cm) pieces. Fold each piece into a pleated fan to form the peacock's crown. Tape the crown on the back of a plastic spoon. Last, cut about eight green and eight blue strips from construction paper, about 4" to 6" (10 cm to 15 cm) long, for each child. Invite older children to help you with some of these preparations.

2. Using markers, have the children color their plate blue or green and their spoon blue or turquoise. Let them attach sticky dots for eyes and a small triangle of paper for a beak; alternatively, let them draw the features using a black marker.

3. Have the children hold their plate with its rounded side up. Tape the spoon handle to the middle of the plate, positioning the spoon itself near the rounded edge of the plate.

4. Show the children how to glue the green and blue strips of paper onto the paper plate, fanning out from the center.

5. Ask the children to add the peacock's eye spots using a marker, then color two clothespins for legs with a marker as well.

6. Attach the clothespins to the bottom of the plate.

7. Show the children how to mold claws or a base from playdough and attach the playdough to the end of the clothespins.

More to do
More art: Paint colorful peacocks at the easel. Use feathers to create a peacock mask or fan.
Movement: Wearing colorful masks and gesturing with fans, dance to a lively selection of music.

Related books
Hunting the White Cow by Tres Seymour
Spooky Tail of Prewitt Peacock by Bill Peet

Tina Slater, Silver Spring, MD

Pizza Puzzles

Materials
Small pizza boxes
Poster board circles that fit in pizza box
Scissors
Materials for "toppings" such as buttons, ribbons, beads, and small pompoms
Glue

What to do
1. Ask the local pizzeria to donate enough small pizza boxes so that each child has one.
2. Give each child a circle cut from poster board that will fit into the pizza box.
3. Invite the children to cut their circles into eight sections (slices).
4. Have each child glue bits of ribbon, beads, buttons, or other materials on their slices for "toppings."
5. After the glue dries, the children can piece their pizza puzzles together and place in their boxes. These puzzles make a great math projects, helping young children to learn geometric shapes and sizes.

More to do
Dramatic play: Using pretend money, have the children play pizza delivery. Help them count out the exact amount to pay for their pizza orders.
Snack: Make mini-pizzas on bagels or English muffins.

Related books
Give Me Half! by Stuart J. Murphy
Hi, Pizza Man! by Virginia Walter
Pete's Pizza by William Steig

Dotti Enderle, Richmond, TX

Pretzel Designs

 3+

Materials
Round pretzels
Stick pretzels
Peanut butter
Paper plates

What to do
1. Give every child a plate with a small amount of peanut butter.
2. Put the pretzels out and ask the children to create a design with their pretzels.
3. Show the children how they can "glue" their pictures with the peanut butter.
4. After they're finished they can eat their creations.

Related books
The Chocolate-Covered-Cookie Tantrum by Deborah Blumenthal
Peanut Butter and Jelly, A Play Rhyme by Nadine Bernard Westcott

Sandra Hutchins Lucas, Cox's Creek, KY

Don't Eat the Tablecloth

3+

Materials
White paper, 4" x 5" (10 cm x 13 cm) sheets
Fabric crayons
Square of fabric, 4' x 4' (1.25 m x 1.25 m) with edges hemmed

What to do

1. Give each child a piece of paper.
2. Encourage the children to use fabric crayons to draw their favorite nutritious food.
3. Using a black fabric crayon, write the children's names and their food choices next to their pictures.
4. Follow the directions on the box of fabric crayons and iron the pictures randomly on the piece of fabric.

More to do

Cooking: Throughout the year, attempt to cook all the food items drawn on the tablecloth.
Dramatic play: Use the tablecloth in the housekeeping area.
Home connection: Let children take turns taking the tablecloth home and share it with their family.

Related books

Daddy Makes the Best Spaghetti by Anna Grossnickle Hines
D. W. the Picky Eater by Marc Brown
Now I Will Never Leave the Dinner Table by Jane Read Martin and Patricia Mark

Sandy Lanes, Silver Spring, MD

Fairytale Cottage

Materials

Hansel and Gretel by the Brothers Grimm
Empty tissue boxes (4½" x 5½" or 11 cm x 14 cm)
Brown sandwich bags
Paper cut into 8½" x 6½" (21 cm x 16 cm) pieces, any color
Paper cut into 5" x 1½" (13 cm x 4 cm) pieces (any color)
Tape
Scissors
Small food items to decorate with (lollipops, jelly beans, popcorn, small pretzels, candy canes, etc.)
Royal frosting (confectioner's sugar and milk)

What to do

1. Read *Hansel and Gretel* by the Brothers Grimm. Tell the children they are going to make their own fairytale houses.
2. Have the children place their empty tissue boxes inside the sandwich bags.

3. Fold top of sandwich bag under, about 1" (3 cm), and tape it down to fasten. This is the base of the house.

4. Fold the larger piece of paper in half. Then open it up and spread over fold of sandwich bag. This serves as the roof.

5. Mark the smaller piece of paper into five equal sections, then fold. Open up and tape the first section on top of last section, so it looks like a block open at the top and bottom.

6. Cut a "V" in the front and back of this block and set on top of the house as the chimney.

7. Invite the children to decorate the fairytale "gingerbread" house using the royal frosting to "glue" the small food items.

Related books
Hansel and Gretel by James Marshall
The House That Drac Built by Judy Sierra
Jelly Beans for Sale by Bruce McMillan
Princess in the Forest by Sibylle von Offers
Scared Silly by Marc Brown
Snow White and Rose Red illustrated by G. G. Eichenauer

Ingelore Mix, Massapequa, NY

Chocolate Marshmallow Pops

Materials
Pretzel sticks
Marshmallows
Almond bark chocolate
Microwave
Wax paper
Sprinkles (optional)

What to do
1. Have the children push a pretzel stick into a marshmallow. Make sure the pretzel is secure in the marshmallow, but still long enough to use as a handle.
2. Melt the chocolate in a microwave oven. Let it cool slightly, but not harden.
3. Invite the children to dip their marshmallows into the chocolate and place them on the wax paper. They can then use sprinkles or small candies for decorating.
4. Let the chocolate harden, then lift from the wax paper. The decorated marshmallow pop is ready to eat.

More to do
Health and safety: Teach them kitchen safety, such as how to use potholders and the importance of letting hot food cool.
Snack: Let the children get creative and think of other foods that would taste good bathed in melted chocolate (cookies, donuts, popcorn balls).

Related books
Cherries and Cherry Pits by Vera B. Williams
The Chocolate-Covered-Cookie Tantrum by Deborah Blumenthal
If You Give a Mouse a Cookie by Laura Joffe Numeroff

Original song

(sing to the tune of "Clementine")
Yummy chocolate, yummy chocolate,
Its my favorite thing to eat.
Ooey-gooey, soft and chewy,
Oh, I love a chocolate treat.

Dotti Enderle, Richmond, TX

Food Hide and Seek

Materials

Paper
Crayons

What to do

1. Invite the children to discuss their favorite foods and group them into categories such as fruits, vegetables, sweets, dairy products, and so on.
2. Suggest to the children that it may be harder to identify a food if we only see part of it. For example, it might be hard to identify a picture of an apple if all we saw was part of a leaf and a stem!
3. Have the children pick different foods and privately draw them.
4. Have them fold their papers over so only a small portion of their drawing can be seen.
5. Invite the children to take turns guessing what the hidden food might be. If the children don't know what category the food is in, tell them.

More to do

Snack: Before serving snack, let the children guess what they are going to have by showing them one item partially hidden under a napkin.

Related books

Lunch! by Denise Fleming
Nanta's Lion: A Search-and-Find Adventure by Suse MacDonald
What Food Is This? by Rosemarie Hausherr
Where's Spot? by Eric Hill

Nancy Dentler, Mobile, AL

food

Candy Jewelry

3+

Materials
Black or red string licorice
Fruit Loops cereal
Lifesavers
Gummi bears
Gumdrops
Toothpicks

What to do
1. Give each child a 20" (50 cm) piece of licorice for a necklace and an 8" (20 cm) piece of licorice for a bracelet.
2. Let children string Fruit Loops and Lifesavers on their licorice strings.
3. Help them poke holes in the Gummi bears and gumdrops and string these as well.
4. Wear or eat!

More to do
More art: Give children real string and nonedible objects to string on to it, such as buttons, beads with holes in the middle, and pieces of straws.

Related books
Feathers for Lunch by Lois Ehlert
Mouse Mess by Linnea Riley
A String of Beads by Margarette S. Reid

Lisa M. Chichester, Parkersburg, WV

Log Cabin Delight

3+

Materials
Picture of a log cabin
Graham crackers
Peanut butter
Pretzel sticks
Plastic knives

What to do
1. Show the children a photograph or drawing of a log cabin, and point out how the logs are laid neatly in rows to create the structure.
2. Set out peanut butter, pretzel sticks, and plastic knives.
3. Invite the children to spread peanut butter on graham crackers.
4. Ask the children to place pretzels so they look like logs.
5. Build a cabin (house), using the peanut butter as "glue."
6. Eat and enjoy!

More to do
More art: Give children craft sticks and glue and invite them to create little cabins. Using clay, they can make creatures or people to live in them.

Related books
A House Is a House for Me by Mary Ann Hoberman
The Little House by Viriginia Lee Burton
My House Has Stars by Megan McDonald

 Joyce E. Meckly, Hanover, PA

Bunny Bread

3+

Materials
Frozen bread dough (thawed in refrigerator one day ahead)
Flour
Raisins

Sesame seeds
Wax paper
Vegetable oil spray
Cookie sheets

What to do

1. Give each child a piece of wax paper. Then have them place one spoonful of flour on it and spread to coat.
2. Give each child one large ball of dough (for head) and two smaller balls (for ears). You should be able to get six bunnies per loaf.
3. Roll the larger ball and then flatten slightly to form the head.
4. Take the two smaller balls and roll on flat surface and shape to form the ears. Attach the ears to the head.

5. Give each child three raisins. Invite the children to place them where they think the bunnies' eyes and nose would be.

6. Have children use sesame seeds to create whiskers for their bunnies.

7. Place on cookie sheets and bake at 350° F (180° C) degrees for 20 to 25 minutes.

8. Watch your little bunnies sniffing the air while these are baking and then nibble away at the finished product.

More to do

Movement: Do the following exercise while the bread is baking.

Mr. Rabbit hop-hop-hopping on my lawn, (hop like a bunny)
When I run out you're always gone. (jog in place)
I wish someday you'd stay and play,
Instead of always hop-hop-hopping away. (hop like a bunny)

Related books

Bunny Cakes by Rosemary Wells
If You Were My Bunny by Kate McMullen
The Little Red Hen by Byron Barton

Constance Heagerty, Westboro, MA

Edible Playdough

Materials
Creamy peanut butter
Measuring spoons
Dry milk
Honey
Margarine tubs (small) and lids
Plastic spoons

What to do
1. Clean the table area where the children will work.
2. Have children wash their hands.
3. Measure one or two tablespoons (15 to 30 mL) of peanut butter, one or two tablespoons (15 to 30 mL) of dry milk, and 1 or 2 tablespoons (15 to 30 mL) of honey into each tub.
4. Give each child a plastic spoon, a tub with the prepared ingredients, and a lid.

Instruct the children to use the spoon to mix the ingredients thoroughly, until the color is even and the dough is not sticky.

5. When the dough is prepared, the children may use the dough as they would regular playdough to create balls, snakes, or other objects.

6. Children may eat their creations for snack, or use the tub and lid to take them home.

Related books
Bread Is for Eating by David Gershator
Green Eggs and Ham by Dr. Seuss

Mary Jo Shannon, Roanoke, VA

What Goes Inside?

Materials
White construction paper
Black construction paper
Old magazines
Glue
Scissors

What to do
1. In a group, talk with the children about why we keep some foods cold. Ask if anyone knows why some foods must even be kept in the freezer.
2. Have children fold a large sheet of white construction paper in half so that it opens like a card.
3. Draw a line across the front half about one-third of the way down. Have children cut the line. The top third represents the freezer, the bottom third, the refrigerator.
4. Cut handles out of black paper and have children glue them on.
5. Have children cut appropriate foods out of magazines to glue into the refrigerators and freezers.

Sandra Suffoletto Ryan, Buffalo, NY

Wormy Treats

4+

Materials
Sugar cookie dough
Rolling pin
Flower-shaped cookie cutter
Baking sheet
Oven
Clear plastic cups
Freezer tape or masking tape
Markers
Oreo cookies
Gummi worms
Tinted canned frosting
Popsicle sticks

What to do
1. Invite the children to help roll out your favorite sugar cookie dough recipe.
2. Ask the children to take turns cutting out the dough with a flower-shaped cookie cutter and placing the flowers on the baking sheet.
3. Bake the cookies.
4. As the cookies are baking, give the children clear plastic cups, tape, and markers, and help them write "My Garden" on their cups (or do it for them).
5. Instruct each child to crumble up the Oreos until they look like soil in the cup.
6. Give each child four Gummi worms and tell them to place these in the dirt.
7. After the cookies have cooled, children ice them with tinted canned frosting.
8. Show the children how to insert a popsicle stick into two flower cookies and then shove the other end of the stick into the cup of dirt.
9. Enjoy your worm garden work of art!

Related books
Apple Pie Tree by Zoe Hall
Bunny Cakes by Rosemary Wells
Jack's Garden by Henry Cole
Mud Pies and Other Recipes: A Cookbook for Dolls by Majorie Winslow

Lisa M. Chichester, Parkersburg, WV

food

Scratch and Sniff Painting

Materials
Newspaper
Several packets of unsweetened drink mix
Small bowls
Paint brushes
Measuring spoons
Spoons for mixing
Pitcher of water
White or light colored paper, 8" x 10" (20 cm x 25 cm)

What to do
1. Ask the children to cover the work area with newspapers.
2. Prepare the "paint" by mixing 1 tablespoon (15 mL) of water with each flavor of drink mix in separate bowls.
3. Invite the children to paint with the drink mixes just as they would with any other kind of paint.
4. Let the paintings dry.
5. After the paintings have dried, encourage the children to "scratch the painting" to reveal the different scents.
6. Explain to the children that if they mix the paint on their papers, they will get a whole new scent! Experiment, and have fun!

Related books
Eat the Fruit, Plant the Seed by Millicent E. Selsam
From Seed to Pear by Ali Mitgutsch
What Was It Before It Was Orange Juice? by Jane Belk Moncure

Cory McIntyre, Crystal Lake, IL

Fun With Food Groups

Materials
Illustration of the food pyramid
Magazines

Scissors
4 sheets of poster board
Glue

What to do
1. Talk to the children about the four food groups. Show them an illustration of the food pyramid.
2. Divide the children into four teams, assigning one of the food groups to each team.
3. Ask each team to look through a stack of magazines to find pictures of their foods and cut those pictures out.
4. Give each team one sheet of poster board and glue, and invite them to make a collage of their food group on the poster.
5. After the teams have completed their posters, let them share their collages with the other children.

More to do
More art: Make one big food pyramid collage by cutting out and pasting the poster board collages together. This might be done on a large bulletin board.
Snack: Each day, offer a food item from a different food group.

Related books
Bread and Jam for Francis by Russell Hoban
Cloudy with a Chance of Meatballs by Judi Barrett
Eating the Alphabet: Fruits and Vegetables from A-Z by Lois Ehlert
Gregory the Terrible Eater by Mitchell Sharmat
The Milk Makers by Gail Gibbons

Lori A. Dunlap, Brandon, MS

Bean Mosaics

Materials
Thin cardboard pieces or poster board
Permanent marker
Various types of dried beans, peas, and feed corn

What to do
1. On each piece of cardboard draw one simple picture such as a tree, flower, pumpkin, turkey, boat, animal, etc., for each child.

2. Invite the child to choose the items to place within the picture's outline.
3. Suggest to the children that their mosaics will look better if they use the same kind of peas/beans/corn in the same area (e.g., black beans for the tree trunk). Younger children will probably mix and match their choices.
4. These mosaics can be as simple as needed or, with older preschoolers, you can add details and use a larger variety of dried food materials to enhance creativity and categorizing.
5. When finished, the beans and peas can be returned to a bowl and later used for soup making.

More to do
More art: Make permanent mosaics by giving children non-food items to glue inside their drawings.

Related books
Growing Vegetable Soup by Lois Ehlert
How a Seed Grows by Helene J. Jordan
Lucy's Picture by Nicola Moon
One Bean by Anne Rockwell
Surprise Garden by Zoe Hall

Tina R. Woehler, Oak Point, TX

Artful Memory Game

Materials
Children's artwork
Scissors
Copy machine
Index cards, 4" x 6" (10 cm x 15 cm)
Glue
Clear contact paper or laminating machine

What to do
1. Choose six or eight pieces of the children's art. Choose more pieces for another artful memory game, so all the children's work is represented.
2. Using a black and white copier (or for best results use a color copier), reproduce the images and reduce or enlarge them to the size of the index cards. Make two copies of each drawing.
3. Cut out the pictures and glue them to the index cards.
4. Laminate the cards or cover them with clear contact paper to protect them.
5. Invite the children to play the Artful Memory Game. Place the cards face down on the table, in rows. Turn the cards over two at a time and find the matching pairs. Deal younger children half of the cards, then have them choose from the remainder of the deck in turn to find a match.

Related books
A Child's Book of Play in Art by Lucy Micklethwait
Monet by Mike Venezia
Pierre August Renoir by Mike Venezia
What Makes a Leonardo a Leonardo? by Richard Muhlberger

 *Virginia Jean Herrod, Columbia, SC*

Frisbee Flyers

Materials
Paper plates of any size, two per child
Decorating supplies such as markers, stickers, crayons, and paint
Stapler

What to do

1. Have the children decorate the bottom of each plate.
2. Staple the edges of plates together with the decorated sides facing out.
3. Take the children outside and invite them to throw their new "frisbees."

More to do

Games: See how far the children can throw their handmade frisbees, then mark the spot and measure the distance. Set up a series of targets, mark their location with little flags, then play a round of Frisbee Golf in teams. Set up small plastic bottles like bowling pins, then form teams and play Frisbee Bowling. Hold Frisbee Relays.

Math: Invite each child to measure and record his or her own distance in the Frisbee Throw. They can design a fun chart to record their first, second, and third attempts in the Frisbee Throw.

Related books

The Magic Moonberry Jump Ropes by Dakari Hru
Shake It to the One That You Love Best by Cheryl Warren Mattox

Original song

"This is the Way We Fling the Frisbee" (sing to the tune of "Here We go Round the Mulberry Bush")

This is the way we fling the frisbee,
fling the frisbee,
fling the frisbee.
This is the way we fling the frisbee,
on a (sunny, windy, etc.) morning.

Lauren Brickner-McDonald, Mountain Lakes, NJ

Rainbow Squares

3+

Materials

Paper
Copy machine
Dice
Crayons

What to do

1. Ahead of time, prepare a five-by-five grid with twenty-five squares on a piece of paper and

make several copies.

2. When you are ready to begin, have the children roll one dice. Ask them to choose a crayon and color the correct number of squares on the grid. Repeat the process until all the squares are filled.

More to do

Math: On a larger grid, have older children use two die and color in the sum of the two numbers. Or, have two children each use their own dice and place a bean or button on the correct number of squares until the grid is covered; count to see which player has the most beans on the grid.
More art: Cut the squares apart and paste them onto colored paper in a design, creating a mosaic. Cut the grid into strips and use them for paper weaving.

Related books

How the Sky's Housekeeper Wore Her Scarves by Patricia Hooper
Planting a Rainbow by Lois Ehlert

Tina Slater, Silver Spring, MD

Grocery Bag Treasure Map

Materials
A special object
Paper grocery bags
Scissors
Markers
Ribbon cut in 1' (30 cm) lengths
Tape

What to do
1. Divide the children into two groups. Ask the first group to hide a special object (the treasure) in the classroom while the second group is not looking.
2. Working with the first group, cut down the sides and around the bottom of a paper grocery bag. Flatten to form a large rectangle. Trim edges and corners to make the bag look like an authentic map.
3. Invite the children in the first group to draw the classroom, then mark an "x" where the treasure is hidden. They may need your help with this.
4. Turn the map over. Tape the ribbon about 2" (5 cm) from the edge of the map at the midpoint of its short side. Roll the map up and tie it closed with the ribbon.

5. Have the children in the first group present the map to the children in the second group. Then invite the children in the second group to follow the map to find the hidden treasure.

6. If the children enjoy the game, they can switch sides and group two can hide the treasure and create the map.

More to do
Math: Older children can count paces or measure distances. Hide several treasures and number their locations, then have the children look for them in sequence.

Related books
As the Crow Flies, A First Book of Maps by Gail Hartman
My Map Book by Sara Fanelli

Leslie Kuehn Meyer, Austin, MN

gardening

Growing Grass

Materials
Styrofoam cups,
  one per child
Black markers
Potting soil
Small hand shovels
  or large spoons
Grass seeds
Small watering can
Water
Child safety
  scissors

What to do
1. Have the children draw eyes, a nose, and a mouth on the outside of the cup.
2. When the children have finished drawing, have them add potting soil to the cup, about two-thirds full.

3. Invite the children to sprinkle grass seeds on top of the soil, then cover the seeds with a small amount of soil.
4. When the seeds are covered, have the children pour a small amount of water into the cup.
5. After several days, when the grass grows and reaches a height of 1" or 2" (3 cm or 5 cm) above the rim of the cup, ask the children to trim the grass with their scissors.

More to do
Dramatic play: Encourage the children to name the characters they have drawn on their cups and create a story or play about them.
Science: Pull up a few of the blades of grass as they grow and let the children examine the root systems. Explain how the seeds opened. Bring in a strip of sod grass for the children to examine

with magnifiers. Create a worm garden in a large plastic container. Keep the container in a dark room or closet, then move it into the light; observe the worms as they move deeper into the soil to avoid the light.

Related books
Hats Off to Hair by Virginia Kroll
How a Seed Grows by Helene J. Jordan
In the Tall, Tall Grass by Denise Fleming
The Carrot Seed by Ruth Krauss

Tina R. Woehler, Oak Point, TX

Corn Painting

Materials
Paint trays
Tempera paints mixed to a medium consistency
Smocks
Construction paper, 12" x 18" (30 cm x 45 cm) in various colors
3 ears of dried Indian corn

What to do
1. Ahead of time, pour the paint into paint trays and place the trays on a protected work surface.
2. Provide each child with a smock and a piece of construction paper.
3. Invite the children to put an ear of corn in the paint and roll it around, covering the kernels with paint.
4. Once the kernels are covered, have the children roll the corn onto their paper as if they were using a rolling pin.
5. Allow the paintings to dry and display them around the room.

More to do
Music: Make corn shakers with empty soda bottles. Fill clean, dry bottles with dried corn kernels and seal the bottle cap with glue.
Science: Grow corn in your room or outdoors by placing whole kernel feed corn in a large container or in the ground. Chart its growth. Examine a few ears of corn, both shucked and unshucked, with magnifiers. Display various kinds of corn: for example, Indian, yellow, and white.
Snack: Make popcorn using a hot air popper and popcorn kernels.

gardening

Related books
Corn Is Maize: The Gift of the Indians by Aliki
Growing Vegetable Soup by Lois Ehlert
Three Stalks of Corn by Leo Politi

Tina R. Woehler, Oak Point, TX

Planting Baggie

Materials
Zip-closure baggies, one per child
Soil
Spoons
Popcorn kernels
Water
Tape

What to do
1. Give each child a baggie and a few popcorn kernels.
2. Invite the children to place several spoonfuls of soil in their baggies, and then to press a couple of popcorn kernels into the soil. They should add a tiny bit of water and seal the baggie.
3. Tape the baggies to a sunny window. Soon the root system will sprout, making a pretty and interesting design against the light.
4. Encourage the children to check their baggies frequently.

More to do
More art: Invite the children to draw what is happening in the baggie.
Science: With your help, children can record the changes in the kernel on a sheet of paper.

Related books
Apples and Pumpkins by Anne Rockwell
Growing Vegetable Soup by Lois Ehlert
Planting a Rainbow by Lois Ehlert

Deana Crider, Danville, VA

gardening

Flower Puff Garden

3

Materials
Cotton balls, various colors
Pipe cleaners
Green Easter grass
Yarn
Markers
Plastic gardening pots or strawberry containers
Construction paper in spring colors
Scissors
Glue

What to do
1. Before class, display the first five materials on the table in plastic gardening pots and strawberry containers.
2. Encourage the children to design a flower garden scene by placing these materials on a paper background.
3. Have the children glue the materials onto the paper and allow to dry.

More to do
Gardening: Plant flowers in your school's garden or in containers, perhaps for Mother's Day or May Day. Plant seeds indoors and place them up on the windowsill in your classroom.
More art: Decorate your bulletin board with puff flowers.

Related books
Alison's Zinnia by Anita Lobel
Planting a Rainbow by Lois Ehlert
The Rose in My Garden by Arnold Lobel

Diann Spalding, Santa Rosa, CA

Flower Headbands

3+

Materials
Construction paper, various colors

gardening

Scissors
Stapler
Glue
Butterfly and ladybug stickers, optional

What to do

1. Ahead of time, cut 2" (5 cm) wide strips of construction paper to form a headband for each child. Cut an assortment of flower shapes for decorating the headbands.
2. Wrap the strips of paper around each child's head, forming a headband. Staple the strips together.
3. Encourage the children to cut out their own flower and leaf shapes from construction paper, adding to the assortment you have cut in advance.
4. When the headbands are made, have the children glue the flowers and leaves to them. Attach stickers of butterflies and ladybugs, if desired.

More to do

More art: Cut the flower and leaf shapes from scraps of wrapping paper or greeting cards for a colorful effect. Substitute geometric shapes, numbers, letters, dinosaurs, or farm animals for the flowers, adapting the project to your subject or theme.

Related books

A Hat so Simple by Jerry Smath
Jennie's Hat by Ezra J. Keats
Mattie's Hats . . . Won't Wear That Hat by Elaine Greenstein
Miss Rumphius by Barbara Cooney

Sandra Nagel, White Lake, MI

gardening

Tie-dye Flowers

3+

Materials
Newspaper
Food coloring, various colors
Water
Cups
Eyedroppers
Coffee filters, one per child
Material for flower stems and leaves such as construction paper, pipe cleaners,
   or painted paper towel tubes
Glue
Stapler

What to do
1. Prepare a work area ahead of time by protecting a flat surface with newspaper.
2. Mix food coloring and water in cups and place the cups on your work surface.
3. Invite the children to place the tip of the eyedropper in a cup and pinch the bulb of the eye-dropper to fill it with the liquid.
4. Have the children squeeze the dropper, applying drops of color onto the coffee filter. Repeat with other colors until the filter is completely covered.
5. Hang the filter or place it on a flat surface to dry.
6. Attach the stems and leaves to the filter with glue or staples.

More to do
More art: Create a garden scene by painting a mural for the classroom wall and applying the tie-dye flowers. Drop melted crayon onto the filter, then add the food coloring to create a different look.
Science: Suspend a coffee filter over a cup of colored water, allowing the tip of the filter's base to sit in the water. Observe the colors move up the filter and separate as the filter absorbs the liquid.

Related books
The Legend of the Indian Paintbrush retold by Tomie dePaola
Miss Rumphius by Barbara Cooney
Planting a Rainbow by Lois Ehlert

Sandra Nagel, White Lake, MI

gardening

Darling Daffodils

3+

Materials
Scissors
Cardboard egg cartons
Construction paper or cardboard
Newspaper
Yellow and green paint
Paint cups and brushes
Paper towel tubes or construction
   paper rolled into a tube
Flower shapes cut from construc-
   tion paper or cardboard
Green construction paper
Glue
Stapler

What to do
1. In advance, cut the egg cartons apart, dividing them into individual egg compartments or holders. Cut flower shapes from construction paper or cardboard.
2. Before the children arrive, cover the work area with newspaper and pour the paint into cups.
3. Invite the children to paint the cardboard flowers and egg compartments yellow and the tubes green.
4. While the pieces are drying, have the children cut leaf shapes from construction paper.
5. When the pieces are dry, glue or staple the flower shape to the top of the tube. Glue or staple the egg holder to the middle of the flower shape.
6. Attach leaf shapes to tube.

More to do
Gardening: Plant bulbs and watch for the flowers to bloom.
More art: Create a mural with a variety of flowers for your spring bulletin board.
Science: Bring in a daffodil bulb and describe how the daffodil grows.

gardening

Related books
The Gardener by Sarah Stewart
Miss Rumphius by Barbara Cooney
Planting a Rainbow by Lois Ehlert

Sandra Nagel, White Lake, MI

Decorator Flower Pots

Materials
Newspaper
Miniature flowerpots, one per child
Craft paint, various colors
Paintbrushes
Glue gun, low-temperature (adult only)
Buttons
Scrap materials such as fabric, yarn, costume jewelry, and ribbon
Paint pens

What to do
1. Cover a work area in advance with newspaper and provide each child with a flowerpot.
2. Have the children paint their flowerpots with craft paint.
3. Invite the children to choose an assortment of buttons and scrap materials to decorate their flowerpots. Using the glue gun, attach the decorations to the pots with glue (adult only).
4. When the glue is dry, have the children use a paint pen to add their name and finishing touches to their pots.

More to do
Gardening: Plant seeds in the flowerpots and place them up on the windowsill in your classroom.
More art: Create a mural or book by drawing the outline of a garden scene on paper and gluing the remaining scrap materials inside the outline.

Related books
Chrysanthemum by Kevin Henkes
The Gardener by Sarah Stewart

Lisa M. Chichester, Parkersburg, WV

health and Safety

Boo-Boo Book

3+

Materials
Writing paper
Pencil or pen
Construction or drawing paper
Markers or crayons
Bandage strips

What to do
1. Tell about an injury, or boo-boo, you have had and ask the children to describe one of their own. Write down each of their stories on a separate piece of paper.
2. Give each child paper and a bandage strip. Ask the children to draw a picture of themselves, showing an injury, then apply the bandage to their picture.
3. Assemble the stories and pictures in a book and display the book in the classroom. The book may be taken apart at a later date, and the pictures and stories sent home individually.

More to do
Language: Take turns sending the book home with the children to read with their families.
More art: Trace the outline of each child's body onto large paper. Have the children color in their outline, draw a boo-boo, and apply a bandage to it.

Related books
Barney Is Best by Nancy White Carlstrom
The Cow Buzzed by Andrew and David Zimmerman
Doctor Dan the Bandage Man by Helen Gaspard
Madeline by Ludwig Bemelmans

Patricia Cawthorne, Lynchburg, VA

Finger Cast Puppets

3+

Materials
Petroleum jelly, optional
Rigid or casting wrap, cut into 4" (10 cm) strips
Bowl of water
Paint
Googly eyes
Glue
Yarn or doll hair, optional
Clay, optional

What to do
1. Choose your first "patient" and apply a small amount of petroleum jelly to the child's finger, if desired. Dip the strips of wrap into the bowl of water and wrap them loosely around the child's finger, forming a cast.
2. Carefully remove the cast before it hardens.
3. When their casts harden and dry, invite the children to paint faces on them. Help the children attach eyes and hair, if desired.
4. Attach some clay to the base of the casts if you want the puppets to stand on their own.

More to do
Circle time: Invite the children to discuss safety and how to avoid accidents.
Dramatic play: Use the puppets to act out a scene in a doctor's office or hospital.

health and Safety

Related books
Curious George by H.A. Rey
I Can Tell by Touching by Carolyn Otto
Maggie and the Emergency Room by Martine Davison
Officer Buckle and Gloria by Peggy Rathmann

Carol Nelson, Rockford, IL

What's Inside Our Bodies

Materials
Construction paper
Wallpaper, large scraps
Scissors
Roll of wide paper
Markers and crayons
Yarn
Glue

What to do
1. Ahead of time, cut heart, lung, and stomach shapes from construction paper for each child. Cut scrap pieces of wallpaper into the shape of a shirt for each child. As you will be tracing the children's outlines onto paper, these shapes should be a realistic size.
2. Trace each child's body onto the wide paper. Cut along the outline, or cut the paper in a rectangle, forming a background for their outline.
3. Have the children color their faces and their clothing from the waist down. Help them glue the yarn hair around the outline of their heads, and the stomach, lungs, and heart in the chest area.
4. Glue the shirts to the outlines at the shoulders only so that the children can lift the shirt and see what is inside their bodies.

More to do
Science: Have the children breathe deeply, filling their lungs with air and expanding their chest; feel their heartbeat or listen with a stethoscope; and fill their stomach with a drink or snack.

Related books
See How You Grow by Patricia Pearse
Your Bellybutton by Jun Nanao
What's Inside My Body by Angela Royston

Cindi Winther, Oxford, MI

Veins and Arteries

3+

Materials
Construction paper
Scissors
Red and blue paint
Marbles
Small cups
Shallow cardboard boxes or baking pans
Plastic spoons

What to do
1. Ahead of time, cut out a paper doll for each child. Pour red and blue paint into small cups and place a marble in each cup.
2. Invite the children to lay their paper doll in the bottom of the box or pan.
3. Ask the children to put one red and one blue marble in the box or pan using a spoon, then roll the marbles around by gently tilting the box side to side. The design they create illustrates the veins and arteries in our bodies.

More to do
Science: Have the children feel their own heartbeat or listen with a stethoscope. Ask them to feel or listen to the beat when they are sitting still, then listen again after they have jumped in place. Use a flashlight to observe the veins and arteries in their ears and fingers.

Related books
A Drop of Blood by Paul Showers
The Magic School Bus, Inside the Human Body by Joanna Cole

Phyllis Esch, Export, PA

Floss Your Teeth

3+

Materials
Egg cartons
Scissors
White paint
Paintbrushes
White yarn, cut in 12" (30 cm) pieces

What to do
1. To prepare, divide the bottom of an egg carton into four sections, providing each child with three compartments. Give each child a section of the carton with the bottom of the carton facing up.
2. Have the children paint the carton white to represent their teeth.
3. When the cartons are dry, give each child a piece of yarn.
4. Talk to the children about how they should care for their teeth. Show them how to floss their egg carton teeth by wrapping the ends of the yarn around their fingers and sliding it between the compartments of the egg carton.

More to do
More art: Create a poster or collage by drawing an outline of two rows of teeth; collect pictures or wrappers of healthy foods and glue them within the outline. Create a second poster with pictures of unhealthy foods.
Snack: Plan a healthy and sugarless menu for a special occasion in class. Talk to the children about why sugar is bad for their teeth.

Original song
(Sing to the tune of "Row, row, row your boat.")

Brush, brush, brush your teeth,
At least two times a day.
Cleaning, cleaning, cleaning, cleaning,
Fighting tooth decay.

Floss, floss, floss your teeth,
Every single day.
Gently, gently, gently, gently,
Whisking plaque away.

h**e**alth *and* Safety

Related books
Doctor Desoto by William Steig
Going to the Dentist by Kate Petty
I Have a Loose Tooth by Sally Noll
The Lost Tooth Club by Shelley Davidson
Rosie's Baby Tooth by Maryann Macdonald

Elizabeth Thomas, Hobart, IN

Soap Balls

3+

Materials
Mixing bowls
Laundry soap flakes
Water
Food coloring
Vanilla, cologne, other scents, optional
Trays

health and Safety

What to do

1. Before the children arrive, pour soap flakes into bowls, using a separate bowl for each color you plan to use.
2. Slowly add water to the flakes until the mixture is the consistency of very stiff dough.
3. Ask the children to add drops of food coloring to each bowl, then mix. Add vanilla or other scents, if desired.
4. Have the children shape large spoonfuls of the soap mixture into balls.
5. Place the balls onto trays, labeling each ball with the child's name. Allow the balls to set and harden for two to three days. Encourage the children to wash their hands with the soap balls in class or at home.

More to do

Holidays: Wrap the soap balls in colorful tissue paper and fasten with yarn for a special gift.
Science: Ask the children about the appearance, smell, and feel of the soap mixture and balls, and discuss how they used their senses of sight, smell, and touch.

Related books

The Cow Buzzed by Andrew and David Zimmerman
My Five Senses by Aliki

Barbara J. Lindsay, Mason City, IA

Gift Bags

3+

Materials
Lunch bags
Spools of gift-wrapping ribbon
Scissors
Glue
Purchased pre-made bows
Markers
Stickers

What to do
1. Provide each child with a paper lunch bag.
2. Give them each one ribbon cut to the length of the bag and one ribbon cut to the width of the bag.
3. Have the children glue the longer ribbons down the middle of the fronts of their bags, from top to bottom.
4. Then have them glue the shorter ribbons across the middle of the longer ribbons, from side to side.

5. Let each child choose a pre-made bow, and stick it to the bag where the two ribbons meet. The bags will now look like wrapped presents.
6. Encourage the children to use magic markers and stickers to decorate the bags. Suggest that they write messages such as "Happy Holidays" or "Happy Mother's Day", depending on the holiday. They might choose to draw pumpkins, wreaths, dreidels, etc.
7. Let the children use these gift bags to take home gifts they have made for family members.

More to do
Blocks: Put wrapping paper, scissors, bows, and cellophane tape in the block area. Encourage the children to wrap the blocks so they look like presents.

Susan Jones Jensen, Norman, OK

holidays

Hand-print Bunnies

3+

Materials
White and pink paint
Markers
Colored paper

What to do
1. Explain to the children that they are going to make a bunny out of their hand.
2. With white paint, paint the child's palm and fingers only.
3. Have the child hold her hand with first and second fingers together and third and fourth fingers together to form ears.
4. With fingers in this position, press the child's hand down on paper.
5. Paint the tip of the child's thumb pink and press it down to make a nose.
6. When dry, add eyes and teeth with markers.

More to do
Circle time: Bring in a pet bunny to show the class

Related Books
Bunny Cakes by Rosemary Wells
Read to Your Bunny by Rosemary Wells
The Runaway Bunny by Margaret Wise Brown

Suzanne Maxymuk, Cherry Hill, NJ

Tissue Paper Hearts

3+

Materials
White construction paper, 12" x 18" (30 cm x 45 cm)
Paintbrushes
Watered-down glue
Tissue paper cut into heart shapes

What to do
1. Give each child a piece of white construction paper.

2. Have the children use the paintbrushes to paint the entire surface of their papers with watered-down glue.
3. Provide the children with tissue paper hearts to lay all over the paper. Suggest that they overlap and layer them.
4. When the entire surface is covered, have the children brush another coat of watered-down glue all over their projects to seal the picture.

More to do
Math: Have the children sort and graph candy "conversation" hearts.
More art: Encourage the children to make Valentine's Day cards.

Related books
Will You Be My Valentine by Steven Kroll
Franklin's Valentine by Paulette Bourgeois
I'll Love You Forever by Robert Munsch

Amy Melisi, Oxford, MA

Pumpkin Party

3+

Materials
White paper
Orange paint in dishes
Lids in different sizes
Plastic blocks
Markers
Clear contact paper, optional
Pumpkin pie ingredients:
    2 cups (500 mL) of mashed pumpkin
    1 can evaporated milk
    ¾ cup (175 mL) sugar
    1 teaspoon (5 mL) cinnamon
    ¼ teaspoon (1 mL) ginger
    ¼ teaspoon (1 mL) cloves
    ¼ teaspoon (1 mL) nutmeg
    2 tablespoons (30 mL) melted butter

2 frozen pie shells
Pie plate
Mixing bowls
Mixing spoons
Oven
Plates and forks
Napkins

What to do

1. On a day prior to your party, have the children make their placements by dipping a lid into paint and pressing the lid onto their paper, leaving a circle or pumpkin shape. Have them make several pumpkin prints across their paper. Let the children dip the block into paint and add a stem to each pumpkin.
2. Encourage the children to draw expressions on their pumpkins using markers. Set the papers aside to dry.
3. When the paint dries, cover the placemats with contact paper or laminate them for protection from spills.
4. Before class on the day of the party, cut up a pumpkin, wrap it in foil, and bake it at 350° F (180° C) until it is soft.
5. Invite the children to scoop out the pumpkin. (As an alternative, use canned pumpkin.)
6. Help the children measure and mix the ingredients: add sugar to the pumpkin first, then the spices. Beat the eggs, then add them to the mixture. Add the milk and the melted butter last.
7. Pour the mixture into the pie shells and bake at 350° F (180° C) until a knife blade inserted in the pie comes out clean.
8. Set your table for the pumpkin party and enjoy a slice of pumpkin pie.

More to do

More art: Make a picture using some of the pumpkin seeds and save the others to plant in the schoolyard.

Related books

It's Pumpkin Time! by Zoe Hall
When the Goblins Came Knocking by Anna Grossnickle Hines
Who Said Boo? by Nancy White Carlstrom

Original poem

Pumpkin Magic

I made a jack-o-lantern,
A jolly one was he,
With two big eyes, and two big teeth
A-grinning back at me!

I lost my jack-o-lantern,
But I'm not sad, not I!
I lost my jack-o-lantern,
But, I made a pumpkin pie!

Mary Jo Shannon, Roanoke, VA

Dreidel Game

3+

Materials
Masking tape
1 square cardboard box
Scissors
1 empty cardboard wrapping paper tube

Chanukah wrapping paper scraps
Glue sticks
Black marker
White paper

What to do
1. Tape the top and bottom of the box closed.
2. Cut a hole in the center of the box top, just big enough in which to insert the wrapping paper tube.
3. Cut a hole in the bottom of the box just big enough to push the tube through.
4. Insert the tube into the box through the holes so that it sticks out evenly on both the top and the bottom.
5. Tape the areas where the tube comes out of the holes to secure it in place.
6. Give the children scissors, wrapping paper scraps, and glue sticks.
7. Have them cut the scraps in any way they wish, and glue them to the box.
8. Encourage them to overlap the scraps and to cover the box as much as possible.
9. Use black marker to draw body parts (such as hand, head, leg, tongue, etc.) on small pieces of white paper.
10. Glue each drawing of a body part on a side of the box.
11. Play this dreidel game by having the children stand in a circle and letting them take turns spinning the dreidel.
12. When the dreidel lands, the children need to move the part of the body that is face up on the box in an interesting way.

More to do
Manipulatives: Put out a few dreidels of different sizes for the children to practice spinning.
Movement: Pretend to be dreidels. Play a Chanukah song and let the children spin. Stop the song intermittently, and the "dreidels" can fall down.

Related song
"The Dreidel Song"

Sandy Lanes, Silver Spring, MD

Holiday Magnets

3+

Materials
Clear contact paper
Scissors
Tissue paper in assorted colors
Photograph of each child
Magnetic tape
Paint in shallow containers
Sponges cut in assorted holiday shapes

What to do
1. Invite the children to choose a holiday shape such as a bell, star, or tree. Cut two identical shapes from contact paper for each child.
2. Have the children tear small pieces of tissue paper and place it on the adhesive side of one of their shapes.
3. Help the children glue their picture in the center of the tissue paper.
4. Show the children how to press the adhesive side of the second shape onto the first shape.
5. When they finish, give each child a sheet of tissue paper.
6. Have the children dip a sponge into paint and briefly press it onto the paper. Encourage the children to create a design using different sponges and colors.
7. While they are working, cut two pieces of magnetic tape and press them onto the back of their photo holder.
8. When the paint is dry, ask the children to wrap their holiday frame in the hand-painted gift paper.

More to do
More art: Design a collage with miniature pinecones, holly leaves, berries, and sprigs of evergreen. Create a winter scene for the classroom—shape miniature pinecones into trees and sprinkle a mirror with artificial snow to resemble an ice-skating pond; have the children add sculpted animals. Create funny characters with pinecones, pipe cleaners, acorns, and bits of fabric.

Related books
The Christmas Tree Tangle by Margaret Mahy
Mr. Willowby's Christmas Tree by Robert Barry

Susan L. Mahoney, Orange Park, FL

holidays

Ghostly Hands

3+

Materials
White tempera paint
Pie tins
Black construction paper
Googly eyes

What to do
1. Pour white paint in pie tins. Give each child a sheet of black construction paper.
2. Encourage the children to dip one hand in the white paint.
3. Have the children press one painted hand on their sheet of black construction paper, holding their fingers together.
4. The children can then glue on googly eyes.

Related books
Go Away, Big Green Monster! by Ed Emberley
Very Scary by Tony Johnston
Who Said Boo? by Nancy White Carlstrom

Lisa M. Chichester, Parkersburg, WV

Ooey Gluey Ghosts

3+

Materials
Wax paper
Paper plates
Bottles of white glue
Permanent markers
Hole punch
Yarn

What to do
1. Give each child a piece of wax paper on a paper plate.
2. Give the children bottles of glue and let them squirt a thick glob of glue onto their wax paper in a "ghost" shape.

3. Allow the glue to dry completely. It will become a nice ghost-like color as it dries.
4. When the glue is dry, have the children peel off their ghosts from the wax paper.
5. Let the children use permanent markers to give their ghosts facial features.
6. Use the creations as an addition to seasonal displays, or make a necklace by punching a small hole near the top and stringing the ghost on a piece of yarn.

More to do
More art: Use colored glues to create other seasonal shapes.

Related books
Georgie's Halloween by Robert Bright
The Monster at the End of This Book by Jon Stone
Scary, Scary Halloween by Eve Bunting

Lyndall Warren, Milledgeville, GA

St. Patrick's Day Pudding

Materials
Pudding recipe written on chart paper
Baby food jars
Measuring spoons
Vanilla instant pudding
Milk
Green food coloring
Spoons

What to do
1. Give each child a baby food jar that contains 2 tablespoons (30 mL) of vanilla instant pudding, ¼ cup (60 mL) of milk, and 3 drops of green food coloring. Make sure to close the lid tightly.
2. Have the children shake their jars until the mixture thickens.
3. Let them eat it right out of the jar.

More to do
More art: Make a shamrock-shaped collage from scraps of green paper, green fabric, and green markers and crayons.
Music: Put on some lively music, possibly Irish fiddle music, and let the children shake their jars to the beat.

holidays

Related books

Fin M'Coul, the Giant of Knockmany Hill by Tomie dePaola
St. Patrick's Day in the Morning by Eve Bunting

Ann Wenger, Harrisonburg, VA

Fireworks Art

3+

Materials
Poster board
Tempera paints
Paintbrushes
Glue
Glitter
Hole punch
Yarn

What to do
1. Give each child a piece of poster board and suggest that they paint with tempera paints in a swooping motion upward, to resemble fireworks bursting in the sky.
2. After the paint has dried, have the children use paintbrushes to paint glue on the picture in the same swooping motion.
3. Let the children sprinkle glitter over their artwork. Shake off the excess, and allow the pictures to dry for several hours.
4. Once dry, punch a hole in the top of each, and string a loop of yarn through the hole for hanging.

More to do
Snack: Make red, white, and blue sundaes. Let the children put strawberries, raspberries, and blueberries on vanilla ice cream.

Related books
The Fabulous Firework Family by James Flora
Hurray For the Fourth of July by Wendy Watson

Tina R. Woehler, Oak Point, TX

Patriotic T-shirts

3+

Materials
Cardboard
1 pre-washed white T-shirt per child
Red and blue fabric paints
Meat trays
Smocks
Star-shaped sponges in various sizes

What to do
1. Have the children wear smocks for this activity.
2. Cut pieces of cardboard to fit inside the T-shirts so that the paint will not bleed through.
3. Pour some fabric paint in meat trays.
4. Give the children star-shaped sponges to dip in the paint and press on their T-shirts to make prints. Show them how to wipe off excess paint before stamping the sponge on the shirt.
5. Encourage them to make creative designs with the stars.
6. Allow the paint to dry for at least 24 hours.
7. Have a special day when all the children wear their patriotic shirts.

More to do
Movement: Put on a patriotic song such as "Stars and Stripes Forever," and have the children march around the classroom, playing rhythm instruments.

Related book and song
Hurray For the Fourth of July by Wendy Watson
"Twinkle, Twinkle Little Star"

 Tina R. Woehler, Oak Point, TX

Handprint Holly Wreath

3+

Materials
Green tempera paint
Meat trays

Construction paper
Red paint
Pre-made bows

What to do

1. Pour green paint in a meat tray.
2. Encourage each child to dip one hand in the paint and press it repeatedly on a sheet of construction paper, so that the handprints form the shape of a circle. Let the pictures dry.
3. Pour red paint in a meat tray.
4. Have the children dip a finger in the red paint and make dots on the handprints to resemble holly berries.
5. Provide the children with pre-made bows to stick on their wreaths once the paint has dried.

More to do

More art: Make a class nature wreath. Have the children look outside for small items to glue or pin to a Styrofoam wreath form.

Related books

The Christmas Alphabet by Robert Sabuda
Hilary Knight's The Twelve Days of Christmas by Hilary Knight
Stories by Firelight by Shirley Hughes

Cindy Winther, Oxford, MI

Valentine Mice

Materials

Red paper hearts
Black felt pen
Bits of string about 3" (8 cm) long
Glue

What to do

1. Fold the paper heart in half and find the mouse. The nose and whiskers are at the tapered end—draw them in.
2. For the tail, glue the string on the inside of the fold (opposite the end with the nose and whiskers), and let it hang out. There's the mouse!
3. Add a greeting on the inside.

More to do
More art: Design greeting cards with fingerprint mice.
Snack: Enjoy a snack of cheese cut in heart shapes.

Related books
Mouse Mess by Linnea Riley
Somebody Loves You, Mr. Hatch by Eileen Spinelli

Carol Petrash, Reprinted from Earthways

Chinese New Year Shindig

Materials
Red and gold paint
Styrofoam trays
Chopsticks
Sturdy white paper

What to do

1. Pour red paint and gold paint in large Styrofoam trays.
2. Give each child a chopstick with which to paint on sturdy white paper.
3. Encourage the children to use the chopstick in different ways, such as painting with the tip of the chopstick, or immersing the entire chopstick in the paint and laying it down or rolling it on the paper.

More to do

Snack: Have a Chinese New Year Tea Party. Boil water and pour over tea bags in a clear container so that the children can see how the tea leaves release their flavor into the water. Add ice cubes to cool the tea for drinking. Serve fortune cookies.

Related books

Cleversticks by Bernard Ashley
D Is for Doufu: An Alphabet Book of Chinese Culture by Maywan Shen Krach
The Dancing Dragon by Marcia K. Vaughan

 Penni Smith, Riverside, CA

Cookie Cutter Wrapping Paper 3+

Materials

Tempera paint, a variety of colors
Styrofoam meat trays
Plastic cookie cutters in Christmas shapes
Large sheets of white butcher paper
Scotch tape
Ribbon

What to do

1. Pour just enough tempera paint in each tray to cover the bottom with a thin layer.
2. Place a few cookie cutters in each tray.
3. Provide each child with a piece of butcher paper.
4. Have the children print designs on the paper by dipping the cookie cutters in the paint and pressing them down on the paper. Suggest that the children print with their cookie cutter several times before returning it to the tray.
5. Encourage them to try printing with different cookie cutters and paint colors.

6. When the wrapping papers have dried completely, provide the children with tape and ribbon for wrapping their parents' Christmas gifts.

Related books
The Elves and the Shoemaker by Paul Galdone
Harvey Slumfenburger's Christmas Present by John Burningham
Marvin's Best Christmas Present Ever by Katherine Paterson

Rebecca McMahon, Mobile, AL

Eggshell Mosaic

3+

Materials
Clean, dry eggshells
Easter egg dye or food coloring
Small bowls
Poster board
Glue

What to do
1. Because you will need approximately 4 eggshells per child, it is helpful to enlist the help of parents in accumulating the needed shells. Request that they rinse empty eggshells, allow the shells to dry, and send them to school for several weeks prior to the scheduled activity.
2. Dye the eggshells a variety of colors, with either Easter egg dye or food coloring.
3. Have the children help you crush the shells into tiny pieces. Fill several small bowls with the pieces, keeping the different colors separate.
4. Give each child an egg-shaped piece of poster board, and encourage the children to glue on the shell pieces in an original design.

More to do
Language: Read and dramatize the nursery rhyme, "Humpty Dumpty."
Science: Crack a raw egg into a clear plastic container and let the children use magnifying glasses to investigate its different parts: shell, membrane, yolk, and albumen.
Snack: Encourage the children to observe what happens when you fry eggs. Eat and enjoy!

Related books
Chickens Aren't the Only Ones by Ruth Heller
The Egg by Gallimard Jeunesse
Egg to Chick by Millicent Selsam
Rechenka's Eggs by Patricia Polacco
The Talking Eggs by Robert D. San Souci

Rebecca McMahon, Mobile, AL

Confetti Tree Ornaments

Materials
Hole punch
Construction paper, in assorted colors
Green construction paper, cut into Christmas tree shapes, about 8" (20 cm) high
Glue in containers
Paintbrushes

What to do
1. Use a hole punch to cut out a class supply of confetti from an assortment of construction paper. Let the children help, if you wish.
2. Give each child a precut Christmas tree.
3. Encourage the children to use a paintbrush to spread glue on their trees in any design they wish.
4. Have them sprinkle the confetti over the glue-covered areas. Shake off the excess.
5. Allow the trees to dry.

More to do
Field trip: Visit a Christmas tree farm where the children can pick out a class tree.
More art: Make the Christmas trees smaller and then hang as ornaments, punching a hole on the top and looping a piece of string through it.

Related books
The Little Crooked Christmas Tree by Michael Cutting
Mr. Willowby's Christmas Tree by Robert Barry
Santa's Favorite Story by Aoki Hisako and Ivan Gantschev

Quazonia J. Quarles, Newark, DE

holidays

Foot Ghosts

3+

Materials
White paper
Black crayons
Scissors
Markers

What to do
1. Have each child place her foot, with the shoe on, on a piece of white paper.
2. Trace the children's feet with a black crayon, or have the children trace each other's feet.
3. Give the children scissors with which to cut out their feet.
4. Encourage the children to draw a face on their "ghost."

Related books
Clifford's Halloween by Norman Bridwell
My First Halloween Book by Colleen L. Reece
Old Devil Wind by Bill Martin, Jr.
Scary, Scary Halloween by Eve Bunting

 Cory McIntyre, Crystal Lake, IL

Tissue Paper Pumpkins

3+

Materials
Pumpkins cut out of tag board
Orange paint
Paintbrushes
Orange squares of tissue paper
Glue
Brown crayon or tissue paper

What to do
1. Have the children paint the pumpkins.
2. Allow them to dry.

215

3. Encourage the children to crumple the tissue squares and glue them on the pumpkin shape.
4. Have the children color or add brown tissue to the stem.

More to do
Field trip: Visit a pick-your-own pumpkin patch and bring home a class pumpkin.

Related books
The Biggest Pumpkin Ever by Steven Kroll
It's Pumpkin Time! by Zoe Hall
Pumpkin, Pumpkin by Jeanne Titherington

Linda Atamian, Charlestown, RI

Dyeing Easter Eggs

Materials
Commercial egg dye kits, 1 kit for every 5 children
Containers for the egg dye
Plastic spoons
Hard boiled eggs, 3-4 per child
Crayons
Puffy paints

What to do
1. Set up three stations: a drawing table, an egg-dyeing table, and a puffy-paint table
2. At the first station, have the children use crayons to color designs or write their names on their eggs.
3. At the second station, set out the prepared egg dyes, and let the children take turns dyeing their eggs.
4. After the eggs are dry, the children may decorate them with puffy paint at the third station.

More to do
Outdoors: Have an Easter egg hunt using real or plastic Easter eggs.

Related books
The Golden Egg Book by Margaret Wise Brown
Good Morning Chick by Mirra Ginsberg

The Egg Tree by Katherine Milhous
The Night Before Easter by Natasha Wing
The Runaway Bunny by Margaret Wise Brown

Barbara Saul, Eureka, CA

Grass Baskets

3+

Materials
Plastic one-gallon milk cartons, one for each child
Scissors
Glue
Scraps cut from colored construction, wrapping paper, and/or wallpaper
Large bag of potting soil
Grass seed
Indelible ink felt-tip pen
Trowels
Strips of pastel card stock, 2" x 12"
   (5 cm x 30 cm), 1 per child

What to do
1. If this is an Easter project, start it 3 weeks before Easter.
2. Cut the tops off the milk cartons, leaving the sides 5" (13 cm) high.
3. Have the children decorate their baskets by gluing on colorful paper scraps. Write their names on their baskets with the pen.
4. Have the children put about 3" to 4" (8 to 10 cm) of the potting soil in the bottom of their baskets using the trowels.
5. Encourage the children take handfuls of grass seed and sow it into the soil.

6. Staple the cardstock handles to the sides of the milk cartons (adult only).
7. Have the children lightly water the seeds and place them in a sunny spot.
8. Encourage them to watch the baskets daily and water when needed.
9. The children can use the baskets for Easter eggs and take them home to share.

More to do
Science: Place one extra basket in a closet and don't water it. After one week, observe and talk about what is different about these seeds.

Related books
Easter Egg Artists by Adrienne Adams
Max's Chocolate Bunny by Charlotte Zolotow
When Spring Comes by Robert Maas

Barbara Saul, Eureka, CA

Christmas Lights

Materials
Green construction paper
Hole punch
Glue
Colored cellophane
Crayons

What to do
1. In advance, cut out Christmas trees from construction paper and the same size shape from colored cellophane.
2. Have the children punch holes in the trees.
3. Give the children glue to stick colored cellophane to the back of the trees, which will resemble Christmas lights on the front of the trees.
4. Encourage the children to turn the trees over and decorate them with the crayons.

Related books
Christmas Tree by Alma Ada
The Christmas Tree Tangle by Margaret Mahy
Mr. Willowby's Christmas Tree by Robert Barry

Star Tree by Gisela Colle
The Twelve Days of Christmas by Jan Brett
Why Christmas Trees Aren't Perfect by Dick Schneider

Original song
I'm a Little Pine Tree (sing to the tune of "I'm a Little Teapot")

I'm a little pine tree—as you can see,
All the other pine trees are bigger than me.
Maybe when I grow up, then I'll be
A great big merry Christmas tree.

Elizabeth Thomas, Hobart, IN

Handpainted Gift Wrap

Materials
Bingo bottles
Liquid watercolor paint
White tissue wrap

What to do
1. Ahead of time, fill bingo bottles with liquid watercolor paint. The mixture should be roughly half paint and half water.
2. Show the children how to fold their sheet of tissue paper until it is about 6" (15 cm) square.
3. Have the children press the bingo bottles to the paper until the paint soaks through all the layers of paper.
4. Set the paper aside to dry, leaving it folded.
5. When the paint dries, unfold the paper and use it as gift wrap.

More to do
More art: Ask the children to make handprints or fingerprints on the paper with paint. Paint broad strokes across the paper with large paintbrushes for an abstract appearance. Wrap the children's handmade gifts in the paper.

holidays

Related books
Badger's Bring Something Party by Hiawyn Oram
The Whale's Song by Dyan Sheldon

MaryAnn F. Kohl, Bellingham, WA

Stamp-a-Doodle

4+

Materials
Styrofoam cup
Play clay or plasticine
Variety of printing materials such as beads, corks, small tiles, buttons, or other small objects
Plaster of Paris mixed to a creamy consistency
Tempera paint
Paper towel in Styrofoam tray
Paintbrush or spoon for spreading paint
Paper

What to do
1. Cut the cup in half. Use the bottom half of the cup.
2. Press some clay into the bottom of the cup.
3. Push various little items into the clay.
4. Adult pours plaster of Paris into the cup until it is about 1" (3 cm) deep.
5. When the plaster has hardened and dried, take it out of the cup. Also remove the clay.
6. The plaster section is the stamp.
7. Pour some paint on the paper towel in the Styrofoam tray.
8. Spread the paint with a brush or spoon.
9. Press the stamp into the paint and then press it on a piece of paper to make a self-created stamp print.

More to do
More art: Use the stamp prints to make wrapping paper, greeting cards, wallpaper, or stationery.

MaryAnn Kohl, Reprinted from Preschool Art

Easter Basket

4+

Materials
Plastic strawberry baskets
Various colors of yarn cut in 12" (30 cm) lengths
Gold or silver twine

What to do
1. Give each child a strawberry basket.
2. Let each child choose a piece of yarn, and have her weave the yarn in and out of the holes of the basket.
3. Once the child has reached the end of the first piece of yarn, encourage her to continue weaving with other colors.
4. Take 2 pieces of twine, approximately 18" (45 cm) each, and tie the ends to the corners of each basket to make handles.

More to do
Outdoors: Let the children use these baskets on an Easter egg hunt. The children can also take these baskets outside to collect items on a nature hunt.

Related books and song
The Country Bunny and the Little Gold Shoes by Du Bose Heyward
Easter Egg Artists by Adrienne Adams
Mr. Rabbit and the Lovely Present by Charlotte Zolotow
"A Tisket, A Tasket"

Leslie Kuehn Meyer, Austin, MN

My Artwork Calendar

 4+

Materials
Markers
White paper, 8" x 10" (20 cm x 25 cm)
Tempera paints
Brushes
Construction paper 12" x 18" (30 cm x 45 cm), 13 sheets per child
Calendar grids, 12 per child
Glue
Hole punch
Yarn

What to do
1. Over the course of 12 days, have each child make 12 pictures with markers on sheets of white paper.
2. Have each child paint a cover for his calendar on a sheet of construction paper.
3. Give each child 12 calendar grids with the names of the months and days written at the tops, and the numbers filled in.
4. Make the pages of the calendar by gluing one artwork to the top of each sheet of construction paper, and one calendar grid to the bottom.
5. Place the cover sheet vertically, painted side down, on the table. Place all 12 of the artwork/calendar pages, facing up, on top of the cover.
6. Fold this pile of pages in half, the short way.

7. Punch two holes very close to the edge at the closed end of the calendar.
8. Thread pieces of yarn through the holes, and tie bows at the top.
9. These calendars make nice holiday gifts.

Related books
Badger's Bring Something Party by Hiaawyn Oram
Chicken Soup with Rice by Maurice Sendak
Marvin's Best Christmas Present Ever by Katherine Paterson

Diane K. Weiss, Fairfax, VA

Star of David Ornament

Materials
Shoeboxes
Utility knife or similar tool, optional
Thin white paper, optional
Old greeting cards and magazines
Scissors
Glue
Popsicle sticks
Blue paint
Gold glitter
Sturdy thread or fishing line

What to do
1. Ahead of time, remove the bottom of each shoebox, if you choose, and replace it with thin white paper. It is not necessary to remove the bottom of the box, but doing so will allow light to filter through the box.
2. Let the children look through greeting cards and magazines and cut out pictures that represent the Jewish holiday and traditions.
3. Distribute the shoeboxes and have the children glue the pictures to the inside of their box. Set the boxes aside to dry.
4. Show the children how to glue three Popsicle sticks together, forming a triangular shape. Make a second triangle with three more sticks. When you are done, glue the two triangles together to form a star. Let the glue dry.
5. Afterward, ask the children to paint the star blue, then sprinkle glitter on the paint before it dries. Set the stars aside again to dry.

6. Return the shoeboxes to the children and ask them to turn their box on its side.
7. Glue a piece of thread to the star and suspend it inside the shoebox.
8. Display the boxes throughout the classroom, then send them home for the families to enjoy throughout the holidays.

More to do
Circle time: Help the children understand the meaning of the Star of David.

Related book and song
Inside Out Grandma: A Hannukkah Story by Jean Rothenberg
"My Dreidel" sung by Raffi

Kimberle S. Byrd, Kalamazoo, MI

Mish Mosh Menorahs

Materials
Crayola Model Magic dough
Craft items such as beads, feathers, pompoms, Popsicle sticks, sequins, buttons, etc.
Trays
Chanukah candles

What to do
1. Place various craft items on trays in the center of the table.
2. Give each child a large hunk of dough to mold into any shape.
3. Encourage the children to stick the craft items all over their dough to decorate it.
4. Give each child Chanukah candles to stick in the dough.
5. Let these menorahs dry for a couple of days.
6. Remind parents that these are decorative menorahs and may not be safe to light.

More to do
Circle time: Have a parent bring in a real menorah to light.
Health and safety: Talk about lighted candles and fire safety.

Related books
Inside Out Grandma: A Hannukkah Story by Jean Rothenberg
The Miracle of the Potato Latkes by Malka Penn

Sandy Lanes, Silver Spring, MD

Jeweled Eggs

Materials
Large plastic Easter eggs
Small paper cups
Sturdy glue that bonds tightly
Paintbrushes
Toothpicks
Glitter in rainbow colors
Sequins

What to do
1. Invite the children to glue one large plastic egg securely to the bottom of a paper cup.
2. Make sure that the egg dries securely and stays in place. Avoid using drinking cups that have wax on the outside or the eggs most likely will not adhere to the cups.
3. With the eggs glued on the cups, allow children to add glitter and sequins freely onto their eggs, using a paintbrush to paint on the glue. Add the glitter onto the eggs first, followed by sequins. These can be put on individually using toothpicks to add dots of glue onto the back of sequins.
4. Allow the eggs to dry completely. This may take some time and patience!

More to do
Snack: Explore the many ways to cook an incredible, edible egg. Fry, poach, scramble, boil, or even bake those eggs.

Related books
Bunny Cakes by Rosemary Wells
Easter Egg Artists by Adrienne Adams

Related song
Sing this to the tune of "Frere Jacques."

Here's a bunny, here's a bunny,
With ten more, with ten more....
See them at the bunny patch,
See them at the bunny patch,
Easter eggs galore, Easter eggs galore.

Gathering Easter eggs, gathering Easter eggs,
Yellow, green, blue, pink and purple too...
See the bunny hop away, see the bunny hop away...
Bringing them to you, bringing them to you.

Penni Smith, Riverside, CA

Make a Piñata!

4+

Materials
Flour
Water
Large mixing bowl and spoon
One large balloon
String
Tarp or newspapers
Newspaper strips, 1"(3 cm) wide
Containers of glue
Paintbrushes
Tissue paper squares, 2"(5 cm)
  wide, in assorted colors
Sharp knife
Wrapped candy and small toys
Broom handle

What to do
1. Have the children mix flour and water together in a mixing bowl, until it reaches the consistency of thin cake batter.
2. Blow up the balloon and tie the end.
3. Tie a string around the end of the balloon and secure it to something in the room, such as the crosspiece of the easel.
4. Cover that area of the floor with a tarp or some newspapers.
5. Let the children pull the strips of newspaper through the flour batter and lay them on the balloon.
6. Encourage them to continue until the entire balloon is covered with two layers of strips.
7. Let the balloon dry for several days.
8. When it is completely dry, set out containers of glue, brushes, and tissue paper squares.
9. Let the children paint glue on the newspaper-covered balloon, and cover it completely with the colored tissue paper.
10. Make a harness of string around four sides of the balloon.
11. Pierce the balloon inside. Cut a hole with a sharp knife in order to fill the piñata with wrapped

candy and small toys.

12. Hang the filled pinata from the ceiling.

13. Let blindfolded children take turns hitting it with a broom handle. It may take an adult to give it the final whack!

Related books and songs

A Christmas Surprise for Chabelita by Argentina Palacios
Children Around the World Celebrate Christmas by Susan Titus Osborn and Christine Tangvald
Hooray, a Piñata by Elisa Kleven
Las Navidades, Popular Christmas Songs from Latin America by Lulu Delacre
(cassette tapes of these songs are also available)
Nine Days to Christmas, a Story of Mexico by Marie Hall Ets
The Piñata Maker by George Ancona

Sandra W. Gratias, Perkasie, PA

Star-spangled Necklace

Materials
Unpainted wooden beads or spools or handmade clay beads
Red, white, and blue craft paint
Paintbrushes
Red satin ribbon
Store-bought toothpick flag
Hot glue gun (adult only)
Red, white, and blue construction paper
Scissors
Fine-point marker
Glue

What to do
1. If you choose to make the beads with the children, follow a recipe for dough made from flour, cornstarch, salt, and warm water. Let the beads harden.

2. Have the children paint their beads or spools. Encourage them to paint stripes on some of the beads or spools if they are able to do so.

3. While the beads are drying, remove the flag from the toothpick and glue it to the center of the ribbon. Secure it to the ribbon with a glue gun, if necessary, reminding the children that only an

adult may touch the glue gun. Alternatively, have the children make a miniature American flag with small pieces of construction paper; add little dots with a fine-point marker for the stars.

4. Have the children string beads onto both ends of the ribbon.
5. Help the children hold the necklace at their neck while you tie a knot in the ribbon. Be sure to leave enough length that the children can put it on and take it off over their heads.

More to do
Field trip: Visit a local historical site.
More art: Design napkin rings in red, white, and blue using pipe cleaners.

Related books
Hurray for the Fourth of July by Wendy Watson
From Sea to Shining Sea by Amy Cohn

Lisa M. Chichester, Parkersburg, WV

Heart-y Straws

Materials
Heart stencils, approximately 2" (5 cm), cut from poster board
Pencils
Pink, red, and white construction paper
Scissors
Hole punch
Markers
Plastic drinking straws
Plastic cups

What to do
1. Have the children trace around the heart stencils on construction paper, and cut out a heart.
2. Invite the children to punch one hole at the top of the heart under the point and one hole at the base of the heart just above the bottom point.
3. Let the children use markers to write their names and decorate the hearts in any way they wish.
4. Insert a plastic drinking straw into the bottom hole from the front side of the heart and back through the top hole. Slide the paper heart to the top of the straw.
5. Use the straws in plastic cups as place cards for the class Valentine's Day party.

More to do
Dramatic play: Set up a post office in your classroom. Encourage the children to write Valentines Day cards, put on stamps, mail them, sort them, and deliver them.

Related books
The Valentine Bears by Eve Bunting, illustrated by Jan Brett
Valentine's Day by Gail Gibbons

Rebecca McMahon, Mobile, AL

Valentine Holder

4+

Materials
Paper plates
Hole punch
Red yarn, cut into 36" (90 cm) lengths
Masking tape
Markers
Stickers

What to do

1. Cut some paper plates in half.
2. Place a half plate upside down on a whole plate, and punch holes about 1" (3 cm) apart around the rims.
3. Wrap one end of each yarn length with masking tape, to form a "needle."
4. Using their yarn, have the children lace the two plate pieces together, leaving about 12" (30 cm) of yarn free at each end.
5. Tie the loose ends in a bow in the middle of the plate.
6. Print each child's name on the upper half of a holder.
7. Let the children decorate the holders with markers and stickers.
8. Hang the holders up on a bulletin board.
9. Encourage the children to deliver their Valentine cards to the appropriate holder.
10. When Valentine's Day is over, the children can take their cards home in their holders by folding over the top halves and tucking them into the bottom. They can use the yarn as handles.

More to do
Language: Set up a table with paper, scissors, and markers, and encourage the children to make Valentine cards to send to a nursing home. Make an extra Valentine holder to put them in.

Related books
Arthur's Valentine by Marc Brown
Bee My Valentine by Miriam Cohen

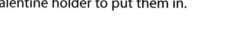

Mary Jo Shannon, Roanoke, VA

holidays

4th of July Picnic Place Mats 4+

Materials
Red, white, and blue construction paper
Scissors
Old magazines, particularly food and travel magazines
Glue
Star and flag stickers
Clear contact paper

What to do
1. Ahead of time, cut out circles in two sizes to represent little plates and glasses, and triangles to represent folded napkins.
2. Ask the children to cut out pictures of picnic food such as hamburgers, watermelon, chicken, and corn on the cob.
3. Have the children arrange, then glue the shapes and pictures on their paper as if they were setting a picnic table on the Fourth of July. Let them add stickers for decoration.
4. When the glue is dry, cover the collage with clear contact paper on one or both sides.

More to do
Field trip: Visit a Revolutionary War-era landmark.
Language: Using books, guests, and other resources, go on an imaginary trip to another part of our country and keep a journal of your adventure.
More art: Create banners or pennants on butcher paper or poster board with magazine pictures or postcards of American landmarks. Create a flag with fabric scraps. Create the appearance of a fireworks display in a crayon etching.
Science: Use magazine pictures to create a food pyramid.

Related books
Celebrate America in Poetry and Art by Nora Panzer
This Land Is My Land by George Littlechild

Penni Smith, Riverside, CA

Sack-O-Lantern

4+

Materials
Brown paper lunch bags
Newspaper
Rubber bands
Orange, yellow, and green paint
Paint containers
Paintbrushes
Black markers

What to do
1. Give each child a lunch bag and have him stuff it with newspaper.
2. Squeeze the top closed, and wind a rubber band around it.
3. Have the children paint their pumpkins with orange, yellow, and green paint.
4. Let the bags dry thoroughly, and then give the children black markers to draw jack-o-lantern faces on their pumpkins.

More to do
Cooking: Scoop out pumpkin seeds from a pumpkin, bake them until they are brown, and let the children taste them.
Movement: Have all the children pretend to be pumpkins in a pumpkin patch. Hold hands to make a vine that connects all the pumpkins.

Related books
Apples and Pumpkins by Anne Rockwell
It's Pumpkin Time by Zoe Hall
Picking Apples and Pumpkins by Amy and Richard Hutchings
Pumpkin, Pumpkin by Jeanne Titherington

Kimberle S. Byrd, Kalamazoo, MI

Christmas Stockings

4+

Materials
Construction paper
Pencils
Stocking patterns, cut out of tag board
Scissors
Paperclips
Hole punch
Yarn, cut into 2' (60 cm) lengths
Markers, glue, glitter, buttons, etc.

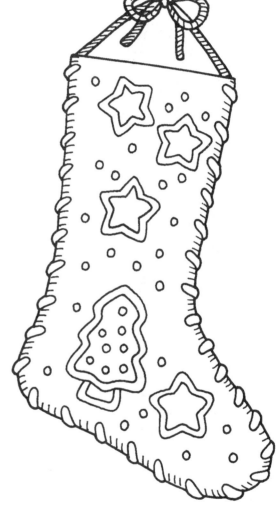

What to do
1. Give each child a sheet of construction paper folded in half horizontally.
2. Have the children trace around the stocking pattern onto the construction paper.
3. Cut out the pattern, going through both pieces of the folded paper. The children should end up with two stocking pieces exactly the same size.
4. Paperclip the two pieces together. Have the children punch holes around the perimeter. Do not punch holes across the top of the stockings.
5. Give each child a piece of yarn and tie it onto the top hole on one side of the stocking. Let the children "sew" the stockings together.
6. When they have completed sewing their stockings, tie off the yarn in the last hole. Loop the remaining yarn across to where the yarn was initially tied on to form a hanger at the top of the stocking.
7. Encourage the children to decorate their stockings using markers, glue, glitter, buttons, etc.

More to do
Bulletin board: Cut out a large paper fireplace and staple it to a bulletin board. Hang the stockings on the "fireplace."
Language: Have the children dictate what they would like to receive in their stockings while you write it down.

Related books
The Best Christmas Pageant Ever by Barbara Robin
The Night Before Christmas by Clement Moore
The Nutcracker by E.T.A. Hoffman
Santa's Favorite Story by Aoki Hisako and Ivan Gantschev

Barbara Saul, Eureka, CA

Tissue Collage Easter Eggs

Materials
Construction paper, in pastel colors
Pencils
Scissors
Liquid starch
Plastic containers
Colored tissue paper, torn into small pieces
Paintbrushes

What to do
1. Have each child draw a large egg shape on the construction paper and cut it out.
2. Pour liquid starch in plastic containers.
3. Have the children lay a piece of tissue paper flat on the egg and paint over it with liquid starch.
4. Encourage them to repeat this process, overlapping the pieces of tissue paper until the egg is covered.
5. Allow the eggs to dry overnight. They will make an attractive bulletin board display.

More to do
Language: Suggest that the children write or dictate stories about what might hatch out of their egg.

Related books
The Golden Egg Book by Margaret Wise Brown
Mr. Rabbit and the Lovely Present by Charlotte Zolotow
The Tale of Peter Rabbit by Beatrix Potter

Barbara Saul, Eureka, CA

Button Pin Gifts

Materials
Unruled index cards, 3" x 5" (8 cm x 14 cm)
Scissors
Thin markers
Glue
Variety of buttons, flat and lightweight
Pin backings (can be purchased in craft stores)

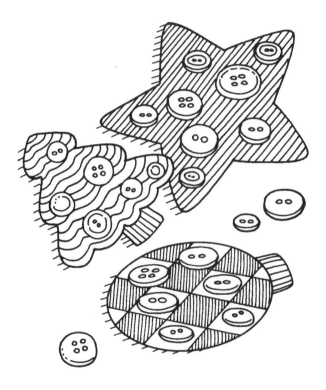

What to do
1. Give each child an index card and invite the children to cut the cards into any shape they want.
2. Have the children color their shapes with thin markers.
3. Then encourage the children to glue buttons all over their shapes.
4. Glue a pin backing on the back of each of their shapes.
5. These pins make great gifts for Mother's Day, Christmas, or Chanukah.

More to do
Games: Play "Button, Button, Who's Got the Button?"
Math: Invite the children to sort the buttons by size, shape, number of holes, color, etc.

Related books
Bit by Bit by Steve Sanfield
Brass Button by Crescent Dragonwagon
The Button Box by Margarette S. Reid
Lucy's Picture by Nicola Moon
Norman the Doorman by Don Freeman
The Perfect Present by Michael Hague
The Yellow Button by Anne Mazer

Sandra Nagel, White Lake, MI

Holiday Board Game

5+

Materials
Markers
Poster board
Holiday stickers
Dice
Colored beads or buttons

What to do
1. Tell the children that they are going to make a board game.
2. Let the children name the game and discuss its rules. Some examples of holiday game ideas are: "Let's Go Trick-or-Treating" (you could use Halloween candy as the playing pieces), "Help the Turkeys Escape From the Farm," and "Help Santa Find His Way Home."
3. Have each child help draw squares on the poster board.
4. Have the children use markers to draw pictures related to the theme of the game on the board. Let them apply stickers also.
5. Then, help them write directions on the squares, such as move forward two spaces, move back one, or lose a turn.
6. Now, use a die, and have the children play the game with different colored beads or buttons as game playing pieces.

Related book
The Three Bears Holiday Rhyme Book by Jane Yolen

 *Lisa M. Chichester, Parkersburg, WV*

Christmas Potpourri

5+

Materials
Pine branches
Shallow cardboard box
Orange peels
Paper plates
Nandina berries

Spoon
Dried whole cloves
Rock salt
Cinnamon sticks
Baby food jars
Red or white nylon net, cut into 4" (10 cm) squares
Rubber bands
Narrow red ribbon

What to do

1. Let the children strip needles from the pine branches and spread them in a shallow cardboard box to dry.
2. Collect orange peels and lay them on paper plates to dry.
3. Have the children remove nandina berries from their cluster and allow them to dry also.
4. Once dry, break the pine needles and orange peels into tiny pieces.
5. Let each child spoon a little bit of the pine needles, cloves, orange peels, and the rock salt into a baby food jar. Have them add a few of the cinnamon sticks and berries.
6. Place a square of nylon net on top of the jar, then secure with a rubber band. Tie a red ribbon around the jar to cover the rubber band.
7. Encourage the children to shake the contents of the jars, and sniff the aromas of Christmas.

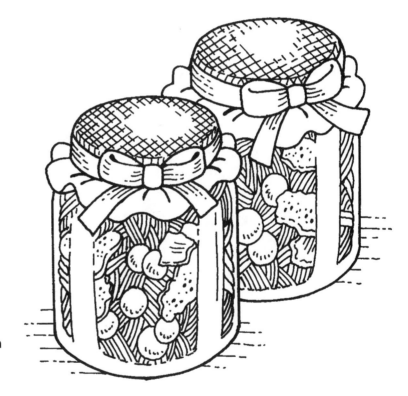

holidays

More to do

Science: Discuss the various textures, colors, and smells with the children.

Related books

Carlos, Light the Farolito by Jean Ciavonne
Santa's Short Suit Shrunk and Other Christmas Tongue Twisters by Nola Buck
Snowballs by Lois Ehlert

Mary Jo Shannon, Roanoke, VA

housekeeping

It's Dust Art

3+

Materials
Cylindrical container or poster board
Cellophane tape
Paint
Paint trays or pans
Paper
Feather dusters

What to do
1. Ahead of time, find a cylindrical container; if you do not have one, roll the poster board into a cylindrical shape and tape it closed.
2. Pour the paints into trays or pans.
3. When you are ready to begin, roll up a piece of paper and place it inside the cylinder.
4. Show the children how to dip the feather duster in the paint and gently shake the excess paint from the duster so the paint is not dripping. Have the children put the feather duster inside the cylinder, then twist the duster by its handle as they pull it out. Let the children repeat the process with as many colors as they choose, using a separate feather duster for each color.

More to do
Math: Introduce the cylindrical shape to the children. Brainstorm about other objects with a cylindrical shape. Collect cylinders and sort them by size.
More art: Paint with feather dusters on a flat piece of paper. Create a mural or wrapping paper using larger sheets of paper.
Sand and water table: Give the children an assortment of cylindrical containers for pouring and measuring.

Related books
Hands by Lois Ehlert
Mouse Mess by Linnea Riley

Ann Gudowski, Johnstown, PA

Quilt Patterns

3+

Materials
White glue or liquid starch
Small containers
Fabric squares, various textures, 1" (3 cm) square
Poster board in any color, 9" x 12" (23 cm x 30 cm)
Paintbrushes

What to do
1. Ahead of time, pour glue or starch into small containers. Lay an assortment of fabric squares on the table.
2. Supply each child with poster board and a brush.
3. Invite the children to select fabric squares for their quilt and lay them in a pattern on their poster board.
4. After they have finished designing their quilt, show them how to lift the squares, a few at a time, and glue them to the poster board.

More to do
Circle time: Bring in a quilt and show the children how one is made. Encourage the children to talk about their own blankets and why they are special. Invite the children to touch the fabric squares and describe the textures and differences they feel. Older children can describe the pattern in the quilt or quilts.
Dramatic play: Pretend it is bedtime and act out a bedtime ritual. Make a cave or fort with blankets. Put baby dolls to bed.
Math: Create patterns with the fabric squares.
More art: Decorate fabric squares with fabric crayons or paints and create a class quilt. Ask older children to tie the quilt. Make a bed for clothespin dolls by folding an 8" (20 cm) square piece of fabric, wrong sides together, leaving a 1" (3 cm) overlap at the top. Then sew side seams and three vertical seams, creating four equal pockets, or beds, for the clothespin babies.

Related books
Five Little Monkeys Jumping on the Bed by Eileen Christelow
Goodnight Moon by Margaret Wise Brown
The Keeping Quilt by Patricia Polacco
No Jumping on the Bed by Tedd Arnold
The Patchwork Quilt by Valerie Flournoy
The Quilt Story by Tony Johnston

Carol J. Mead, Los Alamos, NM

Rolling Pin Painting

3+

Materials
Fingerpaint paper
Spoons
Tempera paints
Rolling pins

What to do
1. Give each child a sheet of fingerpaint paper.
2. Have the children pour a few spoonfuls of paint on their paper.
3. Help the children fold their paper in half.
4. Show the children how to hold their rolling pin and roll it across their paper, back and forth.
5. When they are finished, have them unfold their paper and reveal the symmetrical design they created.

More to do
Cooking: Have the children roll out sugar cookie dough with a rolling pin, then cut and bake.
More art: Roll playdough with rolling pins.
Movement: Let the children gently massage each other's back with a rolling pin.

Related books
Hands by Lois Ehlert
The Little Red Hen by Byron Barton
Mr. Cookie Baker by Monica Wellington
Pancakes, Pancakes! by Eric Carle

Sandy Lanes, Silver Spring, MD

Building a Log Cabin

4+

Materials
Extra-large cardboard box
Utility knife (adult only)
Plastic drop cloth

Brown construction paper
Poster board, optional
Scissors
Glue
Water
Containers, cups, or trays
Wide masking or duct tape

What to do

1. Beforehand, cut a door in one side of the box and a window on the opposite side. The door should be large enough for a child to enter safely.
2. Place a large drop cloth on the floor.
3. Cut log shapes from construction paper in a variety of sizes. Older children will be able to cut these on their own, particularly with the use of patterns cut beforehand from poster board.
4. Mix glue and water to thin the glue slightly. Pour the glue mixture into containers.
5. Have the children apply the glue to the sides of the box, in sections.
6. Help the children paste the logs on the box to create the appearance of a log cabin.
7. Allow four to six hours for the glue to dry.

More to do

Dramatic play: Play a game of frontier make-believe. Add a small rug, some fabric on the window, and household accessories from the pioneer days. Have the children rummage through the dress-up box for period clothing and prepare a meal over the make-believe fire.

Snack: Prepare a simple picnic like the early settlers might have done. Have a snack of cornbread or bread with molasses or syrup.

Related books and song

The Little House by Virginia Burton
The Quilt Story by Tony Johnston
Sewing Quilts by Ann Turner
"Over the River and Through the Woods"

Tina R. Woehler, Oak Point, TX

insects

Painted Rocks

3+

Materials
Rocks, various sizes and shapes
Paint and paintbrushes
Pipe cleaners, beads, felt, and other collage materials
Glue
Markers

What to do
1. Have the children choose a rock that they can decorate as a bug. Encourage the children to consider the size and shape of the rock when making their choice.
2. Have the children paint their rocks and let them dry.
3. When the rocks are dry, invite the children to use the collage materials and markers to create their rock insects.

More to do
Language: Have the children name their insect and dictate a short sentence about it. Assemble the sentences into the children's own bug encyclopedia.
Math: Count and sort a collection of rocks.
More art: Create a bug habitat for the insect creations using natural or artificial materials. Make other objects from rocks, including animals or miniature cars.
Outdoors: Let the children choose their rock while on a walk or have them bring one from home.

Related books
Bugs by Nancy Winslow Parker and Joan Richards Wright
Have You Seen Bugs? by Joanne Oppenheim
Where's That Insect? by Barbara Brenner

 Melissa J. Browning, Milwaukee, WI

Dragonflies

3+

Materials
Tag board in silver or pastel shades

Scissors
Crayons or markers
Pipe cleaners in black and pastel shades
Crayons or markers

What to do

1. Before class, cut wings from tag board. The wings should be cut on a fold.
2. Encourage the children to decorate the wings with crayons or markers. Show the children pictures of butterflies and point out that the design on the wings is symmetrical.
3. Give each child one black and one pastel-colored pipe cleaner. Help the children twist the pipe cleaners together and roll one end to form a head.
4. Puncture a hole in the wing and weave one-half of the pipe cleaner through the opening. Make a loop with two halves of another pipe cleaner where the child can insert her finger.

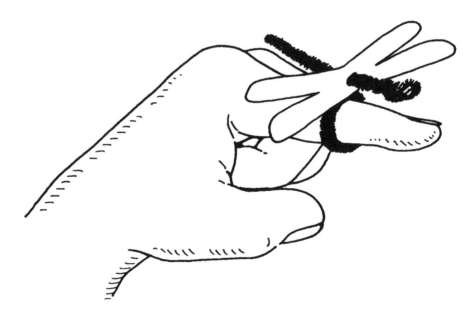

More to do

Circle time: Have a discussion about ponds, the dragonfly's favorite habitat. Introduce new words, such as insects, cattails, marsh, pond, wings.

Music: Listen to a piece of classical music and invite the children to mimic the flight of the dragonfly in dance.

Related books

Dragonfly by Durga Bernhard
The Very Lonely Firefly by Eric Carle

Related song

A Dragonfly (sing to the tune of "Never Smile at a Crocodile")
Up in the sky
With a dragonfly
Fly down low
Where the flowers grow

I will know
Where all the cattails grow
Because I'm flying
With a dragonfly.

Marie L. Wimmer, Holbrook, NY

Create-a-Bug

Materials
Heavyweight construction paper, 9" x 12" (23 cm x 30 cm)
Construction paper cut in various shapes and sizes
Scissors
Glue
Markers

What to do
1. Provide each child with a piece of heavyweight construction paper and scissors. Invite the children to choose scraps of paper, or cut their own, which they will piece together in the shape of a bug.
2. Help the children glue the scraps to the paper.
3. When they have finished their bugs, invite the children to draw and color a background for their bug.

More to do
Field trip: Go on a bug hunt inside the school or outdoors and record the names of the bugs in a journal. Be sure to teach the children to respect the bugs and their habitats.
Language: Older children may write or dictate sentences about their bug.

insects

Related books
Bugs by David T. Greenberg
Have You Seen Bugs by Joanne Oppenheim
Icky Bug Alphabet Book by Jerry Pallota

Amy Melisi, Oxford, MA

Bug Sticker Art

Materials
Large sheets of construction paper
Large round white stickers
Crayons or markers
Dot printers

What to do
1. Have the children place the stickers on the paper in the shape of bugs, real or imaginary.
2. When the designs are complete, ask the children to color the stickers or paint with dot printers.
3. Encourage the children to draw backgrounds for their bugs and to give their bugs names. Encourage creativity.

More to do
Circle time: Have the children describe their insect and dictate a story about it. Talk about the insects we see every day.
More art: Use the stickers to create birds, pets, zoo animals, fish, or dinosaurs.

Related books
How Many Bugs in a Box? by David A. Carter
If You Were a Bug: A Pop-Up Book About Bugs and You by Dawn Bently

Margie Moore, Burke, VA

Munching Caterpillars

3+

Materials
File folders or poster board
Scissors
Egg cartons
Newspaper
Paint and paintbrushes
Small containers
Green construction paper, 12" x 18" (30 cm x 45 cm)
Pencils
Hole punch
Pipe cleaners, cut in half
Stapler

What to do
1. Ahead of time, cut used file folders or poster board to make large leaf stencils. Cut the bottom of the egg cartons in half lengthwise.
2. Cover table with newspaper and set out paints in small containers. Place one-half of an egg carton and a paintbrush at each child's seat.
3. Ask the children to paint their egg carton caterpillars.
4. While the caterpillars are drying, have the children trace the leaf stencils on construction paper, then cut out the leaves.

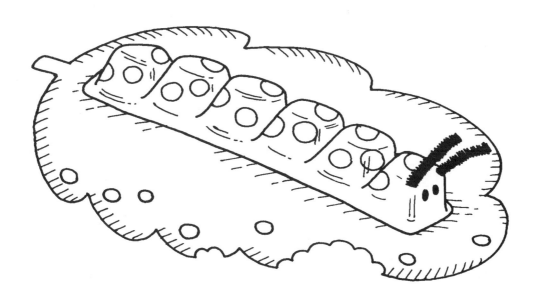

5. Punch out caterpillar nibbles in the leaves with a hole punch. Poke a hole in the top of the caterpillars for the antennae and have the children insert a piece of pipe cleaner.
6. Staple the egg carton caterpillar to the leaf.

More to do
Dramatic play: Wrap children up in a cocoon made from a sheet and encourage them to emerge as a butterfly and "fly" around the room.
Science: Order caterpillar eggs from a teacher supply catalog and observe them in your classroom.

Related books
I Wish I Were a Butterfly by James Howe
The Very Hungry Caterpillar by Eric Carle

Linda N. Ford, Sacramento, CA

Ladybugs!

Materials
Red construction paper
Scissors
Black construction paper or round stickers
Glue
Sponges and black paint, optional
Black markers or crayons

What to do
1. Ahead of time, cut one circle shape from red construction paper for each child. Cut small circular ladybug spots from the black construction paper.
2. Have the children add black dots to their circle by gluing the paper dots or attaching the sticker dots. Show the children how to sponge paint their ladybug, if desired.
3. When the children have finished the spots, encourage them to add details such as eyes or the outline of wings with black markers or crayons.

More to do
Outdoors: Look for ladybugs on leaves and plants around the building.
Snack: Make a ladybug snack by attaching raisins with cream cheese to halves of strawberries. Lay the strawberries on a bed of lettuce.

insects

Related books

The Grouchy Ladybug by Eric Carle
In the Tall, Tall Grass by Denise Fleming
In the Woods: Who's Been Here by Lindsay Barrett George
Lady Bug's Ball by Heather Lowenberg

Susan Rinas, Parma, OH

Papier-mâché Cocoon

Materials
Oblong balloons
Mixing bowl or shallow tub
Water
Flour or liquid laundry starch
Strips of newspaper
Scissors
Brown paint
Paintbrushes
Scarf or pieces of fabric

What to do
1. Blow up the balloons ahead of time.
2. In a bowl or tub, make a mixture of two parts water to one part flour, or one part water to two parts liquid laundry starch.
3. Ask the children to dip strips of newspaper into the mixture and lay them across their balloon, covering it.
4. Allow to dry for one or two days.
5. When the newspaper has dried, cut a flap in the top and pop the balloon.
6. Have the children paint the outside of the balloon "cocoon" brown.
7. Help the children tie a scarf or piece of fabric into the shape of a butterfly.

8. When the cocoon is dry, invite the children to place the butterfly inside.

Related songs

Caterpillar, Caterpillar (sing to the tune of "Teddy Bear, Teddy Bear")

Caterpillar, caterpillar (arms up high)
Turn around. (turn around)
Caterpillar, caterpillar (all fall down)
slither on the ground. (wiggle on the floor)
Caterpillar, caterpillar (stand up)
Spin a co-coon. (twirl around)
Caterpillar, caterpillar (sit down)
Sleep until noon. (pretend to sleep)

Changing Caterpillar (sing to the tune of "Mary Had a Little Lamb")

I eat leaves so green and long, green and long, green and long.
I eat leaves so green and long. They help me grow up big and strong.

Fast I spin so one day soon, one day soon, one day soon,
Fast I spin so one day soon, you'll find I've spun a big cocoon.

My body changes while I lie, while I lie, while I lie.
My body changes while I lie, so I can be a butterfly.

Patricia Moeser

Bumblebee Puppets

3+

Materials
Yellow and black fun foam sheets
Scissors
Hole punch
Black pipe cleaners
Glue
Tongue depressors or smaller craft sticks
Googly eyes

What to do

1. To prepare, cut a bee body for each child from the black fun foam. The body should be as long as the tongue depressor. Punch two holes on the top of each bee for the antennae. Cut a piece of pipe cleaner for each bee long enough to poke through the holes and stand up.
2. Then, cut several yellow stripes for the bee.
3. Ask the children to weave the pipe cleaner through the holes in the foam.
4. When they are finished, have them glue the bee onto the tongue depressor, then add its eyes and stripes.

More to do

More art: Create fingerprint bumblebees with a stamp pad. Add detail with crayons or markers. Use fingerprints to design a flower garden for the bees.
Outdoors: Take a walk and look for bumblebees.
Science: Examine a beehive or honeycomb. Have a beekeeper visit. Talk about bee safety.
Snack: Enjoy a snack of toast and honey.

Related books

Buzz Said the Bee by Wendy Cheyette Lewison
The Honeybee and the Robber by Eric Carle
Winnie the Pooh by A. A. Milne

Tina R. Woehler, Oak Point, TX

Egg Carton Ants

Materials
Cardboard egg cartons
Scissors
Hole punch
Black or brown pipe cleaners
Wire cutters
Black or brown tempera paint
Large paintbrushes
Medium-sized googly eyes
Glue

What to do

1. Ahead of time, divide each egg carton into four sections. Each child's section should have three egg compartments, representing the ant's body.
2. Punch two holes in each egg compartment, one on each side, for the ant legs. Punch two holes on top of the first compartment for the antennae.
3. Cut a 3" (9 cm) piece of pipe cleaner for each child, then ask the children to push their pipe cleaner through the hole in the top.
4. Give each child three whole pipe cleaners. Have the children guide the pipe cleaners through the holes in the sides. Help the children bend the pipe cleaner so the egg carton will stand on its legs.
5. Invite the children to paint the egg carton ants.
6. When the paint is dry, have the children glue the eyes onto the head.

More to do

Outdoors: Observe an ant colony. Leave a few crumbs in the ants' path and predict what will happen.

Science: Keep an ant farm in the classroom and assign the children responsibility for the care of the farm.

Related books

Armies of Ants by Walter Retan
Two Bad Ants by Chris Van Allsburg

Tina R. Woehler. Oak Point, TX

Leaf Eaters

3+

Materials

Green construction paper
Scissors
Leaf shape cut out of tag board for kids to trace
Small pompoms
Glue
Hole punch
Markers

What to do

1. Have the children trace the leaf shapes on green paper and cut them out.
2. Punch three to six holes in the leaf to represent the areas that the caterpillar ate.
3. Glue small pompoms in a row to form a caterpillar on the leaf.
4. With markers, add the antenna.

More to do

Dramatic play: Pretend to be different insects such as worms, caterpillars, spiders, flies, or butterflies.

Field trip: Go for a nature walk and collect leaves that have holes in them. Glue the pom-poms to the real leaves.

Related books

In the Tall, Tall Grass by Denise Fleming
I Went Walking by Sue Williams
The Very Hungry Caterpillar by Eric Carle

 Sandy L. Scott, Vancouver, WA

Ladybug Pencil Holders   3+

Materials

Clean 12 oz. (375 mL) juice cans
White paper
Scissors
Red, black, and green paint
Shallow dishes
Thin paintbrushes
Black fine-tipped marker
Leaves

What to do

1. Beforehand, cut paper to fit around each can.
2. Pour red paint into a shallow dish and invite the children to make ladybugs by dipping a thumb into the paint and pressing it on the paper. Encourage them to print many ladybugs.
3. In the meantime, pour black and green paint into shallow dishes.
4. Have the children paint black spots on their ladybugs using a brush.
5. When the paint dries, have the children add feelers using a black fine-tipped marker. Show the children how to paint the veined side of a leaf with a brush, then press the leaf to the

paper or felt, leaving its impression. Encourage the children to print leaves here and there amid their ladybugs.

6. When it dries, help the children glue the paper to their juice cans.

More to do
More art: Make ladybugs with paper and pipe cleaners and slide them onto a pencil. Create greeting cards and gift wrap with ladybug prints. Design a ladybug pin with felt and buttons.

Related books
In the Tall, Tall Grass by Denise Fleming
What About Ladybugs? by Celia Godkin

Cindy Winther, Oxford, MI

Clothespin Butterflies

4+

Materials
Water
Food coloring
Small bowls
Sturdy paper towels
Newspaper
Old-fashioned clothespins
Pipe cleaners, one per child
Markers

What to do
1. Mix water and food coloring in small bowls.
2. Show the children how to fold their paper towel in half four times.
3. Have the children dip the corners of the folded towel into the bowls of coloring, then help them squeeze the excess water into a spare container.
4. Ask them to carefully unfold the towel and lay it on newspaper to dry.
5. When the towels have dried, have the children gather the mid-section of the towel. Grasp the towel with the clothespin.
6. Have the children attach the pipe cleaner as antennae and create a face using markers.

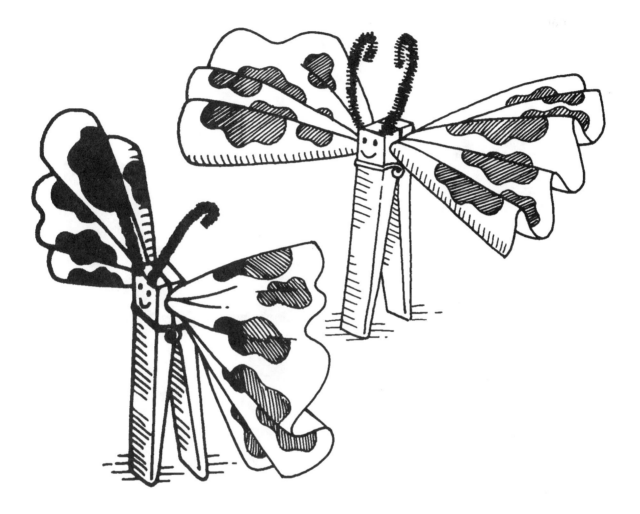

More to do

More art: Make caterpillars from egg cartons and cocoons from toilet paper tubes. Hide the children's butterflies in the cocoons, then have the butterflies emerge in a special celebration. Make caterpillar magnets using clothespins, pompoms, and googly eyes.

Related books

Butterfly Alphabet by Jerry Pallotta
Charlie the Caterpillar by Dom DeLuise
The Very Hungry Caterpillar by Eric Carle

Deborah R. Gallagher, Bridgeport, CT

insects

Clay Bugs

4+

Materials
Clay
Toothpicks
Pipe cleaners

What to do
1. Tell the children to roll the clay into three body segments. Help the children attach the segments with toothpicks.
2. When they are finished, show the children how to insert three pipe cleaners on each side of their bug, then bend the pipe cleaners into a leg shape.

More to do
Science: Design a habitat for the clay insects using rocks, twigs, leaves, and dirt.

Related books
Bugs by David Greenberg
Helpin' Bugs by Rosemary Lonborg
Lady Bug's Ball by Heather Lowenberg

Related song
Sing to the tune of "When the Saints Go Marching In."

On, when the bugs go marching in,
Oh, when the bugs go marching in,
Oh, how I'll see the ants and the beetles,
Oh, when the bugs go marching in.

Oh, when the bugs begin to crawl,
Oh, when the bugs begin to crawl,
Oh how I'll see the roaches and termites,
Oh, when the bugs begin to crawl.

Oh, when the bugs come flying in,
Oh, when the bugs come flying in,
Oh, how I'll see the moths and mosquitoes,
Oh, when the bugs come flying in.

Elizabeth Thomas, Hobart, IN

Sock Caterpillars

Materials
The Very Hungry Caterpillar by Eric Carle
Socks
Wool stuffing/batting
String
Craft items such as googly eyes, yarn, felt, and pompoms
Glue

What to do
1. Read *The Very Hungry Caterpillar* to the children.
2. Give each child a sock and some wool stuffing or batting. Let the children stuff their sock, stopping about 1" (3 cm) from the top.
3. Tightly tie the opening of the sock with a piece of string.
4. Invite the children to decorate their caterpillars as they please with the craft items.

More to do
Dramatic play: Using their puppets, the children can retell the story of the hungry caterpillar or compose their own.
Movement: Have everyone crawl like a caterpillar to the sound of slow, relaxing music.
Outdoors: Look for caterpillars on a walk and observe their behavior.

Linda Atamian, Charlestown, RI

Bug Costumes

Materials
Large paper grocery bags, one per child
Scissors
Glue
Paint
Paintbrushes or sponges
Empty paper towel and toilet paper rolls
Glitter, yarn, pipe cleaners, pompoms, doilies, and other creative art materials

What to do
1. Ahead of time, cut a face and arm holes in the bags.
2. Set out the paint and other art materials on a large table.
3. Give each child a bag to create an insect, imaginary or real, using the art materials.
4. Help the children put on their insect costumes and invite them to march around the room.

More to do
Dramatic play: Engage the children in a game of make-believe while they wear their insect costumes.

Language: Have the children dictate a story about their insect. Read their stories back to the class or assemble them in a book to share at home.

Math: Count, sort, and graph the bugs using categories such as bugs with hair, bugs made by girls, and bugs with legs.

Related books
How Many Bugs in a Box? by David Carter
The Snail's Spell by Joanne Ryder

Ann Gudowski, Johnstown, PA

Insect Mask

Materials
Plastic milk jugs, one per child
Scissors
Paper birthday blowers
Tempera paint
Construction paper scraps
Materials such as pipe cleaners, straws, pompoms, feathers, stickers, yarn, buttons, sequins, and bits of fabric
Glue

What to do
1. Ahead of time, cut away the back half of the milk jug, leaving the base intact. The jug's base is the top of the mask and will sit on the child's head; the front of the jug is the insect face. Cut two openings for the eyes and a hole for the mouth and birthday blower, or insect tongue.
2. Encourage the children to decorate their masks with the paint and craft materials.
3. While the children are working, invite them to imagine how their insect moves, what kind of

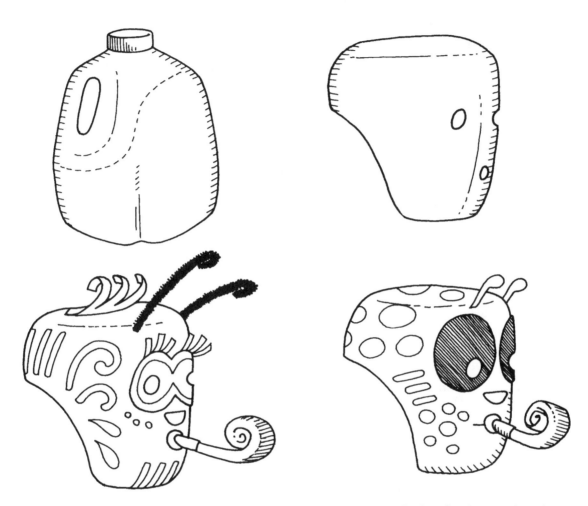

sound it makes, what its habitat is like, who its enemies are, and what food it needs to live.
4. Invite the children to put on their finished masks and behave like insects.

More to do
Dramatic play: Invite the children to put on a play while wearing their insect masks.
Games: Play Insect Tic-Tac-Toe. Divide the class into two groups and ask them to identify the insect in pictures you show them. Correct answers win an X or O on the game board.

Related books
Bugs by Nancy Winslow Parker and Joan R. Wright
Icky Bug Alphabet Book by Jerry Pallotta
Icky Bug Counting Book by Jerry Pallotta
Insectlopedia by Douglas Florian
The Very Quiet Cricket by Eric Carle
Why Mosquitoes Buzz in People's Ears by Verna Aardema

Christine Maiorano, Duxbury, MA

insects

Spotted Butterfly

Materials
White construction paper
Pencils
Paint and paintbrushes
Pipe cleaners
Yarn or string, optional

What to do
1. Have the children stand on the paper with their feet side by side. Ask them to trace their feet with a pencil.
2. When they are finished, ask the children to cut out the pattern of their feet and fold it in half.
3. When the children have pressed a fold in their paper, have them open it and paint spots on one side of the fold.
4. Next, ask the children to fold the paper in half again and gently rub the sides together, then open it and allow the paint to dry.
5. Finally, ask the children to cut a paper shape for the body and glue it in the center of the wings.
6. Attach two pieces of pipe cleaner for the antennae. Attach string or yarn to hang the butterflies, if desired.

More to do
Language: Have the children compose a poem about butterflies individually or as a class; glue the poems on the back of the butterfly wings.

Related books
Fireflies for Nathan by Shulamith Levey Oppenheim
Jack's Garden by Henry Cole
The Very Hungry Caterpillar by Eric Carle

Carla McClure, Hickman, KY

# insects

String Wing Surprises

Materials
Newspaper
Tempera paint in assorted colors
Containers
Construction paper in assorted colors, 9" x 12" (23 cm x 30 cm)
Butterfly templates for a 9" x 6" (23 cm x 15 cm) space
Pencils
Safety scissors
String
Easel brushes

What to do
1. Ahead of time, cover a workspace with newspaper and pour the paint into containers.
2. Ask the children to fold a piece of construction paper in half along its width.
3. Lay the template on the fold and have the children trace the template with a pencil.
4. When they are finished tracing, ask the children to cut out their butterfly with the paper folded, taking care not to cut along the folded edge.
5. Have them open the butterfly.
6. Give each child a piece of string and ask him or her to hold both ends of the string in their hands. Show them how to dip the string in the paint, keeping the ends of the string dry.
7. Help distribute the paint along the string and wipe any excess with a brush.
8. Have the children lay the string on one side of the butterfly, twisting the string as they do. Show them how to hold the ends of the string beyond the edge of the paper.
9. Have the children close the butterfly, then pull the string with one hand while gently pressing down on the paper with their other hand.
10. When they have pulled the string through, have the children open the butterfly and repeat with another color, laying the string in a different position this time.

More to do
Dramatic play: With imagination and movement, act out the metamorphosis of caterpillar to butterfly.
Math: Introduce the concept of symmetry by studying the patterns on butterfly wings.
More art: Create a mobile using the children's butterflies and paintings of the other life-cycle stages.
Science: Prepare matching cards of butterflies, moths, and caterpillars. Keep caterpillars in your class and record observations about their life cycle.

insects

Related books

The Butterfly Alphabet by Kjell B. Sandved
How to Hide a Butterfly by Ruth Heller
Look, a Butterfly by David Cutts
The Very Hungry Caterpillar by Eric Carle

Related rhyme

Fuzzy Wuzzy Caterpillar into a corner crept.
Wound around himself a blanket,
For a long time slept.
Fuzzy Wuzzy Caterpillar, waking by and by,
Found himself with beautiful wings,
He's changed to a butterfly!

Sandra W. Gratias, Perkasie, PA

leaves, trees, and plants

Painting Nature 3+

Materials
Objects from the outdoors such as evergreen branches, leaves, pinecones, berries, acorns
Paper
Paint and paintbrushes
Paint trays

What to do
1. Before class, arrange the objects from the outdoors on a table in an attractive way.
2. Invite the children to choose one or two of the objects to be the subject of their painting.
3. Provide the children with paint, brushes, and paper. Encourage them to create a painting, emphasizing that it need not look exactly like the subject.

More to do
Field trip: Go for a walk and collect objects from nature to paint. Paint outdoors on a pleasant day.
Math: Sort the objects into groups; arrange them in patterns.

Related books
Incredible Ned by Bill Maynard
A Tree in the Wood: An Old Nursery Song by Christopher Manson
A Tree Is Nice by Janice May Udry

Melissa J. Browning, Milwaukee, WI

Pine Needle Paintbrushes 3+

Materials
Pine needles
Twigs
Yarn or twine
Paint and paper

What to do
1. Bring the children outdoors to gather pine needles and straight, sturdy twigs.

2. Help the children gather a bunch of pine needles around one end of their twig.
3. Wrap the needles and twig securely with yarn or twine and tie in a knot.
4. Put out some paint and paper, and encourage the children to paint a picture using their new paintbrushes.

More to do

Dramatic play: Use the brushes as miniature brooms and dusters.

Math: Count the pine needles in a cluster.

More art: Show the children an example of a Native American pine needle basket. Create some of your own with clay and pine needles.

Science: Examine and compare pinecones, evergreen boughs, and an assortment of branches from deciduous trees.

Related books

Apple Pie Tree by Zoe Hall
Have You Seen Trees? by Joanne Oppenheim
A Tree Is Nice by Janice May Udry

Sharon Dempsey, Mays Landing, NJ

Paper Plate Sunflowers   3+

Materials
Real or artificial sunflower, or a picture of one
Yellow construction paper
Scissors
Snack-size paper plates, one per child
Glue
Paintbrushes
Yellow tempera paint or food coloring
Paint cup
Sunflower seeds in their shells

What to do
1. Before class, cut small petal shapes from construction paper. Mix a small amount of yellow paint or food coloring with glue in a paint cup.
2. Invite the children to examine the sunflower or a picture of one. Identify the parts of the flower.
3. Ask the children to paint the entire surface of their plate with the colored glue, then place the petals in the glue around the edge of the plate.
4. After the petals are glued in place, instruct the children to place sunflower seeds in the middle of the plate, representing the seed-filled center of the sunflower.
5. Make an arrangement of the finished sunflowers on your bulletin board for all to enjoy.

More to do
Math: Glue sunflower petals around the edge of a paper plate and write a number in the center. Ask the children to place the correct number of seeds on the plate.
Science: Discuss how plants grow from seeds and invite the children to examine a variety of seeds. Create a chart, matching seeds with pictures of plants and flowers.

Related books
Birdsong by Audrey Wood
Jack's Garden by Henry Cole
Sunflower by Miela Ford

Vicki L. Schneider, Oshkosh, WI

leaves, trees, and plants

Sticky Windowpanes   3+

Materials
Collage materials such as scraps of wallpaper, tissue paper, wrapping paper, foils, construction
     paper, cellophane wrap, magazines, greeting cards, and fabric; pieces of yarn, thread, and rib-
     bon; feathers, sequins, leaves, pressed flowers, small twigs, and thin pieces of bark
Two-sided tape
Clear contact paper
Scissors
Colored masking or trim tape

What to do
1. Prepare a display of the collage materials ahead of time.
2. Apply a piece of two-sided tape to each child's work surface to prevent their paper from moving around while they work.
3. Cut two pieces of clear contact paper the same size. Remove the protective paper from one
   sheet and lay it on the work surface, adhesive side up.
4. Invite the children to choose a selection of collage materials and arrange the materials on their
   contact paper. Older children can cut pieces of material from the scraps you provide. Instruct
   the children to leave space between the materials.
5. When the children have finished designing their collage, remove the protective paper from the
   second sheet of contact paper and lay it on top of the first sheet.
6. Trim the contact paper as needed and frame the edges with masking tape.
7. Hang the collages in front of windows in the classroom and enjoy.

More to do
Math: Cut the contact paper into triangles, circles, and squares before adding collage materials.
More art: Have older children design a quilt pattern using strips of paper as seams to separate
individual squares of contact paper.
Science: Cut the contact paper into the shape of a butterfly and invite children to design identical patterns for each wing. Attach string and hang the butterflies from the ceiling or at the window.

Related books
Good Morning Pond by Alyssa Stain Capucilli
How to Be a Nature Detective by Millicent E. Selslam
Little Blue and Little Yellow by Leo Lionni

Bev Schumacher, Ft. Mitchell, KY

leaves, trees, and plants

Spatter Leaves

3+

Materials
Smocks
Leaves
Cellophane tape or two-sided tape
Paper
Paint
Paintbrushes

What to do
1. Have the children put on their smocks ahead of time.
2. Tape a leaf from underneath to a sheet of paper.
3. Invite the children to dip the brush in paint and run a finger over the tip of brush, causing the paint to spatter.
4. Allow the paint to dry, then remove the leaf and see its impression on the paper.

More to do
More art: Put watered-down paint in a water sprayer and invite the children to spray the paper with the leaf taped on to it. When dry, remove the leaf. Collect an assortment of leaves and make an impression of each, then assemble the sheets of paper into a book of leaves. Design a mural for the bulletin board using an assortment of leaves and spatter paint.

Related books
Look What I Did With a Leaf by Morteza E. Sohi
Red Leaf, Yellow Leaf by Lois Ehlert

Sandra Hutchins Lucas, Cox's Creek, KY

Handprint Tulips

3+

Materials
Green, red, yellow, black, and orange tempera paints
Pie pans or paint trays
Smocks

White construction paper, 12" x 18" (30 cm x 45 cm)
Towels or diaper wipes
Small paintbrushes

What to do

1. Ahead of time, pour the paint into pans or trays, one for each color.
2. Ask the children to put their smocks on before the project begins.
3. Invite the children to place their forearm in the green paint, without touching the paint with their hands; then have them press their forearm onto the white construction paper about three or four times, creating a row of flower stems.
4. When they have finished the stems, ask the children to place their hand in the orange, red, and yellow paints one at a time. Have them press their handprint at the top of each flower stem, holding their fingers together and their thumb above the paper, creating the tulip impression. Wipe or wash hands after each color.
5. Add the pistols using the small brush and black paint.

More to do

Math: Play a tulip counting game with tulips constructed from paper and craft stick stems. The children count the correct number of tulips and place them in laminated file folders that are decorated with a numbered flower pot.

More art: In the spring, put a vase of fresh tulips on a table and invite the children to create a still-life drawing.

Related books

Growing a Rainbow by Lois Ehlert
The Tiny Seed by Eric Carle

Tina R. Woehler, Oak Point, TX

Worms in the Grass

3+

Materials

Brown tempera paint
Pie pans or mess trays
Brown yarn, cut in 8" (20 cm) lengths
Green construction paper

leaves, trees, and plants

What to do

1. Pour mixed paint into pans or trays.
2. Give each child a piece of yarn and one sheet of paper.
3. Ask the children to dip their yarn in the paint and wiggle it back and forth until it is covered with paint.
4. When their yarn is ready, have the children paint a picture of worms in the green grass by dragging the yarn across their paper.

More to do

Science: Add a worm garden to your room by filling a large, clear plastic container with soil. Add apple slices and poke holes in the lid for air. Add worms and keep in a dark place while the children are not in class.

Related books

The Girl Who Loves Caterpillars by Jean Merrill
How My Garden Grew by Anne and Harlow Rockwell
Jack's Garden by Henry Cole

Tina R. Woehler, Oak Point, TX

Dip and Paint

Materials

Objects collected on a nature walk
Paint
White construction paper

What to do

1. Take the children on a nature walk. Encourage them to collect dandelions, leaves, twigs, pinecones, and other interesting and natural objects.
2. When you return to the classroom, have the children dip the objects they have collected in the paint and use them as paintbrushes.

More to do

More art: Create a collage with some of the objects from the nature walk.
Science: Invite the children to feel, sort, and examine the collection.

leaves, trees, and plants

Related books
Autumn by Steven Schnur
The Earth and I by Frank Asch
I Can Tell by Touching by Carolyn Otto
I Went Walking by Sue Williams
The Legend of the Indian Paintbrush retold by Tomie dePaola

Diane Hasenour, Evansville, IN

Leaf Rubbings

3+

Materials
Paper
Cardboard
Two clothespins
Leaves
Crayons with paper removed

What to do
1. Fasten the paper to the cardboard with clothespins to hold the paper in place.
2. Invite the children to feel the raised pattern of veins on the underside of the leaf. Tell them to lay the leaf underside up between the cardboard and the paper.
3. Have the children color the entire sheet of paper, holding their crayon on its side and using broad strokes from top to bottom and left to right.

More to do
More art: Make greeting cards with the leaf rubbings. Let older children make a design of several rubbings or create a border for the bulletin board.

leaves, trees, and plants

Related books
Apple Pie Tree by Zoe Hall
The Ghost-Eye Tree by Bill Martin, Jr., and John Archambault
Red Leaf, Yellow Leaf by Lois Ehlert

Mary Jo Shannon, Roanoke, VA

Leaf Prints

3+

Materials

Leaves
Newspapers
Manila paper or newsprint
Tempera paint, thick
Brushes

What to do

1. Go for a walk with the children to collect leaves or bring in an assortment of leaves ahead of time. Cover the table with newspaper and place the leaves in the middle.
2. Invite the children to select one leaf each for their print.
3. Have them turn the leaf underside up, so they can see the pattern of veins on its surface, and place it on a piece of newsprint or manila paper.
4. Show the children how to lightly brush the leaf with a coat of paint, covering its surface.
5. Once the underside is painted, have the children place the leaf, paint side down, on the paper and press gently, leaving an imprint of the leaf on the paper.

More to do

Math: Use a variety of leaves and compare their sizes and shapes.
More art: Make wrapping paper by covering large sheets of newsprint with leaf prints.
Science: Match the leaf prints with pictures of trees and plants.

Related books

Red Leaf, Yellow Leaf by Lois Ehlert
Why Do Leaves Change Color? by Betsy Maestro

Mary Jo Shannon, Roanoke, VA

Favorite Leaf

3+

Materials
Leaves
Paper
Pencils
Scissors
Tempera paint in fall or spring leaf colors
Cotton swabs

What to do
1. Take the children on a nature walk and tell them that they are going to look for one leaf that they can call their favorite leaf.
2. When they return, invite the children to trace the leaf they selected on a piece of paper with a pencil, holding the leaf in place with tape and being very careful not to damage the leaf as they trace.
3. Then, ask the children to cut out their paper leaf shape.
4. Invite the children to paint their paper leaf shape with cotton swabs.
5. On a larger piece of paper, have the children glue the real leaf and their paper leaf, side by side.

More to do
Movement: Give each child a large, tissue paper leaf and invite them to move to an instrumental recording of "Autumn Leaves" or similar music.

Related books
Autumn Leaves by Ken Robbins
Leaves by Rena Kirkpatrick
Red Leaf, Yellow Leaf by Lois Ehlert

Original poem
Down, down, yellow and brown,
The leaves are falling to the ground.

Diane Billman, Marietta, GA

leaves, trees, *and* plants

Forsythia

3+

Materials
Paper
Pencils
Yellow tissue paper cut in 1" (3 cm) squares
Glue
Markers or crayons

What to do
1. If the children have never seen a forsythia plant, take them on a walk to show them one, or find one in a book to display. Talk about the beautiful yellow flowers that grow on a forsythia plant.
2. Encourage the children to draw lines on the paper, representing the branches of a forsythia plant.
3. Ask them to scrunch the tissue squares.
4. Have the children glue the tissue pieces along the lines.
5. Once their forsythia is complete, ask the children to draw and color a background.

More to do
Field trip: Go for a walk and find a forsythia or other early signs of spring.
Science: Bring in forsythia for the children to see. Ask them to watch for the first signs of spring in their neighborhood.

Related books
Colors Around Us: A Lift-the-Flap Surprise Book by Shelley Rotner and Anne Woodbull
Eeny, Meeny, Miney Mole by Jane Yolen
Growing Colors by Bruce McMillan
Jack's Garden by Henry Cole
Planting a Rainbow by Lois Ehlert

Phyllis Esch, Export, PA

leaves, trees, and plants

Colorful Leaves

3+

Materials
White paper
Scissors
Tissue paper squares in fall colors
Water in bowls
Paintbrushes

What to do
1. Ahead of time, cut leaf shapes from white paper.
2. Ask the children to place tissue squares on the leaf shapes one at a time and brush with water.
3. Allow to dry.
4. When completely dry, remove the tissue squares, leaving a colorful dye imprint on the leaf.

More to do
Math: Hold a contest to see who can find the biggest and smallest leaf. Sort leaves by shape, size, or color.
More art: Make wax-paper transparencies of leaves or press them.
Outdoors: Bring the class outside to play in the leaves and rake them into big piles.

Related books
Red Leaf, Yellow Leaf by Lois Ehlert
The Tree That Grew Through the Roof by Thomas Berger
Why Do Leaves Change Color? by Betsy Maestro

 Linda Atamian, Charlestown, RI

Leaf Bookmarks

4+

Materials
Leaves, ferns, and grasses
Watercolor paper cut into rectangular bookmark shapes
Watercolor paints
Thin paintbrushes

leaves, trees, and plants

Clear contact paper
Hole punch
Thread or yarn

What to do

1. Collect small fall leaves, ferns, and grasses with the children. Lay them on newspaper, or press them between pages of books until they are dry. This may take a few days.
2. Invite the children to paint the bookmark shapes.
3. Let the bookmarks dry.
4. Set out the pressed plants and encourage the children to glue them on to their bookmarks in arrangements of their choice.
5. Laminate or cover each bookmark with clear contact paper.
6. Punch a hole at the top of each bookmark.
7. Have the children tie yarn or thread through the hole.

More to do

More art: Cut the paper into small squares and make gift tags.
Outdoors: Rake autumn leaves into a big pile and let the children jump in.

Related books

Autumn by Steven Schnur
Chicka Chicka, Boom Boom by Bill Martin, Jr., and John Archambault
Red Leaf, Yellow Leaf by Lois Ehlert

Linda Atamian, Charlestown, RI

Fork Print Evergreen Trees

Materials

Green, red, and brown tempera paint
Small containers
Plastic or metal forks
Construction paper, 9" x 12" (23 cm x 30 cm) in white, dark blue, or black
Rectangular sponge, about 1" x 2" (3 cm x 5 cm)
Cotton swabs
Star stickers, optional

What to do

1. Ahead of time, place the paint in individual containers.
2. Before you begin the project, show the children an evergreen tree outdoors or in a book.
3. When the children are ready, show them how to dip the fork tines in the green paint and gently wipe the excess off against the side of the container. Press the fork onto the paper in the shape of an evergreen tree or triangle. Tell them to dip the fork in the paint again, if necessary, adding to the painting until a tree shape is complete.
4. Have the children paint the tree trunk using the sponge and brown paint.
5. Finally, have the children dip the cotton swabs in the red paint and dab on some berries and, if desired, add a star sticker to the top.

More to do

More art: Use different kinds of evergreen branches as paintbrushes.
Movement: Dance to music using small evergreen branches as fans.
Science: Have the children add animals to the painting to reinforce a lesson on habitat. Gather assorted kinds of evergreen branches and discuss how they are different and alike.

Related books

Mr. Willowby's Christmas Tree by Robert Barry
A Tree Is Nice by Janice May Udry

Diane Billman, Marietta, GA

The Wire Giving Tree

Materials

Small block of wood, 3" x 3" (8 cm x 8 cm)
Drill (adult only)
Telephone or craft wire, cut into 18" (45 cm) lengths
Wire cutters
Pre-cut leaf shapes made from "fun foam" with a hole punched in the end

What to do

1. Twist four or five lengths of wire together at the bottom.
2. Drill a hole in the block of wood wide enough for the base of the twisted wire to fit through.
3. Twist the wire into the drilled hole.
4. Invite the children to form "branches" from the wire and attach the leaves to the end of the branches by twisting the ends of the wire through the holes in the leaves.

leaves, trees, and plants

Related books
The Giving Tree by Shel Silverstein
A Tree Is Nice by Janice May Udry

Synthia Scheck, Mesa, AZ

leaves, trees, and plants

Stick Wrapping

Materials
3' (1 m) stick or 1/2"- 3/4" (1.5-2 cm) dowel
Many colors and lengths of yarn, string, ribbon, or streamers, embroidery floss, fabric strips,
    and other string-like materials
Decorations, such as feathers, felt, foil, or flowers with stems
Glue
Masking tape

What to do
1. Start wrapping the stick with yarn. With adult help, tie a half-hitch knot at the beginning or use masking tape to attach the yarn securely to the stick.
2. Continue wrapping the chosen material tightly around the stick.
3. Change colors at any time. The new yarn can either be tied to the previous piece of yarn or taped to the stick. Begin to wrap the stick with the new color, texture or material. Loose ends can be left hanging or neatly tucked in. Encourage creativity.
4. As wrapping continues, other decorative items can be tied, taped, glued, or wrapped into the yarn or string. This gives the wrapping a "surprise" character that makes it unique.
5. Loose ends can also be decorated with any interesting items.

More to do
More art: Find a pole, pillar or column to wrap with larger strips of fabric, colored ropes, and yarn for a large rendition of the wrapped stick.

MaryAnn Kohl, Reprinted from Preschool Art

Mosaic Flowers

Materials
Poster board cut in 6" (15 cm) squares
Old magazines
Scissors
Glue
Water

leaves, trees, *and* plants

Cups
Old paintbrushes
Markers

What to do
1. Invite the children to choose a color for their flower.
2. Have the children cut pictures with shades of that color from magazines, then cut the pictures into small squares.
3. Mix glue and water in a cup and ask the children to apply a coat of glue to their poster board with a paintbrush.
4. Have the children place their color squares on the poster board, overlapping them and covering the entire board.
5. When the children have covered the poster board, instruct them to draw or trace a flower pattern on its reverse side.
6. Help the children cut along the flower pattern.
7. When the children have cut out their flower, have them paint a coat of glue over the top of it.

More to do
Holiday: Attach a pin on the back of the flower and create a piece of jewelry to give as a gift.
More art: Attach a pipe cleaner stem and paper leaves to the flowers.

Related books
Alison's Zinnia by Anita Lobel
Colors Everywhere by Tana Hoban

Nicole Sparks, Miami, FL

Bleached Leaves

Materials
Newspaper
Bleach
Small container with plastic lid with hole for brush or swab
Smocks and rubber gloves
Cotton swabs
Assortment of leaves
Black construction paper, 9" x 12" (23 cm x 30 cm)
Construction paper in fall colors, 12" x 18" (30 cm x 45 cm)

What to do
1. Ahead of time, cover a work area with newspaper.
2. Pour bleach into the container. Secure the lid.
3. Provide the children with smocks and rubber gloves.
4. Have the children dip a cotton swab in the bleach through the hole in the lid. Invite the children to feel the surface of their leaves and the raised pattern of the leaf's veins and stem on the underside. Have them paint this side of their leaves, using the swab.
5. Once the underside is painted, ask the children to turn the leaf over and press it to the black paper, then gently rub the top of the leaf while holding it in place.
6. Tell the children to lift the leaf off the paper and observe the impression it has left.
7. Let the paintings dry, then mat them on the larger paper.

More to do
Math: Cut leaves from construction paper in a variety of sizes, shapes, and colors. Laminate, if desired. Encourage the children to sort and count the leaves.
Outdoors: On a fall day, provide small plastic rakes and wheelbarrows. Bring the children outdoors to rake and gather leaves.
Snack: Make a leafy green salad from a variety of lettuce leaves, including spinach, bib, romaine, and iceberg, and serve with dressing.

Related books
Red Leaf, Yellow Leaf by Lois Ehlert
The Tree That Grew Through the Roof by Thomas Berger
When the Wind Stops by Charlotte Zolotow

Debi Behr and Diana Reed, New Wilmington, PA

Florentine Vase

Materials
Plastic milk jug, quart (1L) or half-gallon (2L) size
Strong scissors
Lightweight cardboard
White squeeze glue
Yarn or heavy string

leaves, trees, *and* plants

Heavy duty aluminum foil
Black tempera paint and brushes
Fine steel wool or kitchen scrubber pad
Clear hobby spray or brush-on coating, optional
Dried or silk flowers and greens

What to do

1. Ahead of time, cut away the top one-third of the milk jug. Cut flowers and other interesting shapes from the cardboard.
2. Have the children glue the cardboard shapes onto the jug, then glue the yarn or string around the cardboard shapes, creating a design or pattern. Allow the glue to dry.
3. Wrap the jug completely in foil, covering the cut-outs and yarn. Ask the children to press the foil to the jug. Their back and forth motion will smooth wrinkles and reveal the shapes and design beneath the foil.
4. Once the foil is smooth, have the children paint the jug, covering the foil completely. Allow to dry.
5. When the paint is completely dry, tell the children to lightly brush the raised areas of the jug with the steel wool or scrubbing pad for an antique effect. Do not brush the jug's flat surface area.
6. Apply a protective coating, if desired.
7. Invite the children to add an arrangement of dried or silk flowers to the vase. Do not use water, as the paint will rub off the vase.

More to do

Field trip: Go for a walk and collect flowers or dry grasses to put in the Florentine box or vase.
More art: Create a Florentine box with a cigar or shoebox. Learn

about Lorenzo Ghiberti, who used a similar technique in the 15th Century to create the sculpted bronze doors of the Baptistry in Florence, Italy. Dry some flowers and greens to use in the vases.

Related books

Art Dog by Thacher Hurd
Grandfather Tang's Story by Ann Tompert

MaryAnn Kohl, Bellingham, WA

Flower Sun Catchers

Materials
Transparent book covers in assorted colors
Scissors
Paint in squeeze bottles

What to do
1. Beforehand, cut out a tulip shape for each child from the book covers.
2. Give the children paint in squeeze bottles and invite them to decorate the shape with painted squiggles, lines, and dots.
3. When the paint dries, remove the adhesive backing from the material and hang the tulips on a sunny window.
4. Cut the book cover material into short, narrow strips and hand them out to the children. Invite the children to cut a grassy fringe along the top of their strip, then peel off the backing and affix the strip of grass below their tulip.

More to do
Gardening: Plant tulip and other bulbs in the schoolyard.
More art: Cut the book covers into small shapes and create the appearance of a stained glass window. Cut paper into shapes, then remove the center and replace it with the book cover material or cellophane; hang the colorful shapes in front of a window.

Related books
Planting a Rainbow by Lois Ehlert
The Reason for a Flower by Ruth Heller
What Is the Sun? by Reeve Lindbergh
When Spring Comes by Robert Maass

Cindy Winther, Oxford, MI

light

Shades of Color

3+

Materials
Colored cellophane, cut in l" to 2" (3 cm-5 cm) pieces
Scissors
2 sheets of contact paper, 3' x 4' (1 m x 1.3 m), per child
Tape
Hole punch
Yarn

What to do
1. Tape a large sheet of contact paper to the table, adhesive side facing up.
2. Invite the children to select pieces of cellophane and arrange them on the contact paper in any design.
3. When they have finished arranging the cellophane, place the second sheet of contact paper over their design, adhesive side down. Press until the layers adhere to each other.
4. Cut the layers of paper into shapes, one for each child.
5. Punch a hole in each child's shape and attach a loop of yarn to it.
6. Hang the color shapes near a window or in front of a light.

More to do
Math: Cut geometric shapes from construction paper, then cut out their middle and glue colored cellophane over the opening. Attach string and hang the sun catcher shapes by the window.
More art: Invite the children to place their finished product on a light table. Cut the layered contact paper into shapes related to the seasons or holidays such as leaves, flowers, hearts, and four-leaf clovers. Layer red, blue, and yellow cellophane to create secondary colors. Create a facsimile of a stained glass window using colored cellophane and construction paper. Construct a kaleidoscope using cellophane and paper towel and toilet paper tubes.

Related books
Colors Everywhere by Tana Hoban
Seven Blind Mice by Ed Young

Peggy Eddy, Johnson City, TN

Window Wonders

3+

Materials
Black permanent markers
Drawing paper
Crayons in vibrant colors
Newspaper
Paper towels
Baby oil or vegetable oil, in a bowl
Tape

What to do
1. Have the children use a black marker to draw the outline of a picture on their paper.
2. When they have finished their outline, have the children color it in with crayons.
3. Ask the children to turn their papers over so their pictures are facedown on newspaper.
4. Show the children how to dip their paper towel into a bowl of oil and rub it on the back of their pictures.
5. When they have finished, have them hold their pictures up to the light. Explain that the oil makes the design transparent.
6. Tape the papers on a window where light will filter through the children's designs.

More to do
Cooking: Fry potato pancakes in oil. Make salad dressing with oil, water, and herbs.
More art: Cut around the outline, punch a hole in the shape, and attach yarn or string to create a window ornament. Introduce the words "transparent" and "opaque".
Science: Mix oil and colored water in a bottle.

 Susan A. Sharkey, La Mesa, CA

Sun Catchers

3+

Materials
Paint or food dye in 3 or 4 colors
3 or 4 bottles of white glue
Polystyrene plates, one per child
String

light

What to do

1. Add a different color of paint or food dye to each bottle of glue.
2. Give each child a polystyrene plate.
3. Have the children squeeze glue from the bottles onto their plate, filling the bottom of the plate. Encourage them to make a design using different colors.
4. Place a loop of string in the glue toward the edge.
5. Set the plates aside for a few days to allow the glue to dry.
6. When the glue has dried and hardened into a disk, help the children gently peel it away from the plate.
7. Hang the disks or sun catchers at a window.

More to do

More art: Create pendants or other jewelry with smaller disks.

Related books

My Many Colored Days by Dr. Seuss
Sun Song by Jean Marzollo
The Very Busy Spider by Eric Carle

Sandra Nagel, White Lake, MI

Sun-faded Art

Materials

Dark construction paper
Small paper cut-outs
Double-sided or ordinary cellophane tape

What to do

1. Have the children choose a paper cut-out and tape it onto their construction paper. Use double-sided tape or roll ordinary tape so the tape does not extend beyond the edge of the cut-out.
2. Hang the paper in a sunny window.
3. After a few days, return the papers to the children and ask them to remove the paper cut-out. Have the children observe how the sun has faded the color of the paper except where the cut-out blocked the sunlight.

More to do

More art: Place small objects such as felt shapes, buttons, and macaroni on the paper and lay it flat on a windowsill for the same results. Have children cut out their initials and lay them on another sheet of paper in a sunny place.

Related books

One Light, One Sun by Raffi
Sun Song by Jean Marzollo
Windsongs and Rainbows by Albert Burton

Sandra Hutchins Lucas, Cox's Creek, KY

Rainbows Galore

Materials

Clear plastic drinking glass filled with water
White paper
Cellophane or masking tape
Watercolors
Brushes
Rinse water

What to do

1. Schedule this project for a sunny day. Position a table near a window where the sun will shine through the window.
2. Place the glass of water just barely over the edge of the table. Adjust the glass until it catches the sunlight and a rainbow appears on the floor.
3. Tape a piece of white paper on the floor where the rainbow appears.
4. Invite the children to trace the rainbow, then paint it using watercolors.

More to do

Science: Position a hand mirror so that it is facing the sun and watch a rainbow appear on the ceiling. Help the children understand that sunlight is many colors in combination; when the sunlight hits the glass or water, it separates into the colors that comprise it: red, orange, yellow, green, blue, indigo, and violet—the colors of the rainbow. Make a rainbow outdoors by spraying a mist into the air with a garden hose while your back is to the sun.

Related books
Look at Rainbow Colors by Rena K. Kirkpatrick
Planting a Rainbow by Lois Ehlert
A Rainbow of My Own by Don Freeman
Windsongs and Rainbows by Albert Burton

Vicki Whitehead, Ft. Worth, TX

Punch-out Art

Materials
Pencils
White paper
Thin pieces of carpet
Corncob holders or large pushpins

What to do
1. Have each child use a pencil to draw a large design on a sheet of paper.
2. The children should place their designs on top of a piece of carpet.
3. Using the point of a corncob holder or pushpin, the children can punch holes in the paper along the lines of their design.
4. Hang the finished artwork in front of a window so children can see how the light coming through the little holes outlines their designs.

More to do
More art: Invite the children to turn their artwork over and feel the raised bumps on the other side. Have the children punch so many holes that their design can be removed from the larger piece of paper. Let the children try punching out their designs using a hole punch. Suggest that the children draw holiday shapes to punch out.

Related books
The Very Hungry Caterpillar by Eric Carle
What the Sun Sees/What the Moon Sees by Nancy Tafuri

Sandra Hutchins Lucas, Cox's Creek, KY

Baked Stubs

Materials
Old crayon stubs, peeled
Matte board or cardboard
Cookie sheet covered with foil
Rocks, shells, felt squares, pieces of wood, and other items
Hot sunny day (or oven)
Craft sticks or coffee stir sticks

What to do
1. Peel the paper from old broken crayons.
2. Place the matte board or cardboard on the covered cookie sheet.
3. Place peeled crayons on the matte board, randomly or by stacking them.
4. Add rocks or shells in and around the crayons if desired.
5. Leave the arrangement in the hot sun to melt, or an adult should place the cookie sheet in a 250° F (125° C) oven for about 10 minutes.
6. An adult should remove the hot sheet from the oven.
7. The artist may wish to push the melted crayon about with the craft sticks before the melted crayon design cools.
8. Cool the design completely. Remove it from the cookie sheet.

More to do
More art: Melt crayon stubs on felt squares, fabric scraps, thin boards, cardboard or other sturdy papers or materials.

Related book
Harold and the Purple Crayon by Crockett Johnson

MaryAnn Kohl, Reprinted from Preschool Art

Light and Shadows

5+

Materials
White paper
Light or lamp
Pencil
Black crayon

What to do
1. Hang a piece of white paper on the wall.
2. Have one child sit in front of the paper, their side toward the wall.
3. Place the light a short distance away, creating a silhouette.

4. Invite a second child to trace the silhouette with a pencil.
5. Have the rest of the class create their silhouettes in turn.
6. When their silhouettes are finished, ask the children to color them in with black crayon.

More to do
More art: Draw outlines of animals or other creatures on overhead transparencies and project them onto a large sheet of white paper. Then have the children trace the outlines and create life-size drawings. Assemble the drawings in a life-size coloring book.
Dramatic play: Show the children how to make shadow puppets with their hands. Encourage the children to perform a skit using only shadows.

Related books
Bear Shadow by Frank Asch
Black on White by Tana Hoban
What Makes a Shadow? by Clyde R. Bulla

Sandra Hutchins Lucas, Cox's Creek, KY

Coin Creations

3+

Materials
Modeling clay
Rolling pins
A variety of U.S. and international coins
Watercolor or tempera paint
Paintbrushes

What to do
1. Give each child a piece of the clay. Have them roll it flat using the rolling pin.
2. Place an assortment of coins on the table and invite the children to choose one coin.
3. When the children are ready, show them how to press the front or back of the coin into the clay, then remove the coin and set the clay aside to dry.
4. When the clay has dried, have the children paint their coin impressions.

More to do
Field trip: Visit a mint or a bank.
Games: Use the coin creations in a matching game. Match a coin to its imprint or the front of a coin to its back.
Math: Sort and count the coins. Bring in extra pennies for practice.
More art: Make coin rubbings with paper and colored pencils.
Science: Inspect the coins with a magnifying glass, looking for similarities and differences.

Related books
Alexander, Who Used to Be Rich Last Sunday by Judith Viorst
Jelly Beans for Sale by Bruce McMillan
Max Makes a Million by Maira Kalman

Ann Gudowski, Johnston, PA

Going Shopping

4+

Materials
Small bags of cereal
Trinkets
Crayons
Snacks
Stickers or labels
Envelopes, 5" x 7" (13 cm x 18 cm)
Yarn
Markers
10 pennies per child

What to do
1. Ahead of time, set up a store display in your classroom. On a table, arrange merchandise such as small bags of cereal, trinkets, crayons, and snacks. Label each item with a price from one to five cents.
2. When class begins, have each child decorate an envelope with markers. To make a pocketbook, help the children attach a loop of yarn at the envelope opening. To make a wallet, have them fold their envelope in half.
3. Give each child 10 pennies and tell them to keep the coins in their wallet or pocketbook.
4. Split the children into two groups and have them practice counting their pennies.
5. Invite the first group of children to shop. Show them around the store and help them read the price tags and calculate how many items they can buy with their money.
6. When the first group has finished, invite the second group to shop.

More to do
Circle time: Talk about the children's trips to the store or shopping mall with their family.
Dramatic play: Encourage the children to set up a make-believe store.
More art: Have the children make some of the merchandise such as ornaments, paintings, and greeting cards, then hold shopping day around the holidays when the children can buy gifts handmade by their classmates.

Related books

Alexander, Who Used to Be Rich Last Sunday by Judith Viorst
Benny's Pennies by Pat Brisson
Bunny Money by Rosemary Wells
Jelly Beans for Sale by Bruce McMillan
Lilly's Purple Plastic Purse by Kevin Henkes
Max's Dragon Shirt by Rosemary Wells

Susan L. Mahoney, Orange Park, FL

Penny Pictures

Materials
Pennies for each child
White paper
Colored pencils

What to do
1. Supply each child with a few pennies, a white piece of paper, and colored pencils.
2. Have the children put a penny under their paper. Show them how to rub the side of their pencil over the coin, reproducing the image of the penny.
3. Encourage the children to make another rubbing using more coins. Tell them they may arrange some or all of their pennies in a design.

More to do
Dramatic play: Provide simple props and let the children run a make-believe store or lemonade stand.
More art: Make rubbings of leaves, interesting buttons, other coins, or decorative carvings. Make a frame for the rubbings from construction paper or poster board, then use glue to affix old pennies, buttons, or small leaves and baby pine cones to the frame.

Related books
26 Letters and 99 cents by Tana Hoban
Jelly Beans for Sale by Bruce McMillan
Let's Count It Out, Jesse Bear by Nancy White Carlstrom

Nancy Dentler, Mobile, AL

money

Money Banks

4

Materials
Cans of frosting or formula with lids, empty and clean
Scissors
Construction paper
Glue
Money stickers
Other decorating items such as yarn, bits of fabric and wrapping paper, and buttons
One penny per child

What to do
1. Beforehand, cut small slots in the lids of the cans.
2. If necessary, cover the cans with construction paper.
3. Have the children decorate the cans with stickers and other decorating supplies.
4. When the children finish decorating their bank, give them each a penny to start their savings account.

More to do
Dramatic play: Make a cash register or money drawer from a shoebox, and supply the children with plastic play coins for banking and shopping.
Field trip: Visit a bank.
Games: Play money lotto.

Related books and song
Bunny Money by Rosemary Wells
Emeka's Gift: An African Counting Story by Ifeoma Onyefulu
"Sing the Piggy Bank" by Greg and Steve on "We All Live Together, Vol. 3"

Linda N. Ford, Sacramento, CA

Auction

5+

Materials
Children's artwork
Labels or blank stickers
10 pennies per child
Gavel and block
Bowl or basket

What to do
1. Have the children select which artwork they would like to sell in an auction. Assemble the collection over the course of several days or weeks. Label each piece with the artist's name.
2. Have the children bring in 10 pennies from home in a plastic bag labeled with their name.
3. Before the auction begins, explain that the pieces of artwork will be sold to the highest bidder. Tell the children that they are to indicate their bid with their fingers, not their voices.
4. When you are ready to begin, name the title of the first piece of artwork and its artist, then describe the work, including the kind of painting (such as portrait, landscape, still-life) and the medium (such as crayons, watercolors, pencil).
5. Invite the children to bid. When you reach the highest bid, bang the gavel and announce the child's name. Have another adult available to write the name and bid on a sticker and place the sticker on the back of the painting. Another adult can collect the money due in a small basket. Try to give all the children ample opportunity to buy a painting.
6. When the auction is over, the student artists keep the pennies they earned, and buyers keep the art they purchased.

More to do
More art: Exhibit the children's artwork during an open house before the auction. Have a local artist come to your class and give a demonstration, then donate a small piece of art to the school. Hold a silent auction so the parents may bid on the donation.

Related books
Art Dog by Thacher Hurd
The Art Lesson by Tomie DePaola
Bonjour, Mr. Satie by Edward Lear and Tomie DePaola
Caps for Sale by Esphyr Slobodkina

Shirley R. Salach, Northwood, NH

Magnetic Painting

3+

Materials
Paper
Shallow cardboard box
Paint in a variety of colors
Small spoons
Small metal objects such as ball bearings, nuts, bolts, and nails
Magnet
Rubber gloves
Tub of water
Towels

What to do
1. Place a piece of paper in the bottom of the box. Ask two children to hold the box.
2. Have a third child spoon a few colors of paint onto the paper.
3. Ask the children to choose a few of the small metal objects and place them in the box.
4. Invite another child to sit under the box and move the magnet across the bottom of the box. Show the children how the magnet pulls the metal objects through the paint, creating a design on the paper.
5. When the design is complete, have the children put on rubber gloves and remove the metal objects, then rinse the paint from them and dry them with a towel for the next group.
6. Put a clean sheet of paper in the box and invite the rest of the class to participate in turn, rotating positions.

More to do
More art: Instead of using a magnet, put a rolling ball into the box and have the children holding the box rock it so the ball rolls around in the paint. Have the children begin the project with only primary colors, then observe which new colors they create as they begin to paint.
Sand and water table: Bury metal objects in the sand and locate them with the magnet.
Science: Encourage the children to experiment with a magnet and an assortment of objects in the box before they add paint and paper. Have them test objects from the classroom or home to see which are attracted to the magnet. Make a chart with pictures of the objects that were or were not attracted to the magnet.

Related books
Archibald Frisby by Michael D. Chesworth
Little Blue and Little Yellow by Leo Lionni

Ann Gudowski, Johnston, PA

movement

Magic Pebbles

3+

Materials
Small pebbles, 10 or more per child
Wet tempera paint, assorted colors
Cups and spoons
Paper plates, 2 per child
Stapler
Staple remover

What to do
1. Help the children write their name on the plates.
2. Have them drop a pebble or two in color cups of paint.
3. Have them then scoop the pebbles out of the paint with a spoon and place them on their paper plate.
4. When all of the pebbles are on the plate, place the second plate facedown over the first to create a pocket.
5. Staple the plates together for the children.
6. Hand the plates back to the children and encourage tambourine action through movement and music.
7. When the child are finished or the song is over, lead the children back to the table.
8. Remove the staples for the children and dispose of them.
9. Reveal the art within by having the children open the plates and see the surprise painting inside. Dispose of the pebbles and allow the plates to dry.

Related books
The Banging Book by Bill Grossman
Crash! Bang! Boom! by Peter Spier
Of Colors and Things by Tana Hoban
Sing a Song of Popcorn edited by Beatrice Schenk deRegniers

Dani Rosensteel, Payson, AZ

movement

Moving Pictures

Materials
Drawing paper—heavy stock—at least 8½" x 11" (20 cm x 28 cm)
Crayons
Scissors
Tape
Support sticks—popsicle or craft sticks, tongue depressors or strips of smooth cardboard
Glue, optional

What to do
1. Have the children draw and color a simple sea scene on the paper. Basically, you want to include the sea, the sky, some fish, sea birds, etc. Don't just make line drawings, but fill in the area with color.
2. Cut a slightly curving line through the paper in the sea, making sure to leave a 1" (3 cm) margin on each side of the paper. Place a piece of tape at each end of this curving cut on the backside of the paper for reinforcement. Also be sure to cut it no higher than the length of your support sticks (keep the cut in the bottom one-third of the paper). The stick needs to reach the cut and still be longer than the bottom edge of the paper.
3. With the children's help, draw a small sailboat on a separate sheet of paper. (Heavy weight paper, e.g., watercolor paper, works well for this.) The boat should be a size that will fit in with the scene—not so big or so small as to seem out of place.
4. Cut out the boat and glue or tape it to one end of the support stick. The boat should be wide enough to cover the width of the support stick, so the support stick does not show.
5. Slip the stick through the hole and down past the bottom of the paper. Set the boat into the slot so that it appears to be part of the scene.
6. You can add extra support to the scene by gluing a piece of paper the same size to the top and two sides of the back of the scene. Leave the bottom open for inserting the stick.
7. Sail the boat along the sea, perhaps stopping to swim or to look for a whale! Endless adventures can develop from such a simple starting place.
8. As you can imagine, this simple technique can be adapted for many different kinds of scenes. You could have a little child on your stick, walking in the woods or up a mountain, or an animal wandering through a meadow. Experiment with new possibilities. The more difficult ones may be too hard for the children to do, but they will love to watch and help you make them for the classroom and to play with them when they're done.

More to do
Storytelling: Have the children compose a short story related to their picture and tell it using their art work as a prop.

Related book
My Life With the Wave by Catherine Cowan

Carol Petrash, Reprinted from Earthways

Mouth Painting

5+

Materials
Tempera paint, (assorted colors)
Smocks
Paintbrushes
Plastic wrap
Tape

What to do
1. Talk to the children about experimenting with other ways to draw or paint besides using hands. Tell them that some artists with disabilities adapt by using other parts of their bodies to accomplish tasks.
2. Wrap handles of the brushes with plastic wrap and tape to the brushes.
3. Place paper on the table or the easel.

4. Invite the children to hold the brush between their teeth and paint freely at the easel or on the table.

5. The children can also try holding the paintbrush with their toes and drawing a picture.

More to do

More art: Have the children draw or paint with their non-dominant hand. Wear a blindfold and try to string beads, do a simple puzzle, or write your name.

Related books

Chuck Close, Up Close by Jan Greenberg and Sandra Jordan
Friends in the Park by Rochelle Bunnett
Katy No-Pockets by Emmy Payne
Let's Celebrate Our Differences by Mary L. Williams
Someone Special, Just Like You by Tricia Brown
We're Different, We're the Same by Bobbi Jane Kates

Sandra W. Gratias, Perkasie, PA

multicultural

Northern Lights

4+

Materials
White drawing or construction paper
Strips of brightly colored tissue paper, 3 or more colors
Wide paintbrushes
Water

What to do
1. Talk to the children about the beautiful lines of colors that can be seen in the night sky near the Arctic Circle. Explain that these are called the Northern Lights or Aurora Borealis.
2. Have the children wet down their paper with the paintbrushes and water.
3. Invite them to lay the strips of tissue across the wet paper.
4. Then have the children lift off the tissue strips to reveal lovely lines of color.

More to do
More art: Have the children make a large picture, using large white butcher paper or bulletin board paper and large strips of tissue paper. Hang it from the ceiling. Turn the lights off and let the children shine flashlights, covered with different colors of sandwich wrap, onto the ceiling.

Related books
The Alaska Mother Goose by Shelley Gill
Northern Lights by Diana Cohen Conway
Northern Lights by Michael Kusugak

Sandra Nagel, White Lake, MI

Mask Making

4+

Materials
Paper plates
Construction paper
Feathers
Beads
Craft sticks

Glue
Tissue paper
Crepe paper

What to do

1. Read a book or show pictures to children to get them thinking about different cultures.
2. Let children design a mask using paper plates (grocery bags work, too).
3. Use crepe paper for streamers or decoration.
4. Cut out construction paper for eyes, mouth, nose, etc.
5. Let children create their own masks using the above materials. You may tie a string around the back, or they may tape a craft stick on the back of the paper plate and hold it up in front of them. If using a paper bag, cut out the eyes and mouth and place the bag over the head.

More to do

Dramatic play: Invite the children dress up in "costumes" from other cultures.

Music and movement: Let the children create a dance set to music or make up their own music. Use crepe paper streamers or feathers to create flow of movement.

Snack: Use any recipe from *Kids Around the World Cookbook* by Deri Robins.

Related books

All the Colors of the Earth by Sheila Hamanaka

Children Just Like Me: A Unique Celebration of Children Around the World by B. Kindersley, A. Kindersley, and Susan Copsey

Color Dance by Ann Jonas

Kids Around the World Cookbook by Deri Robins

Sheryl A. Smith, Jonesborough, TN

German School Cones

Materials

Oak tag
Construction paper
Stapler
Stickers
Markers or crayons
Hole punch and reinforcers
Yarn or string
Small prizes and school supplies such as tiny erasers, sharpeners, stickers, pencils, candy

What to do

1. Show the children how to cut a circle from the oak tag and one to match from the construction paper.
2. Demonstrate how to form a cone shape with the oak tag. Cover this with the construction paper and staple them together.
3. Invite the children to decorate their cones with stickers, markers, and crayons.
4. Next, let the children fill their cones with tiny prizes.
5. After the children have filled their cones, punch holes on each side and reinforce, then hang them with yarn or string for everyone to admire.

6. Explain that in Germany boys and girls take a Schultoten or school cone to school with them on the first day. Each child fills the cone and, at the end of the day, exchanges the cone with another child as a welcome-to-school gift.
7. At the end of the day, invite the children to exchange cones and take them home.

Related books
Busy at Day Care Head to Toe by Patricia Brennan Demuth
Friends at School by Rochelle Bunnett
Margaret and Margarita by Lynn Reiser

Lisa M. Chichester, Parkersburg, WV

multicultural

The Colors We Are

4+

Materials
All the Colors We Are by Katie Kissinger
Multicultural paints
Small disposable cups
Cotton Swabs
Scissors
White paper
Markers
Hair-colored yarn, short pieces
Glue

What to do
1. Read *All the Colors We Are* by Katie Kissinger.
2. Talk with the children about similarities and differences among people.
3. Set out multicultural paints in small disposable cups.
4. Give each child a sheet of white paper and invite them to draw the outline of a head and shoulders.
5. Allow children to mix paints in a separate cup to create any skin tone they wish.
6. Encourage the children to paint their pictures using the multicultural paint.
7. They can add faces using markers and glue on yarn as hair.
8. After the faces dry, hang them on a bulletin board or wall to create the display "Our Rainbow Colors."

Related books
All the Colors of the Earth by Sheila Hamanaka
Bright Eyes, Brown Skin by Cheryl Willis Hudson and Bernette G. Ford
The Garden of Happiness by Erika Tamar
How My Family Lives in America by Susan Kuklin
Welcoming Babies by Margy Burns Knight
Why Am I Different? by Norma Simon

Quazonia J. Quarles, Newark, DE

Rainsticks

3+

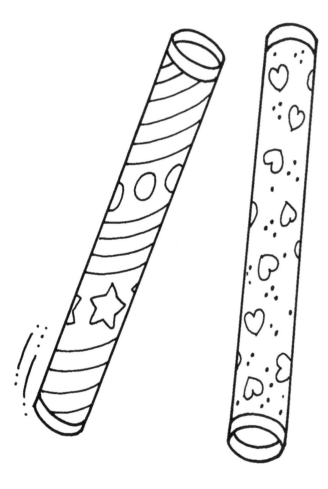

Materials

Cardboard mailing tubes, preferably with metal stoppers
Aluminum foil
Filler, such as sand, pebbles, coins, small plastic objects
Glue
Tempera paint
Paintbrushes

What to do

1. Beforehand, cut sheets of aluminum foil in lengths greater than the length of the mailing tube.
2. Tightly roll a sheet of the foil into a stick shape, then shape it into a coil. Repeat the process with several sheets of aluminum for each rainstick.
3. Make certain that one end of each child's tube is closed securely. Have the children insert the coils in their mailing tube, then add the sand, rice, and beans.
4. Tell the children to close the open end of their tube with the stopper. A bit of glue placed around the edge of the stopper holds it in place.
5. Invite the children to paint their rainstick in a design and color of their choice.

More to do

Music: Play music and invite the children to use their rainsticks as percussion instruments or marching sticks.

Related books

Abiyoyo by Pete Seeger
Five Live Bongos by George Ella Lyon
Meet the Orchestra by Ann Hayes

Su Lorencen, Gray, TN

Rainbow Streamers

3+

Materials
Poster board, cut in 1$\frac{2}{3}$" x 18" (4 cm x 45 cm) strips
Scissors
Crayons
Crepe paper streamers, assorted colors, cut in 8" (20 cm) lengths
Tape or stapler
Recorded music in various rhythms and tempos

What to do
1. Give each child a strip cut from poster board. Invite the children to decorate their strips with crayons.
2. When they are finished, ask them to turn the strip over to the blank side.
3. Put out the colorful streamers and have each of the children choose six streamers, each a different color.
4. Help the children tape or staple one end of each streamer to the strip.
5. When the streamers are attached, staple the ends of the strip together.
6. Play a recording and encourage the children to hold the loops and dance as the streamers float out around them.

More to do
Field trip: Take the children to a dance performance.
Language: Use music to teach opposites: fast/slow, loud/soft, solo/ensemble, choppy/smooth.
More art: Attach streamers to paper towel tubes. Dance with them.

Related books
Angelina Ballerina by Katharine Holabird
Dance Away by George Shannon
Lili on Stage by Rachel Isadora
The Little Band by James Sage
Max by Rachel Isadora

Sandra W. Gratias, Perkasie, PA

Styrofoam Guitar

3+

Materials
Styrofoam food trays, one per child
Markers in assorted colors
Rubber bands in assorted sizes

What to do
1. Have the children color their tray with markers.
2. When they finish coloring, have the children choose five rubber bands in different sizes and stretch them around their tray.
3. Invite the children to strum their new guitar. Encourage them to feel the vibration of the tray and listen to the differences in pitch produced by the rubber bands.

More to do
Music: Bring in a real guitar. Let the children strum the guitar, or play it for them. Make a "junkyard" band with objects you find in the classroom. Play recordings of flamenco guitar and classical guitar by Andre Segovia and Julian Bream; rock and roll by Eric Clapton; and folk guitar by Pete Seeger.
Science: Learn more about pitch by pouring different amounts of water into glasses; gently tap each glass with a spoon, noting the differences in sound.

Related books
The Banza by Diane Wolkstein
Berlioz the Bear by Jan Brett
Max Found Two Sticks by Brian Pinkney

Sandra W. Gratias, Perkasie, PA

What Do You Feel?

3+

Materials
Books or stories concerning feelings
Large sheet of paper
Drawing tools
Musical recordings

What to do
1. Read a number of books or stories about feelings to your class over a period of time. See the suggestions under "Related books" below.
2. Distribute paper and an assortment of drawing tools to the children.
3. Tell them that you are going to play a selection of music and that they are to make a drawing or design that reflects the feelings they experience when the music is playing.
4. When they are finished, ask the children to describe how their drawing portrays their feelings.

More to do
Math: To introduce the concept of a Venn Diagram to the children, draw a happy face and a sad face on the board, overlapping them. When the children listen to a story or piece of music, ask them whether it makes them feel happy, sad, or a mixture of both, then tally their responses on the diagram accordingly.

Movement: Listen to a variety of classical selections that elicit a wide range of emotions and dance to the music with scarves; provide a mirror so the children can watch their own expressions.

Related books
Alexander and the Terrible, Horrible, No Good, Very Bad Day by Judith Viorst
Everybody Has Feelings by Charles E. Avery
Feelings by Aliki
Feelings by Joanne B. Murphy
I Was So Mad by Norma Simon
My Many Colored Days by Dr. Seuss
Rain Song by Lezlie Evans
Sometimes I Like to Cry by Elizabeth and Harry Stanton
The Temper Tantrum Book by Edna Preston Mitchell

Wanda K. Pelton, Lafayette, IN

music

Coffee Can Drums

3+

Materials
Wrapping or construction paper
Scissors
Coffee cans with a plastic lid on each end
Glue
Markers, crayons, or paint
Decorating materials such as stickers, old buttons, sequins, and beads
String or yarn
Mallets or pencils
Masking tape

What to do
1. Ahead of time, cut paper in sheets that will fit around the sides of a coffee can. Remove the top and bottom from the cans.
2. Teach the children the *Drummers' Song*, which is sung to the tune of "One Little, Two Little, Three Little Indians."
   One little, two little, three little drummers,
   Four little, five little, six little drummers
   Seven little, eight little, nine little drummers
   Ten drummers in our band.

3. Help the children cover their can with glue and wrap it in paper. Invite them to decorate their coffee can with a few of the odds and ends.
4. While the children are working, cut lengths of string or yarn that will loop through the can and around the back of the child's neck like a strap. Show the children how to pass the string through one end of the can and out the other, then tie the ends together.
5. Finally, have the children place a lid on each end of their coffee can.
6. For playing the drums, provide mallets or pencils with ends that are protected with a wad of masking tape; some children will prefer to use their hands.

More to do
Games: Have the children sit on the floor in a circle with the drums on the floor in front of them. Play music and have the children beat their drum once, taking turns around the circle. When the music stops, the last drummer moves to the center of the circle and plays along on another hand-made instrument until there is an entire orchestra.

Related books

Five Live Bongos by George Ella Lyon
Pots and Pans by Patricia Hubbell
Thump, Thump, Rat-a-Tat-Tat by Gene Baer

Margery A. Kranyik, Hyde Park, MA

 **music**

Dancing Crayons

 4+

Materials
Clipboards
White or manila paper, 8" x 12" (20 cm x 30 cm)
Crayons or markers in assorted colors
Music recordings in various styles, tempos, rhythms, and moods such as "Fantasia," "Saint Saen's
Carnival of the Animals," Irish ballads, and Latin music

What to do
1. Have each child find a place in the room where she can draw and not disturb other children. Provide the children with clipboards, if necessary.
2. Supply the children with paper and crayons or markers.
3. Play a selection of music.
4. Encourage the children to listen to the music and let their crayons dance, or draw and color, to the rhythm; their drawings will reflect what the music makes them feel. Reassure the children that there is no right or wrong interpretation.
5. After a few minutes, put on a new selection.
6. When the new selection begins, tell the children they may continue working on the same drawing or begin a new one.

More to do
More art: Do the same exercise using different media such as clay, paint, or pastels. Share the children's drawings with the other children and invite the others to guess which music was playing.
Movement: Play a variety of music selections and encourage the children to dance and move.
Music: Listen to a recording such as "Peter and the Wolf" where the story is conveyed through the music. Supply the children with instruments and encourage them to create a story or retell a familiar one.

Related books
All I See by Cynthia Rylant
Be Bop by Chris Raschka
The Little Band by James Sage
The Maestro Plays by Vladimir Radunsky
The Philharmonic Gets Dressed by Jane Kuskin
Zin Zin Goes the Violin by Marjorie Priceman

Sandra W. Gratias, Perkasie, PA

Dream Catcher

Materials
Plastic lids like those from butter tubs
Yarn
Adult scissors

What to do
1. Prepare the lids by cutting slits or notches in the edge, all the way around the outer edge.
2. Show the children how to wrap the yarn around the lid, pulling into the notches.
3. At the end, leave extra yarn to loop and hang the dream catcher from.

More to do
Circle time: Explain the idea behind the dream catcher: The web of the dream catcher filters all dreams. Good dreams pass through the center hole down the feather to the sleeping person. The bad dreams get caught in the web and can't get through. Ask what dreams they might want the catcher to catch, and what dreams they would like to get through.
More art: Feathers, beads, or stones can be hung from the bottom of the dream catcher.

Related books
Dancing With the Indians by Angela Shelf Medearis
Dreamcatcher by Audrey Osofsky
My House Has Stars by Megan McDonald
Raven: A Trickster Tale From the Pacific Northwest by Gerald McDermott
Red Bird by Barbara Mitchell

Sandra Nagel, White Lake, MI

Pattern Headbands

3+

Materials
Sentence strips or construction paper, cut into 3" (8 cm) wide strips
Strips of colored construction paper, 1" (3 cm) wide
Scissors
Glue
Stapler

What to do
1. Show the children how to hold a colored construction paper strip and cut it into square pieces.
2. Next, show the children how to cut each square piece from corner to corner and make triangles.
3. Give the children strips and safety scissors and encourage them to cut squares and triangles so that they have an assortment to choose from for their headbands.
4. Have the children glue the shapes onto the sentence strips in a pattern.
5. Measure the strips around each child's head and staple to make a headband.

More to do
More art: Rubber stamps or vegetable prints can be used in place of the cutout shapes. Watercolors may be used to paint the students' faces with traditional Native American designs.
Music: The headbands may be worn with paper bag costumes. Using rhythm band instruments, have a class performance with some children playing a steady beat on the drums and the others dancing.

Related books
Dancing With the Indians by Angela Shelf Medearis
Did You Hear Wind Sing Your Name? by Sandra De Coteau Orie
My Navajo Sister by Eleanor Schick

Barbara Saul, Eureka, CA

Native American Shield

Materials
String, cut in 10″ to 14″ (23 cm-33 cm) lengths
Brightly colored construction paper cut
    into circles
Feathers
Beads
Hole punch
Scissors
Glue

What to do
1. Have each child choose two circles of construction paper in different colors. Cut the circles in half and then in quarters.
2. Invite the children to make a circle with four of the pieces by gluing them to a complete circle. An alternating pattern can be made here.
3. Punch a hole on the edge of the circle, and use the string to make a loop for hanging.
4. Attach strings with feathers and beads to the loop or glue them directly to the circle pattern.
5. For a more advanced design, use more pieces to make the circle.

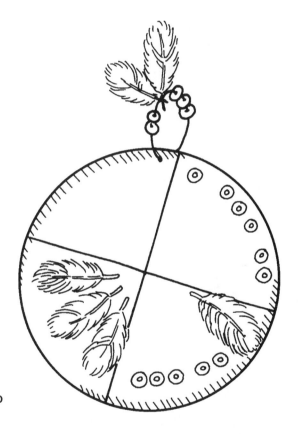

Related books
Dancing With the Indians by Angela Shelf Medearis
Dreamcatcher by Audrey Osofsky
My House Has Stars by Megan McDonald

Sandra Nagel, White Lake, MI

native americans

Making Corn Husk Dolls

Materials
Cornhusks
Pan of warm water
Heavy thread—buttonhole thread or embroidery floss works well
Scissors
Stuffing wool or cotton and material scraps for clothes, optional

What to do
1. Soak the cornhusks in warm water for about ½ hour.
2. Tie 12 husks together tightly at the top.
3. To make the head, tie a neck a short way down from the top. You can stuff a little wool or cotton in here if you like.
4. Separate three husks on both sides, and tie them halfway down for the arms. Trim the excess.
5. To make the body, tie the remaining husks just above halfway down.
6. Make legs by tying three husks on each side, a bit up from the ends. Trim the ends.
7. Add clothing—scarves, hats, shawls, skirts, jackets, etc.
8. Make cornhusk children by starting with shorter husks.

Related books
Corn Is Maize: The Gift of the Indians by Aliki
Knots on a Counting Rope by Bill Martin, Jr., and John Archambault
My Navajo Sister by Eleanor Schick

Carol Petrash, Reprinted from Earthways

Licence Plate Rubbings   3+

Materials
4 or 5 different license plates
Light colored construction
    paper
Chunky crayons in dark colors

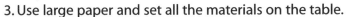

What to do
1. Gather the license plates, crayons, and paper.
2. Peel the paper off the crayons.
3. Use large paper and set all the materials on the table.
4. Invite each child to choose a license plate and a piece of paper.
5. Have each child place the paper on top of the license plate and rub with the long side of a crayon.
6. Repeat with different colors of crayon, or different license plates, or both.

More to do
Language: Help the children learn their phone numbers and addresses.
Math: Set out the flannel board, felt numbers, and felt pieces cut into small shapes.
Example: "1" and one circle, "2" and two squares, "3" and three triangles. Invite the children to put the numbers and shapes together on the flannel board.
More art: Invite the children to roll out playdough and use it to bend and form into numbers.

Related books
Count and See by Tana Hoban
Every Buddy Counts by Stuart J. Murphy
A Million Fish…More or Less by Patricia C. McKissack
Over in the Meadow by John Langstaff

Cory McIntyre, Crystal Lake, IL

numbers

Count and Sprinkle

3+

Materials
Dice
Graham crackers or cookies
Paper plates
Sprinkles in a bowl
Icing
Plastic knives
Small spoon

What to do
1. Give each child a graham cracker.
2. Put a little icing on a knife and show the children how to spread the icing on their cracker.
3. Talk to the children about the dice. Show them how to count the dots.
4. Let each child roll the dice and read the number. They can then fill the spoon with sprinkles as many times as the number they rolled, tipping the spoon over their iced cracker after each filling.
5. Soon everyone is laughing, hoping to roll a six!

Related books
Eating the Alphabet: Fruits and Vegetables From A to Z by Lois Ehlert
If You Give a Mouse a Cookie by Laura Joffe Numeroff
Lunch by Denise Fleming

Sandra Hutchins Lucas, Cox's Creek, KY

Number Book

3+

Materials
Poster board
Scissors
Felt-tipped pen
Glue
Paper

numbers

Crayons without paper wrapping
Stickers
Stapler

What to do

1. Ahead of time, cut poster board into square or rectangular sheets. Write a number on each sheet, then draw the corresponding number of dots next to the number. Trace over the numbers and dots with a thick line of glue. Let the sheets dry until the glue is transparent, or approximately 24 hours.
2. Ask the children to place their paper over one of the number sheets and rub the side of their crayon across the paper, creating a crayon image of the number and dots. When they finish with one number, have them go on to the next, using a clean sheet of paper, until they have completed a full set.
3. Let the children put the correct number of stickers on each paper.
4. Invite the children to design a decorative cover. Fasten the children's papers with a stapler.

Related books

One Is One by Tasha Tudor
Ten Black Dots Donald Crews
Twelve Ways to Get to Eleven by Eve Merriam

BetteJane Grey, Woodbridge, VA

Bean Count

Materials

Washed recycled Styrofoam meat trays
Assorted dried beans and legumes
Large bowl
Marker

What to do

1. Ahead of time, write the numbers 1 through 10 on the Styrofoam trays, one number per tray.
2. Set out the bowl of beans and the 10 Styrofoam meat trays.
3. One at a time, invite the children to count out the number of beans to match the number in each tray, and put those beans in the tray.
4. When everyone has had a chance to count the beans, invite the children to make interesting mosaics or designs with the beans.

More to do
Math: Put all the beans in a large glass jar and invite the children to guess how many are inside.
More art: Give the children small jars and invite them to arrange the colorful beans in interesting layers, much like sand art.
Snack: Make bean soup and enjoy!

Related books
Let's Count It Out, Jesse Bear by Nancy White Carlstrom
More Than One by Miriam Schlein
The Best Bug Parade by Stuart J. Murphy

Dani Rosensteel, Payson, AZ

Sew a Plate

Materials
Paper plates
Crayons and markers
Hole punch
Yarn
Plastic yarn needles
Scissors
Tape

What to do
1. Write a number in the center of each plate. For younger children, draw a corresponding number of circles on the plate.
2. Encourage younger children to color in the circles; invite older children to draw a picture showing the correct number; for example, suggest that they draw three apples for the number 3.
3. When they finish, help the children punch holes around the edge of their plate.
4. Tie a piece of yarn to the first hole or tape it to the bottom of the plate. Help the children thread their needle, if they are using one; if they are not using a needle, wrap a piece of tape around the end of the yarn.
5. Show them how to weave the yarn through the openings. Tie a knot when they finish their border.
6. Invite the children to decorate their plates with markers or crayons.

More to do

Math: Arrange the plates in order while singing a counting song. Play a counting game with books, blocks, plastic animals, or even the children's shoes; place the correct number of objects next to each plate.

More art: Design a colorful number line for your bulletin board. Make movable cardboard or paper figures in the shape of a number using paper fasteners.

Snack: Count the crackers on your plate, then subtract them as you eat them.

Related books

Knots on a Counting Rope by Bill Martin, Jr., and John Archambault
Number One Number Fun by Kay Chorao
One Is One by Tasha Tudor

Tina Slater, Silver Spring, MD

Measuring Fun

Materials

Balls of yarn (red, yellow, blue, green)
Grids made from plastic rings (used with six-packs of canned soda)

What to do

1. Ahead of time, prepare the grid by stapling plastic rings together. Staple several grids together to create a larger one, if you want.
2. Give children the yarn and invite them to measure each other. They can work in groups of three, with one child lying down on the floor, another child holding the yarn at his head, and the third child cutting the yarn at his feet.
3. When all three are measured, invite the children to weave their yarn through the grid.
4. Continue steps two and three until all children are measured, and all the yarn used is woven into the grid.

More to do

More art: Hang the weaving in the hallway and write a note inviting parents and other teachers to add other materials (e.g., dried materials, lace, ribbon, small toys) to the project. Expect a colorful, interesting result. The children love looking for new additions.

Related books

Abuela's Weave by Omar S. Castaneda
Kente Colors by Debbi Chocolate

Cary Peterson, Pittsburgh, PA

Mary, Mary, Quite Contrary

Materials
Pipe cleaners, 12" (30 cm)
Catalogs, specifically doll, children's clothing, and toy catalogs
Scissors
White glue
Construction paper in white and pastel colors
Fine-point black marker
Crayons
Glitter, optional
Spool of sturdy white thread or fishing line

What to do
1. Read the nursery rhyme, "Mary, Mary, Quite Contrary." Tell the children that they are going to make a mobile of Mary.

   Mary, Mary, Quite Contrary
   Mary, Mary, quite contrary,
   How does your garden grow?
   With silver bells and cockle shells
   And pretty maids all in a row.

2. Bend the pipe cleaners into the shape of a small hanger.
3. Have the children cut out pictures of a girl and a flower and glue them to white paper.
4. Help the children draw an oval shape with fine-point marker around both pictures. Set the pictures aside while the glue dries.
5. Trace the shape of a watering can onto pastel-colored construction paper for each child. Invite the children to decorate their watering can with crayons.
6. Help the children draw an oval shape around the watering can.
7. Have them cut out the three oval shapes and decorate them with glitter, if they choose.
8. Attach thread or fishing line to the oval shapes.
9. Tie the thread or line to the hanger.

More to do
Cooking: Cut cookie dough in the shape of nursery rhyme characters and props, then bake them for a special treat.
Dramatic play: Provide simple props such as a watering can, a candleholder, a spider puppet, and doll and cradle. Invite the children to perform their favorite nursery rhymes.

nursery rhymes

More art: Make several mobiles with characters from other nursery rhymes. Design a mural with nursery rhyme characters. Make flannel-backed pieces and use them on a flannel board.

Original poem
How Do Flowers Grow?

There is something I would like to know.
How do tiny seeds into pretty flowers grow?
First seeds need rich brown soil for a flower bed.
So the little tiny buds can poke out their heads.
Second, the warm sun needs to shine every day.
To warm the seeds so they will grow. Hurray!
Last, seeds need many wet warm spring showers.
And at last those seeds become lovely flowers.

Related books
James Marshall's Mother Goose by James Marshall
Mother Goose Favorites, A Pop-up Book by Ernest Nister
My Very First Mother Goose by Iona Opie
The Random House Book of Poetry for Children by Jack Prelutsky

Mary Brehm, Aurora, OH

Little Boy Blues

3+

Materials
4 or 5 shades of blue paint
Paper
Paintbrushes

What to do
1. Teach "Little Boy Blue" to the children.

   Little Boy Blue
   Come blow your horn.
   The sheep's in the meadow.
   The cows in the corn.
   Where is the little boy
   Who looks after the sheep?
   He's under the haystack
   Fast asleep.
   Shall I wake him?
   No! Not I.
   For if I do, he's sure to cry.

2. At the art table, have white paper and many shades of blue paint available.
3. Encourage the children to paint using only the blue colors.
4. Introduce words like "dark blue" and "sky blue" to expand vocabulary.

More to do
More art: Go on a "blue hunt" to look for other blue items around the classroom. Make a blue collage of blue items.

Related books
Jamaica's Blue Marker by Juanita Havill
Little Blue and Little Yellow by Leo Lionni
The Rainbow Fish by Marcus Pfister
Red is Best by Kathy Stinson

Ann Wenger, Harrisonburg, VA

Humpty-Dumpty Put-together 3+

Materials
Construction paper
Glue
Markers or crayons

What to do
1. Cut out patterns (one for each child) for Humpty's parts: egg-shaped body, two arms, and two legs. Depending on the age group, make more or fewer pieces.
2. For a background, draw a brick wall on paper and make copies.
3. Have children put Humpty-Dumpty back together again by gluing the parts together on the brick wall background.
4. Invite the children to draw a face on Humpty Dumpty and add background details such as sun, clouds, a hat, etc.

More to do
Language: Using a flannel board and felt pieces, put Humpty-Dumpty together again while reciting the rhyme with the class.

Humpty-Dumpty sat on a wall.
Humpty-Dumpty had a great fall.
All the King's horses and all the King's men
Couldn't put Humpty together again.

Snack: Crack real eggs and scramble them.

Related books
James Marshall's Mother Goose by James Marshall
Nursery Tales Around the World by Judy Sierra

Suzanne Pearson, Winchester, VA

Peter, Peter, Pumpkin Eater   3+

Materials
Pumpkin shape per child cut from a full sheet of orange construction paper
White paper, one 3" x 3" (8 cm x 8 cm) piece per child
Glue
Crayons or markers

What to do
1. Ahead of time, make a flap in the front of each pumpkin shape. Draw a square door that is about 2" by 2" (5 cm by 5 cm). Make one vertical solid line and three dotted lines. Cut the flap so it will open by cutting on the dotted lines (the solid line is the "hinge" of the door). Glue the piece of white paper onto the backside of the pumpkin so when the children open the flap they know where to draw the picture.

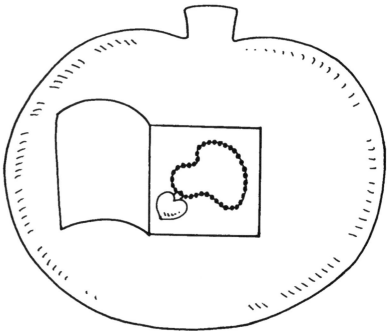

2. Read "Peter, Peter, Pumpkin Eater." Ask the kids what Peter was afraid of losing (his wife) and what he did about it (hid her inside a pumpkin shell).

Peter, Peter, Pumpkin Eater
Had a wife and couldn't keep her.
Put her in a pumpkin shell,
And there he kept her very well.

3. Have them think of something that they are afraid of losing.
4. Give them a pumpkin and have them draw the object they don't want to lose inside the door of their pumpkin.

More to do
More art: Have the kids share their work by changing the nursery rhyme to fit their project. For example:

David, David, pumpkin eater,
Had a dog and couldn't keep her.
He put her in a pumpkin shell and
There he kept her very well.

Related books
Grandmother's Nursery Rhymes/Las Nanas de Abuelita by Nelly Jaramillo
It's Pumpkin Time by Zoe Hall

Vicki Whitehead, Ft. Worth, TX

Plum Pie

Materials
Blue and red (or magenta) tempera paint
Paper plates
Plastic spoons
Paper cups

What to do
1. Read the nursery rhyme "Little Jack Horner" to the children.
2. Give each child two paper cups with a little blue tempera in one and red in the other.
3. Allow children to mix their own purple paint to make plum pies.
4. Then they can "stick their thumb and pull out a plum" and make thumbprint plumbs on their paper plates.

More to do
More art: Write the nursery rhyme on a folded little booklet to put their thumbprints on and take home.

Little Jack Horner sat in a corner,
Eating his Christmas pie.
He put in his thumb
And pulled out a plum.
And said, "What a good boy am I!"

Snack: Make a real pie with the children, or taste plums.

Related books
Each Peach Pear Plum by Janet and Allan Ahlberg
The Missing Tarts by B.G. Hennessy
Richard Scarry's Best Mother Goose Ever by Richard Scarry

Laura Durbrow, Lake Oswego, OR

Old King Cole's Crown

Materials
"Old King Cole"
Pictures of crowns
Assorted faux jewels
Sentence strips
Markers

What to do
1. Read "Old King Cole" to the children. Show the children pictures of crowns and their jewels, noting the shape of the jewels. Invite the children to look over an assortment of faux jewelry.

   Old King Cole was a merry old soul,
   And a merry old soul was he.
   He called for his pipe,
   And he called for his drum,
   And he called for his fiddlers three.

2. Distribute yellow sentence strips and markers.
3. Ask the children to design jewels on their strip, or crown, by drawing a variety of shapes such as squares, rectangles, diamonds, circles, and triangles. Invite the children to color the "jewels" in a variety of colors.
4. When the children finish, fit the strip around their head; holding the ends together, remove the strip from their head, then staple the ends from the inside of the crown.
5. Have the children wear their crowns and recite "Old King Cole" again.

More to do
Games: Cut out shapes from construction paper and divide them in half; give each child one-half of a shape and ask them to find the matching half.

More art: Decorate the crowns with sequins, glitter, or glitter glue for a shiny appearance. Cut sponges in a variety of shapes and create sponge paintings. Draw shapes with stencils, then draw a picture using only shapes. Make crayon rubbings of shapes. Design sun catchers in a variety of shapes using construction paper and colored cellophane.

Snack: Cut fruit and cheese in a variety of shapes.

Related books

King Bidgood's in the Bathtub by Audrey Wood
What Am I? Looking Through Shapes at Apples and Grapes by N.N. Charles

Charlene Woodham Peace, Semmes, AL

There Was an Old Woman

Materials

A variety of old shoes
Tempera paint
Styrofoam trays or aluminum pans, large
Mural paper, 3' x 6' (1 m x 2 m)
Newspapers

What to do

1. Read or recite the nursery rhyme, "There Was an Old Woman Who Lived in a Shoe." Tell the children that they are going to have some fun with shoes.

   There was an old woman who lived in a shoe.
   She had so many children, she didn't know what to do.
   She gave them some broth without any bread,
   And kissed them all soundly and sent them to bed.

2. Make a display of different kinds of old shoes.
3. Cover a large area of the floor with newspapers and lay the mural paper on top of them.
4. Pour different colors of tempera paint in the trays.
5. Invite the children to select a pair of shoes from the different styles and put them on.
6. One by one, encourage the children to select a tray of paint and step into it, then walk on the mural paper. To avoid slipping, hold the child's hand while she walks on the paper.
7. Continue until everyone has had a chance to leave footprints on the paper.

More to do
Math: Make a graph that shows the different types, sizes, and colors of shoes that the children wore for the art activity.
More art: Cut the mural in the shape of a giant shoe.

Related books

All About Alfie by Shirley Hughes
Frogs in Clogs by Sheila White Samton
Shoes, Shoes, Shoes by Ann Morris

Sandra Fisher, Kutztown, PA

Smooth Sailing

3+

Materials
Scissors
Construction paper
Crayons or markers
Stickers
Styrofoam meat trays
Plastic straws
Tape
Plasticene or florist's clay

What to do
1. Ahead of time, cut triangle shapes for sails from construction paper approximately 4" by 4" by 7" (10 cm by 10 cm by 18 cm). Let older children cut out their own triangles.
2. Invite the children to decorate both sides of the sail and the Styrofoam tray with markers, crayons, or stickers.
3. When they are finished, help them tape a straw along one edge of their sail.
4. Show the children how to roll some clay into a ball and press it into the middle of the tray. Have them stand the straw up in the clay.
5. Sail the boats in a sink full of water or a small wading pool.

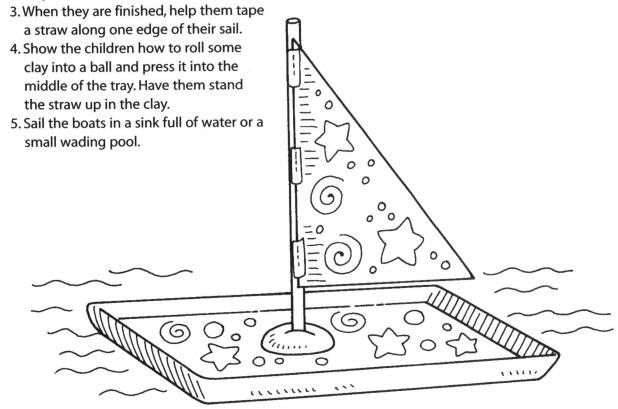

Oceans

More to do
Dramatic play: Put the children's boats in a wading pool and hold a regatta; enjoy lemonade and fish crackers while wearing sunglasses and silly handmade sun hats.
More art: Mold figures from clay to ride in the boat and cut fish shapes out of Styrofoam trays, then float them in the water.

Related books
The Cinder-Eyed Cats by Eric Rohmann
Little Toot by Hardie Gramatky
Noah's Ark by Peter Spier
Salty Dog by Gloria Rand

Tina Slater, Silver Spring, MD

Ocean in a Bottle

Materials
Construction paper
Scissors
Poster board patterns, optional
Pitcher
Water
Blue food coloring
8 or 10 oz. (250 or 300 mL) plastic bottles with screw-on caps
Tiny seashells
Gold glitter
Waterproof tape

More to do
1. Ahead of time, cut fish and sea plants or animals from construction paper. Provide some patterns for older children to trace and cut, if you choose.
2. Fill a large pitcher with water and add a few drops of blue food coloring, then stir.
3. Fill each child's bottle, refilling the pitcher as needed.
4. Help the children put the shapes and seashells into the bottle and sprinkle glitter into the water.
5. Replace the cap on the bottle and secure the cap with tape, then tell the children to give their bottles a shake.
Enjoy watching the fish swim and seashells tumble and toss in the waves.

More to do
More art: Paint seashells and use as paperweights or hanging ornaments.
Sand and water table: Bury seashells and plastic sand creatures in the sand before the children arrive.
Science: Decorate the room with models of undersea creatures and bring in seashells for the children to touch and examine.

Related books
Edward and the Pirates by David McPhail
Is This a House for Hermit Crab? by Megan McDonald
Until I Saw the Sea: A Collection of Seashore Poems edited by Alison Shaw

Cindy Paddock, Palm Bay, FL

Sea Creature Plates

Materials
Blue or white plates, preferably Styrofoam
A variety of construction paper fish, whales, dolphins, and other sea creatures
Glue
2 or 3 shades of green crepe paper or yarn
Tiny seashells
Clear or blue plastic wrap or cellophane
Tape

What to do
1. Have the children glue the paper sea creatures on to their plate, then add yarn or crepe paper seaweed.
2. Let the glue dry completely.
3. Ask the children to select four or five tiny seashells for their ocean scene and set them on the plate. Do not glue the shells onto the plate.
4. Seal the plate with plastic wrap. Use clear wrap if the plates are blue or blue wrap if

the plates are white. Pull the wrap tightly to remove wrinkles and secure with tape on the back of the plate.

More to do

Language: Ask the children to dictate or write a few sentences about the seashore; have them decorate paper cut in the shape of a shell, bucket, seahorse, or the like, then tape their words on the reverse side.

Math: Bring in shells and other objects from the seashore, then make a picture graph of the collection.

Movement: Sit in a circle and toss a large beach ball to each other. Call out a name or word related to the ocean with each toss.

Snack: Serve blue gelatin, with gummy candy sharks and whipped cream.

Related books

The Magic School Bus on the Ocean Floor by Joanna Cole
The Seashore by Gallimard Jeunesse and Elisabeth Cohat
The Underwater Alphabet Book by Jerry Pallotta
Whale and Dolphin by Vincent Serventy

Sheryl A. Smith, Jonesborough, TN

Seashell Frames

Materials

Thin magnetic or cardboard sheets, 3" x 5" (8 cm x 13 cm)
Seashells
Glue
Watercolor paints and brushes
Crayons or markers
Beads or sequins

What to do

1. Ahead of time, cut an opening in the center of the magnetic or cardboard sheet to form a frame for each child. The opening can be in any shape.
2. Have the children glue seashells onto their frame.
3. Supply watercolors, crayons, and markers to the children and encourage them to paint the seashells and color their frame in a design of their choice.
4. When they are finished, have them add a few beads or sequins as decoration.

More to do

Dramatic play: Add props such as sunglasses, a picnic basket, a beach bag, and ball to the play area, then invite the children to pretend they are spending the afternoon at the seashore.

Language: Have the children don gear such as goggles and colorful beach hats, then videotape them as they describe their favorite kind of beach day or what it would be like to swim with dolphins.

More art: Attach a photo and wrap in handmade paper for Father's Day or another special occasion. Glue lightweight shells on paper in a pattern or design. Add fine sand and small shells to a clear plastic bottle. Layer colored sand in a clear bottle.

Sand and water table: Add seashells, buckets, sifters, and shovels to the table.

Science: Weigh seashells and compare their size, texture, and color. Record your observations on a colorful chart.

Related books

Oceans by Katharine Jones Carter
Seashore by David Burnie
The Seashore by Gallimard Jeunesse and Elisabeth Cohat

Sharon Max, St. Louis, MO

Class Octopus

Materials

Tag board or poster board
Scissors
Markers or crayons
Small collage supplies such as buttons, yarn, sequins, beads, and small bits of fabric
Glue
Paper fasteners

What to do

1. To prepare, cut out a large circle from tag board and draw a face on it. Cut out eight tentacles, between 12" and 18" (30 cm and 45 cm).
2. Distribute one tentacle to every two or three children. Have the children decorate the tentacles using crayons, markers, and small collage supplies.
3. When the children are finished, fasten the tentacles around the edge of the circle with paper fasteners.
4. Let the children gently move the tentacles back and forth, then hang the octopus in a display or mural of sea life.

More to do

Games: Cut a large octopus head and tentacles from poster board and play Pin the Tentacles on the Octopus. Or, cut eight small tentacles and a head from cardboard for each team and conduct a relay race; the first team to place all eight tentacles on their octopus wins.

Math: Count the tentacles on the octopus; divide them in half and quarters. Number the tentacles with a magic marker.

Related books

My Visit to the Aquarium by Aliki
Rainbow Fish by Marcus Pfister
Until I Saw the Sea: A Collection of Seashore Poems edited by Alison Shaw

Suzanne Pearson, Winchester, VA

Rainbow Fish

3+

Materials
Rainbow Fish by Marcus Pfister
Fingerpaint paper
Permanent marker
Sweetened condensed milk
Blue shades of tempera paint, regular or neon
Iridescent sequins, small and large
Fine iridescent shades of glitter
Scissors

What to do
1. Before you begin, read *Rainbow Fish* to the children.
2. Using Pfister's subject as a model, draw a large outline of a fish on fingerpaint paper using permanent marker.
3. Drizzle sweetened condensed milk all over the fish outline.
4. add drops of blue tempera paint to the drizzled milk. There should be more milk than paint. That way, when the paint dries it will be shiny and glossy.
5. Invite the children to paint with their fingers, pushing the paint over the surface of the fish.
6. When they are finished, have them wash their hands.
7. While the fish are still wet, have the children sprinkle sequins and "angel dust" glitter over their surface.
8. Allow the fish to dry, then cut along the outline and hang them on the wall or bulletin board.

More to do
Circle time: Use *Rainbow Fish* to reinforce themes of friendship and sharing.
Dramatic play: Equip the play area with beach and diving equipment such as a scuba mask, foot fins, goggles, life jackets, a rocker boat or one-man raft, swim suits, beach towels, sunglasses, flipflops, beach bags, and beach balls.

Related books
Dawn by Uri Shulevitz
Fish Faces by Norbert Wu
My Visit to the Aquarium by Aliki

Shawn Perlich, Burnsville, MN

Stunning Starfish

3+

Materials
Paint cup
Fine sand
Powdered tempera paint
Water
Starfish cut-outs, one per child
Plastic teaspoons
Paintbrushes

What to do
1. In a paint cup, mix sand and tempera paint in a color of your choice. Add water until the mixture has the consistency of oatmeal. Older children can help mix the ingredients.
2. Have the children paint their starfish using a teaspoon or brush.
3. Lay the starfish flat to dry.

More to do
More art: Experiment with other ingredients when mixing paint, including salt, oatmeal, cornstarch, and sawdust. Paint a mural of the beach or sea using various textures of paint. Sand blocks of wood with different grits of sandpaper, and ask the children to decide which is the most effective.

Sand and water table: Let the children experiment and play with fine sand and seashells, using sifters and measuring cups.

Science: Hide smooth and rough objects in a touch-and-guess box and have the children identify them.

Related books
Is This a House for Hermit Crab? by Megan McDonald
Until I Saw the Sea: A Collection of Seashore Poems edited by Alison Shaw

Linda S. Andrews, Sonora, CA

Under the Sea

Materials
Large, lightweight frame or framing mat
Construction paper in a variety of colors
Crayons
Glitter
Sequins
Googly eyes
Glue
Scissors
Hole punch
Strong thread or fishing line
Green and blue crepe paper

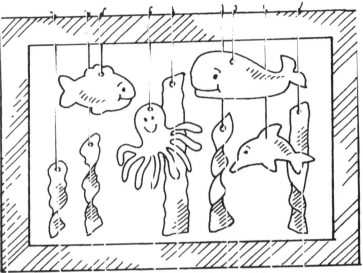

What to do
1. Ahead of time, make or purchase a large, lightweight frame or framing mat. The frame should not have a back.
2. Invite the children to draw and color a picture of a sea creature on construction paper.
3. Have them decorate their creature with sequins, googly eyes, and glitter.
4. When they are finished, have the children cut their creature out, turn it over, and decorate the opposite side.
5. Punch a hole in the top of each child's project. Attach thread or fishing line to each creature, varying the length. Suspend the creatures from the top of the frame. The creatures should hang at different heights.
6. Help the children twist the crepe paper. Fold it over at one end to reinforce it and punch a hole. Use thread or fishing line to suspend the grass from the top of the frame.
7. Hang the frame in an open area or in front of a large window.

More to do
Cooking: Cut seashell shapes from cookie dough, then bake.
More art: Suspend sea creatures from a mobile.

Related books
Animals of the Ocean by Stephen Savage
I Am the Ocean by Suzanne Marshak
The Living Ocean by Robert A. Mattson
Ocean by Seymour Simon
Rainbow Fish by Marcus Pfister

Virginia Jean Herrod, Columbia, SC

Oceans

Fantastic Fish

4+

Materials
Pictures of fish in children's books
White construction paper
Pencils
Scissors
Tissue paper in a variety of colors, cut in small squares
Small containers of water
Paintbrushes

What to do
1. Invite the children to look through books and choose their favorite kind of fish.
2. Have the children draw their favorite fish on construction paper in pencil. Encourage them to cover most of the paper with their drawing. When they are finished, have them cut out their picture.
3. With their pictures lying flat, tell the children to place the tissue paper squares over the entire surface of the fish.
4. When you see that the fish are completely covered, have the children gently brush the tissue paper squares with water.
5. Encourage the children to wait about 20 seconds, then remove the tissue squares from their fish, leaving a colorful imprint of the tissue paper dye.

More to do
Field trip: Visit an aquarium or fish store.
Games: Fish for cardboard cut-outs with a handmade pole; glue a paper clip to each fish and attach a magnet at the end of the fishing line.
Math: Introduce a Venn Diagram to the class by inviting them to taste three varieties of goldfish crackers and choose their favorites. Tally their responses in a diagram with three large, overlapping fish shapes.

Related books
My Life With the Wave by Catherine Cowan from a story by Octavio Paz
Rainbow Fish by Marcus Pfister
Swimmy by Leo Lionni

Kimberle S. Byrd, Kalamazoo, MI

oceans

Deep Blue Sea

Materials
White art paper
Crayons
Small pieces of sponge, one per child
Cups of water
Paper towels
Watercolor sets and brushes
Silver or white glitter or glitter glue
Glue

What to do
1. Give each child a piece of paper and invite him or her to draw an underwater scene with crayons. The scene should include one large fish.
2. Ask the children to color everything in their picture but the water. Encourage them to press hard with their crayons.
3. Show the children how to saturate their sponge with water, then move the sponge across the surface of their paper, pressing water from the sponge as they do so.
4. Have the children wet the blue paint in their watercolor set with the brush, then apply the paint to their picture, creating a blue watercolor wash over their crayon drawing.
5. Allow the paintings to dry.
6. When the paintings have dried, have the children decorate the fins of their fish with glitter.

More to do
Circle time: Brainstorm about ways in which the children share. Record the ideas on an undersea mural or on the reverse side of their underwater scene.
More art: Create a mural of an undersea world using pastels.

Related books
Dazzle the Dinosaur by Marcus Pfister
Rainbow Fish by Marcus Pfister
Rainbow Fish and the Big Blue Whale by Marcus Pfister

Barbara Saul, Eureka, CA

oceans

Stuffed Fish

4+

Materials
Large easel paper
Paper clips
Pencils
Scissors
Stapler
Tempera paints and brushes
Felt-tip pens
Newspaper
String cut in 3' (1 m) lengths

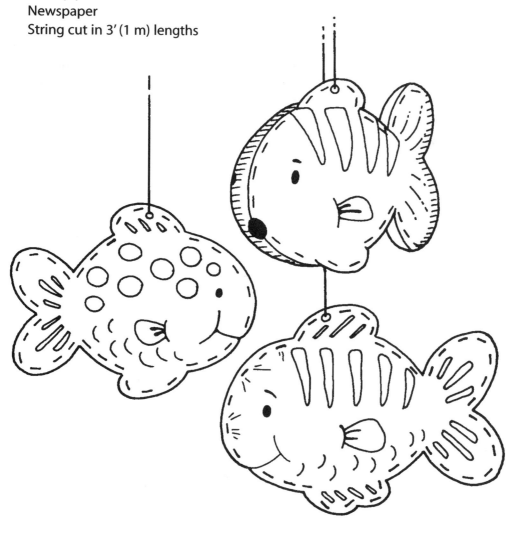

oceans

What to do

1. Beforehand, align two pieces of easel paper so the edges match and hold them together with paper clips. Draw the outline of a large fish on the top paper, then cut along the outline of the fish through both pieces of paper. Staple the papers together around the perimeter of the fish, leaving a 4" or 5" (10 cm or 13 cm) opening. Prepare a fish for each child in the class.
2. Have the children paint one side of their fish.
3. When one side has dried, have them paint the opposite side.
4. Help the children draw scales, fins, gills, eyes, and a mouth using felt-tipped pens.
5. While the paint is drying, tell the children to crumple sheets of newspaper. When the fish is dry on both sides, show the children how to stuff the fish with newspaper through the opening.
6. Close the opening with staples.
7. If a child chooses to use the fish as a kite, attach the length of string to the front of the fish; alternatively, if the child chooses to hang the fish from the ceiling or a mobile, attach the string to the top of the fish.

More to do

Field trip: Visit an aquarium or pet store.

More art: Make a fishing pole from a dowel and fishing line, then decorate cardboard fish cut-outs and hang them along the fishing line. Hang your fishing pole mobile from the ceiling.

Related books

Just Like Daddy by Frank Asch
One Fish, Two Fish, Red Fish, Blue Fish by Dr. Seuss
Rainbow Fish by Marcus Pfister

Barbara Saul, Eureka, CA

Whale Pillows

5+

Materials

Easel paper
Pencils
Large pieces of gray or black felt, two per child
Sewing pins
Scissors
Yarn needles
Yarn

White felt squares or googly eyes
Glue gun
Pillow stuffing

What to do

1. Help the children draw a large whale on easel paper in pencil.
2. Lay two pieces of felt on top of one another and pin the paper pattern to the felt. Cut out the whale shape.
3. Thread the yarn needles and show the children how to sew the two pieces of felt together. Sew around the edge of the whale, leaving an opening where the stuffing will be inserted.
4. Glue a googly eye on each side of the whale using the glue gun (adult only); or, if you choose, help the children cut circles for the eyes from white felt, then attach the eyes with the glue gun.
5. Invite the children to stuff the whale with pillow batting.
6. Stitch the opening with yarn.

More to do

Language and snack: Give each child 10 fish crackers, then have them make up a story about how many fish a whale ate for dinner and invite them to eat that many crackers.
Math: Lay yarn across the playground in the actual dimensions of the whale. Guess and check how many children can fit inside the outline.

Related books and song

Namu by National Geographic Books
Rainbow Fish and the Big Blue Whale by Marcus Pfister
Whale Song by Dyan Sheldon
"Baby Beluga" by Raffi

Barbara Saul, Eureka, CA

Lacing Jellyfish

Materials

Poster board or tag board
Scissors
Hole punch
Colored glue and glitter glue
Yarn cut in 6" to 8" (15 cm to 20 cm) lengths

Beads in assorted colors and sizes, optional

What to do
1. Ahead of time, cut poster board shapes that resemble the top of a jellyfish. Punch holes along the bottom edge of each jellyfish.
2. Invite the children to decorate their poster board jellyfish with colored glue and glitter glue in any design.
3. Set the jellyfish aside to dry.
4. If the children would like to decorate their yarn with beads, show them how to thread the beads onto the yarn and tie a knot around the bead. Encourage younger children to use the extra-large beads.
5. Help the children lace the yarn through the holes, then tie a knot to secure the yarn.

More to do
More art: Cut a jellyfish from felt or other fabric and create a simple marionette using dowels and strings; have the children move the jellyfish through its habitat.
Movement: Play a selection of graceful music and invite the children to mimic a jellyfish pushed along by the waves or swimming by means of jet propulsion.

Related books
Is This a House for Hermit Crab? by Megan McDonald
Splash by Ann Jonas
Until I Saw the Sea: A Collection of Seashore Poems edited by Alison Shaw

Suzanne Pearson, Winchester, VA

Bingo Marker Fish

Materials
White or manila construction paper
Scissors
Glue
Bingo markers in various colors
Large googly eyes

What to do
1. Cut a fish shape from construction paper for each child.

Oceans

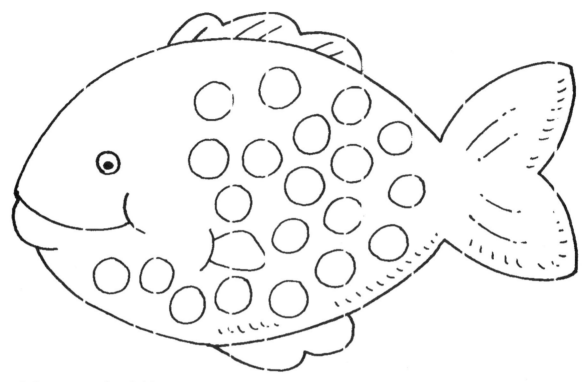

2. Encourage the children to glue the bingo markers onto the fish shapes to make scales.
3. Glue a large googly eye to one side of the fish.
4. Hang to dry.

More to do

Games: Make a set of matching cards in fish shapes, marking them with numbers or letters and corresponding pictures; glue a metal paper clip to each card and place the cards in a dry wading pool. Make a pole from a stick, then attach a magnet to the end of the fishing line. Fish for matching cards and collect them in a plastic bucket.

Sand and water table: Add plastic fish in different sizes and colors to the table.

Science: Maintain an aquarium in the classroom and invite the children to name the fish and care for them.

Snack: Enjoy fish crackers when your project is finished.

Related books and song

Fish Is Fish by Leo Lionni
A Million Fish…More or Less by Patricia C. McKissack
One Fish, Two Fish, Red Fish, Blue Fish by Dr. Seuss
Swimmy by Leo Lionni
"Baby Beluga" by Raffi

Tina R. Woehler, Oak Point, TX

Flying Saucers

3+

Materials

Heavy paper plates, two per child
Markers
Crayons
Scissors
String or yarn
Glue
Stapler
Hole punch, optional

What to do

1. Have the children decorate their plates with markers or crayons. Invite them to draw windows, portholes, numbers, doors, etc.

2. Tell the children to decide which plate will be the top of their spaceship. Attach a string to the middle of the top plate.

3. Glue the plates to each other or sew them together with string or yarn. If you choose to sew the plates together, put one on top of the other and punch holes in both at once so the openings line up. Show the children how to weave the yarn or

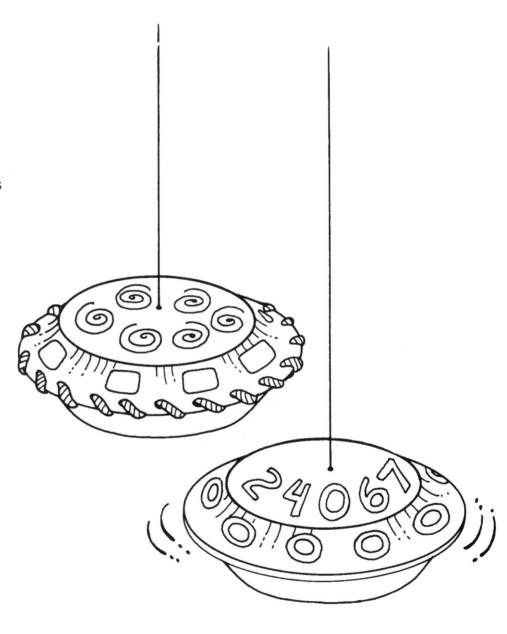

string through the openings, then tie a knot when they are finished.

4. Hang the saucers in the room or throw them like a frisbee outdoors. The children can also run with the saucer, pulling it by the string.

More to do

More art: Ask the children to design a lunar landing vehicle using only a pencil and sheet of paper.

Science: Conduct flight experiments with paper and foam plates by cutting notches or punching holes in the plates and using plates of different sizes and weights. See which ones fly the farthest and highest.

Related books

Big Silver Space Shuttle by Ken Wilson-Max
Floating Home by David Getz
Grandpa Takes Me to the Moon by Timothy R. Gaffney
Moonhorse by Mary Pope Osborne
What Next, Baby Bear! by Jill Murphy
Zoom! Zoom! Zoom! I'm off to the Moon! by Dan Yaccarino

Sandra Nagel, White Lake, MI

Can Constellations

3+

Materials

Potato chip cans with lids, one per child
Black tempera paint and paintbrushes
Books and posters of the stars and constellations
Scissors
Permanent marker
Hammer and nail
White crayon

What to do

1. Ahead of time, cut a small eyehole in each lid.
2. Ask the children to paint the outside of the can and lid.
3. While the paint is drying, invite the children to look at books and posters with pictures and names of the stars and constellations.
4. Have the children choose one constellation. Encourage older children to draw the constellation on paper.

5. Using a permanent marker, mark dots on the bottom of the can following the pattern of the constellation.
6. Use the hammer and nail to punch holes through the dots (adult only).
7. With white crayon, write the name of the constellation on the outside of the can.
8. Invite the children to look through the eyehole and point the bottom of the can toward light to see their constellation.

More to do
Field trip: Plan a trip to a planetarium or observatory.
Language: Read a story about how a constellation got its name, then have the children compose their own stories.
Math: Count the number of stars in each constellation. Older children can find the distance between stars.
Science: Make a list of questions about the stars—what are they made of? Where did they come from? Bring the questions with you to the planetarium or library and help the children find the answers.

Related books
The Children's Giant Atlas of the Universe by Ian Ridpath
Coyote in Love by Mindy Dwyer
Fun Facts About the Solar System by William J. Cromie
Traveling in Space by Sue Becklake
You Among the Stars by Herman and Nina Schneider

Angie Miller, Hilliard, OH

Starry Night   3+

Materials
Fingerpaint paper
Blue fingerpaint
Yellow tempera paint
Paper plates or Styrofoam trays
Sponges cut in star shapes and crescent or full moon shapes
Water

What to do
1. Give each child a sheet of paper and invite the children to create a blue fingerpainting. Let the

paintings dry overnight.

2. Pour yellow paint onto a paper plate or tray. Return the children's finger paintings to them.
3. Wet the sponges and wring out the excess water.
4. Have the children dip the sponges in the paint and apply the star and moon shapes to their painting.

More to do

Dramatic play: Paint a sheet with star-shaped sponges and glow-in-the-dark paint, then turn off the lights on a rainy day and climb under the sheet.

More art: Show the children a picture of Van Gogh's "Starry Night" and compare their paintings to his. Use fingerpaints to create paintings of the planets in outer space. Create a starry mural for the classroom wall or bulletin board.

Related books

My House Has Stars by Megan McDonald
Papa, Please Get the Moon for Me by Eric Carle
Stars by Seymour Simon

Nancy Tatum, Williamsburg, VA

Spectacular Stars

Materials

Star stencils of different sizes
Yellow or gold heavy paper
Pencils
Safety scissors
Glitter glue
Yellow watercolor paint
Iodized salt
String

What to do

1. Have the children trace a star stencil on paper, then help them cut the star out.
2. Invite the children to decorate their star with the glitter glue. Alternatively, have the children do a yellow watercolor wash on the star and, while it is still wet, sprinkle salt over the paint.
3. Encourage the children to name their star as a scientist often does.
4. Let the stars dry overnight.

5. When they are dry, suspend them from the ceiling with string.

More to do
Field trip: Visit a planetarium or observatory.
Language: Share myths and legends about the stars and encourage the children to compose their own stories. Write down their stories and attach them to the back of their Spectacular Stars. Teach the poem "Star Light, Star Bright" and ask the children to think of a wish they would make on a star.
Music: Have the children act out the song "Twinkle, Twinkle, Little Star."

Related books
Draw Me a Star by Eric Carle
Now I Know Stars by Roy Wandelmaier
Twinkle, Twinkle, Little Star by Iza Trapani

Jackie Wright, Enid, OK

Creative Constellations

Materials
Pictures of the Big Dipper and the Little Dipper
Small star stickers
Blue paper
Black markers

What to do
1. Talk to the children about constellations. Show them a diagram of the Big Dipper and the Little Dipper. Point out how they resemble their names. Tell the children they are going to design their own constellations.
2. Have the children affix the stars to their paper in a design of their own creation.
3. Ask them to connect the stars with a black marker.
4. When they have finished, invite the children to name their constellation.

More to do
Cooking: Cut star shapes from cookie dough and bake.
Science: Older children can use a picture of a constellation as a pattern for their design, then look for it in the night sky. Tape the children's pictures to the ceiling. Bring in a telescope and show the children how to look through it.

outer space

Related books
A Book About the Planets and Stars by Betty Polisar Reigot
A Day in Space by Suzanne Lord and Jolie Epstein
My House Has Stars by Megan McDonald

Cindi Winther, Oxford, MI

Wacky Spaceships

Materials
Small Styrofoam bowls
Foil
Decorating materials such as pipe cleaners, coffee stirrers, and pompoms
Glue
Construction paper
Toothpicks
Miniature store-bought flags, optional
Glitter

Outer space

What to do

1. Invite the children to cover the bowls with foil.
2. When they are finished, have the children turn the bowl upside-down so that it resembles a spaceship. Invite the children to choose which materials they would like to use to decorate their ship.
3. Help the children poke holes in the Styrofoam and insert the pipe cleaners or coffee stirrers. Show them how to use glue to attach the pompoms.
4. Demonstrate how to make a small flag on paper, then attach it to a toothpick; as an alternative, use miniature store-bought flags. Poke the toothpick flag into the Styrofoam to attach.
5. When their spacecrafts are almost finished, have the children spread glue sparingly over the surface, then sprinkle with glitter.

More to do

Dramatic play: Invite the children to rummage through the dress-up clothes and pretend to be aliens.

Language: Play "What If?" and ask the children what they would say if a friendly alien landed his spaceship on the playground and wanted to learn about the planet Earth.

More art: Cover a wall with black paper and add glittering star and planet stickers. Hang stars from the ceiling. Spray a box with silver paint to use as a spaceship, then decorate.

Related books

The Earth and I by Frank Asch
The Planets by Gail Gibbons
What the Sun Sees/What the Moon Sees by Nancy Tafuri

Cindi Winther, Oxford, MI

Robots from Outer Space

Materials

Toilet tissue tubes, one per child
Foil
Packing bubble wrap
Glue
Scissors
Straws
Empty spools

outer space

Decorating odds and ends such as sequins, buttons, pipe cleaners, confetti, bottle caps, yarn, bits of wrapping paper and fabric
Glue gun, optional

What to do

1. Give each child a toilet paper tube. Help them wrap it in foil or bubble wrap. Secure the wrap with glue if necessary. Help the children punch a hole on both sides of the tube and feed the straw, or the robot's arms, through the openings.
2. Invite the children to decorate their robot with some of the odds and ends. Have the children affix the decorations with glue. An adult can secure the odds and ends with a glue gun, if desired.

More to do

Dramatic play: Convert an extra-large cardboard box into a rocket ship and play a game of make-believe.

Math: Count backward from 10, preparing for launch.

More art: Cut paper shapes in varying sizes to represent the planets and the sun, then invite the children to create collages with the leftover decorating odds and ends. Create a rocket ship with a paper towel tube and paper cone, then decorate with odds and ends.

Related books

Here Come the Aliens by Colin McNaughton
My Place in Space by Robin and Sally Hirst
Zoom! Zoom! Zoom! I'm Off to the Moon! by Dan Yaccarino

Gryphon House Staff

Blast-off Helmets

3+

Materials
Paper grocery bags
Scissors
Glue
Markers
Crayons
Plastic hosing, optional
Decorating odds and
   ends such as sequins,
   buttons, bottle caps,
   scraps of paper, foil,
   wallpaper, and fabric

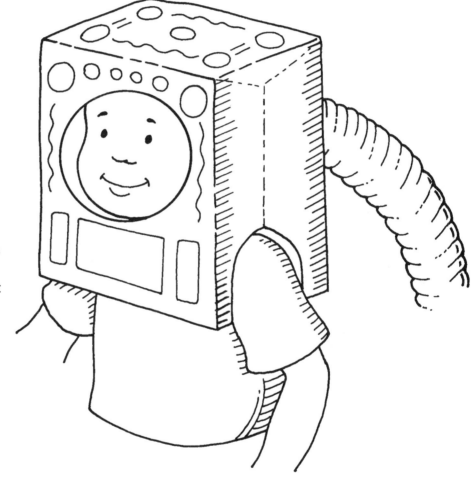

What to do
1. Ahead of time, cut the top 5" (13 cm) off the bag, then cut openings for arms on the sides and a circle in the front for the face.
2. Attach a piece of plastic hosing through a small hole in the back of the helmet, if desired.
3. Invite the children to decorate their space helmet with the crayons, markers, and decorating odds and ends.

More to do
Dramatic play: Have the children act out the first lunar landing.
More art: Make a vest from another paper bag and decorate it as a spacesuit. Create a mural of the lunar landscape. Make alien creatures from pipe cleaners, bead pompoms, and googly eyes.

outer space

Related books
Big Silver Space Shuttle by Ken Wilson Max
Floating Home by David Getz
Grandpa Takes Me to the Moon by Timothy R. Gaffney
I Want to Be an Astronaut by Byron Barton
I Want to Be a Space Pilot by Carla Greene
Moon Horse by Mary Pope Osborne
Richie's Rocket by Joan Anderson
Space Alphabet by Irene Zacks
What Next, Baby Bear! by Jill Murphy
Zoom! Zoom! Zoom! I'm Off to the Moon! by Dan Yaccarino

Sandra Nagel, White Lake, MI

Meteor Shower

Materials
Dishpan
Water
Cheese grater or potato peeler
Colored chalk
White construction paper, cut into large circles

What to do
1. Pour water into a dishpan until it is two-thirds full.
2. Using a cheese grater or potato peeler, scrape different colors of chalk into a bowl.
3. Ask the children to sprinkle the grated chalk on top of the water in the dishpan.
4. Give each child a construction paper circle. Invite the children in turn to gently lay their circle on top of the water, then remove it and set it aside to dry.
5. When the paper dries, the children will see a swirl of colors.

More to do
Movement: Play music and invite the children to rotate and revolve around one child who is pretending to be the sun.

Related books
The Earth and I by Frank Asch
The Planets by Gail Gibbons

outer space

A Tour of the Planets by Melvin Berger
A Trip to Mars by Ruth Young

Kimberle S. Byrd, Kalamazoo, MI

Moon Rocks

Materials
Lunch-size paper bags
Water table or bucket of water
Small brushes such as old toothbrushes
Newspaper
Magnifying glass, ruler, and scale
Florescent color poster paint and paintbrushes
Clear glitter

What to do
1. Bring the children outside and pretend to look for moon rocks. Have each child collect a few rocks in a paper bag labeled with their name and bring them back to the classroom.
2. Tell the children to wash the rocks at the water table, using brushes to remove the dirt from them. Lay them on newspaper to dry.
3. When they are dry, encourage the children to examine the rocks with a magnifying glass. Have them weigh the rocks on a scale and measure them with a ruler.
4. Afterward, invite the children to paint the rocks with florescent paint and shake on clear glitter.
5. When dry, the rocks will have a shiny, extra-terrestrial appearance.

More to do
More art: Decorate a box to collect and sort the rocks in.
Science: Older children can graph and chart the results of their rock study. Cover rocks and the bottom of a shallow box with rust-colored craft sand, replicating the landscape of the Moon, then use odds and ends to make a replica of the Moon landing vehicle.

Related books
Happy Birthday, Moon by Frank Asch
I'll See You When the Moon Is Full by Susi Gregg Fowler
Owl Moon by Jane Yolen

Maxine Della Fave, Raleigh, NC

Alien Art

Materials
Styrofoam trays, blocks, and packing material in varied shapes and sizes
Toothpicks
Popsicle sticks
Straws
Craft supplies such as ribbon, googly eyes, pompoms, pipe cleaners
Safety scissors
Glue

What to do
1. Encourage the children to imagine the variety of creatures that might live in outer space.
2. Invite the children to create a creature from the materials provided. Suggest to the children that they begin with a Styrofoam block or tray and attach the decorations using toothpicks or popsicle sticks and glue.

More to do

Language: Have the children create a story about their alien and record their words on tape; play the stories at circle time and ask the children to guess whose voice is on the tape. Afterward, send the tape home to their families.

Related books

Alistair in Outer Space John Sadler
A Day With Wilbur Robinson by William Joyce
Here Come the Aliens by Colin McNaughton
June 29, 1999 by David Wiesner
The Magic School Bus Lost in the Solar System by Joanna Cole

Ann Gudowski, Johnstown, PA

Galactic Mobiles

Materials

4 cups (1 L) of flour
2 cups (500 mL) of salt
2 1/2 cups (1.3 L) of boiling water
Mixing bowl
Rolling pin
Circle and star cookie cutters
Toothpicks
Baking sheet
Cookie rack
Paints and brushes
Glitter, optional
Yarn or string
Scissors
Clothes hanger

What to do

1. Have the children scoop 4 cups (1 L) of flour into a bowl.
2. Add the salt to boiling water, then ask the children to stand aside while you add the water to the flour and mix the ingredients together.
3. Invite the children to knead the dough until it is pliable. Show them how to roll it flat with a rolling pin.

4. Ask each child to cut two star shapes and two circle shapes with the cookie cutters. Poke a hole with a toothpick at the top of each shape.

5. Place the circles and stars on a baking sheet and bake them at 250° F (130° C) for two to three hours, checking frequently after two hours to prevent the dough from burning. Remove the shapes from the oven when they are brown and hard. Set them on a cookie rack to cool.

6. The next day, invite the children to paint their circles and stars, adding glitter to the paint before it dries, if desired.

7. When the paint dries, thread a piece of yarn or string through the hole in the top of the shape. Tie the shapes to a clothes hanger, varying their height.

8. Hang the mobiles from the ceiling.

More to do

Cooking: Cut shapes from cookie dough, then bake and enjoy a special treat.

More art: Color star shapes cut from poster board with glow-in-the-dark crayons; thread fishing line through an opening in the top, then hang the stars from the ceiling.

Movement: Have the children rotate, spin, and revolve to a selection of relaxing music.

Related books

Coyote in Love by Mindy Dwyer
My House Has Stars by Megan McDonald
Stars by Seymour Simon

MaryAnn F. Kohl, Bellingham, WA

outer space

Papier-mâché Planets

Materials
Flour
Water
Tub or large bowl
Balloons in several sizes
Newspaper cut in strips
Paint and paintbrushes

What to do
1. Ahead of time, mix flour and water until the mixture is the consistency of oatmeal.
2. Inflate 11 balloons to represent the planets, the sun, and the moon.
3. Show the children how to dip the strips of newspaper in the flour and water mixture, then lay the strips across a balloon in several layers. Cover the entire surface of the balloon. Allow sufficient time for drying.
4. When the balloons are dry, have the children paint them. Hang the balloons from the ceiling when finished.

More to do
More art: Make spacesuits from paper bags. Cover with foil and cut openings for the head and arms. Use another bag for the helmet. Trim some length and cut an opening for the face.

Related books
Our Solar System by Seymour Simon
The Planets by Gail Gibbons

Sharon Max, St. Louis, MO

My Own Little Planet

Materials
Sandpaper
Construction paper in light colors
Scissors
Iron
Newspaper

outer space

What to do

1. Beforehand, cut a circle for each child from the sandpaper, about 2" (5 cm) in diameter. Cut the same number of circles from the construction paper, about 2" (5 cm) larger than the first circle.
2. Have the children color the rough side of their sandpaper circle. Tell them to press hard and color the entire circle.
3. When they finish coloring, have the children place their circle, colored side down, on the construction paper circle. Show the children how to center their sandpaper circle on the larger one.
4. Set up the iron on a thick layer of newspaper. The iron should be handled by adults only.
5. Iron the colored circle onto the larger circle, then set the sandpaper and construction paper circles aside to cool.
6. When they have cooled, lift the sandpaper circles from the paper, leaving behind the image of the sandpaper planet.
7. Trim your paper planets, if desired, then hang them from the ceiling.

More to do

Dramatic play: Use a silver thermal camping blanket for a space tent and pretend to live on another planet.

Language: Pretend the class is planning a trip to another planet. Ask the children to list the items they will need to bring with them. Have them dictate a letter to a friend they hope to meet in outer space. Assemble their letters in a book.

Science: Talk to the children about what plants need to live and how planet Earth supports life; in an experiment, put a plant in the freezer, another under a dark cover, and a third in light, but do not water. Predict what will happen, then keep a record of the children's observations.

Related books

I Want to Be an Astronaut by Byron Barton
My Picture Book of the Planets by Nancy E. Krulik
The Planets by Gail Gibbons

Linda S. Andrews, Sonora, CA

outer space

The Swirling Skies of Jupiter 4+

Materials
White poster board
Small plate
Red construction paper
Light corn syrup
Small bowl
Picture of Jupiter
Wide paintbrush or pastry brush
Food coloring in assorted colors
Toothpicks
Plastic wrap, optional

What to do
1. Before class, trace and cut circles from the poster board, using the small plate as a template. Cut small circles or "red spots" from the construction paper. Pour the corn syrup into a bowl.
2. Show the class a picture of Jupiter. Bring their attention to the big red spot and swirling storms on its surface.
3. Help the children cover the poster board circle with corn syrup, using a brush.
4. When they are finished, have the children squeeze a drop or two of food dye, preferably two colors, into the corn syrup and mix the colors gently with a toothpick. Have the children place a red spot on their planet Jupiter. The corn syrup will hold it in place.
5. Let the project dry for a couple of days. If the project must go home before then, cover it with plastic wrap and tape the wrap on the reverse side.

More to do
Movement: Play music and invite the children to move like a swirling storm or an angry red spot.
Snack: Bring in muffins, then squeeze a drop or two of food coloring in frosting and let the children stir, making the colors swirl; frost the muffins and top each with a red cinnamon candy.

Related books
The Planets by Gail Gibbons
On the Day You Were Born by Debra Frasier
Our Solar System and other books by Seymour Simon

Vicki L Schneider, Oshkosh, WI

Pencil Pals

3+

Materials
Scissors
Pencil
Tag board
Felt in assorted colors
Googly eyes
Glue
Markers

What to do

1. In advance, cut a circle pattern from tag board 2" (5 cm) in diameter. Using the pattern, cut a felt circle for each child. Next, cut triangles and tear-drop shapes from felt in a variety of colors for the ears, approximately 1" (3 cm) long. Additionally, cut 1" by 1½" (3 cm by 4 cm) felt strips in any color.

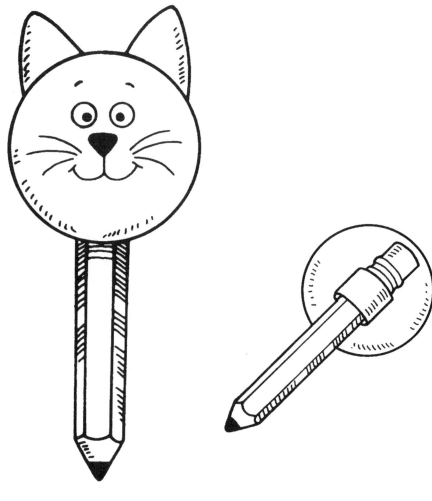

2. Have the children glue the googly eyes and felt ears on the circles. When they are finished, invite the children to draw noses, mouths, and whiskers on their pet's face with markers.

3. Help the children glue each end of the felt strip on the back of their pencil pal, leaving a small opening in the center to slip their pencil through.

More to do

Language: Cut paper in the shape of an animal, then invite the children to compose a few sentences about their pencil pal; record their words on the paper and assemble the pages in a book. Cover the book with a felt animal.

More art: Encourage the children to draw pictures of their pencil pal or their pet at home. Make felt pals for drinking straws. Add a Velcro attachment to the back of the pet pal and wear it on a belt loop or backpack.

Related books
Millions of Cats by Wanda Gag
Some Swell Pup, or Are You Sure You Want a Dog? by Maurice Sendak and Matthew Margolis
Tumble Bumble by Felicia Bond

Dotti Enderle, Richmond, TX

In the Doghouse

Materials
Cardboard box
Exacto or utility knife (adult only)
Duct tape
Large plastic mat or drop cloth
Washable tempera paints
Large brushes

What to do
1. Ahead of time, find a box that is big enough for the children to play inside. Cut a door in one side to resemble a door to a doghouse. Raise the flaps on the top of the box to form a roof and hold them in place with duct tape.
2. Lay a drop cloth on the floor and invite the children to paint the box in any design or color.
3. When it is dry, put the doghouse in the dramatic play area. Add an assortment of stuffed dogs, a food bowl, and other dog accessories.

More to do
Circle time: Invite a dog owner and their child-friendly dog to visit the class; ask questions about the care and training of dogs.
Dramatic play: Provide a variety of props to create the setting in a veterinarian's office.
More art: Make dog finger puppets with older children using felt, needles, and yarn.

Related books
Arthur's New Puppy by Marc Brown
Clifford the Big Red Dog by Norman Bridwell

pets

The Flea Story by Leo Lionni
The New Puppy by Laurence Anholt
Puppies Are Like That by Jan Pfloog
The Puppy Who Wanted a Boy by Jane Thayer

Tina R. Woehler, Oak Point, TX

Turtle Toy

3+

Materials
Green or brown construction paper
Scissors
Paper bowls, one per child
Paint
Paintbrushes
Glue
Hole punch
String or yarn

What to do

1. Ahead of time, cut a turtle head, leg, and tail shapes from construction paper or trace them onto paper.
2. When the children arrive, give them each a bowl. Have them turn their bowl upside-down and paint the bottom and sides.
3. If the shapes are not cut ahead of time, ask the children to follow your outline and cut a head, four legs, and a tail for their turtle.
4. When the bowl is dry, help the children glue or staple the shapes onto the edge of the bowl.
5. Punch a hole near the turtle's head. Tie a string through the hole; the string should be long enough for the child to pull, but not so long that it will tangle easily. Make a small loop at the other end of the string that the child can grasp.

More to do

Field trip: Visit a nature center or nearby pond and watch the turtles swim and sun themselves.
Movement: Have the children pretend they are turtles and hold a turtle relay race.

Related books

Mordant's Wish by Valerie Coursen
Tilly Turtle by Annie Kubler
The Tortoise and the Hare by Janet Stevens
Turtle Day by Douglas Florian
The Turtle Who Lost His Shell by Paul Levy

Sandra Nagel, White Lake, MI

Rabbit Headbands

Materials

White poster board
Stapler
Pink construction paper
Scissors
Glue

What to do

1. Ahead of time, cut poster board into strips 2" (5 cm) wide and long enough to wrap around a child's head. For each child, cut two rabbit ears from poster board and two smaller pink rabbit ear shapes from construction paper.

2. Have the children glue the pink shapes to the poster board ears, then glue the ears to the middle of their headpiece.
3. Set the headpieces aside to dry.
4. When the glue is dry, wrap a headpiece around each child's head. Holding the ends in place, remove the headpiece and staple the ends together.

More to do

Games: In a game of Big Bunny and Little Bunny Hide and Seek, the Little Bunnies must hop back to the bunny den before Big Bunny catches them.
Snack: Make a Rabbit Salad with shredded baby carrots, canned crushed pineapple, and raisins, then serve on a lettuce leaf.

Related books

Goodnight Moon and *Runaway Bunny* by Margaret Wise Brown
Guess How Much I Love You by Sam McBratney
Hush Little Baby by Sylvia Long
I Love You, Little One by Nancy Tafuri

Tina R. Woehler, Oak Point, TX

Snaky Plate

Materials

Thin, dinner-size paper plates, one per child
Scissors
Hole punch
Yarn cut in 8" (20 cm) lengths
Green or brown tempera paint
Small brushes
Googly eyes
Red construction paper
Glue

What to do

1. Cut the plate beginning on one side and moving in a spiral course until you reach the center, leaving a strip, or snake, roughly 1" (3 cm) wide.
2. Punch a hole in the center of each plate and tie a piece of yarn to the hole, forming a handle.
3. Invite the children to paint their snake.

4. Help the children cut tongue shapes from the red paper. When the paint is dry, help the children glue the eyes and tongue to the head of their snake.
5. Hang the snakes to dry.

More to do

Field trip: Visit a nearby zoo or nature center to observe the snakes and learn how to hold them.
Movement: Play music and invite the children to hiss and slither along the ground.
More art: Make a snake puzzle by cutting a long, wide paper snake into pieces with irregular edges; have the children paint or color the pieces, then fit them together. Make a snake puppet from old socks and fabric scraps.
Science: Invite a reptile handler to visit the school and give a demonstration on snakes.

Related books

The Day Jimmy's Boa Ate the Wash by Steven Kellogg
The Greedy Python by Richard Buckley
Snakes and Lizards by Daniel Moreton and Pamela Chanko

Tina R. Woehler, Oak Point, TX

Dalmation Thumbprint Dogs 3+

Materials
White construction paper
Black ink pads
Disposable wipes
Black and red crayons

What to do
1. Beforehand, cut construction paper in the shape of a Dalmatian. Make a shape for each child.
2. Have the children press their thumb on an inkpad, then use their thumbprint to make the Dalmatian's spots and a black nose.
3. Tell the children to clean their fingers with the wipes.
4. When they are ready, have the children draw eyes and a mouth on their Dalmatian.

More to do
Dramatic play: Play a game of pet store with stuffed animals, assorted pet accessories, a cash register, and play money.
Games: Play a matching game with Dalmatians cut from paper and laminated; match the number of spots on the dog with the number of dog bones on a complementary set of cards.
Math: Create a set of flash cards cut in the shape of a Dalmatian, each displaying a different number of spots.
More art: Make paw prints with your fingers and an inkpad or using paint and sponges; decorate greeting cards, gift wrap, and the bulletin board with the prints.
Sand and water table: Add some bubble bath, sponges, and plastic toy animals to the water and encourage the children to bathe their toy pets.

Related books
Dalmatians by Stuart A. Kallen
101 Dalmatians by Walt Disney
Where's Spot? by Eric Hill

Tina R. Woehler, Oak Point, TX

Shape Pets

Materials
Construction paper in various colors
White construction paper, 9" x 12" (23 cm x 30 cm)
Glue

What to do
1. To prepare, cut the colored paper into a wide assortment of shapes and sizes. Leave some paper for the children to cut themselves.
2. Distribute the white paper and encourage the children to create an imaginary pet by arranging the colored shapes on their paper. Let them cut additional shapes if they choose.
3. When the children have finished their arrangement, help them glue the colored shapes in place.
4. Have the children choose a name for their pet. Write the name on their picture.

More to do
Circle time: Talk about the pets that the children have at home, including the children's responsibilities toward the pet and the ways in which the pet contributes to the family. Invite parents to bring small, friendly pets to class for a visit or have the children bring in photos. Invite a veterinarian or representative from an animal shelter to talk to the children.
Math: Make a picture graph of the children's pets or pets they would like to own.

Related books
Can I Have a Stegosaurus, Mom? Can I Please? by Lois G. Grambling
Clifford the Big Red Dog by Norman Bridwell
The Curious Kitten by Linda Hayward
The Great Adventure of Woti (a goldfish) by Nathan Zimelman
Franklin Wants a Pet by Paulette Bourgeois and Brenda Clark
Just Me and My Puppy by Mercer Mayer
Uses for Mooses by Mike Thaler

Sandra W. Gratias, Perkasie, PA

How Did Your Dog Get So Dirty?

3+

Materials
Harry the Dirty Dog by Gene Zion
White paper
Tag board pattern of dog
Fingerpaints

What to do
1. Read *Harry the Dirty Dog* to the class and ask the children to imagine another experience a dog might have that would get him dirty.
2. Hand out the paper and have the children draw a picture of a dog or use a pattern to trace the outline of one.
3. When they are finished drawing, have the children paint their picture, adding details of the messy adventure the dog has gotten into, such as a chocolate cake, a mud puddle, or a pile of wet leaves.
4. While they are painting, have the children describe the adventure. Record their stories on paper.
5. Afterward, share the children's stories with the whole class.

More to do
Language: Laminate the children's papers and assemble them in a traveling book that the children can bring home in turn and share with their families.
Sand and water table: Make a manageable mess with mud and plastic pets, then give the pets a bath.

Related books
A Boy, a Dog, and a Frog by Mercer Meyer
Good Dog, Carl by Alexandra Day
Mouse Mess by Linnea Riley

Debbie Barbuch, Sheboygan, WI

Paper Plate Frog Puppets

Materials
Pictures of brilliantly colored frogs from other parts of the world
Paper plates
White, green, and red construction paper
Scissors
Paint
Paintbrushes
Glue
Pencils for curling

What to
1. Show the children pictures of brilliantly colored frogs from parts of South America and Australia.
2. Invite the children to cut a piece of green construction paper the same size as the plate.
3. Have them fold their paper plate and their paper in half, then cut along the fold on the green paper. Set one of the halves aside for later and ask the children to glue the other onto the underside of the folded plate; have them apply glue only to the outside edges, leaving a pocket between the plate and the paper.

4. Help the children cut a piece of white paper so it is the same size as the top half of the plate. Show them how to glue it to the plate, again applying glue only to the outside edges so you leave a pocket for the children's fingers.
5. Invite the children to paint the frog in the brilliant colors and patterns of frogs from other parts of the world. Let the paint dry.
6. Meanwhile, help the children cut eye shapes out of the remaining green paper. Fold the bottom edge of each eye and ask the children to glue the eyes to their frog. Have them paint the coloring of the frog's eyes.

7. Help the children cut thin strips from red paper for the frog's tongue. Show the children how to wrap the strip around a pencil, then remove the pencil, curling the paper. Have them glue the strip to the back of the frog's mouth.
8. When the glue dries, invite the children to insert their thumb in the lower pocket and their other fingers in the upper pocket to manipulate their frog.

More to do
Dramatic play: Invite the children to put on a frog puppet show.
Games: Play leap frog. Hold a frog-hopping race.

Related books
Frogs by Gail Gibbons
Jump, Frog, Jump by Robert Kalan

Sandra S. Ryan, Buffalo, NY

Baby Rocks

Materials
Rocks
Newspaper
Tempera paint
Googly eyes
Feathers
White plastic bags cut into the shape of diapers

What to do
1. Prepare a work surface with newspaper and set out the paint and other supplies.
2. When the children arrive, take them on a hike outdoors, collecting rocks and small stones along the way.
3. When you return to the classroom, lay the rock collection on the newspaper.
4. Invite the children to paint their rock in any color.
5. When the paint is dry, help the children use the glue to attach eyes, feathers for hair, and small stones for feet.
6. Help the children glue a plastic diaper on their baby rock.

More to do
Math: Keep a collection of rocks in the classroom and sort them by size and shape.

More art: Decorate rocks of different sizes and make a family for the pet rock. Make a home for the pet rocks from a shoebox. Make a family of pets from seashells.

Related books
Animal Dads by Sneed B. Collard III
Oink by Arthur Geisert

Lisa M. Chichester, Parkersburg, WV

Wild Thing Sculpture

Materials
Newspaper strips
5 lb. (2 kg) bag of flour
Water
Toilet paper and paper towel tubes
Large and small oatmeal boxes
Any odd shaped small boxes
Masking tape
Tempera paint
Neat junk (feathers, googly eyes, pompoms, pipe cleaners, straws, Easter grass, lids, buttons, etc.)

What to do
Note: This is a three or four day project.
1. Have the children tape boxes, paper tubes, and odd pieces together to form a "wild thing" structure. You may need to reinforce legs and heads to the body with extra thick tape.
2. Make flour and water mixture in a large bowl by using several cups of flour and slowly adding water to get a thick paste for papier-mâché.
3. Dip newspaper strips in papier-mâché goop. Squeeze out extra paste. Allow the children to cover entire structure with one good layer of newspaper strips and papier-mâché. Let it dry for at least a day.
4. Cover the structure with a second layer of newspaper and papier-mâché. Let this dry another day.
5. When dry, paint the entire "wild thing" with assorted tempera paint colors. Again let the sculpture dry for a day.
6. Encourage the children to glue, stick, or color on various features on the sculpture using any of the listed "junk" and inviting other ideas. Creations are unlimited.

pets

More to do

Music: Have a "wild thing" parade or dance. Play a record of eerie or interestingly moving music (suggestion: Schumann's Finale from Piano Quartet, Opus 44). Encourage children to invent new ways to move their bodies.

Related books

There's a Nightmare in My Closet by Mercer Mayer
Where the Wild Things Are by Maurice Sendak

Debi Behr and Diana Reed, New Wilmington, PA

Saltwater Chalk Prints

Materials
Colored drawing chalk
Light colored construction paper, 8" x 10" (20 cm x 25 cm)
Salt
Water
1 tsp. (5 mL) measuring spoon
¼ cup (60 mL) measuring cup
Small containers

What to do
1. Cover the table with newspaper.
2. Mix one teaspoon (5 mL) salt and ¼ cup (60 mL) of warm water into small containers and stir. Set out the containers and paper.
3. Invite the chldren to hold a piece of chalk in the saltwater for approximately one minute, then draw with the wet chalk on the paper.
4. Encourage the children to dip the chalk into the saltwater as needed.
5. Allow prints to dry. Display for all to enjoy.

More to do
More art: Instead of the usual rectangle shape to paint on, cut paper into shapes such as egg shapes for Easter, butterfly shapes for spring, and heart shapes for Valentine's Day.

Related books
Color Dance by Ann Jonas
Little Blue and Little Yellow by Leo Lionni
Planting a Rainbow by Lois Ehlert

Cory McIntyre, Crystal Lake, IL

Science

"Mouse" Painting

3+

Materials
4 unusable "mice" (chord removed) from computers
4 different colors of thin tempera paint
4 cups for paint
Paintbrushes
Light-colored construction paper, 12" x 18" (30 cm x 45 cm)

What to do
1. Spread newspaper over the working area.
2. Put different colored paint in the four cups with a paintbrush in each.
3. Using the paintbrush, have the children brush the ball-bearing side of the mouse with paint, then encourage the children to push the mouse all over the paper. Use a different mouse to add a second, third, and fourth color.
4. Let the creations dry and label them "Mouse Painting."

More to do
Cooking: Make Mouse Nibbles for the class. Heat oven to 450° F (230° C). Mix 2 cups (500 mL) flour, 2 teaspoons (10 mL) baking powder, and ⅝ teaspoon (2.5 mL) of salt in a bowl. Cut in ½ cup (125 mL) of shortening, using a pastry blender. Stir in 2/3 cup (150 mL) of shredded cheddar cheese. Add just enough milk so that a soft dough forms. Sprinkle a surface lightly with flour. Turn the dough onto the floured surface. Knead it gently 10 times. Place it then on an ungreased cookie sheet. Pat dough into an 8" (20 cm) square and cut the square in half. Then cut each half crosswise into 1" (3 cm) strips. Bake the strips until they are golden, for 12 to 15 minutes. Serve the nibbles with ketchup or mustard dip if you like. This recipe makes 16 sticks.

More art: Follow along the lines of the above project, substituting unusable floppy disks. Children may use the edge or the flat side of the disks to create interesting patterns on recycled computer paper.

Related books
Arthur's Computer Disaster by Marc Brown
The Mouse and the Potato by Thomas Berger and Carla Grillis

Debi Behr and Diana Reed, New Wilmington, PA

Bumpy Snake

Materials
Wallpaper samples
Scissors
Black crayon
Googly eyes
Glue

What to do
1. Give children the wallpaper samples and safety scissors.
2. Invite the children to cut out a worm or snake shape from the samples.
3. Show the children how to fold the snake accordion style, then unfold it so the snake has ridges.
4. The children can then glue on the googly eyes.

More to do
More art: Give children shoeboxes and art supplies, and invite them to create a home for their snakes.
Music: Put on some music and invite the children to slither along like snakes.
Science: Invite a snake expert to bring in a snake and some skin that a snake has shed for the children to touch.

Related books
The Day Jimmy's Boa Ate the Wash by Steven Kellogg
Outside and Inside Snakes by Sandra Markle

Original poem
When you see a snake,
It will slither and slide.
Then under a rock
It may try to hide.

Mariln Harding Grimes, IA

Wormy Art

Materials
String cut in 10" to 14" (25 cm to 35 cm) lengths
Paint
Pie tins
Construction, manila, or drawing paper

What to do
1. Knot one end of the string to make the head of the worm.
2. Have the children hold the knot and dip the string in the paint, then wiggle it around, coating it with paint.
3. Demonstrate how to lay the string on the paper with the knot just beyond the edge of the paper.
4. When their string is lying flat, ask the children to fold their paper in half. Hold the paper down firmly and have the children gently pull the string. The children should pull the knot up and around the edge of the paper.
5. When they have pulled the string out, tell the children to unfold their paper and see the design the string, or worm, has left.
6. Invite the children to repeat the process with several colors until their paper is crisscrossed with lines in a colorful design.

More to do
More art: Use light brown paper to resemble soil or use brown paint on a colored background.

For a whimsical appearance, draw a picture of a garden or other outdoor setting on the top half of the paper, then make the string design on the bottom half.

Science: Keep worms in a transparent container filled with soil.

Related books
The Big Brag by Dr. Seuss
Inch by Inch by Leo Lionni
Lowly Worm's Shapes and Sizes by Richard Scarry
Wonderful Worms by Linda Glaser
Worms Wiggle by David Pelham

Sandra Nagel, White Lake, MI

Plaster of Paris Sculpture

Materials
Plaster of paris
Water (1 L)
Quart-size zip-closure plastic bags, one per child
Paint or food coloring

What to do
1. Place ½ cup (125 mL) plaster of paris in each zip-closure bag and add the appropriate measure of water. Squeeze out the excess air and close the bags securely.
2. Ask the children to mix the powder and water by squeezing the bag.
3. When they are finished, have the children choose two colors. Help them unzip their bag, add the paint or food coloring, then close the bag again.
4. Ask the children to squeeze the bag again to mix the colors and continue squeezing until they have achieved the desired mix of color. A marbleized effect is achieved with less mixing.
5. Once the mixture begins to harden, have the children stop and set their bags aside. Open the bags slightly if you want them to dry more quickly.
6. Once the plaster has set, remove the bag.

More to do
More art: Place small decorative objects in the plaster mixture before it sets.
Science: Have a discussion about the changes that occurred when the materials were mixed together. Produce simple chemical reactions for the children to help them understand.

SCIENCE

Related books
The Art Lesson by Tomie DePaola
Matthew's Dream by Leo Lionni

Sandra Nagel, White Lake, MI

Icy Sculptures

3+

Materials
Clay
Aluminum pie pans, one per child
Water
Food coloring

What to do
1. Have the children roll clay into a long tube shape. The tube should be sufficiently tall and thick to hold water in place as a mold would.
2. Show the children how to place the clay in the pan and mold it into any design. The design may be as simple as a circle or more complicated. Have the children press the clay firmly to the bottom of the pie pan, creating a water-tight seal. Make certain that there are no gaps in the clay mold where water could escape. Mold the clay until it resembles a long connected wall, making sure the walls are high enough to hold a good amount of water.
3. When the mold is finished, fill it with water.
4. Let the children add food coloring, if they choose. If they use more than one color and want to keep the colors in separate compartments of the mold, they must handle their pan as gently as possible.
5. Place the pie pans in a freezer for several hours.
6. Remove the pans from the freezer. Have the children peel the clay away from the ice and remove their ice sculpture from the pan. It might be necessary to gently flex the pan.
7. Keep the ice sculptures outdoors if it is cold enough, or float them in the classroom's water table.

More to do
Sand and water table: Fill ice cube trays, cups, and baking and geletin molds, then put them in the freezer and play with the frozen shapes the next day.
Science: Have the children describe in their words what happens when the water freezes and when it melts. Have older children compare how long it takes for the sculptures to melt under dif-

science

ferent conditions. When possible, bring snow in from outdoors and watch it melt or make snowballs and put them in the freezer; surprise the class with them on a warm spring day.
Snack: Fill reusable popsicle holders with juice for a frozen treat.

Related books
A Drop of Water by Walter Wick
The Polar Express by Chris Van Allsburg
Snowballs by Lois Ehlert
Winter White by Joanne Ryder

Virginia Jean Herrod, Colombia, SC

Rainbow 'Round Me

Materials
Watercolor paints
Paintbrushes
Small cups or shallow trays of water
Large sponge cut into 2" (5 cm) cubes
Scissors
Glue
Cotton or quilt batting
Hole punch
String or yarn cut into 12" (30 cm) pieces

What to do
1. Demonstrate how to dip the paintbrush into the water and squeeze two or three drops of water into each color in the watercolor tray.
2. Have the children dip the small sponge into the water and wet the entire surface of their paper.
3. Before the water dries, tell the children to dip their brush into a warm or cool color, coating it completely.
4. When they are ready, have the children paint a rainbow arch on their paper. Repeat the process with the other colors of the rainbow, blending them.
5. After the paint dries, help the children cut their rainbows out and glue tufts of cotton on each end.
6. Punch a hole in the center of the rainbow and tie the string or yarn through the opening. Hang the rainbows from the ceiling.

More to do
More art: Have the children work cooperatively and create a large rainbow for the bulletin board.
Science: Position a glass of water on a sunny windowsill and demonstrate how the light separates into the colors of the rainbow.

Related books
Planting a Rainbow by Lois Ehlert
Rainbow of My Own by Don Freeman
Skyfire by Frank Asch

Barbara Saul, Eureka, CA

Pendulum Art

Materials
String
Ceiling hook
Masking tape
Wide, washable markers in assorted colors
Large sheets of butcher paper or newsprint

What to do
1. To design the pendulum, cut a length of string that will reach from the ceiling to the floor. Attach one end of the string to a hook on the ceiling. Tie the other end to a roll of masking tape and cover the tape with contact paper.
2. Attach a marker to the pendulum weight so that the tip of the marker just touches the floor.
3. Lay butcher paper or newsprint beneath the marker. Show the children how to swing the pendulum, then watch as the movement of the pendulum creates a design on their paper. Invite the children in turn to choose a marker and place their paper beneath the pendulum.

More to do
More art: Attach paintbrushes to the pendulum for a different effect.
Science: On another day, hang various objects from the pendulum and watch their motion. Experiment with different weights and chart the results. Brainstorm about everyday uses of pendulums.

Related book
The Way Things Work by David Macaulay

Cory McIntyre, Crystal Lake, IL

Monoprints

Materials
Newspaper
Smocks
Tempera paints in 2 colors
Plexiglas boards, 2' x 2' (60 cm x 60 cm)
Glycerin
Spoons
Good quality drawing paper

What to do
1. Beforehand, cover a work area with newspaper and prepare powdered tempera or thickened liquid tempera paint. Set out the boards, paints, and glycerin.
2. When you are about to begin, ask the children to put on their smocks. Have them spoon a small amount of glycerin onto the Plexiglas, then pour a small spoonful of paint next to the glycerin.
3. Tell the children to spread the paint and glycerin over the Plexiglas with their hands.
4. When they are finished with the first color, have them spoon the second onto the Plexiglas, if desired.
5. Invite the children to draw designs, letters, and shapes in paint.
6. When they are finished drawing, place a sheet of paper over the board.
7. Apply pressure to the paper. Ask the children to smooth the paper with their hands.
8. Lift the paper slowly and show the children the mirror image of their finger painting.

More to do
Science: Invite the children to experiment with a mirror. Put a small mark on their faces using washable paint or marker, then have them to point to it using a mirror. Write or draw on paper, then hold it up to the mirror. Write the children's names in reverse, then hold them up to the mirror.

science

Related books
I Can Tell by Touching by Carolyn Otto
My Crayons Talk by Patricia Hubbard

Cory McIntyre, Crystal Lake, IL

science

Laboratory Painting

4+

Materials
Tempera paints
Paint containers
Water
Fingerpaint paper
Pipettes and eyedroppers

What to do
1. Pour the paint into containers, thinning it with a little water.
2. Give each child a piece of finger-paint paper.
3. Supply pipettes and eyedroppers and encourage the children to drip paint on their paper, creating a design.

More to do
More art: Laminate the final product and use as a place mat. Cut the paper in shapes appropriate to the season such as a star, a leaf, a Christmas tree, or Easter egg, then paint.
Snack: Bake or buy muffins or angel food cake, then ask the children to use an eyedropper to squeeze droplets of food coloring from a cup into a bowl of frosting. Frost the baked goods and enjoy a special snack.

Related books
Archibald Frisby by Michael D. Chesworth
George Washington Carver: Scientist and Teacher by Carol Greene

Sandy Lanes, Silver Spring, MD

science

Salt Crystal Prints

Materials
¼ cup (60 mL) of Epsom salt
Shallow flat container such as a microwave snack tray
Warm water to dissolve the salt, about 1 cup (250 mL)
Liquid watercolor
Eyedropper

What to do
1. Have the children stir Epsom salt and water in a small container until salt is dissolved.
2. Let the mixture stand until water evaporates. This process takes several days.
3. When a crystal has formed, invite the children to examine it.
4. The children can squeeze several eyedroppers of liquid watercolor on the crystal, then place a piece of construction paper on top of the crystal and watercolor.
5. Show them how to press down gently, then lift the paper and see the colorful imprint of the crystal on their paper.

More to do
More art: Make greeting cards and decorate with the imprint of the crystal.
Science: Talk to children about other common crystals, such as salt and ice and sugar. Give them samples to examine.

Related books
A Drop of Water by Walter Wick
Look! Snow! by Kathryn O. Galbraith
My Five Senses by Aliki
Science Experiments You Can Eat by Vicki Cobb

Linda S. Andrews, Sonora, CA

Paper Plate Animals

Materials
Two paper plates per child

science

Construction paper (green, black, white, and red)
Tempera paint
Paintbrushes
Scissors
Glue
Stapler

What to do

1. Tell the children they are going to make an animal puppet from paper plates.
2. Invite the children to decide what kind of animal they want to make.
3. Give the children construction paper and paper plates.
4. Tell them they can make eyes out of the green, white, and black construction paper, and a tongue from red construction paper.
5. For each set of plates, cut one plate in half. Staple the edges of the plates together, then fold in half so the plate becomes an animal mouth.
6. The children can then paint the plates.
7. When the paint dries, have the children glue on the eyes and tongue. If the animal is a frog, glue a plastic or paper fly on the tongue.
8. The child places her hand in the plates to make the mouth open and close. The child's thumb goes in the bottom slot and the fingers go into the top slot.
9. Invite the children to name their animal puppets.

Related books

Duck Song by Kenneth Grahame
Frog, Duck and Rabbit by Susanna Gretz
The Frog Who Wants to Be a Singer by Linda Gross

Sandra Nagel, White Lake, MI

Recycle Sculpture

4+

Materials

Assorted, recycled scraps such as small plastic bottles, plastic caps, bottle caps, toilet paper rolls, meat trays, yarn, string, aluminum cans, and anything else handy.
Glue or masking tape
Cardboard, cut into 12" x 12" (30 cm x 30 cm) squares, one per child
Spray paint (metallic, silver, gold, bronze, copper, aluminum, or black), adult only

science

What to do

1. Help the children write their names on the back of their cardboard squares.
2. Encourage the children to select recycled materials for their sculpture.
3. Show the children how to use glue to secure pieces to the cardboard, creating a 3-D sculpture.
4. Allow the sculptures to dry overnight (if using glue).
5. Take the sculptures outside. Then, with the child observing, an adult should spray paint the entire sculpture and allow to dry. Mixing colors gives a great effect, too.

Related books

The Earth and I by Frank Asch
Mr. Willowby's Christmas Tree by Robert Barry
Where Once There Was a Wood by Denise Fleming

Dani Rosensteel, Payson, AZ

Crayon Melting

Materials

Wax paper
Construction paper
Scissors
Iron
Crayons
Dish towels

What to do

1. Ahead of time, cut wax paper into 10" (25 cm) squares and construction paper into 12" (30 cm) squares. An adult can turn the iron's temperature setting to medium.
2. Provide each child with both kinds of paper and some crayons. Have the children make a crayon drawing on the wax paper.
3. When their drawing is finished, tell them to place the square of construction paper on top of the wax paper.
4. Invite the children to watch as you make a crayon melting for them. Place a dish towel on top of the first child's papers. Explain to the children that only an adult may touch an iron. Briefly apply the warm iron to the towel.
5. Remove the iron and pull the wax paper from the construction paper. Show the children how the crayon design has been transferred to the construction paper. Invite the rest of the class, in turn, to have their designs transferred.

science

More to do

More art: Form new crayons by melting crayon pieces.

Movement: Play a dramatic selection of slow music and encourage the children to pretend they are melting.

Science: Leave a decorative candle on a hot, sunny windowsill and observe what happens over several days. Brainstorm about other materials that melt when they are heated.

Snack: Freeze juice in ice cube trays, then serve the cubes in small cups; ask the children to wait for the cubes to melt, then enjoy a cold drink.

Related books

Harold and the Purple Crayon by Crockett Johnson
My Crayons Talk by Patricia Hubbard

Cory McIntyre, Crystal Lake, IL

seasons

Autumn Leaves 3+

Materials
Butcher paper, 6' (2 m) long
Paint in fall leaf colors
Paintbrushes

What to do
1. In the center of the butcher paper, draw the outline of a tree with bare branches.
2. Have the children paint the tree trunk and branches.
3. When they are finished, invite the children to brush paint on the palms of their hands, then press their palms to the paper, making a leaf print in the shape of their hands.
4. Encourage the children to use several different colors, positioning the prints along the branches and falling from the tree.

More to do
Math: Count fresh leaves and sort them by color, then use paint and handprints to create a colorful chart or graph.
More art: Make a hand-print border for the bulletin board. Paint a tree on a smaller sheet of paper and add fingerprint leaves, then frame your leaf print in construction paper and attach small leaves or miniature pinecones to the frame with glue. Create a family tree with photos or drawings of family.

Related books
Apple Pie Tree by Zoe Hall
Have You Seen Trees? by Joanne Oppenheim

 Ivy Sher, Sherman Oaks, CA

Dandelion Painting 3+

Materials
Tempera paint (light blue, yellow, purple, and pink)
Cups for the paint
Freshly picked dandelions
Light green construction paper

What to do
1. Set one or two dandelions next to each color of paint.
2. Have the children dip the dandelions into the paint.
3. Demonstrate how to gently press a dandelion onto the paper, then lift, leaving a flower imprint.
4. Let the children make their own prints and repeat the process with several colors.
5. When the prints are finished, hang them to dry, then frame.

More to do
More art: Use other natural objects to create prints such as leaves, pieces of bark, or a sprig of evergreen. Create wrapping paper or greeting cards imprinted with dandelions and other objects. Bring in cut flowers and hang them upside-down to dry in a warm closet; use the dried flowers for decorating.

Related books
Alison's Zinnia by Anita Lobel
Chrysanthemum by Kevin Henkes
Planting a Rainbow by Lois Ehlert

Inge Mix, Massapequa, NY

3-Dimensional Flower

Materials
Pencil or marker
Poster board
Bowl
White school glue
Water
Colorful muslin or cotton, 14" x 16" (35 cm x 40 cm) pieces

What to do
1. Have the children draw a stem with leaves on the poster board.
2. In a bowl, mix three parts of glue with one part of water.
3. Let the children put the cloth into the mixture and swish the cloth around until it is saturated.
4. Help the children wring the excess liquid from the cloth.
5. Demonstrate how to arrange the cloth at the top of the stem, then invite the children to arrange their own.
6. Set the flowers aside to dry for several hours. The material will stiffen as it dries.
7. Invite older children to make several flowers and arrange them in a bouquet on their paper.

More to do
Cooking: Bake meringue and lemon pudding in a pastry shell, observing the changes in the eggs as they are beaten, then baked.
Gardening: Design a butterfly garden for the schoolyard and start the flowers from seed in the classroom.
More art: Use colorful fabric strips for the stems instead of drawing them.

Related books
Alison's Zinnia by Anita Lobel
The Gardener by Sarah Stewart

Inge Mix, Massapequa, NY

Torn Paper Snowman

Materials
White paper
Glue
Colored construction paper
Markers

What to do
1. This is a great fine motor activity. Give each child a sheet, or half a sheet, of white paper. Invite the children to tear it into pieces.
2. Encourage the children to glue the torn paper onto the colored construction paper in the shape of a snowman.
3. Children can add embellishments, such as a hat, arms, face, etc., with the markers.

More to do
Outdoors: Walk in the snow and make tracks. See if the children can match tracks to the correct shoes.
Sand and water table: Play with snow or ice in the water table. Add shovel and buckets.

Related books
Snowballs by Lois Ehlert
The Snowman by Raymond Briggs
White Snow Bright Snow by Alvin Tresselt

Amy Melisi, Oxford, MA

Mitten Painting

3+

Materials
Tempera paints
Pie pans
Knitted mittens or gloves
Construction paper, 12" x 18" (30 cm x 45 cm)

What to do
1. Bring in a collection of old and unwearable mittens or gloves. Ahead of time, you might invite the children to bring in any mittens or gloves that no longer have a match.
2. Pour paint into pie pans.
3. Invite the children in turn to put on a mitten or glove and dip it in the paint.
4. Have the children make prints on their paper in any design or color, reminding them to change gloves when they want to use a different color.

More to do
Dramatic play: Have the children pretend they are outdoors in the snow and encourage them to don hats, gloves, scarves, and boots on their own.
Math: Play a matching game or make a pattern with pairs of gloves, mittens, and socks in various colors and designs.
More art: Have older children decorate their prints with buttons, paint, or sequins. For each child, cut out a pair of their mitten prints and punch a hole at the base of each mitten; attach the mittens with yarn and use as a hanging ornament.
Outdoors: Take a wintry walk after dressing appropriately.

Related books
Footprints in the Snow by Cynthia Benjamin
Hands by Lois Ehlert
Here Comes the Snow by Angela Shelf Medearis
In the Snow: Who's Been Here? by Lindsay Barrett George
The Jacket I Wear in the Snow by Shirley Neitzel
The Mitten by Jan Brett
Snowballs by Lois Ehlert

Tina R. Woehler, Oak Point, TX

Making Snow People

3+

Materials

Snowballs by Lois Ehlert
White poster board
Scissors
Decorating materials such as scraps of fabric, gift wrap, wallpaper, construction paper, handmade confetti, pompoms, glitter, and miscellaneous sewing notions such as rickrack
Glue

What to do

1. Ahead of time, cut a small, medium, and large circle for each child from poster board.
2. Before you begin the project, read *Snowballs* to the children.
3. Have the children glue the circles together, forming a snow person.
4. Place the decorating supplies within reach and invite the children to glue an assortment of objects on their snow person.
5. Lay the snow people flat until thoroughly dry.

More to do

Games: Cut a wide opening in a large piece of cardboard and prop the cardboard between chairs; toss white Styrofoam or yarn balls through the opening. Paint a funny picture on the cardboard target, if desired.

Outdoors: Catch snowflakes on a dark piece of fabric, then examine the flakes with a magnifying glass.

Sand and water table: Bring snow indoors and play with it at the table while wearing mittens. Ask the children to predict how long it will last.

Related books

Snow Angel by Jean Marzollo
Snowsong Whistling by Karen E. Lotz
The Snowy Day by Ezra Jack Keats

Tina R. Woehler, Oak Point, TX

Hole-punch Snowflakes

Materials

White paper
Scissors
Hole punches in different shapes
Glue
Tissue paper in various colors
Yarn

What to do

1. Cut white paper into 6" (15 cm) squares.
2. Help the children fold their paper in half, then in half again.
3. Cut several free-form shapes on the folded edge of the paper. Encourage older children to cut their own.
4. Have the children unfold their paper and see the snowflake design, then invite them to punch different shapes, adding to the design.
5. When the children are finished, help them glue the tissue paper on back of their snowflake.
6. Glue a piece of yarn at the top of the tissue paper, then let the glue dry.
7. Hang the snowflake in front of a sunny window.

More to do

Circle time: Build a snowman on the flannel board and dress him. Use the snowman's circle shapes to ask the children about small, medium, and large.

Language: Have the children dictate a sentence about playing in the snow and record their words on the top half of a sheet of notebook paper; fold the paper and cut a snowflake design on the lower half. Assemble the papers into a book and make a decorative cover.

Sand and water table: Bring snow in from outdoors.

Related books

A Walk in the Snow by Phyliss Busch
When Winter Comes by Charles Phillip Fox
White Snow, Bright Snow by Alvin Tresselt

Cory McIntyre, Crystal Lake, IL

Winter Wreath

Materials

White tag board
Hole punch
Markers
Winter items such as pinecones,
   bay leaves, cinnamon sticks,
   anise stars, nutmeg, and cloves
Glue
Red or gold ribbon or yarn

What to do

1. To prepare, cut wreath shapes from tag board. Punch a hole at the top of each wreath.
2. Have the children draw on their wreath with markers, then glue a variety of the items on it as decoration.
3. Tie a ribbon through the hole in the top of each wreath to hang.

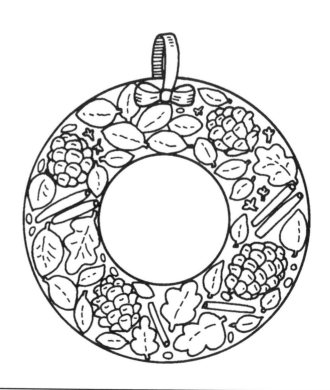

More to do

More art: Place the child's photo in the center of the wreath and wrap in handmade paper for the holidays. Make a wreath for the classroom door from pinecones sprayed with gold paint.

Math: Put extra pinecones in baskets for counting and sorting.

Snack: Enjoy a snack of cinnamon toast and baked apples, or cut cookie dough in holiday shapes, then bake. Serve with hot chocolate.

Related books

Chicken Soup With Rice by Maurice Sendak

Night Tree by Eve Bunting

Linda Atamian, Charlestown, RI

Mystery Mural

Materials

Long, flat table or smooth concrete surface

Broken, unwrapped crayons

Stencils

Butcher paper

Masking tape

What to do

1. Ahead of time and when children are not watching, place stencils randomly on the table or concrete.
2. Cover the stencils with butcher roll paper and tape ends in place.
3. Place the crayons in the center of the paper.
4. Invite the children to rub the sides of crayons over the paper to reveal images of stencils hidden under the paper.
5. When the mural is complete, hang it on a wall or ceiling.

More to do

More art: Let the children do the hiding. Put other things under the paper, such as pennies, textured wallpaper, and leaves. Use chalk instead of crayons.

seasons

Related books
Is It Red? Is It Yellow? Is It Blue? by Tana Hoban
Little Cloud by Eric Carle
My Five Senses by Aliki

Dani Rosensteel, Payson, AZ

Snow Painting

Materials
Dry tempera paint (various colors)
Plain paper
Snow
Shallow cups with spoons

What to do
1. Give each child a piece of paper.
2. Encourage the children to sprinkle tempera on their paper in small quantities.
3. Invite the children to place some snow on their paper and push it around until it melts and the powder tempera is wet. They can make interesting designs.
4. Allow the snow paintings to dry and then display for all to enjoy.

More to do
More art: Do this activity outside on a snowy day. Let children sprinkle dry tempera paint on the snow and, using fingers (with gloves on) or sticks, draw a design.
Outdoors: Take the children out on a snowy day to collect the snow for this project. Use as soon as it is brought into the classroom.

Related books
Little Blue and Little Yellow by Leo Lionni
Look! Snow! by Kathryn O. Galbraith

Dani Rosensteel, Payson, AZ

Leaf Stained Glass

3+

Materials
Assorted leaves and flowers (dried and pressed)
Clear contact paper, 12" x 12" (30 cm x 30 cm) per child
Yarn, cut in 6" (15 cm) lengths
Name of each child written on 2" x 3" (5 cm x 8 cm) pieces of construction paper

What to do
1. Help the children write their names on construction paper. Set aside.
2. Reveal half of the contact paper by peeling back the protective layer and folding it back. Hold paper in place as the child explores the sticky surface.
3. Encourage the children to place their name and the yarn at the top edge, looping the yarn so that it creates a hanger. Then have the children place dry leaves and flowers flat onto the sticky contact paper.
4. When complete, reveal the second half of the contact paper and help the children fold it over and smooth it out flat. Hang the finished work in the window for all to enjoy.

Related books
Planting a Rainbow by Lois Ehlert
Red Leaf, Yellow Leaf by Lois Ehlert
When Spring Comes by Robert Maass

Dani Rosensteel, Payson, AZ

Leaf Chalk Rubbings

4+

Materials
Assorted small- and medium-size leaves
Scrap paper or newspaper
White paper
Paperclips
Thick chalk in various colors
Fixative or hair spray

What to do

1. Invite the children to choose three or four leaves for their rubbing.
2. Have the children arrange the leaves on a sheet of paper or any surface that is identical in size to the paper they will color. Once the children are satisfied with their arrangement, have them place the white paper over the leaves.
3. Attach the top and bottom sheets of paper with clips so the paper will not shift while the children are coloring. Have the children rub the entire paper with chalk, creating an outline of each leaf.
4. When the rubbing is complete, apply the spray to fix the chalk to the paper.

More to do

Field trip: Go for a walk and collect the leaves for the rubbings. Gather several kinds of leaves for a collection.

Language: Assemble the leaf collection in a book, identifying the various kinds of leaves. Use a rubbing as the book cover.

More art: Attach a favorite leaf to the rubbing with glue. Create a unique design by adding different shapes to the leaf arrangement before coloring.

Related books

Red Leaf, Yellow Leaf by Lois Ehlert
Tree of Cranes by Allen Say
Why Do Leaves Change Color? by Betsy Maestro

Original poem

Orange, green and red, (flutter fingers in the air)
Leaves are falling on my head. (cover head)
Red, yellow, brown, (flutter fingers in the air)
Now they're falling on the ground. (point to the ground)

Christina Chilcote, New Freedom, PA

Seeds of Fall

Materials

Sunflowers with their seeds
Indian corn
Trays
Cardboard or tag board
Glue

What to do
1. Let the children examine the sunflowers and corn.
2. When they are ready, have the children remove the seeds from both plants and place the seeds in the trays.
3. Have the children arrange the seeds on their cardboard in any design, then attach them with glue.

More to do
Math: Sort a collection of seeds by kind and count them. Put them in size order.
Outdoors: Go on a nature walk and hunt for acorns and other seeds.
Science: Exhibit the growing stages of a pumpkin in the classroom. Make a bird feeder, fill it with seeds, and keep it near the classroom window.

Related books
The Carrot Seed by Ruth Krauss
How My Garden Grew by Norman Rockwell
Sunflower by Miela Ford

Melissa J. Browning, Milwaukee, WI

Sparkling Snowflakes

Materials
Lightweight cardboard circles, 4" (10 cm) in diameter, one per child
Pencil
Hole punch
Glue sticks
Silver glitter
Zip-closure sandwich bags or a disposable aluminum pie pan
Yarn or thin ribbon, one 8" (20 cm) piece per child
Scissors

What to do
1. Ahead of time, draw a snowflake pattern on each cardboard circle, or invite the children to draw their own snowflake pattern. Punch a hole near the edge.
2. Invite the children to trace over the snowflake pattern with a glue stick.
3. Put some silver glitter in a zip-closure plastic bag, and have the children drop in their circles. Let the children shake the bag, then remove the circle and shake off the excess glitter.

4. Help the children secure or loop the ribbon to the hole in the circle.
5. Hang the snowflakes from the ceiling, on a doorknob, or in front of a window.

More to do
More art: Older children can draw their own snowflake designs and/or cut designs in the cardboard with scissors. Paint a winter scene on mural paper, then sprinkle glitter on a snowman or the snowy branches of a tree.
Sand and water table: Bring snow from outdoors and play with it at the table.

Related books
Look! Snow! by Kathryn O. Galbraith
Snip, Snip...Snow! by Nancy Poydar
Snow Dance by Lezlie Evans

Christina Chilcote, New Freedom, PA

Springtime Baskets

Materials
School milk cartons, one per child
Scissors
Hole punch
Pastel-colored construction paper cut in 4" x 4" (10 cm x 10 cm) squares
Glue in small cups
Brushes
Pipe cleaners
Decorative grass or shredded paper

What to do
1. Ahead of time, wash and rinse the milk cartons, then let them dry. The children can help with this step. Cut off the top of the cartons and punch a hole on opposite sides of each carton for a handle you will attach in a later step.
2. Supply each child with a milk carton, a cup of glue, and a few squares of construction paper in assorted pastel colors.
3. Have the children tear the construction paper into small pieces.
4. When they have finished, ask the children to apply glue to the sides of their carton, then paste the scraps of paper on in any pattern or design.

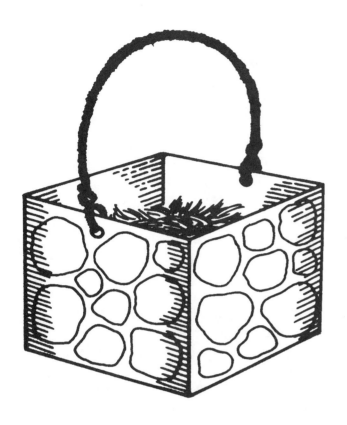

5. When the glue is dry, have the children insert one end of a pipe cleaner into the hole on the side of the carton. Help the children twist the end of the pipe cleaner to secure it. Repeat the process on the opposite side of the carton with the other end of the pipe cleaner.

6. Invite the children to fill their baskets with decorative grass.

More to do

More art: Create collage art with the leftover paper scraps, bits of fabric, and similar odds and ends.

Outdoors: Bring your baskets outside and hunt for decorated eggs or gather dandelions, clover, and buttercups.

Related books

The Boy Who Didn't Believe in Spring by Lucille Clifton

Easter Egg Artists by Adrianne Adams

Max's Chocolate Egg by Rosemary Wells

Anne Lippincott, New Hartford, CT

Tissue Square Trees

Materials

Newspaper

Wax paper in 8" (20 cm) squares

Liquid starch

Small containers

Paintbrushes

Green, red, orange, and yellow tissue cut in 1" (3 cm) squares

Black construction paper

Crayons

Tag board tree patterns, about 7" (18 cm) tall

Scissors

seasons

Glue
Hole punch

What to do
1. Spread newspaper to protect your work surface.
2. When you are ready to begin, ask the children to decide if they would like to make a tree with fall foliage or summer foliage.
3. Give each child a piece of wax paper. Have them apply liquid starch over the surface of the paper, then cover the center of the wax paper with the tissue squares, overlapping them. Help them choose the colors appropriate to their season.
4. When they have covered the center of the paper with tissue, have them apply a coat of starch over the tissue.
5. While the tissue is drying, distribute two pieces of black paper to each child. On one piece, have the children draw an outline of a tree trunk and its foliage in crayon. Help younger children trace the tree pattern.
6. Clip the sheets of black paper together to hold them in place and punch a hole inside the outline, creating an opening for your scissors. Cut along the outline through both sheets of paper.
7. Return the wax paper to the children and have them place it between the two sheets of black paper, positioning the colored tissues at the tree-shaped opening. Glue or staple the three layers together.
8. Display the finished product at a window so the sunlight will filter through the trees, illuminating them.

More to do
More art: Adapt this project for other seasons with appropriate colors and shapes. Set up a gallery space in the room for exhibiting artwork and photographs of foliage through the seasons, using prints, posters, and the children's artwork.
Circle time: Discuss how the weather changes with each season and how it affects our activities, the clothes we wear, and the foods we eat.
Science: Collect and sort pictures of deciduous and evergreen trees.

Related books
Fresh Fall Leaves by Betsy Franco
Red Leaf, Yellow Leaf by Lois Ehlert

Susan O. Hill, Lakeland, FL

Winter Landscape

4+

Materials
Cardboard or poster board
Aluminum foil
Styrofoam shapes
Glue
Toothpicks

What to do
1. Beforehand, place an extra-large piece of cardboard or poster board on a table to form the base of the winter landscape. Cut aluminum foil in irregular shapes to represent lakes and ponds.
2. Give the children a variety of Styrofoam shapes, glue, and toothpicks. Invite them to create a winter scene by making buildings, snowmen, snow forts, or igloos.
3. Encourage the children to place their Styrofoam creations on the winter landscape.

More to do
Dramatic play: Invite the children to play with their winter landscape using imaginary characters or small figures.
Math: Sort Styrofoam balls by size.
More art: Help the children stand twigs or evergreen branches in Styrofoam to resemble trees and position them around the landscape. Mold animals from clay and add them to the winter landscape. Create ice cube paintings.

Related books
Any Room For Me? by Loek Koopmans
The Mitten by Jan Brett
Snowballs by Lois Ehlert
The Snowy Day by Ezra Jack Keats

Sandy L. Scott, Vancouver, WA

Pressed Flower Place Mats

Materials

Wax paper
Fresh flowers such as buttercups, violets, mock orange blossoms, pansies, or any flower
    with delicate petals
Paper napkins
Old telephone books
Iron
Newspapers

What to do

1. Ahead of time, tear wax paper in sheets approximately 28" (70 cm) long and fold them in half.
2. Collect fresh flowers with the children, if possible, or bring flowers from elsewhere. If appropriate, ask the children to bring flowers from home.
3. When you are ready to begin, have the children open a napkin halfway and place a flower face down on it, spreading the petals, then close the napkin again.
4. Have the children place their napkin inside a telephone book with care.
5. When they are finished, stack extra weight on top of the telephone books. Set the books aside for a week, leaving the flowers to dry.
6. Approximately one week later, pre-heat your iron to the appropriate setting. Remind the children that only an adult may touch the iron.
7. Carefully remove the dried flowers from the telephone books. Open the napkins so the children can see them.
8. Place a sheet of folded wax paper on the pad of newspapers and open it. Ask the children to gently arrange several of the dried flowers on the wax paper, then fold the paper again, covering them.
9. Tell the children to move aside, then press the paper with the hot iron to fuse the two sheets of paper. Repeat the process with the remaining flowers.
10. Trim the finished product to the desired size.

More to do

More art: Trim the paper to make bookmarks. Or trim the finished product to fit inside a clear plastic lid; affix with double-sided tape and punch a hole in the lid to make a suncatcher. Wrap in handmade paper for Mother's Day or another special occasion. In the fall, follow the same steps using fresh leaves.

Science: Help the children understand how the drying process has changed the size and texture of the flowers by removing the water from them.

Related books
The Empty Pot by Demi
The Gardener by Sarah Stewart

Mary Jo Shannon, Roanoke, VA

Tomten Winter Garden 5+

Materials
The Tomten and the Fox by Astrid Lindgren
Aluminum pie plates
Jar lids or small bowls
Soil
Moss or gravel
Pinecones
Small branches
Small rocks or crystals
Water
Modeling beeswax or plasticene
Wool, felt, needle, and thread

What to do
1. Before you begin, read *The Tomten and the Fox* to the children.
2. When you are ready, have the children place the lid or small bowl in their pie plate.
3. Show the children how to add soil to the pie plate, filling in around the lid, then add a small amount of moss or gravel.
4. When they are finished, invite them to decorate their garden with a small branch and a pinecone, to represent trees, and small rocks or crystals.
5. Pour a small amount of water into the lid and place the gardens outside when the temperature is below freezing so the water will freeze.
6. Have the children add a bird, fox, or deer that they have sculpted from beeswax or plasticene.
7. Supply the children with scraps of felt and wool and help them sew their own tomten to live in their garden.

More to do
Language: As they work, ask the children to make up a story about meeting a tomten. Write down the stories.

Related books
Annie and the Wild Animals by Jan Brett
The Elves and the Shoemaker by Paul Galdone
The Tomten and the Fox by Astrid Lindgren

Linda Atamian, Charlestown, RI

A Startling Silhouette

Materials
White construction paper
Watercolor paints
Paintbrushes
Water
Cups
Black markers

What to do
1. Demonstrate how to mix watercolor paints on paper to achieve a blend of colors. Mix colors such as orange, red, and yellow or blue, green, and purple.
2. Show the children how to soften the blend of colors by wetting a clean paintbrush and moving the brush across the paper in a sweeping motion.
3. Ask the children to begin painting, encouraging them to cover their entire paper with colors, blending them.
4. When the children have finished, set their paintings aside to dry.
5. When the paint has dried, have the children draw a picture in pencil over the painting. The picture need only be an outline; no details are necessary. If the child's background color is a reddish-orange, suggestions might include a mountain top or a sailboat on the water; if the background colors are a blue-black blend, suggestions might include a house or the thick trunk and barren branches of an old tree. Older children could add a pack of coyote to the mountain top or a vulture to the tree branch.
6. When their drawing is complete, have the children color it in with black marker, creating a silhouette.

7. Have the children share their work and display it in the classroom or hallways.

More to do
More art: Hang white paper on the wall and turn the lights out, then create shadows on the paper using light; invite the children to trace the shadows or silhouettes.
Science: Experiment with shadows using the overhead projector, a bright light, or sunlight.

Related books
It Looked Like Spilt Milk by Charles G. Shaw
My Five Senses by Aliki

Mike Krestar, White Oak, PA

Miniature Spring Garden

Materials
Aluminum pie plates
Large jar lids or small bowls
Soil
Wheat berries or grass seed
Pink tissue paper
Small branches
Glue
Small rocks or crystals
Water
Modeling beeswax or plasticene
Walnut shell halves
Toothpicks
White paper scraps
Scissors

What to do
1. Have the children place the lid or small bowl in their pie plate.
2. Show the children how to add soil to the pie plate, filling in around the lid.
3. Have the children plant wheat berries or grass seed in the soil and show them how to care for it.

seasons

4. When the children have finished gardening, ask them to crumple a few scraps of pink tissue paper. Help the children glue the scraps to the tree branch, then place the branch in the garden.
5. Invite the children to add animals they have sculpted and small rocks or crystals.
6. Pour a small amount of water into each lid.
7. Have the children fill a walnut half with beeswax or plasticene. Help them glue a paper sail on to the toothpick and stand a toothpick inside the walnut. Once it is ready, invite the children to sail their boat in the pond.
8. As the grass grows, trim it with scissors as needed.

More to do
Language: Ask the children what they will do on the first day of spring and record their responses.
Outdoors: Bring your walnut boats outside after a rainstorm and sail them in puddles.
Science: Maintain a terrarium or worm garden in the classroom.

Related books
Eeny, Meeny, Miney Mole by Jane Yolen
Rabbits and Raindrops by Jim Arnosky
The Robins in Your Backyard by Nancy Caroll Willis
When Spring Comes by Robert Maasss

Linda Atamian, Charlestown, RI

self-esteem

Collage Photo Frame

3+

Materials
Tag board
Scissors
Paint
Paintbrushes
Crayons
Glue
Collage materials such as sequins, pompoms, and glitter
Child's Photo or drawing

What to do
1. Beforehand, cut a picture frame out of tag board for each child. Older children might be able to cut out their own frame with some assistance.
2. Have the children decorate their frames with paint, crayons, and the collage materials.
3. Let the frames dry.
4. Have the children choose whether the frame will hold a photo or a favorite drawing. Hang the frames around the classroom or wrap them as gifts for their family.

More to do
Field trip: Visit an art gallery or the art department at a local high school.
More art: Create self-portraits using a variety of media; choose one of the portraits for your collage frame. Make a variety of framing mats from paper; encourage the children to choose a mat for their artwork.

Related books
Art Dog by Thacher Hurd
The Incredible Painting of Felix Clouseau by Jon Agee
Norman the Doorman by Don Freeman

Deborah Hannes Litfin, Forest Hills, NY

Make-a-Wish Magic Wand   3+

Materials
Contact paper in solids or stripes
Scissors
Gold glitter
Zip-closure bag or aluminum pie pan
Plastic straws, one per child
1/8" (3 mm) wide ribbon cut in 12" (30 cm) lengths

What to do
1. Beforehand, cut out two 2" (5") stars for each child from contact paper. Place glitter in a zip-closure bag or aluminum pie pan.
2. When you are ready to begin, help the children flatten one end of their straw.
3. Remove the backing from one star and show the children how to position the flattened end of the straw in the center of the star on its adhesive side.
4. Remove the backing from the second star. Press its adhesive side to the straw and the adhesive side of the first star, without aligning the points of the stars; some of the adhesive on the stars should remain exposed.
5. Ask the children to hold the wand by the straw and move it around in the glitter until the exposed edges of the star are covered with glitter. Have the children shake the excess glitter from their wand and wash their hands.
6. Knot a ribbon around each straw near the base of the star, creating streamers.

More to do
Language: Ask the children to finish the sentence, "If I had a magic wand, I would…" and record their responses.
Outdoors: Make bubble solution and play with bubble wands in the schoolyard.

self-esteem

Related books
Draw Me a Star by Eric Carle
Fanny's Dream by Caralyn Buehner
I Wish I Were a Butterfly by James Howe
Woosh! Went the Wish by Toby Speed

Original rhyme
Abracadabra!
Poof and swish!
With this magic wand
I grant a wish.

Christina Chilcote, New Freedom, PA

"I Can" Collages

3+

Materials
Construction paper
Scissors
All by Myself by Mercer Mayer
Magazines and advertisements
Glue
Crayons
Markers
Photos, optional

What to do
1. Ahead of time, cut each child's initial from large sheets of construction paper. As an alternative, make a paper silhouette of each child by tracing his or her shadow.
2. Read the book *All by Myself* as an introduction to the activity. Encourage the children to talk about their accomplishments.
3. Supply the children with several magazines and advertising fliers, and ask them to find pictures that represent their skills and accomplishments. Examples include a bicycle, if they have learned to ride a bike, or a toothbrush, if they have learned to brush their teeth independently.
4. Have the children glue their pictures onto the construction paper and attach small photos, if they choose.
5. Help the children add short captions to their pictures. Invite them to share their accomplish-

ments with the class.

More to do
Circle time: Make a long list of all the things the children can do.
More art: Create a graph that represents the children's skills and accomplishments.

Related books
Hooray for Me! by Remy Charlip
I Never Did That Before by Lilian Moore
The Little Red Ant and the Great Big Crumb—A Mexican Fable by Shirley Climo

Phillis Esch, Export, PA

My Size Portraits

Materials
A roll of white poster or butcher paper
Pencils or felt-tipped pens
Scissors
Tempera paint in assorted colors, including beige, tan, black, and brown skin tones
Paintbrushes

What to do
1. Ahead of time, cut a piece of poster or butcher paper for each child. The paper should be long enough that the children can make life-size drawings.
2. Distribute the paper to the children and have them choose partners.
3. Ask one child in each pair to lie down on the paper on their back.
4. As the first child lies still, have her partner trace her body with a pencil or felt-tipped pen. When the outline is finished, have the children switch places and the first child makes an outline of the second child.
5. Help the children cut out their pictures. Invite them to add their features, clothing, and other details using paint and markers so that the pictures begin to look like them.
6. When the pictures are dry, display them along a wall.

More to do
Circle time: Have the children guess which outline belongs to each child. Have them introduce their Look-Alike to their class.

self-esteem

Language: Invite older children to describe themselves in their journal.
More art: Have the children trace each other on the playground using chalk. Invite the children to mold clay figures or busts of themselves.
Parent meeting: Ask family members to identify their child's "Look-Alike."

Related books
Every Buddy Counts by Stuart J. Murphy
Oh, the Places You'll Go! by Dr. Seuss
Quick as a Cricket by Audrey Wood

Barbara Saul, Eureka, CA

Mirror, Mirror

Materials
Mirror
Plexiglass
Washable markers

What to do
1. Ahead of time, find a piece of Plexiglas that will fit over the mirror. Place the Plexiglas over the mirror and tape any sharp edges.
2. Have a child sit before the mirror. Encourage the child to draw his face on the Plexiglas with markers.
3. When the child is finished, lift the Plexiglas off of the mirror and place it on the table so the child may review his art.
4. Wipe the Plexiglas clean and invite the next child to draw her portrait.

More to do
Games: Form a circle with the teacher in the center and roll a large ball to each child in turn, asking her to say her name; go round and round the circle, asking the children to name their favorite food, their favorite color, and so on.

Related books
Hooray for Me! by Remy Charlip
When I Grow Up by P. K. Hallinan
When I Was Five by Arthur Howard

Dani Rosensteel, Pason, AZ

self-esteem

Big Boo-Boo Book 3+

Materials
Adhesive bandage strips
Paper
Crayons or markers
Yarn or spiral binder

What to do
1. Give each child a bandage and a piece of paper.
2. Help the children write their name and have them position the bandage strip anywhere on the page.
3. Ask the children to draw a picture of an injury they got and have them describe their experience. Record their words on the paper.
4. Bind the pictures in a Big Boo-Boo Book. Put it where everyone can enjoy.

More to do
Dramatic play: Using simple props, have the children role play in situations where they must make a decision about safety. Set up the play area to resemble a doctor's office or emergency room.

Related books
Barney Is Best by Nancy White Carlstrom
Officer Buckle and Gloria by Peggy Rathmann
Those Mean Nasty…Germs by Judith Anne Rice
The World Is Full of Babies by Mick Manning

Dani Rosensteel, Payson, AZ

Popsicle Stick Frames 4+

Materials
Popsicle sticks
Glue
Markers

Photographs of children
Scissors

What to do
1. Help the children write their names on one of their popsicle sticks.
2. Show the children how to glue the sticks together to form a frame. Invite them to add to the first four sticks, keeping the original corners of the frame intact.
3. Set the frames aside to dry. Meanwhile, ask the families to send in a photo of their child's choice.
4. On another day, have the children color their frame with markers.
5. Glue a photograph to the back of each frame and trim the photo, if necessary.

More to do
More art: Decorate the frames with small collage supplies. Make matching pencil cups with juice cans and popsicle sticks. Make a family of stick puppets with leftover popsicle sticks.

Related books
ABC I Like Me! by Nancy Carlson
Am I Really Different? by Evelien van Dort
Quick as a Cricket by Audrey Wood

Dani Rosenthal, Payson, AZ

Personalized Place Mats

Materials
Clear contact paper, 24" x 12" (60 cm x 30 cm), one sheet per child
Pre-cut letters or child's name printed on 2" x 6" (5 cm x 15 cm) pieces of paper
Assorted small cut-outs
Confetti

Sequins, flat and 1" (3 cm) in size or less
Scissors

What to do
1. Reveal half of the contact paper by peeling back the protective layer and folding it back. Hold paper in place as the child explores the sticky surface.
2. Encourage the children to place their names (or letter cut-outs) onto the sticky paper, then add other decorations, making sure to keep all of the pieces flat and toward the center of the paper with the edges free of debris.
3. When complete, reveal the second half of the contact paper and help the children fold it over and smooth it out flat.
4. These placemats are washable and will last most of the school year.

Related books
D.W. the Picky Eater by Marc Brown
Lunch by Denise Fleming
It Looked Like Spilt Milk by Charles G. Shaw

Dani Rosensteel, Payson, AZ

Punch Pictures

Materials
Number 2 pencils with a dull tip
Construction or plain paper
Large needlepoint screens, wide-point squares
Masking or cellophane tape

What to do
1. Help the children write their names on their papers.
2. Place their paper over a screen. Place tape around the edges of the paper, securing it to the screen. Fold the tape around the back of the screen.
3. Invite the children to punch out the letters of their name with their pencil.
4. When they are finished, remove the paper from the screen and bind the edges of the paper with the tape.
5. Hang the papers in front of a light or a sunny window.

self-esteem

More to do

More art: Create a frame for the Punch Picture from poster board and personalize it with drawings or collage supplies. Punch designs related to the season or holiday.

Related books

Arthur's Neighborhood by Marc Brown
Hooray for Me by Remy Charlip and Lilian Moore
Leo the Late Bloomer by Robert Kraus

Dani Rosensteel, Payson, AZ

Personalized Doorknob Hanger 4+

Materials
Lightweight cardboard
Scissors
Crayons or felt-tipped markers
Hole punch
Narrow ribbon or raffia cut in 18" (45 cm) lengths
Stickers, optional

What to do
1. Ahead of time, cut out a cardboard strip for each child, 8" by 3" (20 cm by 8 cm). Cut out a 2" (5 cm) circle at one end of the strip to form an opening for a doorknob.
2. Before the project begins, invite the children to think of their favorite colors, foods, animals, and interests.
3. When they are ready, have the children turn the doorknob hanger so the opening is at the top. On one side of the hanger, ask them to write their name in their favorite color (help younger children do this), then draw a self-portrait.
4. When they are finished, have them turn the hanger over and draw their favorite foods, animals, and interests.
5. Punch a hole in the bottom of the hanger and string ribbon or raffia streamers through the opening.
6. Let the children decorate their hanger with stickers, if they choose.

self-esteem

More to do
Circle time: Use the hangers to introduce the children to each other at the beginning of school.
Games: Have older children portray their "favorites" by miming them; ask the other children to guess what they are doing.
More art: Make doorknob hangers for holidays and special occasions. Make bookmarks to match the hangers.

Related books
Hooray for Me! by Remy Charlip
I Wish I Were a Butterfly by James Howe
Quick as a Cricket by Audrey Wood

Christina Chilcote, New Freedom, PA

A Book About Me

Materials
White paper
Stapler
Drawing and writing tools
Magazine pictures of foods, beverages, colors, games, activities, and animals
Glue

What to do
1. Ahead of time, using paper of your choice, assemble a book for each child containing six pages. Title the pages in consecutive order: A Book About Me, Owner's Page, I am Growing, My Family Tree, My Favorites, and What is Special About Me? Under the titles on pages one through three, add the following subtitles: This is my name, Here is a picture I drew of myself, I traced around my hand.
2. On the first page, help the children write their name.
3. On the second page, invite the children to draw crayon pictures of themselves.
4. Show the children how to trace their hand and have them practice on scrap paper. When they are ready, invite them to trace their hand on page three.
5. On page four, have the children draw pictures of their family. Help them write the names of their family.
6. On page five, have the children draw or paste pictures of their favorite foods, colors, animals, and interests.

7. For the last page, encourage the children to think of something that is special about them—their birthday, a talent or interest, or extra-special belonging. Help the children put their words on paper or ask them to draw a picture.

8. Use the book to get to know the children at the start of the school year or give it as a gift to their families.

More to do

Circle time: If possible, invite the children to share their special interest or favorite game with the other children.

Snack: Enjoy a combination of the children's favorite foods or invite the children in turn to share their favorite foods with the class.

Related books

I Never Did That Before by Lilian Moore
Oh, the Places You'll Go! by Dr. Seuss
Ruby the Copycat by Peggy Rathmann

Barbara J. Lindsay, Mason City, IA

Newspaper Paintbrushes 3+

Materials
Smocks
Small trays
Tempera paint
Newspaper
Scissors
White construction paper

What to do
1. Pour the tempera paint into small trays and invite the children to put on smocks.
2. Give each child a piece of newspaper and a pair of scissors.
3. Encourage the children to cut or rip the newspaper into smaller pieces and crumple, squeeze, or roll the pieces into shapes to be used as brushes for painting.
4. Invite the children to dip their newspaper paintbrushes in the tempera paint and use them to create designs on the white construction paper.
5. Display the finished artwork around the classroom.

More to do
Math: When the activity is over, encourage the children to count how many different kinds of brushes they made and used.
More art: Try using other materials, such as strips of fabric or pieces of string, as paintbrushes.

Tracey Neumarke, Chicago, IL

Drizzle Goo 3+

Materials
1 cup (250 mL) of flour
¼ cup (60 mL) of salt
¼ cup (60 mL) of sugar
¾ cup (175 mL) of water (more for a thinner consistency)
Mixing bowls and spoons
Food coloring

Squeeze bottles such as detergent or shampoo containers
Paper
Paper products such as egg cartons, paper tubes, paper towels, and paper plates

What to do
1. Help the children combine the first four ingredients in a mixing bowl, stirring well.
2. Divide the mixture into portions. Ask the children to add a few drops of food coloring to each portion until the desired brightness or shade is achieved.
3. Pour each portion into a clean, empty squeeze bottle.
4. Invite the children to drizzle the goo onto paper and other surfaces, such as egg cartons, paper tubes, paper toweling, or paper plates. Encourage them to make interesting shapes and designs.
5. The goo will keep its shape unless the mixture has been really thinned. It takes about a day to harden.
6. After the goo has hardened, invite the children to close their eyes and feel the shapes or designs with their fingers.

More to do
Language: Encourage the children to touch a variety of materials and describe them with words such as soft, hard, smooth, rough, coarse, and slippery; cut out the words from poster board and cover them with the materials they describe.
More art: Before the goo dries, have the children sprinkle it with salt, glitter, or other materials, adding texture and interest. When the goo is almost hard, have the children press an assortment of collage materials into it. Apply the drizzle goo to other media such as tissue paper and cardboard.

Related books
I Can Tell by Touching by Carolyn Otto
First Delights: A Book About the Five Senses by Tasha Tudor

Pam Shelest, Prince George, BC, Canada

Pickle Clay

3+

Materials
15 tablespoons (225 mL) of baking powder
2½ (750 mL) cups of pickle juice or vinegar

5 cups (1.25 L) of flour
5 tablespoons (75 mL) of vegetable oil
Mixing bowl and spoons
Green paint

What to do

1. Help the children measure the baking powder, pickle juice or vinegar, flour, and oil.
2. Invite the children to stir the ingredients together in a bowl, adding a few drops of green paint for effect.
3. Encourage the children to sculpt creatures or other shapes from the clay.

More to do

Cooking: Create salad dressing with a variety of herbs, oil, and vinegar or mayonnaise.
Science: Fill mystery boxes with an assortment of objects and have the children identify what is in the boxes using their sense of smell or touch.
Snack: Enjoy a healthy snack of lettuce, raw vegetables, and the children's homemade dressing.

Related books

I Can Tell by Touching by Carolyn Otto
Sense Suspense by Bruce McMillan
Tasha Tudor's Five Senses by Tasha Tudor

MaryAnn F. Kohl, Bellingham, WA

Sensory Shoebox Collages  3+

Materials

Shoeboxes, one per child
Paper materials with interesting textures cut in small samples, such as sandpaper, foil, tissue, crepe paper, corrugated cardboard, wax paper, bubble wrap
Glue
Scissors

What to do

1. Invite children to touch the different kinds of paper and talk about how they feel the same and how they feel different.
2. Give each child a shoebox and glue. Encourage the children to cover their shoeboxes with the sensory materials.
3. After the samples have been glued and the glue is dry, encourage the children to feel the different textures with their fingertips.

More to do
More art: Invite the children to paint their collages. Have the children build a 3-D structure using the textured materials.

Related books
Fuzzy Yellow Ducklings by Matthew Van Fleet
My Five Senses by Aliki
Windsongs and Rainbows by Albert Burton

Marilyn Harding, Grimes, IA

Paint 'n' Sniff

Materials
Packets of unsweetened soft drink mix in assorted flavors and colors
Paint cups
Water
Paintbrushes
Paper

What to do
1. Combine each packet of drink mix with water in a separate cup.
2. Invite the children to paint a design or picture with the mixtures, using their sense of smell and sight to identify the different flavors.
3. Hang the pictures to dry, then display them where the children can see them and sniff them.

More to do
Gardening: Plant strawberries in a terra-cotta container and enjoy their taste and fragrance as they ripen. Plant fragrant herbs in the classroom.
Music: Ask the children to identify various sounds and musical instruments with their eyes closed.
Snack: Before snack time, blindfold the children and ask them to identify the smell of various fresh fruits and juices.

Related books
Dora Duck and the Juicy Pears by Evelien van Dort
First Delights: A Book About the Five Senses by Tasha Tudor
Fuzzy Yellow Ducklings by Matthew Van Fleet

Susan A. Sharkey, La Mesa, CA

Plastic Canvas Rubbings

3+

Materials
Plastic canvas
Scissors
Lightweight paper such as copy or computer paper
Unwrapped crayons

What to do
1. Before class, cut plastic canvas into various shapes, numbers, and letters.
2. Invite the children to choose a piece of canvas and lay it on the table in front of them. Have them run their fingers over its uneven surface, then lay their paper on top of it.
3. Show the children how to rub the side of their crayon back and forth across their paper, creating a colorful image of the canvas cut-out.
4. Encourage the children to choose a variety of cut-outs and colors.

More to do
More art: Use shapes to reinforce lessons on letters, numbers, clothing, or seasons. Make rubbings using a variety of materials; ask the children to bring materials from home or find them in the classroom and outdoors.

Related books
My Five Senses by Aliki
Sense Suspense by Bruce McMillan

Vicki L. Schneider, Oshkosh, WI

Popsicle Painting

3+

Materials
Paper plates
Paint aprons
Popsicles in assorted flavors
Glue

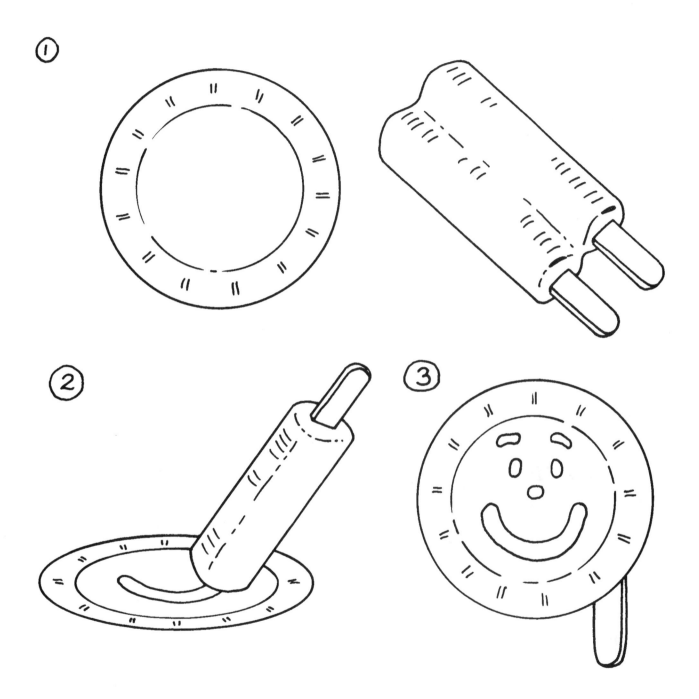

① ② ③

What to do

1. Ask the children to put on their aprons. Give each child a paper plate and a Popsicle in a flavor of their choice.
2. Invite the children to paint a face on their plate with the Popsicle. Encourage them to finish their painting before they eat the Popsicle.
3. When the painting is dry, and the Popsicle is gone, glue the stick to the edge of the plate, creating a mask or a puppet.

More to do

More art: Make paper plate puppets and decorate with a variety of fabrics and collage materials of different textures.

Snack: Freeze juices in different flavors, then ask the children to identify the flavor when blindfolded.

Related books

Fuzzy Yellow Ducklings by Matthew Van Fleet
In the Snow by Huy Voun Lee
My Many Colored Days by Dr. Seuss

Dani Rosensteel, Payson, AZ

Salt Painting

Materials

Salt
Dry tempera paint
Glue in squeeze bottles
Construction paper

What to do

1. Have the children combine salt and dry tempera paint to give the salt color.
2. Invite the children to create a design by squeezing glue from the bottle onto their paper.
3. When they are finished, have them sprinkle salt over the glue.
4. Let the picture dry, then ask the children to gently run their fingers over their artwork.

More to do

More art: Cut paper in leaf, heart, or other shapes, then decorate the shapes with textured glue in conjunction with a holiday or seasonal theme. Create a mural using various paint mixtures.

Sand and water table: Add a variety of materials including beads and buttons, then supply the children with measuring cups, bowls, and spoons.

Related books
I Can Tell by Touching by Carolyn Otto
Walter the Baker by Eric Carle

Sandy L. Scott, Vancouver, WA

Squiggle, Wiggle, and Draw

Materials
6" (15 cm) plastic, disposable plates or small Styrofoam trays, one per child
Aluminum foil
Fingerpaint or tempera paint
Plastic wrap
Tape

What to do
1. Cover each plate with aluminum foil.
2. Spoon about 2 tablespoons (30 mL) of paint onto the middle of the plate.
3. Cover the plate with plastic wrap following the contour of the plate. Do not wrap tightly.
4. Secure the plastic wrap on the back of the plate with tape.
5. Invite the children to mix the paint and create designs or pictures using their fingers.

More to do
Language: Reinforce vocabulary relating to the senses—cold, hot, slippery, rough, coarse, smooth, loud, sweet, sour.
More art: Blend primary colors to create secondary colors. Practice drawing letters or numbers.
Outdoors: Sit outside on a fair day with your eyes closed and listen carefully for sounds.
Science: Put other materials in tightly secured sandwich bags and invite the children to squeeze the bags and compare their texture.

Related books
Little Blue and Little Yellow by Leo Lionni
Mouse Paint by Ellen Stoll Walsh
My Crayons Talk by Patricia Hubbard

Patricia L. Phillips, Evansville, IN

Senses

Scented Playdough

3+

Materials
2 cups (500 mL) of flour
1 cup (250 mL) of salt
2 packages of unsweetened drink mix
Bowl
2 cups (500 mL) of boiling water
3 tablespoons (45 mL) of oil

What to do
1. Have the children mix the dry ingredients in a bowl.
2. Ask the children to step aside, then add the water and oil. Knead the mixture into a brightly colored, sweet-smelling dough, adding more flour, if necessary.
3. Invite the children to play with the dough.

More to do
Circle time: Brainstorm about the senses you use during certain activities.
More art: Add water to drink mix and use the mixture as watercolor paint.
Science: Experiment with slime and flubber.
Snack: Make a fruit kabob and compare the texture and taste of the fruits and their skins.

Related books
Little Mouse, Red Ripe Strawberry, and the Big Hungry Bear by Audrey Wood
My Five Senses by Aliki
Pat the Bunny by Dorothy Kunhardt

 Audrey F. Kanoff, Allentown, PA

Tactile Letters

3+

Materials
Card stock cut into 4" x 5" (10 cm x 13 cm) pieces, one per child
Pencils
Craft or white glue

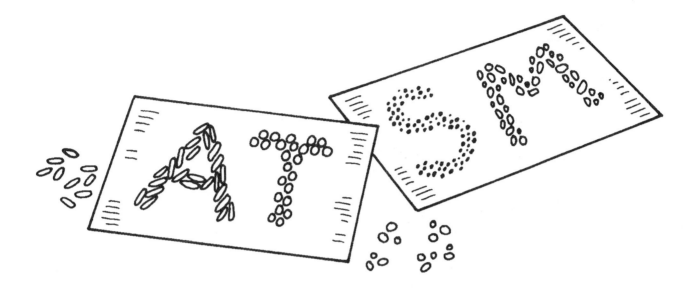

Glue brushes
Decorative materials such as aquarium gravel, coarse sand, sequins, confetti

What to do
1. Help the children write their initials on their card. Encourage them to write in large letters.
2. Instruct the children to apply glue over the letters, then place decorative materials along the strip of glue before it dries.

More to do
Language: Make an entire set of alphabet letters with the class and use the letters in a learning center. Brainstorm about opposites such as hard/soft and hot/cold.
Math: Make a set of number cards for tactile learning. Make a matching set of cards using beans or buttons.
Science: Make a chart of "Things that feel good" and "Things that don't feel good."

Related books
Anno's Alphabet by Anno Mitsmasa
Chicka-Chicka, Boom,Boom by Bill Martin, Jr., and John Archambault
Dr. Seuss's ABCs by Dr. Seuss
On Market Street by Anita and Arnold Lobel

Barbara Saul, Eureka, CA

Amazing String

Materials
Various kinds of string in different colors, cut in 8" (20 cm) lengths
Construction paper
Scissors
Glue

What to do
1. Invite the children to choose a few different pieces of string and arrange them on their paper in a design. They may cut the string in different lengths, if they choose.
2. When they are ready, help the children squeeze glue on their paper in a thin line, then lay the string in the glue.
3. Set the papers aside to dry.
4. When the glue is dry, have the children show their designs to the other children, inviting them to look and touch.

More to do
More art: Substitute fabric for the construction paper, adding another texture to the finished product. Thread various materials such as beads, wooden spools, and pompoms onto yarn or string and compare their textures.
Outdoors: Bring a ball of string onto the playground and create giant string art; trace the contour of the string art with sidewalk chalk or hop and skip in the string shapes you create.

Related books
Come to Your Senses (All Eleven of Them) by Milan Tytla
Golden Books String Games by Michelle Foerder
The Red String by Margot Blair
The Squiggle by Carole Lexa Schaefer

Mike Krestar, White Oak, PA

senses

A Picture to Feel

4+

Materials
Assortment of materials with different textures such as sandpaper, plastic lids and caps, drinking straws, satin, velvet, curling ribbon, felt, fur, corduroy, corrugated cardboard, Popsicle sticks, Styrofoam, small pebbles, screen cloth, bubble packing wrap, feathers, and pipe cleaners
Tag board or cardboard, 12" x 18" (30 cm x 45 cm) sheets, one per child
Glue
Stapler

What to do
1. Place the assortment of materials on the table.
2. Invite the children to arrange the materials in a design or picture on their paper.
3. When they have finished arranging the materials, have the children glue or staple the materials to the tag board. Encourage them to close their eyes and feel their picture, as well as the pictures created by other children.

More to do
Games: Make a set of matching cards by mounting some of the textured materials on cardboard squares, then blindfold the children and ask them to find matching pairs. Make a mystery box and fill it with various objects; invite the children to feel inside the box and guess what the objects are.
Language: Arrange buttons or shape clay into letters of the alphabet. Introduce the Braille alphabet to the children.
More art: Make rubbings with paper and crayons and textured materials such as coins or corrugated cardboard.

Related books
Fuzzy Yellow Ducklings by Matthew Van Fleet
Is it Rough, Is it Smooth? by Tana Hoban
Pat the Bunny by Dorothy Kunhardt

Sandra W. Gratias, Perkasie, PA

Ribbon Weaving

5+

Materials
Lengths of ribbon in various colors and widths
Fabric cut into 2" (5 cm) wide strips
Paper or cardboard
Cellophane tape

What to do
1. Help the children place lengths of ribbon or fabric in rows or columns across their paper.
2. Tape one end of each strip to the paper.
3. Show the children how to weave additional strips over and under the strips on their paper.
4. When the children are finished, tape the opposite ends of the strips to the paper.

More to do
More art: Trim the finished product in a basket shape, then punch two holes and attach a pipe cleaner handle.
Science: Fill a basket with a wide assortment of fabric scraps, ribbons, and string. Invite the children to compare their texture.

Related books
Abuela's Weave by Omar S. Castaneda
Kente Colors by Debbi Chocolate
My Five Senses by Aliki

Dani Rosensteel, Payson, AZ

shapes

Rectangle Art

3+

Materials
White construction paper
Chalk, markers, or crayons

What to do
1. Show the children how to fold their paper in half from top to bottom, then fold again, top to bottom. Next, ask them to fold the paper in half from side to side, then side to side once more.
2. Have them unfold their paper and count 16 rectangles within the folds.
3. Invite the children to color all of the rectangles with chalk, markers, or crayons. Encourage them to vary the colors of the rectangles, or even create a pattern by repeating colors.

More to do
Math: Practice patterns with cards and blocks that depict different shapes.
More art: Assemble the children's papers into a class quilt. Glue a photo of each child on their paper. Cut out pictures of food with different shapes, then assemble the pictures in a collage or food pyramid.

Related books
Of Colors and Things by Tana Hoban
Shapes, Shapes, Shapes by Tana Hoban

Linda S. Andrews, Sonora, CA

Eat a Shape

3+

Materials
Napkins
Crackers and cereal in various shapes

What to do
1. Have the children wash their hands.
2. Give each child a napkin and a mix of snacks. The children can open their napkins and lay the snacks on top.
3. Encourage children to identify the shapes, make a pattern, and sort their snacks by shape and

size, comparing their snacks to those of their classmates.
4. Invite them to enjoy their snack.

More to do
Circle time: Identify shapes around the classroom.
Math: Make a picture graph of objects shaped like circles, squares, triangles, and rectangles.
More art: Make a shape collage on a paper plate using paper and fabric cut-outs and miscellaneous collage materials.
Movement: Invite the children to stretch, twist, and turn into shapes on tumbling mats.
Snack: Freeze juice in molds of various shapes.

Related books
All Shapes and Sizes by John J. Reiss
Circles, Triangles and Squares by Tana Hoban
The Shape of Me and Other Stuff by Dr. Seuss
Shapes, Shapes, Shapes by Tana Hoban

Sandra Nagel, White Lake, MI

Torn Paper Mosaic

Materials
Paper
Construction paper, wallpaper scraps, tissue, and newspaper
Glue

What to do
1. In conjunction with a holiday, season, or lesson plan, cut paper in shapes such as leaves, hearts, bells, letters, numbers, or farm animals.
2. Invite the children to tear construction paper, wallpaper scraps, tissue, and newspaper into strips or scraps.
3. Have them glue the pieces onto the paper shapes, overlapping them. The pieces may be positioned in layers to create an added effect.
4. Hang the decorated shapes around the room.

More to do
More art: Create a mural using torn paper. Glue bits of eggshell or tissue paper to a clay pot or glass votive.

shapes

Related books
Grandfather Tang's Story by Ann Tompert
My Many Colored Days by Dr. Seuss
Rainbow Fish by Mark Pfister

Dani Rosensteel, Payson, AZ

Shape Mobile

Materials
Poster board
Pencil
Construction paper in various colors
Scissors
Hole punch
Markers and/or crayons
Newspaper
Tape
Twist-ties, optional
String or yarn, cut in 12" to 18" (30 cm to 45 cm) lengths

What to do
1. Ahead of time, trace shape patterns cut from poster board onto construction paper. There should be a circle, square, rectangle, and triangle for each child.
2. Help the children cut out the shapes and punch a hole at the top of each one. Invite the children to decorate their shapes with crayons and markers.
3. Ask the children to help you roll sheets of newspaper into narrow cylinders. Secure the paper with tape. Roll one cylinder for each mobile. Alternatively, form a cross bar with two cylinders and secure the intersection with string or a twist-tie.
4. Help the children tie a piece of string to each shape, then attach the other end of the string to the cylinder. Form a loop with string and attach it to the mobile for hanging. Suspend the mobiles from the ceiling.

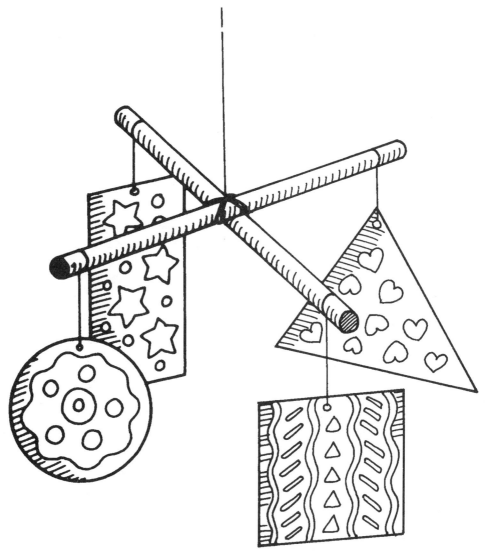

More to do
Games: Form relay teams and carry circles, squares, triangles, and rectangles to the finish line. Hide shapes in the schoolyard and conduct a scavenger hunt.

More art: Attach photos of the children to the shapes.

Related books
Little Cloud by Eric Carle
Shapes, Shapes, Shapes by Tana Hoban
What Am I? Looking Through Shapes at Apples and Grapes by N.N. Charles

Sandra Nagel, White Lake, MI

shapes

Envelope of Shapes 3+

Materials
Construction paper shapes in various colors
Envelopes
Large sheets of construction paper
Glue

What to do
1. Place an assortment of shapes in an envelope for each child.
2. When they are ready, encourage them to create a picture on construction paper using all of the shapes in their envelope. Have them glue the shapes onto the paper.
3. Ask the children to share their pictures with the class.

More to do
Games: Play "I Spy" and identify shapes in the classroom. Build structures with blocks.
More art: Give the children an assortment of collage materials in varied shapes and create three-dimensional art.

Related books and song
Grandfather Tang's Story by Ann Tompert
Shapes, Shapes, Shapes by Tana Hoban
Shapes by Hap Palmer
"Triangles, Circles and Squares" by Greg and Steve

Kaethe Lewandowski, Centreville, VA

See My Pretty Colored Shapes 3+

Materials
Gloves
Small plastic cups
Cooking oil
Food coloring
Multicolored glitter

shapes

Water
16-ounce (500 mL) plastic soda bottle and cap, label removed
Plastic spoons

What to do
1. Wearing gloves, pour cooking oil into small plastic cups.
2. Invite the children to add a few drops of food coloring and to each cup. Have them sprinkle some glitter in each cup.
3. Pour water into the bottle until it is roughly one-half to two-thirds full.
4. Add a few spoonfuls of oil from each cup to the bottle. Close the cap securely.
5. Ask the children to observe the shapes that form in the water.
6. When the oil settles, invite the children in turn to shake the bottle and observe the changing colors and shapes.

More to do
Cooking: Mold gelatin in different shapes.
Science: Create slime or flubber and watch it conform to the shape of its container. Bring a lava lamp to class.

Related song
Sing to the tune of "Shake your Booty."

Shake my bottle,
Shake my bottle,
Shake, shake, shake,
Shake, shake, shake,
Shake my bottle.

Gloria C. Jones, Great Mills, MD

Round and Round

Materials
Paper plates, one per child
Pictures of round objects cut from magazines or advertising fliers
Glue in cups
Paintbrushes

shapes

What to do
1. Put out an assortment of pictures of round objects. These could include pictures of oranges, beach balls, and the sun and moon.
2. Have the children cover their plate with glue.
3. Invite them to glue pictures of round things on the plate, covering its entire surface.

More to do
Circle time: Have the children gather in a circle around you, then roll an indoor ball to each child; when they catch the ball, they name an object that is round or spherical.
Games: Play circle games such as "Ring around the rosy" and "Here we go 'round the mulberry bush."
Math: Sort coins by their size.
More art: Construct a mobile with the plates and hang it in front of a window or outside on a breezy day. Roll clay and sculpt round shapes.

Related books
If You Give a Mouse a Cookie by Laura Joffe Numeroff
What Am I? Looking Through Shapes at Apples and Grapes by N.N. Charles

Cindy Paddock, Palm Bay, FL

Pennant Paintings

Materials
Construction paper
Scissors
Newspaper
Tempera paint in 2 or 3 colors
Paint containers
Paintbrushes
Straw
Tape

What to do
1. Beforehand, cut construction paper into pennant shapes. Cover your work area with newspaper and pour the paint into containers.
2. Ask the children to dip their brush in paint and dab color on the pennant. Show them how to use different strokes to create a variety of shapes and lines that conform to the shape of the pennant.

3. When the paint dries, attach a straw or thin roll of newspaper with tape to form a handle.

More to do
Flannel board: Cut squares and triangles from flannel and fit them on flannel pennants.
Snack: Cut peanut butter and jelly finger sandwiches in pennant shapes. Cut wedges of cheese and serve on triangular-shaped crackers.

Related books
Circles, Triangles, Squares by Tana Hoban
Listen to the Shape by Marcia Brown

Cory McIntyre, Crystal Lake, IL

Bubble Prints

Materials
Tempera paints
Paint containers
Paintbrushes
Bubble packaging wrap
Construction paper

What to do
1. Pour the paint into containers and supply the children with brushes.
2. Have the children paint a sheet of bubble wrap.
3. When they are finished, have them place a sheet of paper over the bubble wrap and gently press the paper to the wrap.
4. Have the children lift the paper, revealing a colorful image of the bubble wrap.

More to do
More art: Cut the bubble wrap in shapes and cut shapes from the bubble wrap prints; attach a string to the prints and use as a hanging ornament. Print on tissue or butcher paper and make gift wrap.
Movement: Let the children stomp on sheets of bubble wrap to pop the bubbles.
Outdoors: Blow bubbles using a variety of bubble wands.

Related books
Bubble Bubble by Mercer Mayer
Soap Bubble Magic by Seymour Simon

 Cory McIntyre, Crystal Lake, IL

Plunger Painting   3+

Materials
Plungers
Large paper
Paint

What to do
1. Lay a large sheet or sheets of paper on the floor.
2. Place paint in shallow trays or paper plates.
3. Have the children place the plungers in the paint and then make circle prints on the paper. (Two children can work together for this.)
4. This is a good activity for any shape unit, and the finished product makes great wrapping paper.

More to do
More art: Take the plunger and a bucket of water outside on a sunny day. Invite the children to make plunger prints on the sidewalk using water.

Related books
Little Blue and Little Yellow by Leo Lionni
Wheels on the Bus by Maryann Kovalski

Audrey F. Kanoff, Allentown, PA

shapes

Shape a Story

4+

Materials
Changes, Changes by Pat Hutchins
Shapes in varying colors and sizes cut from construction paper, fabric, and wallpaper
Construction paper
Glue

What to do
1. Share the book *Changes, Changes* with the class.
2. Allow the children time to brainstorm about a story they could depict using shapes.
3. Provide the children with a variety of shapes, construction paper, and glue.
4. Encourage the children to depict a story, then glue the shapes onto their paper.
5. Ask the children to share their story with the class. Record the stories on paper or audio tape.

More to do
More art: Ask older children to create a set of pictures using shapes, then place the pictures in sequence.
Outdoors: Go for a walk and identify shapes in the natural environment.

Related books
Eating the Alphabet by Lois Ehlert
Have You Seen My Cat? by Eric Carle

Lyndall Warren, Milledgeville, GA

Three-dimensional Collages
4+

Materials
Colored construction paper
Scissors
A pop-up picture book and an ordinary picture book
White art paper
Small scraps of construction paper
Glue

446

shapes

What to do

1. Cut some of the construction paper into strips varying in width from 1" to 1¹⁄₂" (3 cm to 4 cm) and in length from 6" to 8" (15 cm to 20 cm). Cut the rest of the paper into circles, then cut on a diagonal from the edge of each circle toward its center, creating spirals.
2. Show the students an ordinary picture book and a pop-up book and help them understand the difference between two-dimensional and three-dimensional illustrations.
3. Invite the children to make a three-dimensional collage. Demonstrate how to paste one end of a strip of paper onto the art paper and fold a crease in the strip to make it stand upright; then paste the opposite end of the strip on the paper, creating a loop.
4. Help the children create loops, weaving the loops over and under each other, if desired. Show the children how to paste one end of a spiral on the art paper as if it were a spring.
5. Have the children add various scraps of paper to their collage, folding them so they remain upright.

More to do

Dramatic play: Spread a large sheet of butcher paper on the floor and invite the children to make a crayon drawing of the community, then supply blocks of all shapes for building houses, schools, cars, trucks, and more.
Games: Play with slinky toys and learn more about spirals.
More art: Create pop-up greeting cards.

Related books

Glad Monster, Sad Monster: A Book About Feelings by Ed Emberley and Anna Miranda
Pat the Bunny by Dorothy Kunhardt

Barbara Saul, Eureka, CA

 **shapes**

Yarn Designs on Geoboards

Materials

Two 8" (20 cm) square wooden geoboards painted black, with grids of small head nails positioned about 1" (3 cm) apart

Yarn cut in 24" (60 cm) lengths with a small loop tied at each end

What to do

1. Demonstrate how to slip the loop at one end of the yarn over any nail on the geoboard, then wrap the yarn around other nails on the board, forming a design or shape.
2. When you reach the end of the yarn, slip the loop over the last nail in your design to hold the yarn in place.
3. Invite the children to take a turn at the geoboard. Ask them to duplicate your design on the second geoboard using the same color of yarn.
4. When a child's turn is finished, remove the yarn from the board and invite the next child.
5. Switch roles with the children, inviting them to create a design that you will duplicate on the other geoboard, or ask them to work in pairs.

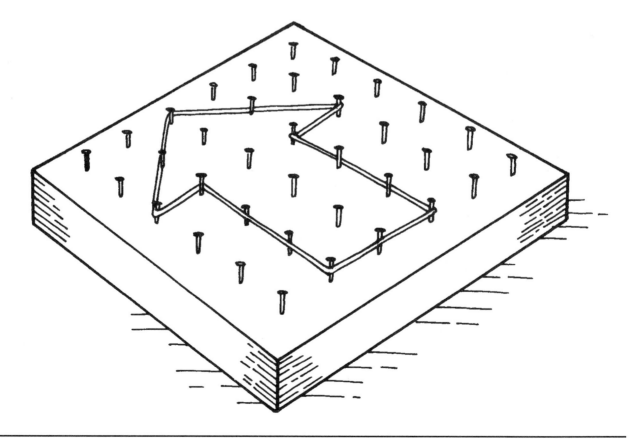

More to do
Games: Create cards showing a picture or shape and challenge the children to duplicate it on the board.

Language: Have the children weave alphabet letters and corresponding words on the geoboards.

More art: Use two or more colors and different lengths of yarn on each board. Make yarn pictures on construction paper, embroider simple designs on embroidery cloth, or make an octopus and other creatures from yarn.

Related books
Abuela's Weave by Omar S. Castaneda
Hands by Lois Ehlert
Kente Colors by Debbi Chocolate

Susan Jones Jensen, Norman, OK

Suncatcher Shapes

Materials
Newspaper
Glue
Shallow containers
Water
Scissors
String or yarn
Tag board
Paintbrushes
Clear plastic disposable lids, 5" (13 cm) or more in diameter, 4 per child
Tissue, cut in 1" (3 cm) squares in assorted colors
Cardboard patterns of triangles, squares, rectangles, and circles
Markers
Hole punch
Stapler

What to do
1. Before class, protect your work surface with newspaper. In shallow containers, dilute the glue with a small amount of water. Cut four lengths of string or yarn for each child, approximately

shapes

5" long. Cut tag board in 2" (5 cm) wide, 16" (40 cm) long strips.

2. When you are ready to begin, have the children brush glue on the first lid, then place tissue squares on the lid, overlapping them. Have the children apply another coat of glue over the tissue squares. When they are finished, ask them to repeat the process with the remaining lids, then set them aside to dry.
3. Later, have the children turn the lids over and trace a cardboard pattern of each shape onto each lid.
4. Cut out the shapes and punch a hole at the top of each one. Form a circle with each strip of tag board and staple the ends together.
5. Help the children punch four evenly spaced holes along the bottom of the circle and two holes along the top.
6. Show the children how to tie one end of each string to a shape and the other end to the bottom of the tag board circle. To hang the mobile, loop the fifth piece of string through the openings on the top of the circle.

More to do
Games: Play "Duck, Duck, Goose," substituting the names of shapes.
Math: Make a picture graph of the children's favorite shapes. Use cut-out shapes to create patterns. Paint shapes using sponges or potato halves.

Related books
Of Colors and Things by Tana Hoban
What Am I? Looking Through Shapes at Apples and Grapes by N. N. Charles
White on Black by Tana Hoban

Susan O. Hill, Lakeland, FL

Straw Necklaces

Materials
Blunt plastic needles
Crochet thread
Straws cut into different lengths
Construction paper, cut in 1" (3 cm) squares

What to do
1. Show the children how to thread their needle, then string the sections of straw and squares of paper, alternating them.

shapes

2. Help the children tie the ends of their thread when they are finished.

More to do
Math: Provide a variety of shapes for older children and invite them to make an interesting pattern.
More art: Work as a team and make decorative garland in holiday colors and shapes.

Related books
The Shape of Me and Other Stuff by Dr. Seuss
Shapes, Shapes, Shapes by Tana Hoban

Sandra Hutchins Lucas, Cox's Creek, KY

shapes

Wood Sculpture

4+

Materials
Wood scraps
Wood glue
Small sponge
Markers or paint and paintbrushes, optional

What to do
1. Give each child an assortment of wood scraps. Encourage the children to arrange the scraps in a variety of designs.
2. When they are satisfied with an arrangement, have them glue the pieces together in a wood sculpture.
3. Wipe away any extra glue, then place the sculpture where it will not be disturbed and let it dry overnight.
4. The following day, let the children color or paint their sculpture, if they choose.
5. Invite the children to name their work of art.

More to do
Field trip: Visit an outdoor sculpture garden or a sculpture exhibit at a local gallery.
Language: Use the sculpture as a "story starter," and encourage the children to compose a story surrounding their sculpture.
More art: Decorate the sculpture with collage materials once it has dried. Use the sculpture as a paperweight or attach a small photo to one of its surfaces. Display the sculptures in an exhibit for others to enjoy. Introduce the work of Alexander Calder to the children.

Related books
Celebrate America in Poetry and Art by Nora Pancer
Construction Zone by Tana Hoban

Susan Jones Jensen, Norman, OK

Totally Tearing

Materials
Scraps of all different kinds of paper, such as construction paper, tissue paper,
 wallpaper, wrapping paper
Glue
Sheets of construction paper

What to do
1. Supply the children with paper scraps, glue, and a sheet of construction paper.
2. Invite the children to create a picture by tearing the scraps of paper into shapes and arranging the shapes on construction paper. The picture may be realistic or imaginary, but the children may not use any other supplies.
3. When they are finished designing their work, have the children then glue the shapes onto the paper.

More to do
Language: Design a book using torn paper collage; have the children write or dictate a few sentences about their collage.
More art: Show the children prints or posters of torn paper collages by Henri Matisse and the work of children's book illustrators Eric Carle and Susan Roth.

Related books
From Head to Toe by Eric Carle
Polar Bear, Polar Bear, What Do You Hear? by Bill Martin, Jr., and Eric Carle
The Very Quiet Cricket by Eric Carle

Nicole Sparks, Miami, FL

Toothpick Sculptures

Materials
Wooden toothpicks
Styrofoam balls, blocks, and packing peanuts
Styrofoam meat trays cut in pieces

shapes

Scraps of construction and wrapping paper
Glue
Scissors

What to do

1. Peruse books and walk outdoors, drawing the children's attention to the many forms of structures. Show them examples of sculptures, particularly outdoor sculptures in a garden or public square.
2. Show the children how to connect the Styrofoam pieces with toothpicks.
3. Encourage the children to create three-dimensional sculptures and structures.
4. When they are finished, let the children decorate the sculptures with paper scraps, if they choose.

More to do

Field trip: Visit a sculpture garden or museum.
Language: Invite the children to describe their sculpture to the class or in their journal.
More art: On neon-colored paper, photocopy textbook pictures of traffic signs with different shapes and attach the pictures to Styrofoam blocks with toothpicks; construct cars, trucks, and buses from Styrofoam blocks.

Related books

Celebrate America in Poetry and Art by Nora Pancer
Getting to Know the World's Greatest Artists Series by Mike Venezia

Barbara Saul, Eureka, CA

Me and My Shadow   3+

Materials
Large sheet of black butcher paper
White chalk
Scissors

What to do
1. Spread the butcher paper on the floor.
2. Choose two to five children at a time to lie side by side with their chest, head, and shoulders on the paper.
3. Ask the children to put their arms around the shoulders or waist of the children on either side of them as friends would do when walking together.
4. Invite a few of the other children in the class to draw a chalk outline of the children on the paper.
5. When the outline is drawn, ask the children to stand up carefully, revealing the facsimile of their shadow. Repeat the process with the rest of the children.
6. When all of the children have had a chance to create a shadow, cut along the chalk lines and hang the shadows on the wall.

More to do
Games: Ask the children to bring in a game from home that they can share with their classmates.
More art: Decorate the shadows with glitter, sequins, colored glue, and bright yarn. Find and trace shadows around the classroom or on the playground; cut out the shadows and arrange them in a shadow montage. Create spooky shadow forms for Halloween. Make strings of paper dolls and have the children decorate them in small groups, sharing a limited amount of supplies.

Related books
Shadowgraphs by Phila Webb and Jane Corby
Shadow Play by Paul Fleischman
Shadows by Dennis Haseley

Virginia Jean Herrod, Columbia, SC

Sharing

Buddy Paintings

4+

Materials
Smocks
Yarn
Tempera paints
Large paintbrushes
Easel paper

What to do
1. Encourage the children to wear old clothing and art smocks.
2. Ask the children to choose a buddy or painting partner.
3. Tie the partners' arms together at the wrist with yarn, securing one child's left arm to the other's right arm.
4. Give the children one or two paintbrushes and ask them to paint a picture at the easel together. They may hold a brush in their free hand or their tied hand, or hold one brush together.
5. When they finish their picture, encourage the children to try again with another partner. Label the pictures carefully so the children can find their artwork.

More to do
Games: Have a three-legged race.
More art: Have the children work in the same pairs and design a frame for their artwork.
Outdoors: Bring the easels outside on a nice day.
Snack: Have the children bring a snack from home for their partner.

Related books
Frog and Toad Are Friends by Arnold Lobel
Lizzie Logan Wears Purple Sunglasses by Eileen Spinelli
Margaret and Margarita by Lynn Reiser

Virginia Jean Herrod, Columbia, SC

Butterfly Art in Sign Language

Materials needed

White paper
Pencil
Crayons

What to do

1. Talk about and practice the sign for butterfly in sign language. Show children how to cross their wrists and hook their thumbs together with palms facing inward.
2. Have the children each make the sign for butterfly when their hands are on top of a white sheet of paper.
3. Trace around their butterfly hand shapes with a pencil.
4. Invite the children to decorate their own hand shapes with crayons to resemble a unique butterfly.

Related books

The Butterfly Alphabet by Kjell B. Sandved
The Kissing Hand by Audrey Penn
Simple Signs by Cindy Wheeler

Nancy Dentler, Mobile, AL

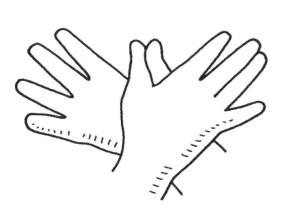

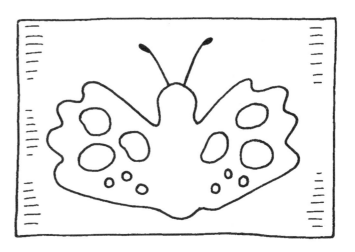

Sign Language Alphabet Book 4+

Materials
The Handmade Alphabet Book by Laura Rankin
Paper
Copy machine
Crayons
Felt-tipped pen
Hole punch
Brads or notebook binder rings
Tag board

What to do
1. Share *The Handmade Alphabet Book* or a similar book with the children.
2. Reproduce a picture of the sign language for the letters *A* through *Z* on individual sheets of paper. Distribute the papers to the children.
3. Help the children think of an object that starts with the letter on their page and invite them to draw a crayon picture of the object.
4. With a felt-tipped pen, write a sentence on each page such as "*A* is for alligator."
5. Punch holes in the pages and bind them with brads or rings, adding a decorative tag board cover.
6. Let the children bring the book home for a few days at a time to share with their families.

More to do
Guest: Invite a group that performs using sign language, inspiring the children to learn the language.
Music: Sign while singing the ABCs.

Related books
The Handmade Alphabet Book by Laura Rankin
Simple Signs by Cindy Wheeler

Nancy Dentler, Mobile, AL

Sign Language Initial Plate (Sign Your Name)

Materials
Paper
Copy machine
Glue
Paper plates
Crayons
Markers
Hole punch
Scissors
Yarn, cut in approximately 1′ (30 cm) lengths

What to do
1. Ahead of time, reproduce pictures of the alphabet in sign language on individual sheets of paper. Copy a sufficient number of your children's first initials.
2. Help each child find her first initial in the sign language alphabet.
3. Have the children paste their initial in sign on a paper plate and color it.
4. Next to or under the picture, write the words "…is for (child's name)", forming a rebus.
5. Punch two holes in the top of the plate and attach a length of yarn.
6. Hang the children's plates around the room or near their cubbies.
7. Practice signing initials with the children.

More to do
Language: Recite a poem using words and sign language. Teach the children to communicate a familiar phrase in sign language each day.

Related books
Handtalk: An ABC of Finger Spelling and Sign Language by Remy Charlip and Mary Beth Miller
Handsigns: A Sign Language Alphabet by Kathleen Fain
The Handmade Alphabet Book by Laura Rankin

Nancy Dentler, Mobile, AL

Pizza Party

3+

Materials
Tag board circles
Glue
Red tempera paint
Paintbrushes
Collage items (yarn, Styrofoam peanuts, felt, beads, etc)
Scissors

What to do
1. Give each child a tag board circle for the "crust."
2. Make a "sauce" mixture of one-half glue to one-half red tempera paint.
3. Have the children paint the "sauce" on the tag board circle.
4. Put collage items and scissors on the table, and ask the children to use them to make the "cheese" and the "toppings," and to stick them on the "sauce."

More to do
Cooking: Make bagel pizzas.
Dramatic play: Set up a pizza parlor in the classroom.
Fine motor: Use playdough to make pizzas.

Related books
Curious George and the Pizza by Margaret Rey
Hold the Anchovies by Shelley Rotner
There's a Party at Mona's Tonight by Harry Allard

 Sandy Lanes, Silver Spring, MD

Mardi Gras Backdrop

3+

Materials
White bulletin board paper
Aluminum pie pans
Various colors of tempera paint
Soft bath sponges

What to do

1. Hang the bulletin board paper on a wall, at the children's level.
2. Fill the pie pans with the paint.
3. Have small groups of children dip the soft bath sponges into the paint and press them all over the bulletin board paper.
4. Upon completion, the children will have created a colorful, festive bulletin board or wall backdrop.

More to do

Dramatic play: Encourage the children to dress up with colorful beads and masks and have a Mardi Gras parade.

More art: String beads for Mardi Gras necklaces. Make Mardi Gras masks out of paper plates and colorful feathers to hang on the bulletin board.

Related books

Jenny Giraffe's Mardi Gras Ride by Cecilia Dartez
Mardi Gras in the Country by Mary Alice Fontenot

Donna Kobal, Lansford, PA

Birthday Candle Holder

Materials

Flour 1 cup (250 mL)
Water ½ cup (125 mL)
Salt ½ cup (125 mL)
Oil ¼ teaspoon (1 mL)
Bowl
Food coloring, optional
Paint and paintbrushes
Small birthday candles

What to do

1. Mix the first four ingredients in a bowl, adding the food coloring, if desired.
2. Invite the children to take a turn kneading the dough. Continue kneading the dough until it is smooth.
3. When the dough is ready, divide it among the children and ask them to shape it into any kind of crawling creature.

4. When they are done, show them how to make a hole for a candle with their index finger.
5. Bake the dough creatures at 375° F (190° C) for 45 minutes or set them aside for one day to dry on their own.
6. When the dough is dry and hard, have the children paint their creatures, then set them aside again to dry.
7. Insert the birthday candles and use for a special celebration.

More to do
Language: Blow the candles out, inviting the children to wish for a journey to anywhere, real or imaginary; record their responses in a book of wishes or their journals.
Math: Shape the candle holders in a number for the children's age at their next birthday.
Science: Make the creepy crawly creatures in conjunction with a unit on insects.

Related books
Birthday Monsters by Sandra Boynton
The Grouchy Ladybug by Eric Carle
The Very Hungry Caterpillar by Eric Carle

Inge Mix, Massapequa, NY

special days

Happy New Year!

Materials
Balloon
Glitter, sequins, and confetti
Funnel
String
Contact paper or ordinary paper sprayed with adhesive
Noisemakers and musical instruments
Pin taped to a ruler or yardstick

What to do
1. Using a funnel, help the children fill a balloon with glitter, sequins, and confetti.
2. Inflate the balloon and hang it by a string from the ceiling.
3. Place a sheet of contact or adhesive paper on the floor below the balloon, adhesive side facing up.
4. Have the children gather around the paper. Supply them with noisemakers and instruments.
5. Count down to the New Year. At zero, pop the balloon with a pin, releasing the glitter and other materials from the balloon in a sparkling display.
6. Encourage the children to welcome the New Year with cheers and noise-making while they watch the sparkles fall from the air and settle on the paper in a colorful pattern.
7. Use the paper to decorate a bulletin board or cut it into shapes.

More to do
Math: Ahead of time, practice counting backward from 10 and moving the hands of the clock toward midnight. Design a calendar for the coming year.
Sand and water table: Provide the children with funnels and an assortment of plastic cups, bowls, and utensils.

Related books
Celebrations by Myra Cohn Livingston
Dumpling Soup by Jama Kim Rattigan
How My Family Lives in America by Susan Kuklin

Carol Nelson, Rockford, IL

Wild West Vests

Materials

Paper grocery bags
Scissors
Markers
Crayons
Odds and ends such as rickrack, pompoms, sequins, yarn, and patches
Glue

What to do

1. Ahead of time, cut a paper bag in the shape of a vest for each child. To do so, cut a circle in the bottom of the bag for the child's neck and cut an armhole on each side. Cut an opening along the length of the bag forming the front of the vest.
2. Invite the children to decorate their vest using markers, crayons, and various odds and ends.
3. Show the children how they can snip the bottom edge of their vest with scissors, creating fringe.
4. Put out some cowboy hats and stick horses, and encourage the children to play Wild West.

More to do

Cooking: Make cornbread, applesauce, or other simple treats dating from long ago.
Dramatic play: Supply a few props and invite the children to set up a pioneer home or community in the play area.
Social studies: Place an oversize map of our country on the floor and invite older children to trace the route of the early pioneers.

Related books

Cowboy Cal by Jim Kraft
Cowboy and the Black-Eyed Pea by Tony Johnson
Matthew the Cowboy by Ruth Hooker

Sandra Nagel, White Lake, MI

special days

Flag Art

3+

Materials
Flag of any kind
White poster board cut into rectangular pieces
Construction paper in various colors
Glue
Shallow containers
Small paintbrushes

What to do
1. Beforehand, draw the design of the flag onto a small piece of poster board for each child. Tear construction paper in the colors of the flag into small bits. Display a real flag where the children can easily see it.
2. Pour glue into shallow containers. Have the children apply glue to their poster board using a brush.
3. Ask the children to follow the design of the flag and position the pieces of construction paper on the poster board.
4. Set the flags aside for several hours to dry. Display around the room.

More to do
Circle time: Talk about the colors and meaning of small flags that the children bring from home.
Games: Make a floor puzzle from a crayon drawing of a flag on large poster board; laminate the board and cut it into pieces. Provide the children with small flags from around the world and pretend you are in the Olympic Games; have an opening processional and ask the children to represent a country in various Olympic events.
More art: Make flags of all sizes to celebrate the seasons and holidays with scraps of fabric.
Outdoors: Take a walk in the neighborhood and see how many flags are displayed.

Tina R. Woehler, Oak Point, TX

Birthday Cupcake

3+

Materials

Cupcake pattern
Construction paper
Scissors
White glue
Popsicle sticks or spoons
Confetti or shredded paper
Markers or pencils

What to do

1. Ahead of time, cut out cupcake shapes from construction paper, or invite the children to cut out their own using a pattern.
2. Have the children use a stick or spoon to spread glue on the top of the cupcake as if they were frosting it. Before the glue dries, ask the children to sprinkle confetti on their cupcake.
3. When the glue dries, help the children write their name and birthday on the bottom half of the cupcake.
4. Hang the cupcakes on a bulletin board. Add photos of the children and their birthday celebrations.

More to do

More art: Make a special crown for the birthday child. Design a colorful birthday flag with fabric scraps and display it on the children's birthdays. Build a simple castle for the birthday prince or princess with cake frosting, graham crackers, and sugar cones, then decorate with a few candies.

Related books

Carl's Birthday by Alexandra Day
Gorilla by Anthony Browne
Happy Birthday Moon! by Frank Asch
Little Gorilla by Ruth Bornstein
On the Day You Were Born by Debra Fraser
Spot's Birthday by Eric Hill

Tracie O'Hara, Charlotte, NC

special days

Birthday Crowns

3+

Materials
New or used bulletin border
Scissors
Markers, crayons
Assorted supplies such as sequins, buttons, and miscellaneous parts from old costume and play jewelry
Glue
Tape or stapler

What to do
1. Measure and cut the strip of border to fit the birthday child's head.
2. Allow the child to decorate her crown with markers, crayons, and assorted supplies.
3. Tape or staple the crown together.

More to do
Language: Ask older children to write a letter to the birthday child using invented spelling. Assemble their letters in a book and present it as a gift.
More art: On another day, make hats representing community workers.

Related books
The Birthday Swap by Loretta Lopez
Happy Birthday, Moon by Frank Asch
Hats, Hats, Hats by Ann Morris

Tracie O'Hara, Charlotte, NC

Mother's Book Bag

3+

Materials
Canvas bags, one per child
Newspaper
Fabric markers in a variety of colors

What to do

1. Place a few sheets of newspaper inside each bag so color will not transfer from one side to the other.
2. Invite the children to draw a picture for their mother on the bag, using fabric markers.
3. Let the bags dry and send them home to the children's mothers for special occasions, such as Mother's Day.

More to do

Cooking: Make a special heart-shaped treat and send it home in the bag.

Language: Make a book about mothers, then reproduce it and send it home in Mother's Book Bag.

More art: Decorate tissue or cellophane wrap with the children's handprints using paint. Mold ring-holders from clay and paint them.

Related books

Lots of Moms by Shelley Rotner
Mama Zooms by Jane Cowen-Fletcher
Mommies Don't Get Sick by Marilyn Hafner
Mr. Rabbit and the Lovely Present by Charlotte Zolotow

Debbie Barbuch, Sheboygan, WI

CD Picture Frame 3+

Materials

Construction paper or poster board in bright colors
Scissors
Photos
Compact disk cases, one per child
Fabric paint
Assorted supplies such as sequins, beads, and buttons
Glue

What to do

1. Ahead of time, cut backing from paper or poster board for each case. Insert the backing in each case. Take photos of the children during class or have them bring a photo from home.
2. Invite the children to decorate the border of the case with fabric paint and an assortment of

supplies.

3. Insert the photo in the case. Make a framing mat from paper or poster board, if desired.

More to do
More art: Frame the miniature photos that accompany developed film to make pendants or magnets using bottle caps, large buttons, or any flat disk. Or, affix the miniature photos to wooden building blocks.

Related books
Badger's Bring Something Party by Hiawyn Oram
January Rides the Wind: A Book of Months by Charlotte F. Otten

Ellen Forte, Mesa, AZ

Rustic Frame

3+

Materials
Photo of each child
Sturdy twigs or sticks, 6" (15 cm) long
Leather cord or yarn, cut into 6" (15 cm) lengths
Clear contact paper
Scissors
Hole punch
Yarn
Plastic lacing needles

What to do
1. Beforehand, take photos of the children in class or have them bring photos from home.
2. Have the children arrange four sticks in the shape of a frame. Help the children secure the corners of the frame with yarn or leather cord.
3. Cut two pieces of contact paper for each child that will extend 1" (3 cm) beyond the edges of their photo.
4. Place one piece of contact paper, adhesive side up, in front of each child and help the children center their photo on the contact paper; then, have the children place the second piece of contact paper over the photo, adhesive side down. Smooth any bubbles and trim raw edges while maintaining the 1" (3 cm) margin.
5. Have the children punch three or four holes in the margin on each side of their photo.

6. When they are done, ask the children to place their frame over their photo.
7. Tie yarn to each frame and thread a lacing needle for each child. Show the children how to whip stitch through the holes in the contact paper and around the stick frame, securing the photo to the frame.
8. When they have finished, tie a knot in the yarn.

More to do
More art: Glue miniature pinecones and dried berries to the frame. Lace yarn through large wooden beads or fun foam, creating necklaces or key chains. Sew simple designs on embroidery cloth with yarn.

Related books
Badger's Bring Something Party by Hiawyn Oram
Josefina by Jeanette Winter

Dani Rosensteel, Payson, AZ

special days

Moon Landing Celebration

Materials
Gray clay or playdough
Coffee can or similar lids
Store-bought toothpick flags
Glue
Shoe from 11" (28 cm) male fashion doll or army character
Marbles
Flat cardboard squares

What to do
1. Have the children press clay or playdough into the lid of a coffee can.
2. When they are done, have the children press a flag into the clay. It might be necessary to add a dot of glue to the bottom of the toothpick.
3. Have the children make footprints in the clay using the doll shoe. Have them create the appearance of craters by pressing a marble into the clay. Set the moon replica aside to dry.
4. When the project is dry, ask the children to gently remove the clay from the lid and place it on a small square of cardboard.
5. Label the project with the date of the first moon landing, July 20, 1969.

More to do
More art: Create a mobile with balls or flat circles representing the Earth, sun, and moon.

Related books
Astronauts Are Sleeping by Natalie Standiford
Owl Moon by Jane Yolen
What the Sun Sees/What the Moon Sees by Nancy Tafuri
Zoom! Zoom! Zoom! I'm Off to the Moon by Dan Yaccarino

Original song
We are Astronauts (sing to the tune of "We are Little Ants" on the Hap Palmer album)
We are astronauts
We are launched into space,
In a rocketship…heading for another place.
We will rock and we'll roll,
To the moon that's our goal,
We'll explore and look around,
Picking moon rocks from the ground.
We'll sleep in our spacesuits and helmets, our boots and our socks,
Talk to the Earth on a radio box.

We'll count stars and moonbeams, watch comets streak past.
This is our first trip, it won't be our last!
We are astronauts.
We are launched into space,
In a rocketship…heading for another place.
We'll be back again!

Penni Smith, Riverside, CA

Butterfly Napkin Ring

Materials
Construction paper
Scissors
Toilet paper tube
Pipe cleaners
Tissue paper in assorted colors
Glue
Protective sealant
Hole punch

What to do
1. Ahead of time, fold a piece of paper for each child and, using a pattern, draw the outline of a butterfly's wing. Also, cut each toilet paper tube in half and cut pipe cleaners into short segments.
2. Have the children cut out two butterfly wings each.
3. Distribute tissue paper and ask the children to tear the paper in small pieces, then glue the pieces on the wings in a pattern or design.
4. Hand each child a toilet paper tube and some tissue paper. Ask the children to tear tissue paper in small pieces, then paste them to the tube, covering its surface. Let the tubes dry.
5. Afterward, apply a protective seal over their surface (adult only).
6. When the sealant dries, help the children glue the wings onto the tube.
7. For the butterfly's head, show the children how to cut a round shape attached to a "neck." Have them glue the neck inside the tube.
8. Let the children punch some holes in tissue paper and glue on the punched circles for their butterfly's eyes.
9. Ask the children to attach two short pieces of pipe cleaner to the tube for antennae.
10. Demonstrate how to roll up a napkin and slide it inside the butterfly napkin ring.

More to do
Math: Introduce the concept of symmetry.
More art: Cut paper in different shapes, then fold it to create a crease, open again and paint one side; fold again, transferring the design to the other side.

Related books
The Butterfly Alphabet Book by Jerry Pallotta
The Butterfly Jar by Jeff Moss
The Very Hungry Caterpillar by Eric Carle

Lisa M. Chichester, Parkersburg, WV

Flower Centerpiece

Materials
Flowers
Newspaper
Heavy book
Green construction paper
Scissors
Glue
Clear adhesive paper, optional

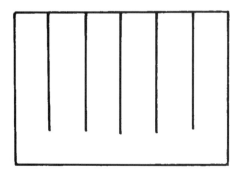

What to do

1. A few weeks in advance of the project, collect flowers for pressing.
2. Have the children gently place the flowers on newspaper, arranging the petals so they are lying flat. Ask the children to place several sheets of newspaper over the flowers. Place a heavy book on top of the newspaper and leave the flowers to dry for three or four weeks.
3. When you are ready to begin the project, draw five or six lines from the bottom of each child's paper to about 2" (5 cm) from the top.
4. Ask the children to cut along the lines.
5. Place the dried flowers within reach and have the children carefully glue one at a time to the strips on their paper. Let them glue a few flowers to each strip and a few along the 2" (5 cm) band at the end of their paper.
6. When the children are done, cover the strips with clear adhesive paper, if you choose.
7. Show the children how to pull the two ends of the paper together, letting the flower stems fall outward. Glue or staple the two ends together.
8. Hold a tea or luncheon for a special occasion and decorate your tables with the children's centerpieces.

More to do

More art: Design note cards or bookmarks with pressed flowers. Hang fresh flowers in a sunny corner of the room to dry, then use them to create wreaths and other ornaments.

Science: Plant seeds and keep a journal of the plants' progress.

Related books

The Gardener by Sarah Stewart
Planting a Rainbow by Lois Ehlert
The Tiny Seed by Eric Carle

Deborah R. Gallagher, Bridgeport, CT

Mother's Day T-Shirt

Materials

White T-shirt or sweatshirt, 50% or more polyester content
White copy paper cut into 8" x 8" (20 cm x 20 cm) squares
Several packages of fabric crayons
Newspaper
Iron
Sponges
Tempera paint and trays

Tissue paper
Construction paper
Pencil
Scissors
Crayons or markers
Stickers
Curling ribbon
Tape

1. Ahead of time, ask parents to send in a white T-shirt or sweatshirt whose fabric content is at least 50 percent polyester. Label each shirt with the child's name.
2. Invite the children to make a crayon drawing on the paper square. Advise the children not to write on the square as words will appear backward once they are transferred onto the shirt.
3. Ask the children to stand a safe distance from the iron. Following the instructions on the package of crayons, iron the children's designs onto their shirts. As an alternative, iron the shirts at home or after class.
4. In the meantime, invite the class to create gift wrap and a greeting card to accompany their Mother's Day gift. Have the children dip a sponge into paint and apply it to a sheet of tissue paper in a design of their choice. Set the tissue paper aside to dry.
5. Fold a piece of construction paper in half for each child. Help the children trace their hand with their wrist positioned along the fold.
6. Have the children cut along the outline of their hand, creating a card. Invite them to decorate the card with markers and stickers.
7. When the tissue paper dries, help the children wrap their shirt and adorn the package with curling ribbon, then attach their card with tape.

More to do

Guests: Invite the mothers to a tea and present them with the handmade gifts.
Language: Have the children write or dictate stories about their mothers, then compile the stories in a book or record them on videotape.
Math: Cut the sponges in geometric shapes and reinforce a lesson on shapes; ask the children to paint a pattern with the sponges.
More art: Cut out pictures of women's clothing from magazines, catalogs, and advertising fliers, then invite the children to draw a picture of their mother, grandmother, and other important women in their lives and dress them up by gluing on the cut-out fashions.
Science: Help the children understand how their crayon design is transferred using heat.

Related books
Are You My Mother? by P. D. Eastman
Mama, Do You Love Me? by Barbara M. Joose
Mr. Rabbit and the Lovely Present by Charlotte Zolotow
The Runaway Bunny by Margaret Wise Brown
What Mommies Do Best by Laura Numeroff

Ann M. Ferruggia, Voorhees, NJ

Button Broach

4+

Materials
Plastic lids from coffee, yogurt, and similar containers
Scissors
Broach pin backs
Glue in squeeze bottles
Buttons in an assortment of sizes, colors, and shapes

What to do
1. Ahead of time, trim plastic lids to 2" or 3" (5 cm or 8 cm) shapes. Label the lids with the children's names.
2. Secure the pin backs in a closed position, then help the children glue the pin to the back of their lid, using small dots of glue.
3. Invite the children to select a number of buttons and arrange them in a design on their lid, then attach them with glue.
4. Allow the broaches to dry. These make great gifts for special occasions.

More to do
More art: Make a colorful wreath of buttons for the classroom door. Cut bear shapes from felt and dress them up in fabric scraps, then attach buttons with glue or yarn.

Related books
Mr. Rabbit and the Lovely Present by Charlotte Zolotow
Emeka's Gift by Ifeoma Onyefulu

Dani Rosensteel, Payson, AZ

special days

School-year Timeline

5+

Materials
White paper trimmed to 6" x 6" (15 cm x 15 cm) or 5" x 4" (13 cm x 10 cm)
Markers, crayons, or colored pencils
Stamp with the date shown
Folders, store-bought or handmade
Roll of paper such as adding machine or cash register tape
Glue

What to do
1. Beginning early in the school year, ask the children to make a "picture of the week" that shows something special or interesting about the prior week of school. Have the children write or dictate a few words or a sentence describing their picture. Label the pictures with their names.
2. Stamp each picture with the date.
3. Provide folders where the children can store their pictures throughout the school year.
4. Near the end of the school year, perhaps in time for a spring open house or family day, return the folders to the children. Ask the children to choose their favorite picture from each month. (In a more ambitious alternative, the children use all their pictures, placing them on a timeline or assembling them in a booklet.)
5. When they are ready, invite the children in turn to glue their cards in chronological order to the roll of paper. The edges of the cards should touch so paper is not wasted. When one child has finished pasting his cards to the paper, cut the timeline from the rest of the roll and have the next child begin.
6. Hang the timelines around the classroom, then send them home as a keepsake at year's end.

More to do
Math: Ask the children about a milestone, such as choosing and raising a pet or learning to ride a bike; record the process on a timeline. Ask the children to put their morning or evening rituals in sequential order.

Related books
Busy at Day Care Head to Toe by Patricia Brennan Demuth
Minerva Louise at School by Janet Morgan Stoeke
Miss Bindergarten Gets Ready for Kindergarten by Joseph Slate
Now Soon Later by Lisa Grunwald

Susan Jones Jensen, Norman, OK

special days

Foil Vases

Materials
Long-necked bottles, one per child
Roll of tin foil
Thinned black and brown tempera paint or liquid shoe polish
Paintbrushes
Rags
Real or artificial flowers

What to do
1. For each child, tear a sheet of foil long enough to cover their bottle. Show the children how to wrap their bottle in foil, shaping the foil to the contour of the bottle and pinching it so it adheres.
2. Paint the bottle in sections, immediately wiping some of the paint off with a rag, creating an antique appearance.
3. Arrange real or artificial flowers in the vases and let the children present them as gifts for special occasions such as Mother's or Father's Day.

More to do
Field trip: Visit a florist and watch a demonstration of flower arranging.
Gardening: Plant flowers from seeds and keep them on a sunny windowsill; label the seeds, using their names to reinforce the alphabet as in *A* for Aster, *Z* for zinnia.
More art: Practice floral arranging with blocks of Styrofoam and artificial flowers and greenery.

Related books
Alison's Zinnia by Anita Lobel
Emeka's Gift by Ifeoma Onyefulu
The Gardener by Sarah Stewart

Barbara Saul, Eureka, CA

Merry Mardi Gras

5+

Materials
Poster board
Pencil
Scissors
Paper plates or store-bought masks, optional
Ribbon or elastic
Hole punch
Green, gold, and purple paint
Paintbrushes
Glitter, feathers, sequins, and ribbon
Glue
Green, gold, and purple crepe paper
Old costumes
Wrapped candies

What to do
1. Ahead of time, draw a simple mask shape on poster board and cut one out for each child. As an alternative, use paper plates or store-bought white masks.
2. Have the children paint their mask in the colors of Mardi Gras. When they are dry, invite the children to decorate them with sequins, feathers, glitter, and ribbons, lending your assistance when it is needed.
3. Punch holes in the sides of mask and attach elastic or ribbon to fit child's head.
4. During February, preferably coinciding with Mardi Gras, have the children decorate the classroom in green, gold, and purple streamers.
5. Invite the children's families to come for a Mardi Gras celebration. Encourage the children to wear an old Halloween costume or colorful clothing.
6. Play music and have the children parade in their costumes and masks, tossing wrapped candies to the parade spectators.

More to do
Circle time: Explain the meaning of Mardi Gras and invite the children's questions about the holiday.
Outdoors: Bring the parade outside and invite the families to bring wagons, tricycles, and bicycles. Decorate the vehicles with crepe paper in the colors of Mardi Gras.
Snack: Serve grape juice with green and yellow gelatin dessert in keeping with the holiday's colors.

Penni Smith, Riverside, CA

Rolling Ball Spider Webs

Materials
Paper
Drawing tools such as crayons, markers, and pencils
Shallow box
Marbles
Paint
Spoon
Hole punch
String

What to do
1. Ahead of time, cut the outside outline of a spider web shape from paper for each child, varying the shapes, if you choose. Encourage older children to cut their own shapes with some guidance.
2. Protect a work surface with newspaper and supply the children with drawing tools. Provide a shallow box and place a few marbles in a cup of paint.
3. Invite the children to create a pattern of lines across their web by laying their paper in the box, scooping up the marbles with a spoon, and rolling them across their paper in a crisscross pattern.
4. When the children have finished their web, have them dip their index finger into black paint and make two fingerprints on the web to represent the body of the spider. Have them draw the spider's eight legs.
5. Punch a hole near the edge of the web and tie a string through it.

More to do
More art: Create webs in different shapes and colors and create a mobile. Design greeting cards with spiders made from fingerprints. Embroider a simple spider or web design on embroidery cloth.
Outdoors: Hunt for spider webs around the schoolyard.

Related books
And So They Build by Bert Kitchen
Bugs by Nancy Winslow Parker and Joan R. Wright
Chickens Aren't the Only Ones by Ruth Heller
The Very Busy Spider by Eric Carle

Inge Mix, Massapequa, NY

spiders

Yummy Spider Treats 3+

Materials
Jumbo marshmallows
Black string licorice cut into 2" (5 cm) lengths
Miniature chocolate chips

What to do
1. Invite the children to insert four pieces of licorice into each side of the marshmallow.
2. When they have attached the legs, have the children add four chocolate chips for eyes.
3. Eat and enjoy!

More to do
More art: Have the children decorate the back of their hand with a spider design using face paint. Have the children paint a web with string; use white paint on black or colored paper cut in the shape of a web. Sculpt spiders and other insects from clay.
Movement: Play a selection of music and invite the children to crawl like a spider or weave an imaginary web.

Related books
The Bug Parade by Stuart J. Murphy
Miss Spider's New Car by David Kirk
Miss Spider's Tea Party by David Kirk
Spiders by Gail Gibbons

 Phyllis Esch, Export, PA

Sticky Spider's Web 4+

Materials
Glue
Bowls
Water
Pieces of embroidery or other strong thread
Wax paper

spiders

What to do

1. Pour glue into small bowls and dilute it with a small amount of water. Hand a sheet of wax paper and several pieces of thread to each child.
2. Have the children dip the pieces of thread in the glue one by one and lay them on a piece of wax paper, crisscrossing them.
3. Set the webs aside while the glue dries.
4. When dry, have the children gently pull the web from the wax paper.
5. Tie a piece of the thread to the web for hanging.
6. Display the webs in front of a window.

More to do

Language: After a walk outdoors to look for spider webs, have the children write a journal entry or dictate a few sentences describing what they saw.

More art: Construct mobiles with sticky webs. Design a cover for a spider journal, using fingerprint spiders or a collection of pictures from magazines.

Outdoors: Go on a nature hunt early in the morning, if possible, and look for spiders and their webs; gather small objects to attach to the handmade webs.

Related books

I Wish I Were a Butterfly by James Howe
Miss Spider's Wedding by David Kirk
Spiders, Spiders Everywhere by Rozanne Williams
The Very Busy Spider by Eric Carle

Ann Gudowski, Johnstown, PA

Paper Plate Spider Webs

Materials

Large and small Styrofoam balls, one each per child
Black spray paint
Black paper plates
Scissors
White yarn
Toothpicks
Black pipe cleaners, cut in half
Googly eyes
Craft glue

spiders

What to do

1. Ahead of time, spray the Styrofoam balls with black paint and let them dry. Cut small slits around the edge of each plate.
2. Help the children weave the yarn across their plate and through the slits, forming a web.
3. Have the children attach a large Styrofoam ball to a small ball with toothpicks or glue.
4. When the spider's body is assembled, ask the children to attach four pipe cleaner legs on each side and four eyes on top.
5. Help the children attach the spider to its web with craft glue.

More to do

Circle time: Gather the children in a circle on the floor, then roll a ball of yarn to the child across from you, holding onto the end of the yarn; have the children continue to roll the yarn across the circle, creating an intricate web pattern.

Language: After observing spiders in the classroom and outdoors, record your observations in handmade journals or on a colorful chart.

Math: Use a model of a spider to practice counting its legs.

More art: Cut out pictures of spiders and paste them on shoeboxes; apply a protective coating or sealant.

Science: Observe a spider in its habitat and another in a jar or terrarium in the classroom.

Related books and song

How Many Bugs in a Box? by David A. Carter
Spiders by Gail Gibbons
Spider's Web by Christine Back and Barrie Watts
The Very Busy Spider by Eric Carle
"Spider on the Floor" by Raffi

Kimberle S. Byrd, Kalamazoo, MI

Dancing Spiders

4+

Materials
Poster board
Scissors
Hole punch
Paint and paintbrushes
Bits of dark-colored felt or other fabric
Black or brown pom-poms
Glue
Pipe cleaners, 5 per child, cut in half

What to do
1. Draw a figure-eight shape 8" to 12" (20 cm to 30 cm) in length for the spider's body and cut one out of poster board for each child. Punch five holes on each side of the body.

2. Have the children paint their spider, then set it aside to dry.

3. When the spiders are dry, invite the children to paste bits of fabric on their spider's body. Have them glue four pom-poms to the top of the spider, representing its four eyes.

4. Show the children how to create a loop with a pipe cleaner on the underside of the body by inserting the ends of the pipe cleaner through the third hole on either side. Twist the pipe cleaner to secure it to the body, leaving a loop large enough to accommodate a child's hand.

5. Have the children attach the remaining eight pipe cleaner segments through the other holes.

6. Invite the children to put their hands through the loop and make their spiders dance.

More to do

Dramatic play: Invite the children to put on a puppet show using their spiders.

Science: Have the children bring in pictures of spiders and add them to your collection in a spider scrapbook; add photos from nature walks and an insect hunt.

Snack: Spread a round cracker with peanut butter and add pretzels for legs.

Related books

Eency Weency Spider by Joanne Oppenheim

Forgetful Spider by June Woodman

Spider Watching by Vivian French

The Very Busy Spider by Eric Carle

Elizabeth Thomas, Hobart, IN

Let's Play Ball

Materials
Large sheets of paper
Balls of different sizes and textures
Trays of paint
Smocks

What to do
1. Cover a table and the floor with large sheets of paper. Place the balls into trays of paint and have the children put on their smocks.
2. Invite the children to gently roll a ball across the table to a partner, leaving an impression on the paper.
3. After they have rolled a ball once or twice, ask the children to move to the next ball and tray.
4. Use the paper as background for a mural or bulletin board; alternatively, cut the paper into smaller sheets and use it as gift wrapping paper.

More to do
Language: Invite the children to finish the story: "There were two minutes left in the game…"
Math: Make a picture graph of a collection of sports equipment. Play a ballgame and keep a record of runs or goals scored and similar statistics.
More art: Make a collector's or storage box by covering shoeboxes with sports pictures from newspapers and magazines; apply a protective coat or sealant over the pictures. Make a puppet athlete with newspaper and masking tape, then attach strings to its arms and legs so the children can manipulate it.

Related books
Gina by Bernard Waber
A Million Fish…More or Less by Patricia C. McKissack
Play Ball, Amelia Bedelia by Peggy Parish

Melissa J. Browning, Milwaukee, WI

Pompoms

3+

Materials
Newspaper
Stapler
Wooden paint stirrers
Masking tape
Markers

What to do
1. Have the children tear newspaper into strips. Each pompom requires about 20 strips.
2. Staple the strips together on one end. Ask the children to hold the strips by that end while you attach a wooden stirrer with masking tape. Wrap the pompom and handle securely.
3. Have the children decorate the pompoms with markers.

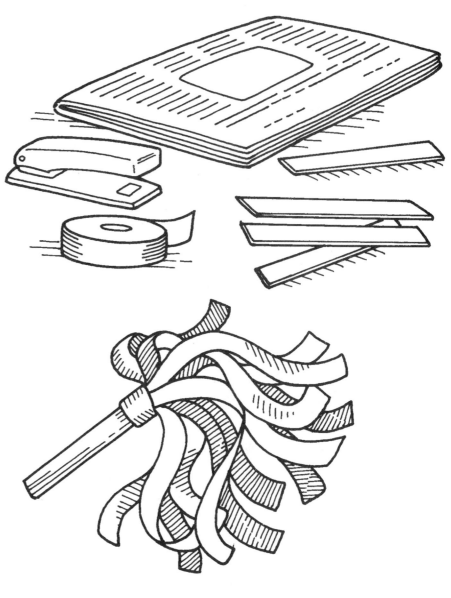

More to do
More art: Paste magazine and newspaper pictures to poster board shapes and construct a mobile; attach photos of the children jumping rope, tumbling on a mat, or dribbling a ball. Use paper fasteners to make movable sports characters from poster board.
Movement: Teach the children a pompom or jump rope routine to the tune of lively music.
Science: Measure heart rates before and after dancing or jumping rope.

sports

Related books
Angelina Ballerina by Katharine Holabird
Dance, Tanya by Patricia Lee Gauch
Dancing Feet by Charlotte Agell
Shy Charles by Rosemary Wells
The Tortoise and the Hare by Janet Stevens

Sandy Lanes, Silver Spring, MD

Sports Mural

Materials
Magazines
Scissors
Glue
Butcher paper, mural paper, or poster board

What to do
1. Ahead of time, cut pictures of athletes and sporting equipment from magazines. Ask older children to cut the pictures out on their own. Try to represent a wide array of sports and athletes of all ages and racial backgrounds.
2. Have the children glue the pictures on a giant poster or mural. If the children choose, help them write their name next to a picture of a favorite sport or athlete.

More to do
Math: Use colorful Venn diagrams or charts to characterize sports as team or individual, indoors or outdoors, using balls or other equipment. Make a bar graph of the sports that the children play or enjoy watching.
More art: Design banners or pennants with a sports theme using fabric and wallpaper scraps; ask families to send in old athletic T-shirts and shorts with team emblems to supplement your scrap collection.
Movement: Play lively music and do an aerobic routine.

Related books
Casey at the Bat by Ernest Lawrence Thayer
I'm Gonna Be by Wade Hudson

Suzanne Pearson, Winchester, VA

Friendship Book

3+

Materials
Camera or photographs
Paper or notebook
Crayons

What to do
1. At the start of school, photograph the children or ask them to bring a special photo from home.
2. Ask the children about their family and pets, their favorite color, their interests, and any special memory or information the child would like to share with the class.
3. Invite the children to make a crayon drawing that they will share with their classmates; encourage the children to include themselves in the picture.
4. Create a separate page for each child. Record the information they shared and attach their photo. On the facing page, insert the child's drawing.
5. Assemble the pages in a "Friendship Book."
6. Design an interesting cover for the book.
7. Share the "Friendship Book" in class, and let the children have a turn sharing it with their families.

More to do
Circle time: Gather the children in a circle around you, then roll a large ball to the children, inviting them to say their name and roll the ball back to you. Invite older children to tell you something special about themselves that you record on a piece of paper; place the papers in a basket and pull them out one at a time, asking the children to guess who the information is about.

Related books
Best Friends by Steven Kellogg
Friends by Helme Heine
Jamaica's Find by Juanita Havill
Little Blue and Little Yellow by Leo Lionni
My New School by Harriet Hains

Sandra Hutchins Lucas, Cox's Creek, KY

Collector's Case

3+

Materials
Cardboard boxes, one per child (unused pizza boxes work well)
Markers
Newspaper
Smocks
Paint
Large paintbrushes
Crayons
Assorted craft materials such as feathers, sequins, and scraps of paper and fabric

What to do
1. Write the children's names on their boxes in bold print, using colorful markers.
2. Cover the floor or a large surface with newspaper and ask the children to wear smocks.
3. Have the children color or paint the outside of their boxes in solid colors or a design of their choice.
4. When the boxes are dry, invite the children to decorate them with an assortment of materials.
5. Use the boxes to store the children's artwork and to transport fragile materials home over the course of the year.

More to do
Circle time: Invite the children to bring a stuffed friend from home, then share a story about the stuffed friend with the class.
More art: Decorate labels for the children's cubbies or coat hooks with crayons or markers, then laminate. Create a border for the bulletin board with the children's handprints using fingerpaint.

Related books
Busy at Day Care Head to Toe by Patricia Brennan Demuth
Madeline by Ludwig Bemelmans
Miss Bindergarten Gets Ready for Kindergarten by Joseph Slate

Bev Schumacher, Ft. Mitchell, KY

My Very Own Place Mat

3+

Materials
Camera or photographs
Colored paper in flesh tones
Scissors
White paper, the size of a place mat
Glue
Felt-tipped pen
Stickers
Crayons
Clear contact paper

What to do
1. Ahead of time, photograph the children or ask them to bring a special photo from home. Help the children trace their hand onto colored paper and cut out the hand shapes. Affix the photo and the hand shapes to the center of the white paper. Write the children's names below their photo.
2. On the day of the project, invite the children to decorate their paper with crayons and stickers.
3. When they are finished, write the child's birthday on one hand shape and their favorite color (or other favorite) on the other shape.
4. Laminate the place mat, if possible, or apply contact paper. Invite the children to use their personal place mats at snack time.

More to do
Games: Hold a scavenger hunt in the classroom and around the school.
More art: Cover a shoebox or cigar box with a photo and cut-out pictures or the children's drawings; store their crayons and pencils inside it. Create mobiles with photos and pictures depicting information the children would like to share with their new classmates.

Related books
Hooray for Me! by Remy Charlip
I Like Me! by Nancy Carlsson
Little Blue and Little Yellow by Leo Lionni
Peter's Chair by Ezra Jack Keats
Pezzettino by Leo Lionni

Tracie O'Hara, Charlotte, NC

starting School

Coming to School

4+

Materials needed
Paper chart
Crayons

What to do
1. Talk to the children about how they come to school. Ask if the walk, ride in a car, or take a bus.
2. Make a class chart with the label "Coming to School." Label one column "Walk," a second column "Car," and a third column "Bus or Van." Write the children's first names along the side, making a grid.
3. Put out the crayons and invite the children to come up, one at a time, and draw a picture of how they come to school in the correct column. (For example, if they walk they could draw a stick figure or a shoe, if they come by automobile they could draw a car or truck, etc.) Some children may need to draw in two columns, if they sometimes walk and sometimes ride.
4. Display the chart in your classroom.

Coming To School			
	Walk	Car	Bus
Susan	👟		
Sam		🚗	
Angel		🚗	
Heather			🚌
Mark	🏃		
Tim			
Jenna			
Amy			
Levi			

Related books
Busy at Day Care Head to Toe by Patricia Brennan Demuth
Friends in the Park by Rochelle Bunnett
Friends at School by Rochelle Bunnett
School Bus by Donald Crews

Nancy Dentler, Mobile, AL

Walnut Boats

3+

Materials

Walnut shells—you want perfect half-shells, so crack them carefully
Small bits of beeswax or clay (beeswax works better as it doesn't dry out)
String cut in 9" to 12" (22 cm to 30 cm) lengths
Paper scraps
Scissors
Toothpicks
Water table, tub, large dishpan, or creek
Buttons, optional

summertime

What to do

1. Crack nuts and have the children help you remove the nut meats. This may mean snack time to them! Save the rest for a baking project. Note: A friend told me that an oyster shucker is great for opening walnuts when you don't want to break the shells. Just stick it in the little opening often found at the flat end of the walnut and wriggle it open.
2. Place one end of the string in the bottom of any walnut shell and press a small ball of beeswax (or clay) over it to hold it in place.
3. Cut a tiny sail shape from a scrap of paper and poke a toothpick through it. Now the boat has a sail on its mast.
4. Stick the bottom end of the toothpick into the ball of beeswax.
5. If you want, attach a button to the loose end of the string. This gives the children more to hold on to as they pull their sailboats around the water.

More to do

More art: Make boats of paper or wood scraps.

Related books

Harbor by Donald Crews
Sail Away by Donald Crews
Where the Wild Things Are by Maurice Sendak

Carol Petrash, reprinted from Earthways

Mud Puddle Painting

Materials

Blanket
Paintbrushes
Paper
Mud puddle

What to do

1. After a rainfall, when the weather has turned fair, bring a few blankets, paper, and paintbrushes outside and find a mud puddle.
2. Invite the children to find a spot on a blanket alongside the puddle and lay their paper beside them.
3. Have them dip their brush into the mud puddle and paint a picture using mud.
4. Let the pictures dry in the sun.

More to do
More art: Make sailboats from walnut shells, toothpicks, and paper and float them in puddles. Create pictures with muddy handprints.
Outdoors: Explore puddles around the schoolyard.
Science: Measure and chart rainfall.

Related books
Mud Pies and Other Recipes: A Cookbook for Dolls by Marjorie Winslow
Peter Spier's Rain by Peter Spier
The Pig in the Pond by Martin Waddell

Jean Potter, Charleston, West Virginia

Flower Mask

Materials
Paper plates
Scissors
Tempera paint
Paintbrushes
Green construction paper
Small scraps of wallpaper or gift wrap
Popsicle sticks
Glue

What to do
1. Beforehand, cut a circle in the middle of each plate big enough for the child's eyes, nose, and mouth.
2. Invite the children to paint the rest of the plate, encouraging them to use more than one color.
3. While the paint is drying, help the children cut leaf shapes from green paper and glue them to the Popsicle stick.
4. When the mask is dry, let the children attach snips of flowery wallpaper and gift wrapping paper.
5. Help the children glue their mask to the stick.

More to do
More art: Paint the children's faces to complement their mask.
Movement: Play music and invite the children to wear their masks and move as if they were flowers growing from seeds.

summertime

Related books
The Empty Pot by Demi
Jack's Garden by Henry Cole
Planting a Rainbow by Lois Ehlert

Lisa Chichester, Parkersburg, WV

Bird Feeder Ornaments 3+

Materials
Bread
Cookie cutters
Birdseed
Lard or peanut butter
Yarn
Pencils

Plastic butter knives

What to do

1. Have the children cut out shapes in the bread with the cookie cutters. Set the excess bread aside for breadcrumbs later.
2. Invite the children to poke a hole at the top of the shape with a pencil (well within the edge of the shape).
3. Show the children how to thread the yarn through the hole and tie a knot creating a loop hanger.
4. Encourage the children to spread the peanut butter or lard onto the shape with the butter knife.
5. Then have the child sprinkle birdseed onto the shape and gently pat into place.
6. Allow the ornaments to dry and then, on a sunny day, hang the feeders in a nearby tree for the wild birds to enjoy.

Related books

The Listening Walk by Paul Showers
The Robins in Your Backyard by Nancy Carol Willis
Where Once There Was a Wood by Denise Fleming

Dani Rosensteel, Payson, AZ

The Fishing Hole

Materials
Butcher paper
Scissors
Rubber worms, one per child
String cut in 12" (30 cm) lengths
Pencils or twigs
Small containers of paint in various colors
Small cups of water

What to do

1. Beforehand, cut butcher paper into a shape that resembles a pond. Tie a worm on the end of a string for each child and tie the string to a pencil or twig.
2. When you are ready to begin, lay the butcher paper on the floor and set the containers of paint on top of the paper.

3. Gather the children around the fishing hole.
4. Invite them to dip the worm in a container of paint and make a design on the paper. Remind the children to rinse the paint from the worm before they change colors.
5. Move the containers of paint around the circle periodically so the children can reach all the colors.

More to do

Games: Design your own set of cards for a memory game; cut fish shapes in duplicate from poster board in a variety of shapes, sizes, and colors. Create a challenging set for older children, requiring them to match more than one characteristic; as an example, the child would have to locate two fish that are long and blue.

More art: Use the finished product as background for a mural. Supply sponges cut in the shape of fish and frogs and invite the children to sponge paint as well. Cut matching fish shapes from paper and staple them together, leaving one opening; stuff the fish with newspaper and decorate them with paint or bits of fabric or tissue paper.

Related books

Fish Is Fish by Leo Lionni
Just Me and My Dad by Mercer Mayer
A Million Fish…More or Less by Patricia C. McKissack
Wonderful Worms by Linda Glaser

Carol Nelson, Rockford, IL

Bubbly Butterflies

3+

Materials
Butterfly pattern
Heavy white construction paper
Scissors
Pipe cleaners
Several small bowls
Water
Food coloring
Liquid dish soap
Straws
Tape
Glue

What to do

1. Before class, use a pattern to cut a butterfly shape from construction paper for each child. Cut pipe cleaners in 2" (5 cm) lengths or longer, depending on the size of your butterflies.
2. Pour water into small bowls until they are half full.
3. Add a few drops of food coloring and liquid soap to the water.
4. Ask the children to mix the ingredients with straws.
5. Set the bowls aside.
6. Give each child a butterfly shape.
7. Using a straw, blow bubbles in each bowl until the bubbles rise over the top of the bowl, stopping just before they spill down the sides. Ask older children to blow the bubbles with their own straws, then discard the straws.
8. Have the children place their butterfly on top of the bowl of bubbles, then lift it to see the results. Encourage the children to repeat the process on one or more bowls until their butterfly is splashed with color.
9. Hang the butterflies to dry.
10. Afterward, attach pipe cleaners for the antennae with tape or glue.

More to do

Circle time: Design one wing of a butterfly on the flannel board and ask the children to duplicate it using flannel pieces.

Gardening: Plan a butterfly garden with the other classes and start the flowers from seed on a sunny windowsill.

Math: Decorate pre-cut butterfly shapes with polka-dots, then count the dots and have the butterflies light upon a colorful number line; challenge older children to combine the dots on two or more butterflies to produce a higher number.

More art: Write the child's name on the reverse side of the butterfly and attach a Popsicle stick; use as a gift card for a potted plant on Mother's Day or another special occasion.

Outdoors: Make bubble solution and bring an assortment of wands outdoors to create bubbles in a variety of shapes and sizes.

Related books

The Bubble Book by Lisa Feder-Feitel
Bubble, Bubble by Mercer Mayer
The Bubble Factory by Tommie dePaola
Butterfly by Susan Canizares
The Butterfly Alphabet Book by Kjell B. Sandved
The Butterfly Counting Book by Jerry Pallotta

Lisa LaFayette, Evansville, IN

summertime

Shadow Drawing

4+

Materials
Large sheet of butcher paper
Felt pens, paints and brushes, crayon or chalk
Sunny day outside
4 rocks, optional

What to do
1. Go for a walk looking for shadows on the ground.
2. Find a shadow that is appealing in design.
3. Place the large sheet of butcher paper on the shadow. Adjust the paper so the shadow is captured on the paper.
4. If the day is windy, place a rock on each corner of the paper to keep it from blowing away.
5. Using any choice of drawing or painting tools, trace, outline, color in, or decorate the paper using the shadow as the design.
6. When complete, remove the paper and observe the shadow drawing.

More to do
More art: Cut the design out and glue it on another sheet of paper contrasting in color. Make a shadow drawing of a friend's shadow. When using crayon, place textured surfaces behind the paper to add design to the shadow drawing. A wire mesh screen, sheet of plywood, bumpy scrap of vinyl flooring, or scrap of Formica make interesting textures.

Related books
Bear Shadow by Frank Asch
What Is the Sun? by Reeve Lindbergh

MaryAnn Kohl, Reprinted from Preschool Art

summertime

Pinwheels

4+

Materials

Colored construction paper or heavy white watercolor paper that the children decorate with crayons

Scissors

Straight pins

New, unsharpened pencils with erasers

Scraps of paper, tape, optional

What to do

1. Cut the paper into 7" (18 cm) squares. You can vary the size with a larger square, but the pinwheel will be more floppy. Don't make it bigger than 8½" (21 cm).
2. Determine the center of the square. This is done by lightly folding tip number one to tip number three and tip number four to tip number two. You don't need a strong crease. The center is where the two folds intersect.

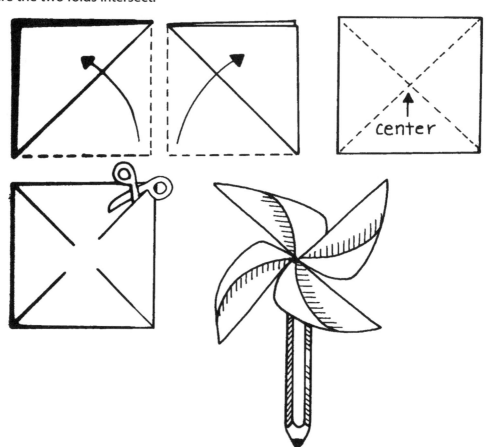

502

3. Now, using the scissors, cut in on each fold line about three-forths of the way to the center. Leave the last inch of each fold uncut.

4. With a pin and pencil ready, fold every other tip (you now have eight) into the center and over-lap them. Push the pin through these overlapping tips, through the center of the pinwheel and into the eraser. Don't let the pin stick out the other side of the eraser. Note: A little paper washer reinforces the center of the pinwheel. Cut a small circle of colored paper (about 1" to 1½" or (3 cm to 4 cm in diameter). This doesn't have to be a perfect circle—just do it freehand. Put a tape loop on the back of the circle and press it onto the overlapping tips of paper at the pinwheel's center. Then insert the pin. This provides extra support at the stress point.

5. Show the children how to make the pinwheel turn by blowing on it. Then let them take the pin-wheels outdoors and see what the wind can do.

More to do
More art: Design a windsock with fabric scraps and streamers. Make a wind chime with wood or stones.

Related books
Snowsong Whistling by Karen E. Lotz
When Spring Comes by Robert Maas
When the Wind Stops by Charlote Zolotow

Carol Petrash, reprinted from Earthways

Pack Your Bags

Materials
Brown construction paper, 12" x 18" (30 cm x 45 cm)
Scissors
Magazines or newspaper sales inserts from department stores
Glue or glue sticks
Crayons

What to do
1. Talk to the children about summer vacation and traveling. Ask them if they have ever gone far away and needed to pack a suitcase before leaving.
2. Make a suitcase for each child by folding the construction paper in half. At the open end, cut the shape of a handle.

3. Encourage the children to pretend that they are about to go on a trip and to look through the magazines or supplements for items that they would like to pack in their suitcases.
4. Have them cut out and glue the pictures in their paper suitcases.
5. Let the children decorate the outsides of the suitcases with crayons, and suggest that they make a luggage tag for identification.

More to do

Circle time: Play the game "My Grandmother's Trunk."
Dramatic play: Place real suitcases in the dramatic play area. Encourage the children to pack them with some of the dress-up clothes.
Language: Write stories about taking a trip.
Field trip: Visit an airport or train station.

Related books

Freight Train by Donald Crews
Grannie Jus' Come by Ana Sisnett
Richard Scarry's Cars and Trucks and Things That Go by Richard Scarry
The Train to Grandma's by Ivan Ghantschev

Linda N. Ford, Sacramento, CA

Nuts and Bolts

Materials
Paint smocks
Tempera paint in various colors
Foam meat trays
Dishwashing liquid, optional
Assorted nuts and bolts
Construction paper

What to do
1. Ask the children to put on their paint smocks.
2. Pour a small amount of paint into the trays, covering the bottom of each tray with a thin layer. A small amount of dishwashing liquid added to the paint minimizes clean-up and clothing stains.
3. Place a few nuts and bolts in each tray.
4. Invite the children to print designs on paper with the nuts and bolts, reminding them to return each nut or bolt to the tray where it belongs.
5. Encourage the children to experiment with the technique, overlapping designs and colors.

More to do
Math: Count and sort nuts, bolts, screws, and washers. Classify tools by their use on a chart.
More art: Add finishing touches to the prints with markers or crayons. Cut the printed paper into the shape of various tools. Design wrapping paper with the nuts and bolts technique. Create collages with discarded nuts, bolts, and similar materials.

Related books
Tool Book by Gail Gibbons
Tool Box by Harlow Rockwell
Tools by Ann Morris, photos by Ken Heyman

Rebecca McMahon, Mobile, AL

Brush Away Art

3+

Materials
Newspaper
Mural paper, 3'x 6' (1 m x 2 m)
Tempera paint in assorted colors
Styrofoam or aluminum trays
Different kinds of brushes such as hair, dog, tooth, basting, vegetable, clothing, scrub, and
   paintbrushes in varied widths

What to do
1. Cover the floor with newspaper. Place mural paper on top of the newspaper.
2. Pour the paint into trays.
3. Invite the children to paint a mural, centered on a particular theme, if desired, using a variety of
   brushes.
4. Encourage the children to experiment with several brushes and colors, noting the difference in
   appearance.

More to do
Circle time: Brainstorm about the uses for each brush and how their size and design relates to
their purpose.
Dramatic play: Supply the children with a variety of brushes and invite them to play.

Related book
Harry the Dirty Dog by Gene Zion
The Legend of the Indian Paintbrush retold by Tomie DePaola
Stephanie's Ponytail by Robert Munsch

 Sandra Fisher, Kutztown, PA

Textured Glue Art

3+

Materials
Funnels of different sizes
Squeeze bottles

Spoons
White or colored glue
Bowls
Glitter, sand, very small bits of yarn, and other textures
Spoons
Paper

What to do
1. Pour glue into several small bowls. Ask the children to add glitter, sand, and other textures to the glue in separate bowls.
2. Have the children create a design or picture by squeezing a bottle of ordinary glue as they move it over their paper.
3. When they are finished, show the children how to drizzle textured glue over their picture using funnels and spoons.
4. Let the pictures dry completely, then invite the children to run their hands over the surface of their artwork.

More to do
Math: Sort a collection of objects by their texture and make a colorful picture graph.
Science: Let the children touch and examine a wide assortment of textures. Place objects with different textures in a box, then ask the children to identify them without looking; surprise the children with some squiggly and slimy objects.

Related books
Fuzzy Yellow Ducklings by Matthew Van Fleet
Sense Suspense by Bruce McMillan

 Ann Gudowski, Johnstown, PA

Kitchen Tools 3+

Materials
Kitchen tools such as forks, spoons, nylon scrubbies, and sponges
Tempera paint in a variety of colors
Paint cups or trays
Newsprint

tools

What to do

1. Have a conversation about tools that are used in the kitchen. Let the children touch and ask questions about an assortment of kitchen gadgets and tools.
2. Pour the paint into cups or trays and give each child a large piece of newsprint.
3. Invite the children to paint a picture or design using the kitchen tools and gadgets. Encourage the children to experiment and observe the different results they can achieve with various tools.

More to do

Circle time: Brainstorm about tools used in the yard, in an office, in a factory, and other settings.
Math: Make a picture chart of tools used in various settings.
More art: Put out playdough and invite the children to use kitchen tools such as a rolling pin, garlic press, measuring cups and spoons, and cookie cutters to create playdough art.

Related books

Hands by Lois Ehlert
Pots and Pans by Patricia Hubbell
Who Uses This? by Margaret Miller

Lyndall Warren, Milledgeville, GA

Hammer and Nails

Materials
Small, lightweight hammer
Nails
Soft wood such as pine, one 6" x 4" (15 cm x 10 cm) piece per child
Fabric scraps
Glue
Child's photograph

What to do
1. Demonstrate how to safely hammer a nail into a piece of wood.
2. Invite the children one at a time to select a piece of fabric. Hand them a piece of wood, a couple of nails, and the hammer.
3. Under your close supervision, have the first child place the fabric on top of the wood, then hammer the nails through the fabric into the wood.
4. When the nails are pounded into the child's strip of wood, securing the fabric, invite the rest of the class to take a turn, under continued supervision.
5. Encourage the children to glue their photographs in the middle of the wood, against the fabric background.

More to do
Guest: Invite an upholsterer or a carpenter to class and ask them to demonstrate their trade. Invite a parent or carpenter to help the class build birdhouses.
More art: Substitute hooks for the nails and make a key rack; drill holes through two corners and insert twine or wire to hang. Create miniature flannel boards with wood, felt, and a staple gun.

Related books
Construction Zone by Tana Hoban
Tool Book by Gail Gibbons

Susan Rinas, Parma, OH

Cotton Balls and Tweezers

Materials
Tweezers, one per child
Construction paper
Tempera paint in assorted colors
Shallow paint trays
Cotton balls

What to do
1. Provide the children with tweezers and paper.
2. Pour the paint into trays and set some cotton balls on the table.
3. Have the children pick up a cotton ball with tweezers, then dip the cotton in the paint and dab color on their paper. Encourage the children to paint a picture using this technique.
4. Remind the children to use a new cotton ball when they switch to a new color or when the old ball is saturated; suggest that the children leave the cotton balls on their paper for an interesting effect.

More to do
Dramatic play: Set up the play area as a doctor's or veterinarian's office.
Games: Transfer small objects from one container to another using tweezers; do the same with larger objects using tongs and chopsticks.
More art: Use toothbrushes, cotton-tipped swabs, and other materials to paint.

Related books
Barney Is Best by Nancy White Carlstrom
Curious George Goes to the Hospital by Margaret and H.A. Rey
Going to the Hospital by Fred Rogers

Sandra W. Gratias, Perkasie, PA

Juice Lid Punch

5+

Materials
Frozen juice can lids, one per child
Permanent markers
Template or stencil
Workbench or stack of newspapers or magazines
Safety goggles
Nails with large flat heads
Lightweight hammers
Yarn

What to do
1. Give each child a frozen juice can lid.
2. Ask the children to draw a picture on their lid with a permanent marker, working freehand or using a stencil.
3. Tell the children to place their lid on the workbench or a stack of newspapers or magazines.
4. Wearing safety goggles, have the children position the nail on the line of permanent marker and hammer the nail, punching a hole through the lid; have them move the nail along the outline of the drawing, punching holes through the entire design.
5. Punch a larger hole at the top of the lid and thread a piece of yarn through the opening. Hang the lids in front of a window or on a Christmas tree.

More to do
Field trip: Visit a carpenter or woodworker.
Games: Show the children a set of carpentry tools and name them; cover the display and remove one of the tools, then ask the children to identify the missing tool. Play a memory card game, matching tools to their job.
More art: Nail scraps of wood together, creating a sculpture. Design a set of matching cards for a memory game showing tools and their uses.

Related books
Hands by Lois Ehlert
Tools by Ann Morris
Who Uses This Tool? by Margaret Miller

Sandra W. Gratias, Perkasie, PA

Creative Construction 5+

Materials
Hammer
Nails
Piece of soft wood
Toothpicks
Styrofoam balls
Cork
Glue
Plastic hammers
Miscellaneous materials such as pipe cleaners, parts of old toys, buttons, empty spools, Styrofoam packaging, and bottlecaps
Paint and paintbrushes
Glitter

What to do
1. Demonstrate how to safely hammer a nail into wood. While an adult holds the nail, let the children practice hammering it into a piece of soft wood.
2. When you are ready to begin the project, supply the children with toothpicks, styrofoam balls, and pieces of cork.
3. Invite the children to build their own structure by connecting the balls and cork with glue, toothpicks, and nails.
4. Encourage the children to use the remaining materials to decorate or supplement their design.
5. Ask the children to name their project.
6. Display the projects in an exhibit.

More to do
Cooking: Build a structure with graham crackers and cake frosting.
Dramatic play: Supply a few props and invite the children to pretend they are at a construction site. Play with building blocks.
Language: Have the children compose a story or narrate a description of their structure, monument, or invention. Record their words on paper or videotape.

Related books
Construction Zone by Tana Hoban
Mike Mulligan and His Steam Shovel by Virginia Lee Burton
Moon Cake by Frank Asch

Sheryl A. Smith, Jonesborough, TN

All Aboard, Animals!

3+

Materials
Paper, 12" x 18" (30 cm x 45 cm)
Scissors
Tape
Tempera paint
Shallow containers
Newspaper
Rectangular and small circular sponges
Cotton balls
Glue
Pictures of animals from magazines, catalogs, advertising fliers, and old books

What to do
1. Ahead of time, cut the paper in half lengthwise, then tape the two strips together to form one long strip. Pour paint into shallow containers and protect your work surface with newspaper. Supply a sponge for each color.
2. When you are ready to begin, invite a child to dip a rectangular sponge into paint and apply it to the paper, leaving its impression. Then, have another child dip a second sponge into a different color and print a rectangle next to the first, leaving a small space between the rectangles.
3. Ask the other children to take turns printing train cars until they reach the end of the paper. Ask them to use the small, circular sponge to add train wheels to the bottom of each train car.
4. Cut one of the rectangular sponges in half and have a child print the engine's smokestack on top of the first car.
5. When the paint is dry, have one or two of the children glue cotton balls over the smokestack.
6. Invite the children to arrange pictures of animals just above the train cars; help them trim the bottom half of the pictures so that the animals appear as if they are riding in the open cars.

More to do
Dramatic play: Line up chairs and pretend you are riding on a train; sell tickets, punch the tickets with a hole punch, and encourage the children to play the roles of conductor, passenger, and snack bar attendant.

Related books
Freight Train by Donald Crews
Hey! Get Off Our Train by John Burningham
Peter Spier's Circus! by Peter Spier
Train Song by Diane Siebert

Tina Slater, Silver Spring, MD

Car Painting

3+

Materials
Tempera paint in assorted colors
Shallow dishes
Small toy cars with wheels that roll
Smocks
Construction paper
Tray
Sponge

What to do
1. Pour the paint into dishes and place a small car in each dish.
2. After the children have put on their smocks, call them in turn and ask them to place their paper on the tray.
3. Have them set the car in the dish of paint, then carefully lift the car and let the excess paint drip into the dish.
4. Tell the children to roll the car across the paper, tracking paint as it goes. Encourage them to create a painting by rolling the car in any direction, adding layers of patterns and colors.
5. Wipe spilled paint from the tray with a sponge between turns.
6. When the children finish, lay the paintings flat to dry.
7. Afterward, hold a car wash with the children and rinse the paint from the cars.

More to do
Language: Ask the children to compose a story or a few sentences about their picture; attach the story to their painting.
More art: Use a variety of vehicles with different tire sizes. Substitute plastic toy animals such as dinosaurs or farm animals and leave animal tracks on the paper. Use the technique to design gift wrap or framing mats.

Related books
The Adventures of Taxi Dog by Sal and Debra Barracca
Go, Dog, Go! by P.D. Eastman
Richard Scarry's Cars and Trucks and Things That Go by Richard Scarry
Sheep in a Jeep by Nancy Shaw

Susan Jones Jensen, Norman, OK

Box Cars

3+

Materials
A variety of large boxes
Newspaper or drop cloth
Paint
Paintbrushes
Circle stencils
Colored paper
Scissors
Glue

What to do
1. Ahead of time, collect a variety of boxes large enough that the children can fit inside.
2. Cover the floor with newspaper or a drop cloth.
3. Supply the children with paint and the other materials and invite them to create a fun mode of transportation.
4. When it is dry, invite the children to climb in and go!

More to do
Dramatic play: Have the children use large building blocks to build a community and use their homemade vehicles for transportation.
Math: Sort pictures of vehicles by land, air, and water transportation.

Related books
Flying by Donald Crews
How Many Trucks Can a Tow Truck Tow? by Charlotte Pomerantz
Things That Go by Anne Rockwell

Ann Gudowski, Johnstown, PA

Torn Paper Ship at Sea

Materials
Discontinued wallpaper sample book
Artwork of ships at sea
Corrugated cardboard
Crayons
Scissors
Construction paper, 12" x 18" (30 cm x
    45 cm) in black, blue, purple, and gray
Glue

What to do
1. Ahead of time, select wallpaper samples with dark, preferably solid colors and a texture that has a swirling or wavy pattern.
2. Show the children artwork of ships at sea and invite them to create a work of their own.
3. Have the children tear the wallpaper, leaving a ragged edge and creating the appearance of a rough sea.
4. Show the children how to tear off the thin outer layer of a piece of corrugated cardboard, exposing the ridges. On the reverse side, have the children draw the shape of a boat and cut it out. Let the children cut out a mast or other features, if they choose.
5. When they are finished cutting, have the children hold the boat with its ridged side facing up and position it on their construction paper as though it were angled precariously in a stormy sea. Have them place the wallpaper along the bottom of the paper. Glue the boat and the sea to the paper.

More to do
More art: On butcher paper, draw the outline of a number of historic ships to scale; invite the children to decorate them and compare their size.

Related books
All Kinds of Ships by Seymour Reit
The Harbor Book by Bryna Stephens
Little Toot by Gramatky

Susan O. Hill, Lakeland, FL

Fluffy Clouds

3+

Materials
White paper
Scissors
Glue
Silver tinsel
Soft craft filler
Hole punch
Thread

What to do
1. Ahead of time, cut out two identical cloud shapes for each child. Older children can cut out their own clouds.
2. Have the children lay the shapes side by side and spread glue over the top of each one.
3. Show the children how to attach the tinsel along the bottom of one shape; have them leave space between the icicles, lending the appearance of a rain shower.
4. When the tinsel is in place, have the children press the front and back of their clouds together.
5. Have them spread glue on one side of the cloud and affix filler to it, then turn the cloud over and repeat the process on the other side.
6. Punch a hole in the top of each cloud and attach a length of thread. Hang the clouds from the ceiling or in front of the window.

More to do
Outdoors: Bring paint or pastels and paper outside and make a picture of the clouds. Identify shapes you see in the clouds.
Science: Observe the weather or the forecast over several days and plot the weather on a picture graph.

Related books
The Cloud Book by Tomie DePaola
Cloudy With a Chance of Meatballs by Judi Barrett
Come a Tide by George Ella Lyon
Little Cloud by Eric Carle

Lesley S. Potts, Franklin, TN

weather

Musical Weather 3+

Materials
Paint
Paintbrushes
Paper
Varied selections of music

What to do
1. Supply the children with paint, brushes, and paper.
2. Play selections of music that call to mind different kinds of weather such as snowfall, a thunderstorm, and a hot, sunny day.
3. Encourage the children to listen to the music and paint a picture that reflects what they hear and how they feel.

More to do
Language: Record the weather in a journal; ask the children to describe something they do on a rainy day, on a windy day, in the snow, or during a thunderstorm.
More art: Design a colorful weather journal.

Related books
Cloudy With a Chance of Meatballs by Judi Barrett
It Looked Like Spilt Milk by Charles G. Shaw
When Spring Comes by Robert Maass
When the Wind Stops by Charlotte Zolotow

Amy Melisi, Oxford, MA

Watching the Wind 3+

Materials
Paper
Markers
Clipboard or other writing surface

What to do

1. On a windy day, give each child a clipboard, marker, and paper.
2. Bring the children outside, sit on the ground, and watch the wind moving objects around you.
3. Talk with the children about how they know the wind is blowing today.
4. Encourage the children to draw pictures of what they see blowing in the wind.
5. Have the children write a description of their picture below it, or ask them to dictate a description so that you can record it for them.

More to do

Games: In "Lion Wind, Lamb Wind," one person calls out "Lion Wind" or "Lamb Wind" and the children mimic the wind, running quickly or moving lazily, with streamers in their hands.

More art: Make a windsock or a brightly colored fan.

Outdoors: Bring some streamers outside; hold them up high and down low to see where the wind is stronger. Hang a wind chime outside the classroom window.

Related books

The Listening Walk by Paul Showers
When the Wind Stops by Charlotte Zolotow
The Wind Blew by Pat Hutchins

Ann Wenger, Harrisonburg, VA

Painting With Rain

Materials

Powdered paint in assorted colors
Containers with holes in the lids such as a grated cheese container
White construction paper
Spray bottles of water, optional

What to do

1. Ahead of time, pour powdered paint into shaker containers.
2. Invite the children to sprinkle powdered paint onto their paper. Encourage them to mix some of the colors together.
3. Place the papers outside in a light rain for a few minutes. If possible, let the children stand outside to watch the rain mix with the paint. Bring the papers inside before they become soaked.
4. If you choose, have the children spray their papers with water instead of putting them out in the rain.

More to do

Cooking: Make a gelatin dessert with water and powdered mix.

More art: Cut the paper in the shape of umbrellas and then paint with powdered paint and rain. Design gift wrap using paper, powdered paint, and a sprayer bottle.

Related books

In the Rain With Baby Duck by Amy Hest
Just a Thunderstorm by Gina and Mercer Mayer
Rain Song by Lezlie Evans
Thundercake by Patricia Palacco

Sandra W. Gratias, Perkasie, PA

Simple Sun Catchers

Materials

Colored glue or white glue tinted with food dye
Plastic lids
Plastic drinking straws cut into 2" (5 cm) pieces
String or yarn cut into 3" (8 cm) pieces

What to do

1. If you are going to dye your own glue, pour a few drops of food coloring in it and stand the bottle upside down overnight.
2. When you are ready to begin, give each child a plastic lid.
3. Have the children cover the bottom of their lid with a layer of glue, using different colors to create an interesting design.
4. When the children are finished, have them stand a piece of a drinking straw in the glue near the edge of the lid. The glue will harden around the straw, leaving an opening for the yarn.
5. Place the lids in a safe place to dry overnight.
6. Once the glue is dry, carefully remove the lid and the straw.
7. Insert a piece of yarn or string into the opening and tie the ends together.
8. Suspend the sun catchers in front of a window.

More to do

More art: Make sun catchers in different sizes and assemble them on a mobile. Arrange small objects on a piece of dark red or navy blue poster board and place the paper in direct sunlight for

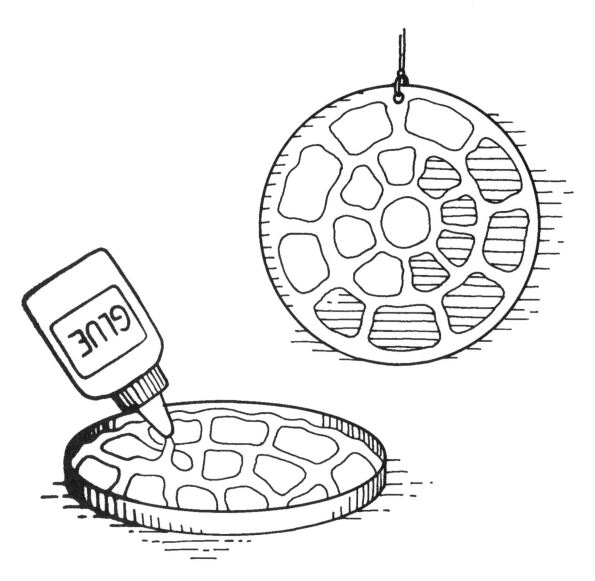

several hours, then remove the objects and see their impression on the faded paper.

Related books

The Sun by Seymour Simon
What Is the Sun? by Reeve Lindbergh
What the Sun Sees/What the Moon Sees by Nancy Tafuri

Rebecca McMahon, Mobile, AL

weather

Go Fly a Kite

Materials
Large paper shopping bags, one per child
Scissors
Hole punch
Hole reinforcements
Watercolors and brushes
Markers
Tissue paper
Glue
String or yarn cut in 3' (1 m) lengths

What to do
1. Open up each bag and cut out the bottom.
2. Punch two holes near the opening 2" to 3" (5 cm to 8 cm) apart and secure the holes with reinforcements.
3. Invite the children to decorate the bag with paint, markers, or pieces of tissue paper.
4. Attach string or yarn through the holes.
5. Bring the kites outside and let the children run, pulling the kites by the string.

More to do
More art: Paint pictures of windjammers. Make a pinwheel.
Music: Play wind instruments.
Science: Chart wind velocity over time on a graph.

Related books
Abuela by Arthur Dorros
Did You Hear the Wind Sing Your Name? by Sandra De Coteau Orie
When Spring Comes by Robert Maass
Windsongs and Rainbows by Albert Burton

Eileen Bayer, Tempe, AZ

Cloud Pictures

3+

Materials
Little Cloud by Eric Carle
White paint
Paintbrushes
Blue construction paper

What to do
1. Read *Little Cloud* by Eric Carle.
2. Bring the class outside to look at the clouds. Invite the children to lie on their backs and talk about the pictures they see in the clouds.
3. When you return to the classroom, invite the children to paint their own cloud pictures with white paint on blue construction paper.

More to do
Movement: Put on some quiet music and invite the children to move gracefully to it, pretending they are clouds.

Related books
Cloudland by John Burningham
Cloudy With a Chance of Meatballs by Judi Barrett
It Looked Like Spilt Milk by Charles G. Shaw
The Water Cycle by David Smith

Barbara Fischer, San Carlos, CA

Colors of the Rainbow

3+

Materials
Butcher paper
Pencil or marker
Paint in rainbow colors
Sink or bucket of clean water

weather

What to do

1. Beforehand, draw arcs on the butcher paper.
2. Invite the children to paint the colors of the rainbow with their handprints. Have them press their hands into red paint and paint the first arc, taking turns.
3. When they finish, have them rinse their hands and begin again with the orange paint. Repeat until all the colors of the rainbow are printed.
4. Let the rainbows dry and hang them to display.

More to do

More art: Make a border of handprints for the bulletin board. Design greeting cards with handprints. Pour colored water into ice cube trays, then arrange the cubes in a rainbow.
Science: Compare your fingerprints with each other.

Related books

How the Sky's Housekeeper Wore Her Scarves by Patricia Hooper
Huff and Puff's Hawaiian Rainbow by Jean Warren
Planting a Rainbow by Lois Ehlert
Sky Fire by Frank Asch

Elizabeth Thomas, Hobart, IN

Animal Clouds

Materials

It Looked Like Spilled Milk by Charles G. Shaw
Beach towel or mat for each child
Blue and white construction paper

What to do

1. Read *It Looked Like Spilled Milk* by Charles G. Shaw.
2. Have the children find a shady spot to lie down on their mats and watch the clouds.
3. Ask the children to imagine that the clouds are pictures and to observe how the wind changes the shape of the clouds.
4. Give each child one sheet of blue construction paper and a half-sheet of white construction paper. Have the children tear the white paper into the shapes they see in the clouds.
5. Let the children arrange the white shapes on the blue paper.
6. Help the children identify the shapes with words.

weather

More to do

More art: Invite the children to create a mural depicting what they saw in the sky, then suspend the mural from the ceiling.

Related books

Cloud Book by Tomie de Paola
Cloudy With a Chance of Meatballs by Judi Barrett
Hi, Clouds by Carol Greene
Little Cloud by Eric Carle
Thundercake by Patricia Polacco

Vicki Whitehead, Ft. Worth, TX

Walk-on Book

Materials

The Jacket I Wear in the Snow by Shirley Neitzel
Butcher paper
Markers
Patterns of clothing shapes such as scarves, hats, gloves, winter and rain coats, long- and short-sleeved shirts, shorts and pants, socks, bathing suits, shoes, umbrellas, and sunglasses
Patterns of weather symbols such as storm clouds, puffy white clouds, sunlight, mud puddles, tornadoes, snow, rain, and lightening
Construction paper or fabric samples
Scissors
Cement glue
Laminating machine

What to do

1. Ahead of time, draw lines on butcher paper to divide the paper into pages, creating one page for each kind of weather you want to include in your book. Identify the kind of weather at the top of each page in bold letters. Trace the patterns of clothing articles and weather symbols onto the construction paper or fabric, then cut them out; let older children cut out some of the shapes themselves.
2. Read *The Jacket I Wear in the Snow* by Shirley Neitzel to the children.
3. Assign a page of the Walk-on Book to each child or group of children. Read them the weather words at the top.

4. Ask the children to choose the kind of clothing and weather symbols they need for their page.

5. When the children are ready, have them glue the shapes onto the paper.

6. When the glue is dry, feed the pages through the laminating machine, last page first (adult only).

7. Trim the edges of the book, but do not cut between each page. Fold the book accordion-style.

8. Invite the children to spread the book out on the floor and "read" it.

More to do

Dramatic play: Provide a few props and invite the children to rummage in the dress-up box and pretend they are going to the beach on a hot, sunny day or playing in the snow on a brisk day.

More art: Mold funny characters from clay and dress them for hot and cold weather. Create mobiles with shapes cut from cloth or molded from clay for different kinds of weather. Dress large paper dolls with fabric scraps.

Related books

Jesse Bear, What Will You Wear? by Nancy W. Carlstrom

Just a Thunderstorm by Gina and Mercer Mayer

Rain Song by Lezlie Evans

Thundercake by Patricia Polacco

Vicki Whitehead, Ft. Worth TX

Grocery Bag Kites

Materials

Recycled plastic grocery bags, one per child
Markers
Lightweight sticks about 12" (30 cm) long
Kite string or masking tape

What to do

1. Show the children how to put two sticks together, forming an "X," then hold the sticks in place with string or tape.

2. Let the children decorate their bags with markers.

3. Help the children open the bag as wide as possible and attach the X-shape at the opening of the bag with masking tape.

4. Tie a 10' (3 m) length of string to the X-shape at its midpoint.

5. Go outside on a windy day and invite the children to run, trailing their kite behind them, coaxing it to fly.

weather

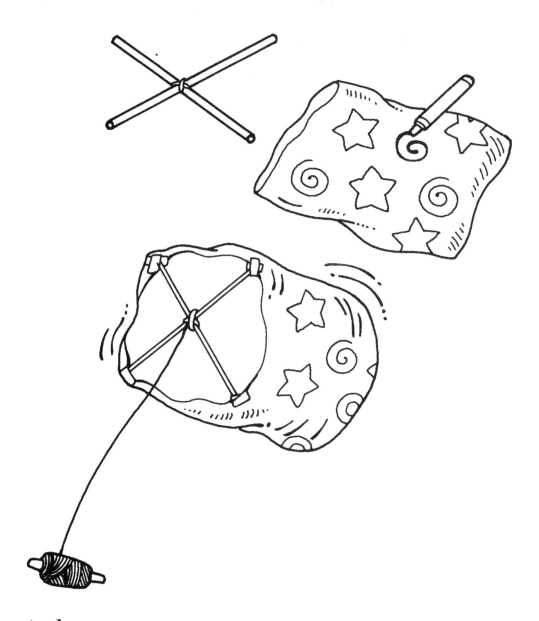

More to do
Science: Place pinwheels and a windsock outside the classroom window and record your observations.

Related books
When Spring Comes by Robert Maass
When the Wind Stops by Charlotte Zolotow
Windsongs and Rainbows by Albert Burton

Dani Rosensteel, Payson, AZ

weather

Weather Dolls

4+

Materials
Poster board
Scissors
Fabric scraps such as wool, canvas, faux suede and leather, vinyl, lightweight knits, and cotton material
Glue
Buttons, rickrack, and yarn

What to do
1. Beforehand, cut doll figures out of poster board that are approximately 20" to 24" (50 cm to 60 cm) tall and 10" (25 cm) wide. Cut one doll for every three or four children.
2. Divide the children into groups and assign them a particular kind of weather such as rainy and cool, snowy and cold, and sunny and hot. Let the children think about the clothing they would wear in that kind of weather.

3. Set out a wide assortment of fabric scraps and invite the children to choose the appropriate kind of fabric for their doll's clothing.
4. Help the children sketch a waistline and sleeve and pant length so they can readily position the clothing.
5. Provide them with scissors, then invite them to cut bits of the fabric and glue them to the doll.
6. When they are finished dressing the doll, ask them to attach buttons, rickrack, and yarn for the eyes, nose, mouth, and hair.

More to do

More art: Decorate a clear plastic jar and set it outside for measuring rainfall.
Science: Record the daily outdoor temperature on a colorful chart. Make a picture graph of the weather over a period of time.

Related books

Jesse Bear, What Will You Wear? by Nancy W. Carlstrom
Snowsong Whistling by Karen E. Lotz
Windsongs and Rainbows by Albert Burton

Lisa M. Chichester, Parkersburg, WV

Snow Measuring Person

4+

Materials

½ gallon (2 L) plastic bottles with caps, one per child
Poster board
Scissors
Permanent markers
1" (3 cm) wide strips of fabric in 18" (45 cm) lengths
Fabric circles, 7" (18 cm) in diameter
Yarn or ribbon cut in 12" (30 cm) lengths

What to do

1. Ahead of time, cut 1" (3 cm) off the bottom of each bottle and remove the cap. On poster board, design a template of a ruler that will fit inside the bottles: draw a straight line, mark off 1" (3 cm) intervals, and number them one to six.
2. When the forecast calls for snow, help the children insert the template in their bottle. Show them how to trace the ruler onto the side of the bottle with a marker.
3. Have the children tie a fabric strip, or the snowman's scarf, around the bottle at the 6" (15 cm) mark.

4. Above the scarf, ask the children to draw eyes and other features.
5. Have the children screw the cap onto the bottle and center the fabric circle, the snowman's hat, over the cap. Secure the fabric with a rubber band and tie a length of yarn over the rubber band.
6. After a snowfall, stand the snowmen in the snow and measure the accumulation.

More to do

Math: Graph snowfall on a picture graph using paper snowflakes. Hang adding machine tape in the classroom and measure the children and objects around the room.

Music: Play soft music and tap a drum, play a triangle, or ring a bell and dance, pretending you are a snowflake.

Science: Bring some snow inside and measure one cupful (250 mL), then let it melt and measure it in its liquid form.

Snack: Mix shaved ice and fruit juice.

Related books

The Big Snow by Berta and Elmer Heder
Geraldine's Big Snow by Holly Keller
Katy and the Big Snow by Virginia Lee Burton
Look! Snow! by Kathryn O. Galbraith
Snowballs by Lois Ehlert
White Snow Bright Snow by Alvin Tresselt

Martha Warren, Fairmont, WV

Raincoat Finger Puppets

Materials
Yellow rubber gloves
Felt
Scissors
³/₁₆" (5 mm) googly eyes
Yarn cut into 1" (3 cm) pieces
Glue
Thin-line markers

What to do
1. Before the children arrive, cut the fingers off the gloves. Cut felt into circles for the puppets' faces.
2. Give each child a rubber finger from the glove.
3. Let the children attach googly eyes and yarn hair to the face and add other features with markers.
4. When the children are finished making the face, have them glue it to the finger.

More to do
Dramatic play: Have the children compose and perform a finger puppet show.
Field trip: Take the children to see a puppet performance.
More art: Make finger puppets with garden gloves and wool gloves. Introduce the children to different kinds of puppets such as rod and marionettes.

Related books
Piggies by Don and Audrey Wood
Peter Spier's Rain by Peter Spier
Rabbits and Raindrops by Jim Arnosky
Rain Talk by Mary Serfozo

Dotti Enderle, Richmond, TX

Weather Sticks

Materials

Paper towel tubes or other long cardboard
   tubes, one per child
Thin cardboard or poster board
Scissors
Masking tape
Nails or straight pins
Hammer
Tiny pebbles

Colored tissue paper
Liquid starch
Cup
Paintbrush
Yarn
Glue

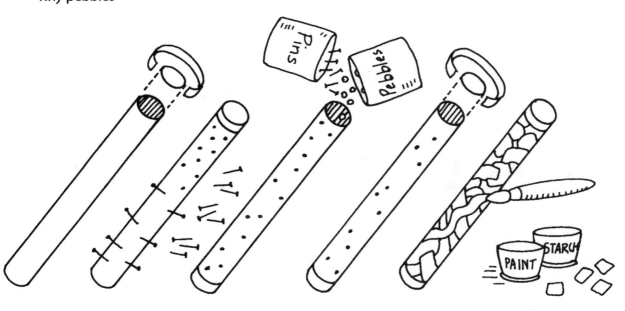

What to do

1. Ahead of time, cut cardboard into circles that will fit on the end of the tubes.
2. When you are ready to begin, have the children place a cardboard circle over one end of the tube. Help them tape it securely.
3. Under your supervision, have the children insert straight pins into the tube. Older children can hammer nails into the tube, especially one with a thicker consistency.
4. When the pins are in place, ask the children to pour some of the tiny pebbles into the tube.
5. Help the children close the tube by placing another cardboard circle over the open end and securing it with tape.
6. When the tube is secure, have the children cover the pins with masking tape.
7. Supply the children with liquid starch, a paintbrush, and tissue paper squares. Invite the children to cover the tube with the squares, attaching them with starch.

8. Let the tubes dry.

9. Afterward, invite the children to decorate the rain sticks with yarn, if they choose.

More to do

Movement: Gather the children in a circle and make a rainstorm together; have them mimic your motions, each for about a half-minute: rub your hands together, then snap your fingers, clap your hands, slap your knees, and stomp your feet. After the storm reaches a crescendo, make the motions in reverse order until the storm is over and the room is quiet.

Music: Create sound cylinders by placing various objects in juice cans and sealing the cans with tape; wrap the cans in contact paper to decorate.

Related books

Bringing the Rain to Kapiti Plain by Verna Aardema

Five Live Bongos by George Ella Lyons

Shake It to the One That You Love Best by Cheryl Warren Mattox

Melissa J. Browning, Milwaukee, WI

Foggy Landscapes

Materials

Examples of landscape art

Scraps of colored construction paper

Scissors

Glue

Blue construction paper

Sheets of waxed paper the same size as the blue paper

Liquid starch

Paint containers

Large paintbrushes

What to do

1. Show the children examples of landscape art.

2. Have the children rip or cut construction paper scraps into shapes that represent land and water formations such as a river cutting through a mountain or a stand of trees on a hilltop.

3. When they are ready, ask the children to glue their landscape onto blue paper.

4. Pour liquid starch into a paint container.

5. Invite the children to lay waxed paper on top of their landscape and apply liquid starch over it.
6. When dry, the overlay will give the appearance that the landscape is shrouded in fog.
7. To add dimension, glue more land formations on top of the waxed paper, creating a fore-ground.

More to do

More art: Invite the children to sit by the window on a foggy day and make a picture of what they see, using various media.

Movement: Read the poem "Fog" by Carl Sandburg and creep around the room like fog.

Related books

Cloudy With a Chance of Meatballs by Judi Barrett
If… by Sarah Perry
When Spring Comes by Robert Maass
Where Once There Was a Wood by Denise Fleming

Barbara Saul, Eureka, CA

Terrific Tortoise

3+

Materials
Paper plates or paper bowls, one per child
4 plastic forks, 1 plastic spoon, and 1 plastic knife for each tortoise
Tape
Newspaper
Brown, yellow, and green tempera paint in containers
Paintbrushes
Brown, tan, orange, and yellow construction paper

What to do
1. Help the children tape the spoon, the forks, and the knife to the inside of the plate or bowl for the tortoise's head, legs, and tail, respectively.
2. Have the children place their tortoise on a piece of newspaper. Encourage them to paint the tortoise, experimenting with a mix of colors.
3. Lay brown paper on the floor to represent sand or soil, the tortoise's habitat. Have the children tear paper to create a mound of dead leaves where the tortoise can burrow for hibernation.

More to do
Field trip: Visit a local pond, canal, or nature center and watch the turtles swim and sun themselves.
Outdoors: Challenge the children to race as if they were turtles, moving slowly but deliberately toward the finish line.
Science: Mold round white tortoise eggs from clay and bury them in sand; if available, mold the clay around small plastic turtles, then keep them on a sunny windowsill and let them "hatch."

Related books
Tortoise Brings the Mail by Dee Lillegard
The Flying Tortoise: An Igbo Tale retold by Tololwa Mollel
The Tortoise and the Hare adapted by Janet Stevens
Turtle Spring by Deborah Turney Zagwyn

Tina Slater, Silver Spring, MD

Paper Towel Tube Alligators 3+

Materials
Paper towel tubes, one per child
Pinking shears
Green construction paper
Green paint and paintbrushes
Glue
Googly eyes

What to do
1. Before class, shape an alligator's mouth from each tube with pinking shears. Cut out four legs and one tail for each alligator using the pinking shears.
2. Have the children paint the tube green.
3. When the paint is dry, ask the children to glue the legs, tail, and googly eyes onto the tube.

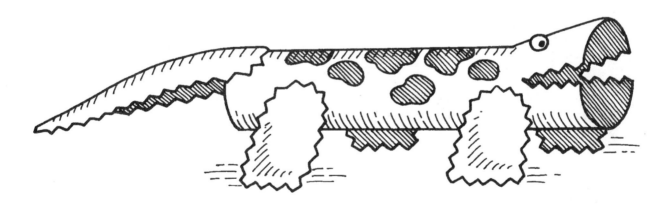

More to do
Movement: Have the children ride a scooter board on their stomach, using their arms and legs to propel themselves as if they were alligators.

Related books
Alligators All Around: An Alphabet by Maurice Sendak
Alligator Baby by Robert Munsch
Frogs, Toads, Lizards and Salamanders by Nancy Winslow Parker and Joan Richards Wright
Lyle, Lyle Crocodile by Bernard Waber

Sandra Suffoletto Ryan, Buffalo, NY

Zoo Animal Mural

4+

Materials
Roll of white poster or butcher paper
Pencils
Tempera paint and brushes

What to do
1. Spread a sheet of butcher paper about 6' (2 m) in length on the floor.
2. Talk to the children about what animals they have seen at a zoo or read about being in a zoo. Tell the children that they are going to design their own zoo on the butcher paper.
3. Divide the children into small groups and encourage them to choose the part of the mural they would like to design. Have them start with pencil and encourage them to spread out so they can have lots of room to work.
4. When the children are satisfied with their design, invite them to paint their portion of the mural.
5. Display the mural in a hallway or on a large wall.

More to do
Dramatic play: Have the children set up an imaginary zoo in the classroom and let them play the roles of zookeepers, visitors, and animals.
Math: Sort small plastic animals by kind or size.
More art: Make murals in circus, community, or transportation themes.

Related books and song
Diego by Jeanette Winter and Jonah White
Diego Rivera by Mike Venezia
Good Night, Gorilla by Peggy Rathmann
My Visit to the Zoo by Aliki
"Momma's Taking Us to the Zoo, Tomorrow" sung by Raffi

Barbara Saul, Eureka, CA

Shape Penguin Puppet 4+

Materials

White paper lunch bags, one per child
Black, white, and orange construction paper
Glue
Large googly eyes
White and black craft feathers and bits of felt

What to do

1. Ahead of time, cut out the shapes that the children will use to assemble their puppet. Older children can cut out some of the shapes on their own. For each puppet, cut a black oval for the penguin's belly and a smaller white oval for the white on its belly. Cut a black circle for each head, two long, thin black triangles for the flippers, two orange triangles for the beak, and two orange triangles for the penguin's webbed feet.

2. When you are ready to begin, have the children place their bag on the table in front of them; tell them to leave the bag folded flat and turn it so the bottom flap, or the penguin's head, is at the top.

3. Ask the children to glue the black oval onto the bag, tucking part of it under the bottom flap, then glue the white oval on top of the black.

4. Have the children glue the circle onto the flap of the bag and attach the penguin's eyes.

5. To attach the beak, show the children how to lift the flap and glue one triangle on top of the belly; glue the other triangle to the penguin's head, directly over the first triangle.

6. When they finish the head, have the children glue the wings to the underside of the belly, positioning them so that they protrude.

7. Tell the children to glue the wider orange triangles with their pointed corner facing down along the bottom edge of the bag.

8. Invite the children to attach feathers or bits of felt to their penguins with glue, then set the puppets aside to dry.
9. Afterward, invite the children to put their hand inside the bag and play with their penguin puppets.

More to do

Dramatic play: Invite the children to put on a puppet show with their paper bag penguins.
More art: Make other animal pictures or puppets with shapes.
Movement: Play some music and have the children pretend to be penguins, waddling on land or swimming swiftly after their prey.
Sand and water table: Add small plastic arctic animals and a few ice cubes to the table.

Related books

Cinderella Penguin by Janet Perlman
Counting Penguins by Betsey Chessen and Pamela Chanko
The Emperor Penguin's New Clothes by Janet Perlman
Looking at Penguins by Dorothy Henshaw Patent
Penelope Penguin: The Incredibly Good Baby by John Bianchi
Tacky the Penguin by Helen Lester

Tina R. Woehler, Oak Point, TX

Bats!

Materials

Cardboard toilet tissue tube, one per child
Construction paper
Scissors
Glue
Pencil
String

What to do

1. Ahead of time, cut out a circle for each child that is slightly larger than the end of the toilet tissue tube. This will be the bat's face. Cut out pointy ears and other features from construction paper that the children can glue on the circle. Cut out a set of wings and two small bat feet for each child.
2. Invite the children to cover their toilet tissue tubes with construction paper.
3. Have the children glue a circle for the face on one end of the tube. Older children can glue

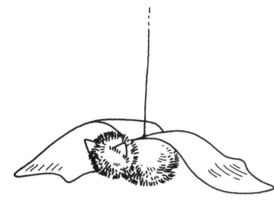

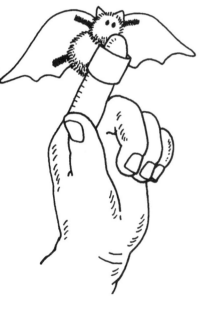

on pointy ears and other features made from construction paper; younger children may need your help with this.

4. Show the children how to glue the wings to the tube.

5. Demonstrate how to fold the wings up and down to resemble bat wings.

6. Have the children glue on the feet so they stick out of the back of the wings.

7. Add string to hang.

More to do

Games: Gather the children in a circle around one blindfolded child in the middle, the bat; one child in the circle creates a sound using a bell, drumsticks, or the like, and the "bat" must locate the source of the sound. Repeat until all the children have had a turn as the bat and as the source of a sound.

Outdoors: Find a quiet spot and have the children shout, then listen for their echo; help them understand how bats used echolocation to find flying insects and other food.

Related books

Bat in the Boot by Annie Cannon
Bat Jamboree by Kathi Appelt
Bats!: Creatures of the Night by Joyce Milton
Batty Riddles by Katie Hall
Stellaluna by Janell Cannon

Elizabeth Thomas, Hobart, IN

Marshmallow Mania

Materials needed
Colored toothpicks
Small and large marshmallows

What to do
1. After a trip to the zoo or following the reading of a book about the zoo, ask the children to decide which animals are their favorites.

2. Give the children colored toothpicks and small marshmallows, and invite them to create that animal. They may need you to demonstrate how to connect the marshmallows with the toothpicks.
3. When they are finished, or at a later time such as snack time, invite the children to disassemble their animal creations and enjoy eating the marshmallows.

More to do

Field trip: Take the children to a zoo or animal park.

More art: Give the children art supplies and invite them to create habitats for their animal creations. Invite them to make other things besides animals from the marshmallows and toothpicks.

Related books

Animal Action ABC by Karen Pandell
Good Night, Gorilla by Peggy Rathmann
I Love Animals by Flora McDonell
Little Elephant by Tana Hoban and Miela Ford
Where Do Bears Sleep? by Barbara Shook Hazen

Vicki Whitehead, Fort Worth, TX

materials index

materials index

materials index

materials index

materials index

materials index

materials index

materials index

materials index

materials index

materials index

activities index

activities index

activities index

activities index